Chapter 1

Why Do We Need Standards?

Many, if not most, educators are unaware of the impact the very discussion of standards, let alone the reorganization of schools around standards, has had on American education. Education policy analyst Anne Lewis (1995) notes that "whether lauded as a sign of progress or scorned as anathema" (p. 745), the standards movement is one of the most talked about issues in school reform. Researchers Robert Glaser and Robert Linn (1993) assert that it might be only in retrospect that we recognize the importance of the current discussion of standards in American education:

> In the recounting of our nation's drive toward educational reform, the last decade of this century will undoubtedly be identified as the time when a concentrated press for national education standards emerged. The press for standards was evidenced by the efforts of federal and state legislators, presidential and gubernatorial candidates, teacher and subject-matter specialists, councils, governmental agencies, and private foundations. (p. xiii)

When and where did the discussion of standards originate? What is the rationale for standards?

A Brief History Of The Modern Standards Movement

Former Assistant Secretary of Education Diane Ravitch is commonly recognized as one of the chief architects of the modern standards movement. In her book *National Standards in American Education: A Citizens Guide* (1995), Ravitch explains the rationale for standards in a straightforward manner:

> Americans . . . expect strict standards to govern construction of buildings, bridges, highways, and tunnels; shoddy work would put lives at risk. They expect stringent standards to protect their drinking water, the food they eat, and the air they breathe. . . . Standards are created because they improve the activity of life. (pp. 8-9)

Ravitch (1995) asserts that just as standards improve the daily lives of Americans, so, too, will they improve the effectiveness of American education: "Standards can improve achievement by clearly defining what is to be taught and what kind of performance is expected" (p. 25).

Many educators see the publication of the now-famous report *A Nation at Risk* (National Commission on Excellence in Education, 1983) as the initiating event of the modern standards movement. Ramsay Seldon, director of the State Assessment Center at the Council of Chief State School Officers, notes that after this highly damaging exposé on public education, educators set out to change what they could through new policies, such as those that increased the rigor of graduation requirements. When these efforts produced disappointing results, education leaders turned to national goals and standards:

> We found that this first wave of reform didn't have dramatic effects. So there was a feeling of urgency that the education system needed to be stronger, and that in addition to what states and districts and individual schools were doing—we needed a stronger presence at the national level. . . . We recognized that we didn't need a national curriculum, so national goals and voluntary national standards came to be seen as a good mechanism for providing a focus. (in O'Neil, 1995, p. 12)

Researcher Lorrie Shepard also cites *A Nation at Risk* as a critical factor in the modern standards movement. Shepard (1993) notes that with the publication of the report, the rhetoric of education reform changed drastically. Proponents of reform began to make a close link between the financial security and economic competitiveness of the nation and our educational system. Who will soon forget the chilling words often quoted from *A Nation at Risk*: "The educational foundations of our society are presently being eroded by a rising tide of mediocrity that threatens our very future as a nation and a people. . . . We have, in effect been committing an act of unthinking, unilateral educational disarmament" (National Commission on Excellence in Education, 1983, p. 5).

These growing concerns about the educational preparation of the nation's youth prompted President Bush and the nation's governors to call an education summit in Charlottesville, Virginia in September, 1989. Shepard (1993) explains that at this summit, President Bush and the nation's governors, including then-governor Bill Clinton, agreed on six broad goals for education to be reached by the year 2000. These goals and the rationale for them are published under the title *The National Education Goals Report: Building a Nation of Learners* (National Education Goals Panel [NEGP], 1991). Two of those goals (3 and 4) related specifically to academic achievement:

> **Goal 3:** By the year 2000, American students will leave grades four, eight, and twelve having demonstrated competency in challenging subject matter, including English, mathematics, science, history, and geography; and every school in America will ensure that all students learn to use their minds well, so they may be prepared for responsible citizenship, further learning, and productive employment in our modern economy.

> **Goal 4:** By the year 2000, U.S. students will be first in the world in science and mathematics achievement. (p. 4)

A COMPREHENSIVE GUIDE TO

Designing

Standards-Based

Districts,

Schools, and

Classrooms

ROBERT J. MARZANO AND JOHN S. KENDALL

ASSOCIATION FOR SUPERVISION AND CURRICULUM DEVELOPMENT
ALEXANDRIA, VIRGINIA

MID-CONTINENT REGIONAL EDUCATIONAL LABORATORY
AURORA, COLORADO

Association for Supervision and Curriculum Development
1250 N. Pitt Street • Alexandria, Virginia 22314-1453
Telephone: 1-800-933-2723 or 703-549-9110 • Fax: 703-299-8631

2550 S. Parker Rd., Suite 500 • Aurora, Colorado 80014
Telephone: 303-337-0990 • Fax: 303-337-3005

Barbara B. Gaddy, Editor
Mary Lee Barton, Editor's Assistant
Jeanne Deak, Desktop Publisher
Shelly Wasson, Research Assistant
Jennifer Norford, Research Assistant
Lisa Schoch-Roberts, Research Assistant
Michael Shea, Research Assistant

Printed in the United States of America.

ASCD publications present a variety of viewpoints. The views expressed or implied in this book should not be interpreted as official positions of the Association.

ASCD stock no.: 196215
ASCD member price: $24.95   nonmember price: $29.95

To order additional copies of this book, please contact ASCD.

Library of Congress Cataloging-in-Publication Data

Marzano, Robert J.
     A comprehensive guide to designing standards-based districts, schools, and classrooms /
     Robert J. Marzano and John S. Kendall.
       p.   cm.
     Includes bibliographical references (p.).
     ISBN 0-87120-277-8 (pbk.)
     1. Education—Standards—United States—Handbooks, manuals, etc. 2. Educational evaluation—United States—Handbooks, manuals, etc. 3. Educational accountability—United States—Handbooks, manuals, etc. 4. Grading and marking (Students)—United States—Handbooks, manuals, etc. 5. Educational change—United States—Handbooks, manuals, etc. I. Kendall, John S. II. Title.
LB3060.83.M37 1996
279.158'0973—dc21

96-36835
CIP

00 99 98 97 96   10 9 8 7 6 5 4 3 2 1

Table of Contents

This book is dedicated to Ron Brandt.

Soon after the summit, two groups were established to implement the new education goals: the National Education Goals Panel (NEGP) and the National Council on Education Standards and Testing (NCEST). Collectively, these two groups were charged with addressing unprecedented questions regarding American education such as, What is the subject matter to be addressed? What types of assessments should be used? What standards of performance should be set?

These efforts engendered a flurry of activity from national subject-matter organizations to establish standards in their respective areas. Many of these groups looked for guidance from the National Council of Teachers of Mathematics (NCTM), which preempted the public mandate for standards by publishing *Curriculum and Evaluation Standards for School Mathematics* in 1989. As *Education Week* reporter Karen Diegmueller (1995) explains, the NCTM standards "redefined the study of math so that topics and concepts would be introduced at an earlier age, and students would view math as a relevant problem-solving discipline rather than as a set of obscure formulas to be memorized" (p. 5). The National Academy of Sciences used the apparent success of the NCTM standards as the impetus for urging Secretary of Education Lamar Alexander to underwrite national standards-setting efforts in other content areas. According to Diane Ravitch, then an assistant secretary of education, Alexander "bankrolled the projects out of his office's discretionary budget" (in Diegmueller, 1995, p. 5). The National Science Teachers Association (NSTA) and the American Association for the Advancement of Science (AAAS) quickly launched independent attempts to identify standards in science. Efforts soon followed in the fields of civics, dance, theater, music, art, language arts, history, and social studies, to name a few. An overview of the movement to establish standards in the core subject areas is reported in Exhibit 1.1.

Exhibit 1.1 The Standards Movement

1983	*A Nation at Risk* is published, calling for reform of the U.S. education system.
1983	Bill Honig, elected state superintendent of California public schools, begins a decade-long revision of the state public school system, which will encompass the development of content standards and curriculum frameworks.
1987	The National Council of Teachers of Mathematics (NCTM) writing teams begin to review curriculum documents and to draft standards for curriculum and evaluation.
1989	The first education summit is held in Charlottesville, Virginia. The nation's fifty governors and President Bush adopt National Education Goals for the year 2000. One goal names five school subjects—English, mathematics, science, history, and geography—for which challenging national achievement standards should be established.
1989	NCTM publishes *Curriculum and Evaluation Standards for School Mathematics.*

Exhibit 1.1 The Standards Movement

1989	Project 2061 of the American Association for the Advancement of Science (AAAS) publishes *Science for all Americans*, describing what "understandings and habits of mind are essential for all citizens in a scientifically literate society."
1990	In his State of the Union address, President Bush announces the National Education Goals for the year 2000; shortly thereafter, he and Congress establish a National Education Goals Panel (NEGP).
1990	The Secretary's Commission on Achieving Necessary Skills (SCANS) is appointed by the Secretary of Labor to determine the skills young people need to succeed in the world of work.
1990	The New Standards Project, a joint project of the National Center on Education and the Economy and the Learning Research and Development Center, is formed to create a system of standards for student performance in a number of areas.
1990, Fall	The Mid-continent Regional Educational Laboratory (McREL) begins the systematic collection, review, and analysis of noteworthy national and state curriculum documents in all subject areas.
1991	SCANS produces *What Work Requires of Schools*, which describes the knowledge and skills necessary for success in the workplace.
1991, June	Secretary of Education Lamar Alexander asks Congress to establish the National Council on Education Standards and Testing (NCEST). The purpose of NCEST is to advise on the desirability and feasibility of voluntary national standards and tests and make recommendations regarding them.
1992, Jan	NCEST releases its report *Raising Standards for American Education* to Congress, proposing an oversight board, the National Education Standards and Assessment Council (NESAC), to establish guidelines for standards setting and assessment development.
1992, Jan	The National Council for the Social Studies names a task force to develop curriculum standards.
1992, Spring	The National History Standards Project receives funding from the National Endowment for the Humanities and the U.S. Department of Education.
1992, Spring	The National Association for Sport and Physical Education begins work on *Outcomes of Quality Physical Education Programs*, which will form the basis of standards in Physical Education.
1992, June	The Consortium of National Arts Education Associations receives funding from the U.S. Department of Education, the National Endowment for the Arts, and the National Endowment for the Humanities to write standards in the arts.
1992, July	The Center for Civic Education receives funding from the U.S. Department of Education and the Pew Charitable Trusts for standards development in civics and government.
1992, July	The Geography Standards Education Project, funded with grants from the U.S. Department of Education, The National Endowment for the Humanities, and the National Geographic Society, creates the first draft of geography standards.
1992, Oct	The Committee for National Health Education Standards is funded by the American Cancer Society.

4

Exhibit 1.1 The Standards Movement

1992, Nov	The Bush administration awards funds to create English standards to a consortium of three organizations: the National Council of Teachers of English, the International Reading Association, and the Center for the Study of Reading at the University of Illinois.
1993, Jan	The National Standards in Foreign Language Education Project becomes the seventh and final group to receive federal funds for standards development.
1993, April	McREL publishes its first technical report on standards, *The Systematic Identification and Articulation of Content Standards and Benchmarks: An Illustration Using Mathematics.*
1993	AAAS's Project 2061 publishes *Benchmarks for Science Literacy.*
1993, Nov	NEGP's Technical Planning Group issues *Promises to Keep: Creating High Standards for American Students*, referred to as the "Malcom Report." The report calls for the development of a National Education Standards and Improvement Council (NESIC), which would give voluntary national standards a stamp of approval.
1993, Nov	The National Research Council, with major funding from the U.S. Department of Education and the National Science Foundation, establishes the National Committee on Science Education Standards and Assessment (NCSESA) to oversee standards development in content, teaching, and assessment.
1994, Jan	McREL publishes *The Systematic Identification and Articulation of Content Standards and Benchmarks: Update, January 1994*, which provides a synthesis of standards for science, mathematics, history, geography, communication and information processing, and life skills.
1994, Feb	The Standards Project for English Language Arts, a collaborative effort of the Center for the Study of Reading, the International Reading Association, and the National Council of Teachers of English, publishes the draft *Incomplete Work of the Task Forces of the Standards Project for English Language Arts.*
1994, March	President Clinton signs into law Goals 2000: Educate America Act. Among other provisions, this legislation creates the National Education Standards and Improvement Council (NESIC) to certify national and state content and performance standards, opportunity-to-learn standards, and state assessments; funds a grant program for reform plans from participating states; and formally authorizes the National Education Goals Panel. In addition, the legislation names four additional school subjects—foreign languages, the arts, economics, and civics and government—in which students should demonstrate competency.
1994, March	The U.S. Department of Education notifies the Standards Project for the English Language Arts that it will not continue funding for the project, citing a lack of progress.
1994, March	The Consortium of National Arts Education Associations publishes the arts standards (dance, music, theatre, and the visual arts).
1994, Fall	The National Council for the Social Studies publishes *Expectations of Excellence: Curriculum Standards for Social Studies.*

Exhibit 1.1 The Standards Movement

1994, Oct	Lynne Cheney, past chair of the National Endowment for the Humanities (NEH), criticizes the U.S. history standards in the *Wall Street Journal* two weeks before their release. (NEH, with the U.S. Department of Education, funded development of the U.S. history standards.)
1994, Oct	U.S. history standards are released; world history and K-4 history standards are released shortly thereafter.
1994, Oct	The Geography Education Standards Project publishes *Geography for Life: National Geography Standards*.
1994, Nov	The Center for Civic Education, funded by the U.S. Department of Education and the Pew Charitable Trusts, publishes standards for civics and government education.
1995, Jan	Gary Nash, National History Standards Project codirector, indicates that the history standards may be revised. The U.S. Senate denounces the current history standards in a 99-1 vote.
1995, April	The U.S. Department of Education withdraws assurance of a $500,000 grant to the National Council on Economic Education for the development of standards in economics.
1995, May	The Joint Committee on National Health Education Standards releases *National Health Education Standards: Achieving Health Literacy*.
1995, Summer	The National Association for Sport and Physical Education publishes *Moving Into the Future: National Standards for Physical Education*.
1995, Oct	The National Council on Economic Education, using funds from private sources, convenes a drafting committee to develop standards; projected publication is winter 1996.
1995, Nov	The New Standards Project releases a three-volume "consultation draft" entitled *Performance Standards* for English language arts, mathematics, science, and "applied learning."
1995, Dec	McREL publishes *Content Knowledge: A Compendium of Standards and Benchmarks for K-12 Education*, a synthesis of standards in all subject areas, including behavioral studies and life skills.
1996, Jan	The National Standards in Foreign Language Education Project publishes *Standards for Foreign Language Learning: Preparing for the 21st Century*.
1996, Jan	The National Research Council publishes *National Science Education Standards*.
1996, March	The second education summit is held. Forty state governors and more than 45 business leaders convene. They support efforts to set clear academic standards in the core subject areas at the state and local levels. Business leaders pledge to consider the existence of state standards when locating facilities.
1996, March	The National Council of Teachers of English and the International Reading Association publish *Standards for the English Language Arts*.
1996, April	Revised history standards are published. Asserting that the revision does not go far enough, Lynn Cheney renews her criticism of the history standards. A review in the *Wall Street Journal* by Diane Ravitch and Arthur Schlesinger, professor emeritus at City University of New York, endorses the standards.

Troubled Times

Despite the federal support for standards and the enthusiasm of educators from various subject areas, critics of the standards movement captured the public's attention. Criticism of the standards fell into four broad categories: (1) resource and equity issues, (2) relationship to previous, failed reform efforts, (3) objectionable content in the standards, and (4) volume of material.

Resources and Equity Issues

Some educators saw the standards movement as a major drain on resources that should have been used for more pressing needs such as basic educational materials. For example, Theodore Sizer, founder of the Coalition of Essential Schools, stated that "the maps on the walls [of classrooms] still call [Zaire] the Belgian Congo. Those are the things that just cry out for attention" (in Diegmueller, 1995, p. 5). Others noted that the drain on resources predictably would adversely affect some students much more than others. Specifically, the standards movement was viewed as another burden that would be placed on the shoulders of those who traditionally do not do well in schools. Curriculum professor Michael Apple noted that "national standards and national testing are the first steps toward educational apartheid under the rhetoric of accountability" (in Diegmueller, 1995, pp. 5-6).

Relationship To Previous, Failed Reform Efforts

Others saw the standards movement as a thinly veiled attempt at a type of education reform that has been tried a number of times before. For example, researcher and theorist Elliot Eisner (1995) noted the similarity of the standards movement to the efficiency movement of the early 1900s:

> The efficiency movement, which began in 1913 and lasted until the early 1930s, was designed to apply the principles of scientific management to schools. Its progenitor, Frederick Taylor, the inventor of time-and-motion study, was a management consultant hired by industrialists to make their plants more efficient and, hence, more profitable. By specifying in detail the desired outcomes of a worker's efforts and by eliminating "wasted motion," output would increase, profits would soar, wages would rise, and everyone would benefit. (p. 159)

According to Eisner (1995), school administrators soon found that the basic concept underlying the efficiency movement—namely, that one could mechanize and routinize teaching and learning—did not work. Educators would no doubt come to the same conclusions about standards, opined Eisner.

The standards movement was also likened to the failed behavioral objectives movement of the 1960s. Like the efficiency movement, the basic notion behind behavioral objectives was to define education goals in terms that were sufficiently specific to determine without ambiguity whether or not students had achieved them. Measurement expert Robert Mager (1962) is commonly credited as the initiator of the movement, although Ralph Tyler (1932/1989, 1949), considered by many to be the father of modern-day curriculum theory, laid much of the foundation for the concept. Based on his extensive research, Tyler (1932/1989) concluded that learning objectives must be highly specific if instruction is to be effective:

> To define the behavior to be evaluated is essentially to determine all of the kinds of behavior which are particularly significant for the purposes under consideration. The reactions of any human organism are so many and varied that it is necessary to isolate the particular reactions which are significant for a given purpose. (p. 77)

Through his book *Preparing Instructional Objectives*, published in 1962, Mager routinized and popularized the process of constructing behavioral objectives to such an extent that teachers all across the country, in virtually every subject area, at every grade level, were writing behavioral objectives during the 1960s. For Mager, an objective must identify the expected behavior in detail, the conditions in which the behavior is to be displayed, and the criterion that makes it possible to measure the student's performance. An example of a behavioral objective following Mager's criteria would be "At the end of a 50-minute period of instruction, students will be able to complete eight out of ten problems in two-column addition within a five-minute period."

This level of detail, although effective instructionally, created a system that was overwhelming for teachers. As Eisner (1995) notes, the approach required that schools construct hundreds, and sometimes thousands, of behavioral objectives to specify the outcomes of instruction. Soon, schools and districts became bogged down by the sheer number of objectives. This led even ardent supporters of behavioral objectives, such as assessment expert James Popham (1972, 1994), to realize that the movement was doomed to failure.

Objectionable Content In The Standards

In addition to its association with the flawed efficiency and behavioral objective movements of the past, the standards movement received a fair amount of criticism for the very content it promoted. Perhaps the lowest point in the standards movement was the debate over the history standards. In the fall of 1994, Lynne Cheney, a fellow of the American Enterprise Institute, unleashed a blistering attack on the History Standards Project, which, along with science, was the first standards project to receive funding from the U.S. Department of Education in 1991. Cheney alleged that the history standards portrayed the United States and its white, male-dominated power structure as an oppressive society that victimizes minorities and women. She further charged that the history standards ignored such traditional historical figures as George Washington and Robert E. Lee in order to placate proponents of multiculturalism. Diegmueller (1995) notes that suddenly the rather academic discussion of standards burst onto the national scene:

Cheney's views won such exceptionally wide exposure because, as chairwoman of the National Endowment for the Humanities, she had lobbied for history standards, funded the project, and selected its leaders and many of the people on its 29-member board. Soon it became evident that the criticism was not about to subside—even though there were far more supporters than detractors. The U.S. Senate even weighed in, denouncing the history standards by a vote of 99 to 1. (p. 8)

To date, the history standards have not recovered from the negative public perception generated by Cheney's criticisms, even though a revised edition that attempted to address the criticisms was published in 1996 (National Center for History in the Schools [NCHS], 1996).

Volume Of Material

Perhaps the death blow to the federally funded efforts to establish standards was the charge that, once developed, they were simply too cumbersome to use. In the beginning, policymakers and educators had expected to see concise standards. However, as the standards drafts and final documents were produced, it became clear that the standards were far from concise. Education researcher Chester Finn, Jr. noted that "the professional associations, without exception, lacked discipline. They all demonstrated gluttonous and imperialistic tendencies" (in Diegmueller, 1995, p. 6).

At the time of Finn's statement in 1995, the standards documents, taken together, weighed about 14 pounds, stood six inches tall, and contained over 2,000 pages. Since then, more documents, more pounds, and more inches have been added to the total mass of standards. By contrast, the Japanese national curriculum fits into "three slender volumes, one for elementary schools, one for lower secondary schools, and one for upper secondary schools" (Ravitch, 1995, p. 15). Ron Brandt (1995), executive editor of the Association for Supervision and Curriculum Development (ASCD), acknowledged the problem of the sheer volume of the standards:

> I would describe them as an ambitious conception of what professional educators, most of whom are advocates or specialists in the various school subjects, want students to learn in those subjects. It's the classic curriculum dilemma faced by every principal, central administrator, and generalist teacher: specialists naturally expect a lot; they love their subject and they know its possibilities. Taken as a whole, however, such statements of aspirations are overwhelming. (p. 5)

In summary, the once-bright promise of subject-area standards, born from a desire to improve the rigor and effectiveness of American education, has quickly faded under a wide array of criticisms. As Finn notes, "If this were a play, I'd put it on the shelf with tragedies" (in Brandt, 1995, p. 5).

Is The Standards Movement Still Alive?

Given the intense criticism of the modern standards movement, there are some who believe that, for all practical purposes, it is dead. Brandt (1995) explains:

> Now that some of the original sponsors are disappointed in the new standards because they are not what was expected, what does that mean for educators? Apparently, these standards will not soon become a national curriculum or the basis for a set of high-stakes tests. Under the circumstances, educators can breathe a sigh of relief and, with discretion, put them to use in the endless task of improving curriculum and instruction. (p. 5)

Similarly, Paul Gagnon, a senior research associate at Boston University's School of Education, notes that the national movement to create standards is "dead of multiple wounds, some self-inflicted, others from our culture wars, still others from congressional antipathy to any federal initiative, and most from American educators who have long resisted establishing a common core of academic learning" (in "National Update on America's Education Reform Efforts," 1995, p. 1).

In general, we agree with Brandt and Gagnon that America will not soon have a set of national standards. In addition to the problems with standards cited above, the impetus for reform at the federal level has been halted because of a changing political climate. This has been dramatically illustrated by the demise of the National Education Standards and Improvement Council (NESIC). Created as part of the Goals 2000 legislation passed in 1994, NESIC was charged with overseeing the development of voluntary national content standards and "certifying" the standards created by states. But by June of 1995, education policy analyst David Cohen wrote that the NESIC was a casualty of a changing Congress:

> NESIC seems to be dead on arrival. Barely half a year after Goals 2000 was signed into law, Republicans took control of Congress. Although many Republicans had supported the legislation in the previous Congress, the new faces were generally more conservative and had little use for any sort of national school reform. They had especially little use for an agency that would devise, promulgate and certify national education standards. (p. 752)

At the same time, the standards movement at the state level has also been problematic. Campaigns have been mounted to stop the identification of state standards in Virginia, Colorado, Oregon, Pennsylvania, and Washington, to name a few. Studies by the American Federation of Teachers (AFT) have concluded that state standards are, for the most part, weak. For example, in a 1995 study (Gandal, 1995a), the AFT concluded that "only 13 states have standards that are strong enough to carry the weight of the reforms being built upon them" (p. 13). By 1996, the AFT found, significant improvements had been made, but state standards were still lacking: "Only 15 states have standards in all four core subjects that are clear, specific, and well-grounded in content" (Gandal, 1996, p. 13).

Standards: A Powerful Option For Reform

In spite of a plethora of problems at the national and state levels, we do not believe that the standards movement is dead. In fact, we assert that the logic behind organizing schooling around standards is so compelling that schools and districts will implement standards-based school reform even in the absence of federal or state mandates or incentives. Indications are that the standards movement, though "fallen from grace" at the national level, is rising through reform efforts at the local level; over the last year, the Mid-continent Regional Educational Laboratory (McREL) has seen a greater than three-fold increase in the number of districts and schools that have contracted for assistance in the development of standards and benchmarks. Even the 1995 AFT study (Gandal, 1995a) concluded that it is not too late "in most states for changes to be made that will strengthen their standards and enhance their efficacy in improving student achievement" (p. 31). Standards-based reform encompasses not only content knowledge and skills but how courses and subjects are defined, how student performance is described, and how student performance is graded and reported. These areas benefit directly from standards development. There appear to be at least four reasons that standards represent one of the most powerful options for school reform: (1) erosion of the Carnegie Unit and the common curriculum, (2) variation in current grading practices, (3) lack of attention to educational outputs, and (4) success in other countries.

Erosion Of The Carnegie Unit And The Common Curriculum

Although 90 years old, the Carnegie unit is still a basic structural feature of American education. The history of the Carnegie unit dates back to 1906 when the president of the Carnegie Foundation for the Advancement of Teaching, Henry S. Prichett, defined a "unit" as "a course of five periods weekly throughout an academic year" (in Tyack & Tobin, 1994, p. 460). By convention, these periods had come to be thought of as 55 minutes long. The impetus for this categorization came from an attempt by a blue-ribbon panel of trustees of the Carnegie Foundation to establish criteria for distinguishing between colleges and universities. At that time, there were over 600 institutions of higher education in the country ranging in character from struggling small academies to major research institutions such as the University of Chicago and Columbia University. Any of the institutions within this range might have used the title of "university." However, the Carnegie committee decreed that to truly be considered a university, an institution must have at least six full-time professors, a course of study of four, full years in the liberal arts and sciences, and require of entering students no less than four years of academic or high school preparation. Researchers David Tyack and William Tobin (1994) explain that the Carnegie committee also set what became well-established standards for the content and duration of specific courses:

> It was not enough simply to prescribe four years of secondary instruction. . . .
> It was also necessary to develop a standard measurement of time and credit for
> each subject—the Carnegie unit—and to demand that a college require at least
> fourteen of these units. The Foundation did not stop there: it also went on for

eight pages specifying in great detail the content of units in subjects like English, mathematics, Latin, Greek, foreign languages, history and science. Thus, they standardized not only time and credits, but gave pride of place to traditional academic subjects. (p. 461)

The Carnegie unit was almost immediately adopted by high schools and quickly became required as one of the criteria for high school accreditation by regional associations such as the North Central Association of Colleges and Secondary Schools. State laws also built the Carnegie unit system of credits into the requirements for secondary schools.

Initially, then, the Carnegie unit represented an implicit set of standards. It required high schools to cover specified content in a specified period of time. For decades, this system worked fairly well.

By the 1930s, even before compulsory education laws were established, most children went to school. However, although education during this period had substantial drawing power, it had little staying power. According to Ravitch (1983), by the middle of the 1940s, educators were concerned that for every 1,000 children who entered fifth grade in 1932, only 455 graduated from high school. To remedy the problem, high schools began to offer a wide array of courses to cater to the various academic and vocational interests of students. This move away from a central core of knowledge and skills was exacerbated by the acceptance of the progressive movement in education. By the mid-1940s, notes Ravitch (1983), "it was no longer referred to as progressive education, but as 'modern education,' the 'new education,' or simply 'good educational practices'" (p. 43).

A central feature of the progressive education movement was a rejection of an emphasis on specific knowledge and skills to an emphasis on the child as learner. Ravitch (1983) adds that progressive education rejected many of the basic features of schooling that previously had provided such stability to the Carnegie unit. Among the features rejected by progressive education were

> the belief that the primary purpose of the school was to improve intellectual functioning; emphasis on the cultural heritage and on learning derived from books; the teaching of the traditional subjects (i.e., history, English, science, and mathematics) or such; the teaching of content dictated by the internal logic of the material. (p. 44)

From the 1940s until the mid-1970s, the emphasis on serving the interests of individual children generated a geometric expansion of the number of courses that constituted the high school curriculum. By the mid-1970s, the U.S. Office of Education reported that more than 2,100 different courses were being offered in American high schools (see Ravitch, 1995).

This trend toward ever-expanding offerings and ever-decreasing uniformity in the school experience still exists today. This is evident in studies that have focused on how teachers use textbooks. Specifically, studies (Doyle, 1992; Stodolsky, 1989; Yoon, Burstein, & Gold, n.d.) indicate that even when highly structured textbooks are used, teachers commonly make independent and idiosyncratic decisions regarding what should be emphasized, what should be added, and what should be deleted.

The lack of uniformity in the curriculum is also evident in the research on how teachers use time. To illustrate, in a study of the content that teachers emphasize within reading and the language arts, researcher David Berliner (1979, 1984) found that one fifth-grade teacher allocated 68 minutes a day of instruction in reading and language arts; another teacher allotted 137 minutes a day. At the second-grade level, one teacher set aside 47 minutes a day for reading and language arts; another teacher set aside 118 minutes a day, or $2\frac{1}{2}$ times more per day, to teach reading and language arts.

Recently, the National Education Commission on Time and Learning (1994) reported the same disturbing results in the use of time in American education. When compared to eight other countries in terms of the amount of time allocated for instruction, the United States ranks in the top half. This finding, however, provides false comfort because, as the commission's report noted, the use of instructional time in American schools is "markedly different." Calling its results "startling," the commission reported that "students can receive a high school diploma—often sufficient in itself for university entrance—if they devote only 41 percent of their school time to core academic work" (p. 23).

In summary, although the content covered and the manner in which time is spent were at one time fairly uniform in American education, today there is little consistency in how much time students spend on a given subject or the knowledge and skills covered within that subject area.

Variation In Current Grading Practices

Most educators and noneducators assume that grades are precise indicators of what students know and can do in a subject area. Additionally, it is assumed that current grading practices are the result of a careful study of the most effective ways of reporting achievement and progress. In fact, current grading practices developed in a fairly serendipitous manner. As early as 1913, researcher I. E. Finkelstein sounded the alarm regarding the subjectivity of grades:

> When we consider the practically universal use in all educational institutions of a system of marks . . . to indicate scholastic attainment of the pupils or students in these institutions . . . we can but be astonished at the blind faith that has been felt in the reliability of the marking system. School administrators have been using with confidence an absolutely uncalibrated instrument . . . variability in the marks given for the same subject and to the same pupils by different instructors is so great as frequently to work real injustice to the students. (in Durm, 1993, p. 294)

Education historian Mark Durm (1993) provides a detailed description of the history of grading practices in American universities. Briefly, marking or grading in American education first began at Yale University in the 1780s when a four-point scale was used. "In all probability," Durm notes, "this was the origin of the 4.0 system used by so many colleges and universities today" (p. 295). There is no record of William and Mary using a numerical scale until 1850. Harvard University's first numerical scale was initiated in 1830; however, this was a 20-point scale instead of a 4-point scale. As a precursor to letter grades, Harvard began classifying students into "Divisions" in 1877:

- Division 1:   90 or more on a scale of 100
- Division 2:   75-89
- Division 3:   60-74
- Division 4:   50-59
- Division 5:   40-49
- Division 6:   below 40

In 1897, Mount Holyoke College began using the letter grade system, which is so widely used in education today:

- A: Excellent - equivalent to percents 95-100
- B: Good - equivalent to percents 85-94
- C: Fair - equivalent to percents 76-84
- D: Passed (barely - equivalent to percent 75)
- F: Failed - below 75

Perhaps the most interesting point about grading practices at these institutions is that prior to utilizing a numeric scale, all three institutions relied solely on written descriptions of students' performance—what today are commonly called anecdotal reports.

For the most part, this 100-year-old system is still in place today. Unfortunately, although the system has been in place for a century, there is still little agreement as to the exact meaning of these letter grades. This was rather dramatically illustrated in a nationwide study by researchers Glen Robinson and James Craver (1989) that involved over 800 school districts randomly drawn from the 11,305 school districts that have 300 or more students. One of Robinson and Craver's major conclusions was that districts stress different elements in their grades. Although all districts stress academic achievement, they also stress elements such as effort, behavior, and attendance. Table 1.1 lists the percentage of districts that include each of these variables in their grades.

Table 1.1 Percentage of Districts Reporting Use of Effort, Behavior, and Attendance in Determining Grades

Grade Level	Effort	Behavior	Attendance
K	26%	4%	6%
1-3	26%	4%	7%
4-6	26%	4%	7%
7-9	32%	7%	14%
10-12	33%	8%	17%

Note: Summarized from *Assessing and Grading Student Achievement*, by G.E. Robinson and J. M. Craver, 1989, Arlington, VA: Educational Research Service.

The Robinson and Craver study was done using the official policies of school districts. In a separate study, McREL polled individual teachers on the extent to which they include effort, behavior, and attendance as well as cooperation in their grades. These findings are shown in Table 1.2.

Table 1.2 Percentage of Teachers Reporting Use of Effort, Behavior, Cooperation, and Attendance in Determining Grades

Grade Level	Effort	Behavior	Cooperation	Attendance
K (n = 79)	31%	7%	4%	8%
1-3 (n = 110)	29%	8%	4%	8%
4-6 (n = 158)	30%	8%	8%	10%
7-9 (n = 142)	36%	10%	8%	18%
10-12 (n = 151)	36%	14%	9%	24%

Note: From Teacher Report of Use of Variables When Constructing Grades, unpublished data, by R. J. Marzano, 1995, Aurora, CO: Mid-continent Regional Educational Laboratory.

Tables 1.1 and 1.2 imply that there is great discrepancy in the factors that teachers consider when they construct grades. In effect, grades given by one teacher might mean something entirely different from grades given by another teacher, even though the teachers preside over two identical classes with identical students who are assigned identical work. For example, one teacher might count effort and cooperation as 25% of a grade; another teacher might not count these variables at all. In spite of the overwhelming evidence that current grades are highly suspect (see Guskey, 1996a, for a review of the research), the general public maintains a tenacious view of the sacred nature of the current grading system.

Lack Of Attention To Educational Outputs

Perhaps the most compelling argument for organizing education reform around standards is the current emphasis on what schools put into the process of schooling as opposed to what students get out of schools—an emphasis on educational "inputs" as opposed to educational "outputs." Finn (1990) describes this shift in perspective in terms of an emerging paradigm for education:

> Under the *old* conception (dare I say paradigm?), education was thought of as process and system, effort and intention, investment and hope. To improve education meant to try harder, to engage in more activity, to magnify one's plans, to give people more services, and to become more efficient in delivering them.

> Under the *new* definition, now struggling to be born, education is the result achieved, the learning that takes root when the process has been effective. *Only* if the process succeeds and learning occurs will we say that *education* happened. Absent evidence of such a result, there is no education—however, many attempts have been made, resources deployed, or energies expended. (p. 586)

Finn (1990) asserts that the shortcoming of the old "input" paradigm of schooling came to light in the mid-1960s when the country nobly set out to offer disadvantaged and minority students better opportunities by providing them with better education. The U.S. Office of Education was commissioned by Congress to conduct a study of the quality of educational opportunity. Researcher James Coleman was the chief author of the resulting report, the celebrated "Coleman Report," released in 1966. Finn explains that the report concluded that the cherished "input" variables might not actually have all that much to do with educational equality when equality was conceived of in terms of what students actually learned as opposed to the time, money, and energy that were expended. In later years, Coleman (1972) summarized the importance of his study in the following way:

> The major virtue of the study as conceived and executed lay in the fact that it did not accept the [traditional] definition, and by refusing to do so, has had its major impact in shifting policy attention from its traditional focus on comparison of inputs (the traditional measures of school quality used by school administrators: per-pupil expenditures, class size, teacher salaries, age of building and equipment, and so on) to a focus on output, and the effectiveness of inputs for bringing about changes in output. (pp. 149-150)

Finn (1990) notes that President Richard Nixon was perhaps the first public official with significant power to recognize the need for an emphasis on learning. "As we get more education for the dollar," Nixon stated in 1970, "we will ask Congress to supply many more dollars for education" (in Finn, 1990, p. 588).

16

Finn (1990) explains that although many school reform efforts are still grounded in the old paradigm, some are beginning to embrace the output view of accountability. Among these new efforts, Finn cites the national goals established at the education summit in 1989:

> Perhaps even more portentous was the 1989 "education summit" held in Charlottesville, Virginia, at which the nation's governors and President Bush actually agreed to develop a set of national "goals" for education—goals that, as they were hammered out and made public in early 1990, have far more to do with outcomes than with service delivery. They also pledged to issue annual "report cards" on progress toward those goals. President Bush seemed to epitomize the basic philosophy of the summit—and to echo Nixon's words of almost two decades before—when he said, "We'll judge our efforts not by our intentions, but by our results." (p. 591)

In summary, the new, more efficient and accountable view of education is output-based; success is defined in terms of students learning specific standards.

Competing Countries Do It

A final reason for considering a standards-based approach is that most of the other countries that U.S. policymakers and critics of education say we should emulate rely on policies and structures that fundamentally are standards-based in nature. For example, in their study of standards-setting efforts in other countries, researchers Lauren Resnick and Kate Nolan (1995) note that "many countries whose schools have achieved academic excellence have a national curriculum" (p. 9).

Although Resnick and Nolan (1995) caution that a well-articulated national curriculum is not a guarantee of high academic achievement, they offer some powerful illustrations of the effectiveness of identifying academic standards and aligning curriculum and assessments with those standards. France is a particularly salient example:

> In texts and exams, the influence of the national curriculum is obvious. For example, a French math text for 16-year-olds begins by spelling out the national curriculum for the year so that all 16-year-olds know what they are expected to study. The book's similar table of contents shows that the text developers referred to the curriculum. Moreover, the text makes frequent references to math exams the regional school districts have given in the past. Students practice on these exams to help them prepare for the exam they will face; they know where to concentrate to meet the standard. (p. 9)

In a similar vein, a report published by NESIC (1993) details the highly centralized manner in which standards are established in other countries. For example, in China, standards are set for the entire country and for all levels of the school system by the State Education Commission in Beijing. In England, standards setting was considered the responsibility of local schools until 1988 when the Education Reform Act mandated and outlined the process for establishing a national curriculum; the School Examinations and Assessment Council was established to carry out this process. In Japan, the ministry of education in Tokyo (Manibushi) sets the standards for schools, but allows each of the 47 prefectures (Ken) some latitude in adapting those standards. According to the NESIC report, "most countries embody their content standards in curriculum guides issued by the ministries of education or their equivalents" (pc-51). Additionally, "a national examination system provides a further mechanism for setting standards through specifications of examinations, syllabuses and regulations, preparations of tests, grading of answers, and establishment of cutoff points" (pc-51).

What Have We Learned?

From history and from our work with schools and districts, we have learned at least two very important lessons about organizing schools around standards. First, setting standards is a very technical process that should not be taken lightly. A school or district that sets content-area standards by convening groups of teachers to identify standards, without serious up-front consideration of technical issues, is asking for trouble. Second, organizing schooling around standards is not a cookie-cutter process—one size does not fit all. Standards-based approaches must be tailor-made to the specific needs and values of individual schools and districts. In fact, the basic purpose of this book is to articulate a process by which schools and districts across the country can design their own standards-based system of education. Additionally, this book attempts to provide clear models of how standards-based education can be implemented. The remaining chapters discuss specific questions that a school or district should address when designing a standards-based system.

The Where, What, And Who Of Standards

In this chapter we consider three of the initial questions a district or school should ask about standards: Where will we get our standards? What type of standards will we have? Who will be involved in setting our standards? The manner in which each of these questions is answered drastically affects the manner in which a district or school organizes itself around standards. We begin with a consideration of the first question, Where will we get our standards?

Where Will We Get Our Standards?

One of the first issues a district or school must address is the source or sources that it will use to construct standards. Currently, most districts and schools rely on two primary sources: national and state efforts to identify standards. We first consider efforts at the national level.

National Efforts To Identify Standards

As described in chapter 1, the impetus for setting standards at the national level can be indirectly traced back to the 1983 publication of *A Nation at Risk* (National Commission on Excellence in Education) and directly linked to the first education summit in Charlottesville, Virginia, in September 1989. Standards-setting efforts by a number of national organizations representing various subject areas resulted in the publication of numerous documents. The documents listed in Exhibit 2.1 are the result of efforts by groups that either were funded by the U.S. Department of Education or identify themselves as representing the national consensus in their subject areas. Thus, these documents could be said to articulate the "official" version of standards in the respective subject areas. For a detailed discussion of the status of standards development in various subject areas, see Kendall and Marzano, 1996.

Exhibit 2.1 "Official" Standards Documents

Science	National Research Council. (1996). *National Science Education Standards*. Washington, DC: National Academy Press.
Foreign Language	National Standards in Foreign Language Education Project. (1996). *Standards for Foreign Language Learning: Preparing for the 21st Century*. Lawrence, KS: Allen Press, Inc.
English Language Arts	National Council of Teachers of English and the International Reading Association (1996). *Standards for the English Language Arts*. Urbana, IL: National Council of Teachers of English.
History	National Center for History in the Schools. (1994). *National Standards for History for Grades K-4: Expanding Children's World in Time and Space*. Los Angeles: Author National Center for History in the Schools. (1994). *National Standards for United States History: Exploring the American Experience*. Los Angeles: Author. National Center for History in the Schools. (1994). *National Standards for World History: Exploring Paths to the Present*. Los Angeles: Author. National Center for History in the Schools. (1996). *National Standards for History: Basic Edition*. Los Angeles: Author.
Arts	Consortium of National Arts Education Associations. (1994). *National Standards for Arts Education: What Every Young American Should Know and Be Able to Do in the Arts*. Reston, VA: Music Educators National Conference.
Health	Joint Committee on National Health Education Standards. (1995). *National Health Education Standards: Achieving Health Literacy*. Reston, VA: Association for the Advancement of Health Education.
Civics	Center for Civic Education. (1994). *National Standards for Civics and Government*. Calabasas, CA: Author.
Economics	National Council on Economic Education. (1996, August). *Content Statements for State Standards in Economics, K-12* (Draft). New York: Author.
Geography	Geography Education Standards Project. (1994). *Geography for Life: National Geography Standards*. Washington, DC: National Geographic Research and Exploration.
Physical Education	National Association for Sport and Physical Education. (1995). *Moving into the Future, National Standards for Physical Education: A Guide to Content and Assessment*. St. Louis: Mosby.
Mathematics	National Council of Teachers of Mathematics. (1989). *Curriculum and Evaluation Standards for School Mathematics*. Reston, VA: Author.
Social Studies	National Council for the Social Studies. (1994). *Expectations of Excellence: Curriculum Standards for Social Studies*. Washington, DC: Author.

One might assume that to construct standards at a local level, a district or school need only consult these subject-specific national documents and copy the standards verbatim. Unfortunately, this is not the case because the various national standards documents vary conceptually in a number of important ways. For example, the manner in which standards are described or defined by a document in mathematics, for example, might be quite different from the manner in which standards are described or defined in a document in science. In fact, a district or school wishing to construct local standards from the national documents must address at least four problems: (1) multiple documents, (2) differing definitions of standards, (3) varying levels of generality, and (4) varying levels of subordination.

The Problem Of Multiple Documents

A number of subject areas have multiple documents that address the standards in that domain. For example, *Curriculum and Evaluation Standards for School Mathematics*, published by NCTM (1989), is certainly considered the "official" description of what students should know and be able to do in the field of mathematics. However, mathematics standards and benchmarks are also explicitly and implicitly articulated in each of the following documents:

- *Benchmarks for Science Literacy* (1993), by Project 2061 of the American Association for the Advancement of Science (AAAS);

- *Framework for the 1994 National Assessment of Educational Progress Mathematics Assessment* (1992), by the National Assessment of Educational Progress (NAEP);

- *What Work Requires of Schools: A SCANS Report for America 2000* (1991), by the Secretary's Commission on Achieving Necessary Skills (SCANS); and

- *Workplace Basics: The Essential Skills Employers Want* (1990), by Carnevale, Gainer, and Meltzer.

Science provides another example of multiple documents. At least three documents have gained recognition as descriptions of what students should know and be able to do in science. The official effort to identify science standards was led by the National Committee on Science Education Standards and Assessment (NCSESA) and published in 1996 by the National Research Council (NRC) as *National Science Education Standards*. The document contains some 200 pages of standards written at three levels: K-4, 5-8, and 9-12. Twenty-five standards are articulated at the K-4 level, 28 standards at the 5-8 level, and 34 standards at the 9-12 level. A second science standards document comes from AAAS's Project 2061: *Benchmarks for Science Literacy* (1993). This publication articulates 60 "literacy goals" across four levels: K-2, 3-5, 6-8, and 9-12. In addition to these publications, the National Science Teachers Association (NSTA) has published the *Scope, Sequence, and Coordination of National Science Education Content Standards* (Aldridge & Strassenburg, 1995) as an addendum to *Scope, Sequence, and Coordination of Secondary School Science, Volume I: The Content Core: A Guide for Curriculum Designers* (Pearsall, 1993).

In short, a district or school would need to consult a number of documents to review even a single subject area comprehensively. For example, it would need to review 12 documents in history, 4 documents in mathematics, and 28 documents in English language arts. Appendix A lists the various documents that should be consulted in order to comprehensively review standards in each subject area.

The Problem Of Varying Definitions

A second issue a district or school must address if it wishes to use the national documents is that the various documents sometimes treat standards in very different ways. To illustrate, consider the following elements taken from the NCTM document *Curriculum and Evaluation Standards for School Mathematics* (1989):

a. Students use estimation to check the reasonableness of results.

b. Students describe, model, draw, and classify shapes.

These elements are stated as standards in the NCTM document but are very different in nature. Element *a* describes a skill or ability a person might use to solve a real-life problem. For example, you might use estimation to check the reasonableness of your calculations as to the amount of lumber to purchase in order to build a fence around your back yard. Conversely, the skills and abilities delineated in element *b* are not commonly used in real-life situations. It is difficult to imagine many day-to-day situations that would demand that one be able to model or classify shapes. Activities such as those described in element *b* are best described as instructional devices to help students understand shapes. Element *b* is most accurately referred to as a curriculum standard, whereas element *a* is most accurately referred to as a content standard.

It is our strong opinion that curriculum standards should not be mixed with content standards. We have two overarching reasons for recommending against this. First, content standards describe the goals for individual student achievement. Curriculum standards, on the other hand, provide supplemental information that contributes to helping students reach these goals. Including both types of standards in a single standards document mixes means with ends. Second, including curriculum standards, which usually focus on activities, projects, or techniques (if interpreted rigidly), could leave teachers little or no room for instructional diversity. Unfortunately, many of the national documents mix content and curriculum standards, which makes the task of adapting these standards to local needs a difficult and complex one.

The Problem Of Varying Levels Of Generality

Another problem with the national documents that a school or district must address deals with the level of generality at which standards are stated. Even a cursory review of the standards generated by different groups reveals very different perspectives on the level of generality at which standards should be stated. For example, the *National Standards for Arts Education* (Consortium of National Arts Education Associations, 1994) provides the following as a standard:

- Understanding the arts in relation to history and cultures

In contrast, a document from *National Standards for United States History: Exploring the American Experience* (NCHS, 1994b) lists the following standard:

- Students should understand the causes of the Civil War.

The example from *National Standards for United States History* is obviously more specific than that from *National Standards for Arts Education*. In addition, the history document provides more detailed information for each of its standards than does the arts document. The degree to which standards are articulated in specific terms is critical because the level of specificity adopted by a school or district will affect the level of detail within the standards, the degree of comprehensiveness the standards aim for, and the number of standards created.

The Problem Of Varying Levels Of Subordination

National standards documents vary in a number of ways. They perhaps differ most in the levels of subordination they use. For example, the history standards documents use a fairly complex structure in terms of levels of subordination. To illustrate, consider the K-4 standards from the document *National Standards for History for Grades K-4: Expanding Children's World in Time and Space* (NCHS, 1994a). The highest level of generality is the "topic," of which there are four. Below the topic level are "standards." In all, the four topics encompass eight standards. Each standard is further subdivided into what are referred to as "understandings." For example, standard 3 in the document states:

> Students should understand the people, events, problems, and ideas that were significant in creating the history of their state.

This standard is divided into five understandings:

> The student should be able to
>
> 3A   demonstrate understanding of the history of indigenous people who first lived in their state or region;
>
> 3B   demonstrate understanding of the first European, African, and/or Asian-Pacific explorers and settlers who came to their state or region;
>
> 3C   demonstrate understanding of the various other groups from regions throughout the world who came into the students' own state or region over the long-ago and recent past;
>
> 3D   demonstrate understanding of the interactions among all these groups throughout the history of their state; and
>
> 3E   demonstrate understanding of the ideas that were significant in the development of the state and that helped to forge its unique identity.

Each of these understandings is then subdivided into two elements, both of which are at about the same level of subordination. One type of element is called a "component," which exemplifies the understandings in further detail. The other type of element is called an "example of student achievement," which provides an illustration of how students might apply their knowledge and skill. Components are coded with either "K-4" or "3-4" to indicate the grades in which each standard "can appropriately be developed" (NCHS, 1994a, p. 9). Examples of student achievement are given for grades K-2 and 3-4.

The hierarchic structure of the history standards, then, might be depicted in the following way:

Level 1: Topic
    Level 2: Standard
        Level 3: Understandings
            Level 4: Components
                Level 5: K-4
                Level 5: 3-4
            Level 4: Examples of student achievement
                Level 5: K-2
                Level 5: 3-4

Contrast this structure with that used in the document *Benchmarks for Science Literacy* (Project 2061, 1993). This document is organized into twelve chapters, each of which is divided into a number of topics. For example, chapter 5, entitled The Living Environment, is divided into six topics:

- Diversity of Life
- Heredity
- Cells
- Interdependence of Life
- Flow of Matter and Energy
- Evolution of Life

Content knowledge in each of these topics is then exemplified at four levels: K-2, 3-5, 6-8, and 9-12. These statements of expectations about students' knowledge and skill at the end of each of the four levels are referred to as "benchmarks." The hierarchic structure of this science document might be depicted in the following manner:

Level 1: Chapter heading
    Level 2: Topic
        Level 3: K-2 benchmarks
        Level 3: 3-5 benchmarks
        Level 3: 6-8 benchmarks
        Level 3: 9-12 benchmarks

Our experience indicates that the simpler the hierarchic structure, the better. In fact, we recommend that local schools and districts construct only two levels. The highest level of generality is a standard. The level below a standard is a benchmark. To illustrate, consider the following statement, which a district or school might identify as a content standard within mathematics: "The student demonstrates number sense and an understanding of number theory." In keeping with the nature of a standard, this statement maps out a very general area within mathematics. Benchmarks for this standard appropriate at the high school level might include the following expectations of a student's knowledge:

- Understands characteristics of the real number system and its subsystems
- Understands the relationship between roots and exponents
- Models numbers using three-dimensional regions

Benchmarks appropriate for middle school might include the following:

- Understands the relationship of decimals to whole numbers
- Understands the relationship of fractions to decimals and whole numbers
- Understands the basic difference between odd versus even numbers
- Understands the basic characteristics of mixed numbers
- Models numbers using number lines

Benchmarks, then, describe the specific developmental components of the general subject-area knowledge identified by a standard. Theoretically, benchmarks could be identified at all grade levels. In fact, the number of levels at which benchmarks will be written is a major consideration for a district or school. We consider this issue in depth in chapter 4.

State Efforts To Identify Standards

In addition to national documents that identify standards and benchmarks in various content areas, most states have identified standards and benchmarks or are in the process of identifying standards and benchmarks (Gandal, 1995a, 1995b). State efforts to create standards were given an impressive endorsement at the second education summit in Palisades, New York, in March 1996 when the state governors committed to designing standards and sharing conceptual and technical information regarding their efforts (National Governor's Association, 1996). These actions are consistent with the opinions of those educators who believe that it is at the state level that the standards movement will either succeed or fail. As education reporter Lynn Olson (1995a) notes:

> The U.S. Constitution makes it clear: States bear the responsibility for educating their citizens. They decide how long students continue their education and how the schools are financed. They control what is taught, what is tested, which textbooks are used, and how teachers are trained.

> Thus, despite all the talk about national education standards, it is the 50 individual states that ultimately will determine what students should know and be able to do. (p. 15)

It is probably accurate to say that most states would prefer not to simply adopt standards set by national organizations. For example, Fred Tempes, an associate superintendent in the California Department of Education explains, "I guess like most states we'd like to feel that we can set our own standards" (in Olson, 1995a, p. 15). Olson notes that 46 states have applied for federal grants under the Goals 2000: Educate America Act. Thirty-one states began work on identifying standards in 1991. As of April 1995, most of those states were still in the process of drafting or reviewing their standards.

In spite of these impressive findings, state efforts to set standards are inconsistent. According to studies conducted by the American Federation of Teachers (AFT) (see Gandal, 1995a, 1996), there is both good news and bad news regarding state efforts to set standards. "The good news," AFT President Albert Shanker says, "is that the movement to upgrade academic standards has taken hold all across the country" (in Innerst, 1995, p. A4). The bad news is that the state-level attempts vary in terms of quality and level of effort. To date, the AFT has completed two studies of state efforts to construct standards. The first, entitled *Making Standards Matter: A Fifty-State Progress Report on Efforts to Raise Academic Standards*, was published in 1995 (see Gandal, 1995a). That initial study reported the following findings:

- Every state except Iowa is engaged in developing academic standards. Iowa has not set standards, opting for standards to be set by local schools and districts.
- Thirteen states have standards that are clear and specific enough to form the basis of core curriculum. The states with the clearest standards are California, Colorado, Georgia, and Virginia.
- Thirty-one states have or will have students' assessments linked to standards, but many of those standards are too vague.
- Seven states have taken steps to evaluate their standards against those of countries with high-achieving students. (in Innerst, 1995, p. A4)

The second report, entitled *Making Standards Matter, 1996: An Annual Fifty-State Report on Efforts to Raise Academic Standards*, was published in 1996 (see Gandal, 1996). On the positive side, the report noted that a great deal of work had been done since the first report:

> The tremendous amount of activity we've seen in the states over the past year is another strong indicator of the national commitment to raising academic standards. Over two-thirds of states have developed new or revised documents since we issued our report last year. Most of these states have come out with new documents in all four core subjects while some states have issued new standards in a few subjects. (p. 13)

However, the report concluded that state efforts are still far from acceptable. The report (see Gandal, 1996) noted the following:

- Forty-eight states are engaged in developing academic standards. (In addition to Iowa, since the publication of the 1995 report, Wyoming has decided against the construction of state standards.)

- Fifteen states have standards in all four core subject areas (i.e., English, history, mathematics, science) that are clear and well grounded in content.

- Forty-two states either have assessments or are in the process of developing assessments linked to their standards, but the standards are not strong enough in most of these states to provide a solid foundation for the assessments.

- Only twelve states have looked at what is expected of students in other countries, while developing their own standards, although more states recognize the need for internationally competitive standards.

(McREL surveyed standards-setting efforts in each state. Appendix B provides a thumbnail sketch of the results of this survey.)

The most damaging finding in both reports is that most state documents simply have weak standards. To illustrate, the 1996 report offers the following as an example of a strong mathematics standard: "The student will differentiate between area and perimeter and identify whether the application of the concept of perimeter or area is appropriate for a given situation" (Gandal, 1996, p. 16). Conversely, a weak mathematics standard from another state document is "Students should be able to represent and solve problems using geometric models" (Gandal, 1996, p. 16).

This lack of specificity in state documents has caused significant opposition to the standards movement. Standards expert Matthew Gandal (1995b) explains that the 1992 "Common Core of Learning" standards in Virginia and the 1991 "Student Learning Outcomes" in Pennsylvania were so vague as to be judged as nonacademic by the constituents of those states. This perception led to the defeat of the entire reform package in those states and the redrafting of more specific standards in both states.

If we accept the findings of the AFT reports, then the support and guidance that can be expected from state-level documents is relatively limited. The vast majority of states have standards that are so vague that they will probably have to be reworked—or even totally rewritten—by schools and districts in those states. Even in the 15 states whose standards were judged to be specific enough, districts still most likely will have to supplement their state standards. For example, Colorado was judged by AFT to have standards that are specific enough to be used by schools and districts. However, the Colorado standards are stated at four levels: K-2, 3-5, 6-8, and 9-12. If a school or district in Colorado wishes to construct grade-level benchmarks (i.e., separate benchmarks for each grade level), it will have to extrapolate the four Colorado levels to 12 levels. Finally, most state documents are presented as "guidelines" to be used by local districts rather than as mandated standards that must be followed without alteration. Only three states will hold students accountable for meeting standards prior to high school graduation; less than half of the states require or plan to require students to pass high school graduation exams linked to their standards, and only nine states will require students to pass graduation exams linked to their standards in all four core subjects (Gandal, 1996). Consequently, even where a sound state- standards document exists, the schools and districts in that state might still find it necessary to engage in a great deal of standards writing and redesign if they wish to implement a standards-based approach.

The McREL Database: A Tool For Constructing Local Standards

From the discussion above, one can easily surmise that the process of constructing local standards, even in states that have sound state documents, is highly labor intensive. What school or district has the resources to wade through the myriad of documents cited above and resolve technical issues such as the level of generality at which standards and benchmarks will be articulated? Fortunately, there are resources that are available. In this section, we consider one specific resource: the McREL database. However, before considering this resource in depth, it is important to note a similar effort by the Council for Basic Education (CBE) in Washington, D.C. In December 1995, CBE announced the initiation of its project called Standards for Excellence in Education. Sponsored by the Carnegie Corporation of New York, the Pew Charitable Trusts, and the MacArthur Foundation, the project's purpose is to analyze standards documents in mathematics, science, civics, history, geography, the arts, English, and foreign languages to make them more useful to teachers and parents. The McREL database had a similar goal as its impetus.

The Mid-continent Regional Educational Laboratory (McREL), located in Aurora, Colorado, is a nonprofit education organization specializing in applied educational research and development. In part through its funding from the U.S. Office of Educational Research and Improvement, McREL has developed a resource database that should greatly lessen the amount of work a district or school must undertake if it wishes to design its own standards based on the national documents or to augment state standards. Simply stated, McREL has analyzed all relevant documents across the various content areas—standards drafts as well as relevant subject-area materials—to produce a database that translates the available information into a common format, one we believe will be easily used by schools and districts. The database is reported in full in the document *Content Knowledge: A Compendium of Standards and Benchmarks for K-12 Education* (Kendall & Marzano, 1996). It is also available on the World Wide Web (Uniform Resource Locator: www.mcrel.org/standard.html).

In all, the McREL database contains 252 different standards and their related benchmarks. (Appendix C lists all of the standards in the McREL database.) These standards are organized into thirteen major categories representing traditional subject areas:

- **Mathematics:** 9 standards, 349 benchmarks
- **Science:** 18 standards, 324 benchmarks

- **History:**
  - *K-4 History:* 8 standards, 109 benchmarks
  - *U.S. History:* 31 standards, 423 benchmarks
  - *World History:* 39 standards, 471 benchmarks
  - *Historical Understanding:* 2 standards, 42 benchmarks
- **Language Arts:** 13 standards, 372 benchmarks
- **Geography:** 18 standards, 238 benchmarks
- **Arts:**
  - *Dance:* 6 standards, 62 benchmarks
  - *Music:* 7 standards, 80 benchmarks
  - *Theatre:* 6 standards, 72 benchmarks
  - *Visual Arts:* 5 standards, 42 benchmarks
  - *Art Connections:* 1 standard, 13 benchmarks
- **Civics:** 29 standards, 427 benchmarks
- **Economics:** 10 standards, 173 benchmarks
- **Foreign Language:** 5 standards, 86 benchmarks
- **Health:** 10 standards, 136 benchmarks
- **Physical Education:** 5 standards, 105 benchmarks
- **Behavioral Studies:** 4 standards, 100 benchmarks
- **Life Skills:**
  - *Thinking and Reasoning:* 6 standards, 117 benchmarks
  - *Working With Others:* 5 standards, 51 benchmarks
  - *Self-Regulation:* 6 standards, 59 benchmarks
  - *Life Work:* 9 standards, 90 benchmarks

These standards were constructed from the content of 85 documents. (A list of these can be found in Appendix D.) These documents range from nationally funded efforts, such as the history standards developed by the National Center for History in the Schools, to state documents, such as the California Department of Education science framework, to documents developed through privately funded efforts, such as the elementary and junior high school standards developed by the Edison Project. Quite obviously, it would take a school or district an inordinate amount of time to analyze these 85 documents at the level of detail McREL has undertaken.

To obtain a sense of the standards in the McREL database, consider the following 18 standards in geography. Note that these standards have been organized into categories that some documents refer to as "strands" (see, e.g., Florida Department of Education, 1996).

The World in Spatial Terms

1. Understands the characteristics and uses of maps, globes, and other geographic tools and technologies
2. Knows the location of places, geographic features, and patterns of the environment
3. Understands the characteristics and uses of spatial organization of Earth's surface

Places and Regions

4. Understands the physical and human characteristics of place
5. Understands the concept of regions
6. Understands that culture and experience influence people's perceptions of places and regions

Physical Systems

7. Knows the physical processes that shape patterns on Earth's surface
8. Understands the characteristics of ecosystems on Earth's surface

Human Systems

9. Understands the nature, distribution, and migration of human populations on Earth's surface
10. Understands the nature and complexity of Earth's cultural mosaics
11. Understands the patterns and networks of economic interdependence on Earth's surface
12. Understands the patterns of human settlement and their causes
13. Understands the forces of cooperation and conflict that shape the divisions of Earth's surface

Environment and Society

14. Understands how human actions modify the physical environment
15. Understands how physical systems affect human systems
16. Understands the changes that occur in the meaning, use, distribution, and importance of resources

Uses of Geography

17. Understands how geography is used to interpret the past
18. Understand global development and environmental issues

Each standard contains benchmarks written at four levels: primary, upper elementary, middle school/junior high, and high school. For example, below are the benchmarks for level 3 of standard 5, "understands the concept of regions." Level 3 indicates that the information is appropriate for grades six through eight:

- Knows regions at various spatial scales (e.g., hemispheres, regions within continents, countries, cities)

(GE,152;NI,56-57)

- Understands criteria that give a region identity (e.g., its central focus, such as Amsterdam as a transportation center; relationships between physical and cultural characteristics, such as the Sunbelt's warm climate and popularity with retired people)

(GE,152)

- Knows types of regions such as formal regions (e.g., school districts, circuit-court districts, states of the United States), functional regions (e.g., the marketing area of a local newspaper, the "fanshed" of a professional sports team) and perceptual regions (e.g., the Bible Belt in the United States, the Riviera in southern France, the Great American Desert)

(GE,153;NE,64-65)

- Knows factors that contribute to changing regional characteristics (e.g., economic development, accessibility, migration, media image)

(GE,153;NI,56-57)

- Understands the influences and effects of particular regional labels and images (e.g., Twin Peaks in San Francisco; Capitol Hill in Washington, D.C.; the South; the rust belt; "developed" vs. "less-developed" regions)

(GE,153;NI,56-57)

- Understands ways regional systems are interconnected (e.g., watersheds and river systems, regional connections through trade, cultural ties between regions)

Note that each benchmark has a detailed code called a *citation log*. (For ease of discussion here, we have not included all the information contained in the citation log for each benchmark. For a detailed discussion, see Kendall and Marzano, 1996.) The citations in the log specify the documents in which the benchmark appears and the explicitness of the benchmark within those documents. To illustrate, consider the citation log for the first benchmark: (GE,152;NI,45). The letter *G* indicates that the benchmark is found in *Geography for Life: National Geography Standards* from the Geography Education Standards Project. The letter *E* means it is explicitly stated, and the number *152* designates the page on which it is found. The letter *N* indicates that the benchmark is also found in *Item Specifications: 1994 National Assessment of Educational Progress in Geography* (NAEP, 1992). The letter *I* indicates that it is implicit in that document, and the number *45* identifies the page number on which the benchmark is implicitly stated.

Obviously, this brief illustration cannot provide a thorough understanding of the coding system in the McREL database. However, it does provide a sense of the level of detail present within that database. Specifically, using the McREL database, a school or district should be able to construct its own standards and benchmarks or augment standards developed by the state, based on a synthesis of the standards and benchmarks found in a vast array of national- and state-level documents.

What Types Of Standards Will We Have?

The issue of the type of standards a district or school will address is so basic that it should be dealt with at the outset. In this section we consider four issues regarding types of standards: (1) world-class versus literacy standards, (2) traditional subject-area standards, (3) thinking and reasoning standards, and (4) lifelong learning standards.

World-Class Versus Literacy Standards

Some of the early discussions of standards advocated a world-class approach. Educators and noneducators agreed that American students should achieve academic standards that made these students second to none. Indeed, Goal 4 of the six goals set at the 1989 Education Summit explicitly set this level of expectation:

> Goal 4: By the year 2000, U.S. students will be first in the world of achievement in science and mathematics achievement. (NEGP, 1991, p. 4)

This emphasis on raising the performance of American students to a level that matches or exceeds those of other countries has also been articulated by the American Federation of Teachers (see Gandal, 1995a, 1995b). Finally the state governors endorsed the push for world-class standards at the second education summit in March 1996, at Palisades, New York: "As Governors, we commit to the development and establishment of internationally competitive academic standards" (National Governors Association, 1996, p. 4).

Some of the national standards documents have made noble attempts to keep this world-class perspective. For example, the Geography Education Standards Project (1994) describes its standards in the following way:

> These geography standards identify what American students should learn—a set of voluntary benchmarks that every school and school district may use as guidelines for developing their own curricula. The standards for grades K-4, 5-8, and 9-12 specify the essential subject matter, skills, and perspectives that all students should have in order to attain high levels of competency. The standards provide every parent, teacher, curriculum developer, and business and policy leader with a set of challenging expectations for all students. (p. 9)

Although we applaud efforts to write world-class standards, such efforts represent a daunting task, especially in light of the research finding that there is an increasing disparity between the performance of American students and the performance of students from other countries on international tests. Ravitch describes this widening gap in her book *National Standards in American Education: A Citizen's Guide* (1995). A summary of Ravitch's synthesis of the research is presented in Table 2.1 on the next page.

Although Ravitch's interpretation of these international comparisons has been questioned (see Berliner & Biddle, 1995), the goal of achieving world-class standards by the year 2000 appears to be an ambitious endeavor—perhaps an overly ambitious one. Research on skill development provides a useful metaphor regarding the amount of energy and resources it might take to achieve world-class standards. Specifically, researchers William Frederick and Herbert Walberg (1980) explain that swimming workout data indicate that 1,000 yards of practice per day produces 75 percent of maximum attainment and 2,000 yards produces 85 percent of maximum. However, it takes 10,000 yards of practice per day to produce 95 percent of maximum. In other words, the amount of energy and resources required to effect positive changes in achievement escalates geometrically as expectations reach an optimum level. Consequently, those who design standards must ask if the amount of energy it will take for students to reach world-class standards is worth the end result, just as the swimmer must ask if the extra 9,000 yards of practice per day (a 900% increase) is worth the gain of 20 percent in skill development.

Although some of the national standards documents aspire to world-class standards, most have adopted what might be called a "literacy" approach. In a literacy approach, standards are written at a level required to be a functioning adult in American society. For example, AAAS's Project 2061 describes the standards in its *Benchmarks for Science Literacy* (1993) as "levels of understanding and ability that *all* students are expected to reach on the way to becoming science-literate" (p. xiii).

If a district or school wishes to identify world-class standards, it can adopt the approach used by NCTM. In its *Curriculum and Evaluation Standards For School Mathematics* (1989), NCTM identifies literacy standards for all students. However, it additionally identifies standards, such as those listed below, for those who wish to pursue mathematics study at an advanced level:

- construct proofs for mathematical assertions, including indirect proofs and proofs by mathematical induction,
- use circular functions to model periodic real-world phenomena; and
- analyze the graphs of polynomial, rational, radical, and transcendental functions. (pp. 143, 163, 180)

Table 2.1 Comparison of Performance of U.S. Students and Students From Other Countries

Test	When	Given To	Number of Countries/ Educational Systems Participating	Results
First International Mathematics Study	1960s	13-year-olds	12	U.S. students scored significantly lower than students in 9 other systems, ahead of students in only one system.
		High School seniors	12	On a test given only to seniors enrolled in a math course, U.S. students scored last, behind students in 11 other countries.
				On a test given to seniors not enrolled in a math course, U.S. students scored last, behind students in 7 other countries.
Second International Mathematics Study	1981-82	13-year-olds	15	U.S. students placed at or near the median on most tests.
		High School seniors who had taken at least 2 years of algebra and 1 year of geometry	15	U. S. students placed at or near the bottom in number systems, algebra, geometry, and calculus.
First International Science Study	1960s-1970s	10-year-olds	16	Only Japanese students scored higher than American students.
		14-year-olds and students in last year of secondary school	18	14-year-old students in 5 systems scored higher than American students; U.S. students in last year of secondary school scored last among students in 11 systems.
Second International Science Study	1983-86	10-year-olds	15	U.S. students scored at the median.
		14-year-olds	17	U.S. students scored in the bottom quarter.
		Students in last year of secondary school	14	U.S. seniors were an elite group enrolled in a second-year science course, yet they scored at or near the bottom in biology, chemistry, and physics.
International Assessment of Educational Progress in Mathematics and Science	1988	13-year-olds	6 (12 systems)	Students in 8 systems had significantly higher scores than U.S. students in science. In mathematics, students in 10 systems scored significantly higher than U.S. students.
Second International Assessment of Educational Progress in Mathematics and Science	1990-91	9-year-olds	15*	U.S. students placed near the bottom of 10 countries in math, but third in science.
		13-year-olds	15*	U.S. students placed in the bottom quarter in both subjects.

*Students in 20 countries were tested; however, comprehensive populations were tested in 15 countries.

Note: Summarized from *National Standards in American Education: A Citizen's Guide* (pp. 84-86), by D. Ravitch, 1995, Washington, DC: Brookings Institution.

Traditional Subject-Area Standards

Most of the state documents focus on the subject areas of English, mathematics, science, history (or social studies), and geography. Most educators and noneducators would consider these subject areas to be traditional staples of the curriculum. Not coincidentally, these are the subject areas identified in Goal 3 of the Goals 2000 initiative, which came out of the 1989 education summit meeting in Charlottesville, Virginia. Recall from chapter 1 that Goal 3 stated that by the year 2000, American students will demonstrate competence in these subject areas.

That standards should address the traditional subject areas seems self-evident. However, some people believe that organizing standards into the traditional subject areas is a practice that has outlived its usefulness. For example, theorists Arthur Costa and Rosemarie Liebman (1995) articulate two reasons that the traditional subject areas have outlived their usefulness:

> First, the disciplines, as we have known them, no longer exist. They are being replaced by human inquiry that draws upon generalized, transdisciplinary bodies of knowledge and relationships. Researchers today are searching for patterns in the chaos of minds, machines, animals, and societies in order to discover important connections.
>
> Second, curriculum, based on discrete disciplines, emerged from a largely male- and western-oriented way of thinking. As we learn to listen to the female voice, gain greater understanding of the perspectives of indigenous peoples, and become more global, our curriculum will need to reflect richer views of how humans construct meaning. (p. 23)

Similar criticisms of the traditional subject-area approach have been leveled by other theorists (see Pinar, Reynolds, Slattery, & Taubman, 1994; Spady, 1988).

In spite of these intriguing arguments, there appears to be no compelling reason that a school or district should ignore subject-area standards. In fact, as Gandal (1995b) notes, ignoring them can have negative consequences:

> When standards-setters abandon the disciplines, content suffers. Standards become vaguely worded and loosely connected, making the job of curriculum designers, assessment developers, and teachers all but impossible. (p. 17)

This is not to say that standards from different subject areas cannot be "bundled" or "packaged" together in unique, timely courses. For example, selected mathematics standards can be bundled with selected science and history (or social studies) standards within a course that deals with the technical and societal implications of a local project. Such an approach is commonly referred to as interdisciplinary (see Drake, 1993; Fogarty, 1991; Jacobs, 1989; Tchudi, 1991). However interdisciplinary courses are designed, it is important to identify the precise knowledge and skills from the domains that are being integrated. For example, if a district or school decides to develop a course that integrates standards and benchmarks from mathematics, science, history, and literature, it must still identify the important information and skills within those subject areas. Consequently, we recommend that districts and schools first identify standards and benchmarks within the traditional subject areas and then think of unique ways to bundle selected standards and benchmarks in an integrated fashion.

Thinking And Reasoning Standards

In our study of the national and state standards documents used to construct the McREL database, we found that virtually all of them either implicitly or explicitly acknowledged the importance of thinking and reasoning. This is not surprising given the historical emphasis educators have placed on thinking and reasoning. Over 80 years ago, education philosopher John Dewey (1916) wrote, "The sole direct path to enduring improvement in the methods of instruction and learning consists in centering upon the conditions which exact, promote, and test thinking" (p. 6). Similarly, in 1961, the National Education Association identified the improvement of thinking and reasoning as central to American education:

> In the general area of the development of the ability to think, there is a field for new research of the greatest importance. It is essential that those who have responsibility for management and policy determination in education commit themselves to expansion of such research and to the application of the fruits of this research. This is the context in which the significant answers to such issues as educational technology, length of the school year, and content of teacher education must be sought and given. (Educational Policies Commission, 1961, pp. 14-15)

More recently, calls for the enhancement of thinking and reasoning in American education have come from the National Science Board Commission on Precollege Education in Mathematics, Science and Technology (1983), the College Board (1983), the National Education Association (Futtrell, 1987), and the American Federation of Teachers (1985). Additionally, the need to enhance students' abilities to think and reason is explicitly stated in Goal 3 of six national education goals established at the first education summit in Charlottesville, Virginia. (See chapter 1 for a discussion of the summit.) As mentioned previously, Goal 3 explicitly targeted the subjects of English, mathematics, science, history, and geography. In addition, it noted that "every school in America will ensure that all students learn to use their minds well so they may be prepared for responsible citizenship, further learning, and productive employment in our modern economy" (NEGP, 1991, p. ix).

Although there is agreement as to the importance of enhancing thinking and reasoning, there is not much agreement on the manner in which thinking and reasoning should be articulated in standards. One approach is to establish a set of standards on generic reasoning. For example, the document *Workplace Basics: The Essential Skills Employers Want* (Carnevale, Gainer, & Meltzer, 1990), identifies Creative Thinking as one of the 16 skills that are important to the workplace. Similarly, the New Standards Project (New Standards, 1995) includes a category of standards called Applied Learning, which involves a variety of forms of problem solving. Thinking skills identified in this manner are stated as generic mental processes that cut across all content areas. A second approach is reflected in the NCTM's *Curriculum and Evaluation Standards* (1989), which articulates a standard entitled Mathematical Reasoning. Within this category, those reasoning processes presumed to be specific to mathematics, but useful within the various subdisciplines of mathematics, are identified. Similarly, *National Standards for United States History* (NCHS, 1994b) includes a category called Historical Thinking. This involves such abilities as chronological thinking, historical research, and historical comprehension. Finally, the third perspective is exemplified by the *Geography for Life: National Geography Standards* (Geography Education Standards Project, 1994). Here no set of standards nor any one specific standard addresses thinking and reasoning. Rather, the benchmarks are stated in terms of performance tasks. (This format for articulating standards and benchmarks is discussed in depth in chapter 3.) These performance tasks implicitly contain thinking and reasoning abilities. To illustrate, consider the following benchmark, which makes explicit the need to make inferences—an important reasoning process:

- [Students] make inferences about differences in the personal geographies of men and women.

A cursory review of the literature in cognitive psychology would seem to favor the latter two positions concerning an approach to thinking and reasoning skills. Specifically, strong arguments have been made against the isolation of thinking and reasoning skills (Glaser, 1984; Resnick, 1987b). However, it is important to note that these arguments focus upon instruction, not upon the identification of standards. The case has been well articulated that thinking and reasoning should not be taught in isolation of specific content. Quite obviously, one cannot think about nothing. Thinking and reasoning processes and strategies must be used with content, and to use any content other than that important to specific disciplines makes little sense.

However, articulating thinking and reasoning standards is quite another matter. Under the assumption that the primary purpose of standards is to give educators direction about the skills and abilities that should be the focus of instruction and assessment, one can infer that it is critical to identify explicit thinking and reasoning standards. If important thinking and reasoning approaches are only found embedded in content, there can be no way to ensure that students have explored content in as many thoughtful ways as possible. To illustrate, consider the following performance task, again taken from *Geography for Life* (Geography Education Standards Project, 1994):

> Compare the economic opportunities for women in selected regions of the world using culture to explain the differences. (p. 203)

This performance task describes one way in which a student might demonstrate knowledge of a content standard in geography. The important knowledge within the performance task, however, could be demonstrated in a variety of different ways. For example, the student could be asked to predict where women will have the most freedom and opportunity in the next decade. But what of the ability to make comparisons? If the ability is considered important enough that a student should be able to apply this skill in geography, then making comparisons should be identified and addressed as systematically as the content, rather than as an incidental part of a performance task embedded in a geography standard. Otherwise, whether a student uses comparison or not will be determined by the luck of the draw, that is, only if he or she is asked to perform this particular performance task. Clearly, such a hit-or-miss approach will characterize any effort that does not fully articulate and address the thinking and reasoning skills that should be brought to the study of content. Thus, the third approach to thinking and reasoning skills—embedding them in performance tasks—has severe limitations.

The second approach found in the various national reports—identifying thinking and reasoning skills within specific subject areas—also proves problematic. Many of the thinking and reasoning skills and abilities identified within specific subject areas are, in fact, quite general. For example, the NCTM standard of mathematical reasoning primarily specifies such general thinking and reasoning abilities as making conjectures, making inferences, and making corrections. These processes are as important in science and history (and so on) as they are in mathematics.

Given the inherent problems with two of the three approaches, we recommend that schools and districts identify explicit thinking and reasoning standards that cut across all content areas. In our analysis (see Kendall & Marzano, 1996), we have found that the following standards are good representations of the thinking and reasoning skills and abilities found in the national documents:

1. Understands and applies basic principles of presenting an argument
2. Understands and applies basic principles of logic and reasoning
3. Effectively uses mental processes that are based on identifying similarities and dissimilarities (compares, contrasts, classifies)
4. Understands and applies basic principles of hypothesis testing and scientific inquiry
5. Applies basic trouble-shooting and problem-solving techniques
6. Applies decision-making techniques

As a further indication that these thinking and reasoning standards have a construct validity of their own, each of these has identifiable content that is unique to them. To illustrate, consider the middle and junior high school benchmarks for standard 2, the thinking and reasoning standard that deals with logical reasoning:

- Uses formal deductive connectors ("if...then," "not," "and," "or") in the construction of deductive arguments
- Understands that some aspects of reasoning have very rigid rules but other aspects do not
- Understands that when people have rules that always hold for a given situation and good information about the situation, then logic can help them figure out what is true about the situation
- Understands that reasoning by similarities can suggest ideas but cannot be used to prove things
- Understands that people are using incorrect logic when they make a statement such as "if x is true, then y is true; but x isn't true, therefore y isn't true"
- Understands that a single example can never prove that something is true, but a single example can prove that something is not true
- Understands that some people invent a general rule to explain how something works by summarizing observations
- Understands that people overgeneralize by making up rules on the basis of only a few observations
- Understands that personal values influence the types of conclusions people make
- Recognizes situations in which a variety of conclusions can be drawn from the same information

The knowledge and skills articulated in these benchmarks must be specifically taught. They will not simply emerge as a result of studying a subject area. For example, understanding and use of the formal deductive connectors "if...then," "and," "not," and "or" is content that must be taught directly. This knowledge will surely not be an incidental byproduct of studying a traditional subject area. Consequently, we recommend that the six thinking and reasoning standards described above (or some variation of them) be an explicit category of standards.

Lifelong Learning Standards

As their name indicates, lifelong learning standards deal with information and skills that are used throughout life in a variety of contexts. Such information and skills are commonly associated with the world of work. Lifelong learning standards gained national prominence when the Secretary's Commission on Achieving Necessary Skills (SCANS) published the report *What Work Requires of Schools: A SCANS Report for America 2000* (1991). The commission spent 12 months "talking to business owners, to public employees, to the people who manage employees daily, to union officials, and to workers on the line and at their desks. We have talked to them in their stores, shops, government offices, and manufacturing facilities" (p. v). The strong message from all quarters was that American students must be taught a variety of skills and abilities to be productive members of the work force. Many of these skills and abilities went beyond the traditional academic subjects commonly found in the curriculum. For example, the SCANS report identified a "three-part foundation of skills and personal qualities" (p. vii). The first part of the foundation involved traditional academic content, such as reading, writing, arithmetic and mathematics, speaking, and listening. The second part of the foundation involved the thinking skills of "thinking creatively, making decisions, solving problems, seeing things in the mind's eye, knowing how to learn, and reasoning" (p. vii). The third part of the foundation involved lifelong learning skills, such as individual responsibility, self-esteem, sociability, self-management, and integrity.

A complimentary work to the SCANS report, entitled *Workplace Basics: The Essential Skills Employers Want* (Carnevale, Gainer, & Meltzer, 1990), was published by the American Society for Training and Development (ASTD), which represents "approximately 50,000 practitioners, managers, administrators, educators, and researchers in the field of human resource development" (p. xiii). The set of skills identified in this work was almost identical to that articulated in the SCANS report. From these two reports, one can infer that the American work force is giving America's educators a strong message: Teach and reinforce lifelong learning skills.

This same message has also been heard from parents. The polling firm Public Agenda surveyed a representative sample of parents regarding what should be taught in the schools. Their report is entitled *First Things First: What Americans Expect From Public Schools* (Farkas, Friedman, Boese, & Shaw, 1994). It noted that 88% of those surveyed said, among other things, that schools should teach and reinforce work-related competencies, such as punctuality, dependability, and self-discipline.

Finally, it appears that educators have reached the same opinion about lifelong learning skills. Specifically, the American Association of School Administrators polled 55 noted educators, referred to as the "Council of 55," regarding what schools should teach to prepare students for the 21st century. The council identified interpersonal skills, including being part of a team, as critical to success in the next century (Uchida, Cetron, & McKenzie, 1996).

In summary, there is a great deal of agreement regarding the importance of generic skills useful within the workplace. Ironically, it was the emphasis on this same type of skills that led to the demise of outcome-based education, or OBE. The problems with OBE are discussed in some depth in chapter 7. Briefly, however, OBE emphasized these skills in lieu of traditional academic subject matter. This is obviously a critical omission. However, when sound academic standards are firmly in place, it appears that parents and community members are quite supportive of teaching and reinforcing general lifelong learning skills.

One serious question commonly raised about lifelong learning standards and benchmarks is, Can they be objectively assessed? At first glance, it would appear that skills and competencies such as contributing to the overall effectiveness of a group are open to too much interpretation to be accurately assessed. However, we have found that if these areas are defined in specific behavioral terms, they can be assessed with a remarkably high level of reliability (see Marzano, 1994; McREL Institute, 1994).

In summary, identifying lifelong learning skills is a viable option for schools and districts. We have found that the following list represents a fairly comprehensive record of the lifelong learning skills identified in national and state documents.

Working With Others

1. Contributes to the overall effort of a group
2. Uses conflict-resolution techniques
3. Works well with diverse individuals and in diverse situations
4. Displays effective interpersonal communication skills
5. Demonstrates leadership skills

Self-Regulation

1. Sets and manages goals
2. Performs self-appraisal
3. Considers risks
4. Demonstrates perseverance
5. Maintains a healthy self-concept
6. Restrains impulsivity

Who Will Be Involved In Setting Standards?

The final question addressed in this chapter is, Who will be involved in setting standards? Most schools and districts with which we have worked assumed that the more people involved from the onset the better. There is a certain intuitive appeal to this notion because of the premise that standards should reflect the values and beliefs of the local community. Indeed, Grant Wiggins (1993a, 1993b), director of programs for the Center on Learning, Assessment, and School Structure, and Ruth Mitchell (1992), former associate director of the Council for Basic Education, both of whom are acknowledged experts in the curricular and assessment implications of standards, make compelling arguments for the need to involve community members in the construction of standards.

However, we have found that when community members are involved can be critical. Specifically, for a number of reasons, involving too many people in the beginning stages of the standards-setting process can have catastrophic results. First, some community members, although well intended, do not have the technical expertise to set standards in content areas such as physics, calculus, and history. Second, some community members might volunteer to work on standards but have personal agendas that are antithetical to the standards-setting process. Third, setting standards can be a messy process, particularly in the beginning stages. If a school or district makes its initial drafts of standards too public, it runs the risk of having draft work perceived as the final product. A process we have found to be effective involves the following eight components:

1. Organize a steering committee to guide the standards-setting efforts in the district.

This committee should be highly knowledgeable about the technical aspects of standards. The committee's job is to oversee the development of subject-area standards to ensure that they are written at the same level of generality and that the same format is used.

2. Ensure that the subject-area standards and benchmarks are written by subject-area specialists.

Specifically, mathematics teachers should draft the mathematics standards, science teachers should draft the science standards, and so on. The collective work produced by these specialists should be considered the first draft of the district's standards.

3. Present the first draft of the standards to a group that is comprised of educators and community members who are noneducators.

4. Ask this group to suggest additions, deletions, and changes to the first draft of the standards.

5. Give suggested additions, deletions, and changes to the steering committee and the subject-area specialists to produce a second draft.

6. Present the second draft to all teachers in the district or a representative sample of teachers for review and comment.

One district we worked with—Douglas County, Colorado—surveyed teachers regarding each benchmark within each standard. Exhibit 2.2 depicts part of the survey form the district used to poll its teachers on the standards and benchmarks that had been generated by subject-area specialists.

Notice that the teachers were asked to comment on a number of aspects of the standards and benchmarks including their clarity, their appropriateness in terms of level of generality, and their thoroughness in covering essential knowledge and skills.

Exhibit 2.2 Survey on Standards: Primary Level

Check below all that apply:

Position: Teacher ☐ Administrator ☐ Parent/Community Member ☐ Accountability Committee ☐ Student ☐

Subject area you believe you are comfortable in and knowledgeable about:
Geography ☐ History ☐ Language Arts ☐ Mathematics ☐ Science ☐

Importance
RQ — This is an important benchmark/standard and should be required of every student.
OP — This is an important benchmark/standard, but should be optional.
NS — This should not be a benchmark/standard.

Clear & Specific
Y (Yes) or N (No) — Is this benchmark/standard clear and specific?

Coverage
Y (Yes) or N (No) — Are the essential knowledge and/or skills for this area covered?

GEOGRAPHY	Importance	Clear & Specific	
1. The student demonstrates an understanding of how to locate groups of people, places, and environments on the Earth.	RQ OP NS		
Primary			
• Knows the location of home, school, neighborhood, community, state, country	RQ OP NS	Y N	
• Knows various landforms (e.g., mountains, foothills, valleys, plateaus)	RQ OP NS	Y N	
• Knows local environmental features (e.g., hills, forests, streams, plants, animals)			
• Knows how to orient a map with a directional symbol	RQ OP NS	Y N	
• Knows terms related to location, direction, distance (e.g., up/down; miles; near/far	RQ OP NS	Y N	
• Knows the Cardinal and Intermediate directions (e.g., N,S,E,W; NW,SW,NE,SE)	RQ OP NS	Y N	
• Understands the difference between maps and globes	RQ OP NS	Y N	
• Knows how to use a letter-number grid on a map	RQ OP NS	Y N	
• Knows how to build simple models and maps of an area	RQ OP NS	Y N	
• Knows how symbols are used to represent things on a map (e.g., shape, size, color)	RQ OP NS	Y N	
Do these benchmarks cover this standard? Comments:			Coverage Y N

7. Use teacher input on the second draft to create a third draft.

8. Present the third draft to the community at large.

At this stage in the process, as many community members as possible should be involved in this review. To illustrate, the Douglas County, Colorado, district we worked with published the third draft of its standards and benchmarks in a special pull-out section of the local newspaper. The headlines in that section read "School district launches effort to establish academic standards" (News Press, 1995, p. 1B). Accompanying articles explained the rationale for standards and the work that had gone into their development:

> After more than a year of research and development, proposed academic standards in the subjects of language arts, math, science, geography and history are ready to be unveiled to the public for review and suggestions for improvement. The goal of the proposed standards is to improve student achievement through a set of clear academic expectations.

> This blueprint for learning in Douglas County was developed over the course of the last year by a group of 80 people representing parents, teachers, administrators, students, community members and college personnel. The proposed standards are based on national and international research and outline specific academic expectations for students from kindergarten through twelfth grade.

> This special supplement is being delivered to nearly every household in Douglas County to give readers the opportunity to review the proposed standards and voice their opinions. Copies will also be available at all schools, the school district administration building, libraries and recreation centers across the county. (News Press, 1995, p. 1B)

Given the effort that had been put into the standards and benchmarks and the multiple reviews they had undergone, it is no wonder that there was little resistance to the standards and benchmarks within this community.

Certainly community involvement is critical to the development of standards and benchmarks. However, the development process is a technical one making the premature involvement of the community at large a precarious endeavor.

Summary And Recommendations

In this chapter we have considered three important questions that a district or school must address if it wishes to organize itself around standards: Where will we get our standards? What types of standards will we have? Who will be involved in setting standards?

The options related to the first question include national documents and state documents. Both present problems. The national documents have little commonality relative to such important factors as level of generality and definitions of standards and benchmarks. Many state documents have been judged as too general to provide districts and schools with adequate guidance. Even when strong state documents exist, districts and schools frequently must do a great deal of rewriting and adapting to meet their local needs. As an aid to this end, the McREL database has been developed. It synthesizes information from over 80 national and state documents into a uniform format that is easily used by districts and schools.

Relative to the second question, there are three types of standards a district or school might construct: (1) subject-area standards, (2) thinking and reasoning standards, and (3) lifelong learning standards. Subject-area standards are absolutely necessary to any district or school. Additionally, it is highly useful to design explicit thinking and reasoning standards because these abilities are critical components of every content area. Lifelong learning standards, although somewhat controversial because of their association with OBE, are useful additions. However, they are probably best approached cautiously at this point in time. Finally, a district or school must decide if it will write standards at a world-class level or at a literacy level.

The third question deals with who should be involved in the process of setting standards. Although, ultimately, the community at large should have a great deal of input into the design of standards, it is best to develop a series of drafts before input from the general public is sought.

Chapter 3

What Format Will We Use To State Our Benchmarks?

The phrase "the medium is the message," popularized by communications theorist Marshall McLuhan, has particular significance in a discussion of standards and benchmarks. This is because the format a school or district selects to articulate its standards and benchmarks has a profound impact on how those standards and benchmarks are used. In this chapter we consider the many ways in which a school or district can articulate its standards and benchmarks. First, however, we consider the nature of standards and benchmarks in more depth.

The Nature Of Standards And Benchmarks

In chapter 2, we briefly described benchmarks as statements of developmental levels of information and skill that define the general categories of knowledge articulated by the standards. In our studies of national and state documents, we have found that these categories of information and skill, which we call standards, are much more subjective than we had imagined or hoped. Specifically, at the operational level, standards are fairly subjective ways of organizing knowledge within a subject area. One school or district might validly organize knowledge within a domain into one set of categories; another school or district might validly organize the same knowledge within that domain into different categories. This explains why different documents organize the same subject matter in very different ways. For example, the *National Science Education Standards* (1996), published by the National Research Council (NRC), identifies seven different categories of standards:

1. Science as inquiry
2. Physical science
3. Life science
4. Earth and space science
5. Science and technology
6. Science in personal and social perspective
7. History and nature of science

Seventy-two standards are embedded in these seven categories. In contrast, the document *Benchmarks for Science Literacy*, published by Project 2061 of the American Association for the Advancement of Science (AAAS) (1993), organizes standards into the following 12 categories, which contain 65 different standards:

1. The nature of science
2. The nature of mathematics
3. The nature of technology
4. The physical setting
5. The living environment
6. The human organism
7. The human society
8. The designed world
9. The mathematical world
10. Historical perspective
11. Common items
12. Habits of mind

Even within seemingly similar categories, the scope and level of detail of the knowledge covered by the standards are different. For example, consider the category Physical Science from the NRC document and the category The Physical Setting from the AAAS document. Below are the standards from the Physical Science category in the NRC document (1996, p. 106):

Levels K-4
- Properties of objects and materials
- Position and motion of objects
- Light, heat, electricity, and magnetism

Levels 5-8
- Properties and changes of properties in matter
- Motion and forces
- Transfer and energy

Levels 9-12
- Structure of atoms
- Structure and properties of matter
- Chemical reactions
- Motions and force
- Conservation of energy and increase in disorder
- Interactions of energy and matter

In contrast, the AAAS (1993) document identifies the following standards in its category The Physical Setting:

- The universe
- The earth
- Processes that shape the earth
- Structure of matter
- Energy of transformations
- Motion
- Forces of nature

Not only does the AAAS document articulate standards at a much higher level of generality within The Physical Setting category than does the NRC document, but it also includes information about the universe and the earth that the NRC document ascribes to a different category. Both the NRC and AAAS documents were designed by consensus of a vast array of experts in science education. Yet, these experts came up with different ways of organizing the knowledge and skills within their domains.

Another example of the idiosyncratic nature of standards comes from the subject area of language arts. In fact, the area of language arts is the prototypic example of how strongly groups can differ on the nature of standards and benchmarks. To illustrate, the North Dakota Department of Public Instruction (1996) identifies the following seven standards in language arts:

Standard 1: Students gather and organize information.

Standard 2: Students engage in the reading process.

Standard 3: Students comprehend literature.

Standard 4: Students engage in the writing process.

Standard 5: Students write for a variety of purposes and audiences.

Standard 6: Students engage in speaking and listening processes.

Standard 7: Students understand and use principles of language.

In contrast, the state of Virginia, whose standards were identified as among the best of the state-level efforts (see Gandal, 1995a), organizes language arts into four general standards: oral language, reading/literature, writing, and research (Board of Education, Commonwealth of Virginia, 1995). Although there is quite a bit of difference between the seven general categories of language arts knowledge (i.e., standards) articulated in the North Dakota document and those articulated in the Virginia document, both documents do list specific elements of information and skills as benchmarks within each standard. However, the "official" language arts document developed at the national level takes exception to this practice.

Specifically, the document *Standards for the English Language Arts* (1996), developed and published by the National Council of Teachers of English (NCTE) and the International Reading Association (IRA), lists 12 broadly articulated standards that cover such skills and abilities as reading a wide range of literature, using a variety of writing strategies, developing an appreciation for differing language patterns and dialects, and applying knowledge of such conventions as spelling and punctuation to create texts. However, the document does not identify specific elements of information and skill as benchmarks for the standards. Additionally, NCTE and IRA do not authorize the reprinting of these 12 standards without also printing the entire text of the chapter in which the standards appear. In that chapter the overall intent of each standard is discussed in detail without reference to specific information or skills. This is in keeping with the philosophy of the authors of the NCTE/IRA standards that providing explicit detail regarding the information and skills of the language arts destroys the robust and holistic nature of the language arts. In short, NCTE and IRA have adopted the position that to dissect the language arts into benchmarks violates basic principles of language learning and communication. This position has not met with unanimous acceptance. In fact, this position is one of the primary reasons that NCTE and IRA lost federal funding supporting the development of the language arts standards.

The Standards Project for English Language Arts (SPELA) was initially funded by the Fund for Improvement and Reform of Schools and Teaching (FIRST) of the U.S. Office of Educational Research and Improvement. SPELA was designed to be a three-year collaborative effort (beginning in September 1992) of the Center for the Study of Reading (CSR), the International Reading Association, and the National Council of Teachers of English. SPELA produced one complete draft of its standards, entitled *Incomplete Work of the Task Forces of the Standards Project for English Language Arts*. That draft contained five strands (Reading/Literature, Writing, Language, Real World Literacy, and Interconnections), each listing two or three standards described at a general level. This draft was to go through a number of iterations until a final document was produced. However, on March 18, 1994, the U.S. Department of Education notified SPELA that it would not continue funding for the project. According to NCTE, funding for the project was halted because of a number of "philosophical differences" between SPELA and the federal agencies. These differences included a disagreement over the inclusion of delivery standards, which was supported by SPELA, and the lack of attention to a specific canon of children's literature, which was not supported by SPELA. However, the primary reason for cessation of funding appears to be the federal government's assertion that SPELA was not attending to the basic task of identifying what students should know and be able to do in the English language arts. As noted by Janice Anderson, interim director of FIRST at the time the funding was halted, SPELA had not made "substantial progress toward meeting the objectives" of the project. The proposed standards, she stated, "are vague and often read as opinions and platitudes," focus too much on process rather than content, and lack "a coherent conceptual framework" ("NCTE, IRA Say," 1994, p. 4).

NCTE and IRA were undaunted by criticisms. They vowed to complete the project in spite of the loss of federal funds and, in fact, did so in 1996 with the publication of *Standards for the English Language Arts*. Given its lack of specificity, this document has also met with criticism. For example, in 1995, an article in *Education Daily* (which was based on a prepublication draft of the NCTE/IRA 1996 document) noted that the standards "deliberately say little more than that students should be able to read a wide range of texts and write effectively using various strategies. . . .The document elaborates on each standard, but doesn't break down specific competencies students should show at various grade levels, as do standards in other disciplines" ("Draft Standards Tackle," 1995, p. 1).

Our point here is not to criticize the position taken by NCTE and IRA so much as it is to use the controversy surrounding their standards as an illustration of the highly subjective nature of the process of standards design.

In summary, standards are general categories that organize the knowledge within a subject area. There is no single set of standards for any domain, because the component information and skills can be organized in a number of ways, each of which is valid.

Do Standards Have To Span Grades K-12?

One common misconception about standards is that every standard must have benchmarks that span thirteen grade levels, K-12. This misconception is based on the assumption that all standards represent expectations about what students should know and be able to do by the time they graduate from high school. Many districts and schools reason that once these "exit" expectations are identified, then we can "map backwards" to determine what students should know and be able to do at lower levels to prepare them for these exit competencies. This relationship between exit expectations and the knowledge necessary to meet the expectations implies a tacit process for generating standards and benchmarks.

Fundamentally, this process of mapping backwards from exit outcomes is what William Spady (1995), principle architect of outcome-based education (OBE), refers to as "designing down":

> OBE's "Design Down" principle raises a number of issues and ironies that go to the heart of the concept. . . . "Design Down" is about designing back from the place teachers want student learning to culminate. The common message in OBE is, "Design down from where you want students to end up." (p. 381)

The "design down" principle is also reinforced by Wiggins (1993a), who makes the point by using the analogy of a cross country trip. If we wish to travel from Los Angeles to New York, we need to identify intermediate destinations that tell us we are on the right track. If New York is the destination, we would map backwards to Los Angeles to identify the most appropriate route. Mitchell has made similar arguments in her book *Testing for Learning* (1992).

These arguments have a strong, intuitive appeal. Indeed, the "design down" principle can be a useful construct when developing standards and benchmarks. However, to use the principle as a hard-and-fast rule can lead to problems because it does not apply universally. This is because the strength and utility of the "design down" principle is a function of the extent to which a subject matter can be organized in a hierarchic fashion with commonly agreed upon "big ideas" or "big tasks" at the top of the hierarchy. If such consensus "big ideas" or "big tasks" did in fact exist within a subject, the districts and schools could easily identify them as their exit outcomes or exit standards. The prerequisite information and skills to understand these big ideas or accomplish these big tasks would then be the benchmarks that support the exit standards.

Unfortunately, we have already seen that experts within a single domain commonly organize the content within their domains in very different ways—witness the different standards and categories of standards that AAAS and NRC have constructed in science. If the field of science had a strong, implicit, hierarchic structure, we would expect more agreement regarding the top-level constructs. That is, we would expect the AAAS and NRC documents to organize the content of science around the same big ideas and the same big tasks. Obviously, they do not. Consequently, when a school or district first identifies the "big ideas" or "big tasks" within a subject area and then "designs down" to identify benchmarks, it should realize that the big ideas and big tasks might constitute a rather idiosyncratic view of a given content area. In short, the assumption of a hierarchic structure to subject areas, which is so crucial to the validity of the exit outcome/design down strategy, simply does not hold up well in the operational world of developing standards and benchmarks.

Given the lack of evidence for a strong, implicit, hierarchic structure within subject areas, there seems to be no compelling reason that all standards must have benchmarks that span grades K-12. Consequently, if a district or school wishes to construct different standards for different levels within a subject area, there is no cognitively based reason that this approach cannot be taken. Indeed, in some subject areas, there might be a strong logic to this discontinuous approach. The national history standards developed by the National Center for History in the Schools (1994a, 1994b, 1994c) are a good case in point. The standards for grades K-4 (1994a) deal with very general concepts such as

- living and working in families and community,
- diverse cultures, and
- democratic values and principles.

From grade five on, however, the standards deal with explicit eras in U.S. history (1994b) and world history (1994c). For example, the eras in U.S. history are

Era 1: Three Worlds Meet (Beginnings to 1620)

Era 2: Colonization and Settlement (1585-1763)

Era 3: Revolution and the New Nation (1754-1820s)

Era 4: Expansion and Reform (1801-1861)

Era 5: Civil War and Reconstruction (1850-1877)

Era 6: The Development of the Industrial United States (1870-1900)

Era 7: The Emergence of Modern America (1890-1930)

Era 8: The Great Depression and World War II (1929-1945)

Era 9: Postwar United States (1945-early 1970s)

Era 10: Contemporary United States (1968-present)

Within history, then, a discontinuous approach to standards makes sense. Grades K-4 can have standards that focus on broad concepts, such as diverse cultures, whereas grades 5 through 12 might have standards that focus on specific eras.

In summary, one of the conclusions from our theoretical and practical work is that schools and districts should feel free to create their own standards and benchmarks. The only "rules" that should be followed are that the standards and benchmarks should provide teachers with guidance regarding what should be taught and should provide students with clear feedback on how well they are progressing.

Benchmark Formats

Given that standards are generally broad and even somewhat arbitrary categories of knowledge, one could correctly surmise that benchmarks, and the form in which they are written, represent the real substance of standards construction. In other words, a school or district can overcome poorly constructed standards but not poorly constructed benchmarks. In general, there are three formats in which benchmarks can be written: (1) as statements of information and skills, (2) as performance activities, and (3) as performance tasks. We consider each of these formats in the following sections.

Benchmarks As Statements Of Information And Skills

The most straightforward way of writing benchmarks is as statements of information and skills. For example, assume that a district or school is writing benchmarks for the following standard in dance:

Identifies and demonstrates artistic movements and skills in performing dance.

The following are benchmarks for this standard, written as specific elements of information and skills that might be appropriate at the upper elementary level:

a. Understands names for basic nonlocomotor/axial movements (e.g., bend, twist, stretch, swing).

b. Moves to a rhythmic accompaniment (e.g., drumbeat) and responds to changes in tempo.

c. Uses movement in straight and curved pathway.

d. Understands basic actions (e.g., skip, gallop) and movement elements (e.g., height of dances in relation to the floor, directions) and how they communicate ideas.

One very useful distinction to keep in mind when constructing benchmarks of this type is the distinction between declarative knowledge and procedural knowledge. This distinction is a basic one made by many cognitive psychologists who study the structure of knowledge (Anderson, 1982, 1983, 1990a, 1990b, 1993, 1995; Fitts, 1964; Fitts & Posner, 1967; Frederiksen, 1977; Newell & Simon, 1972; Norman, 1969; Rowe, 1985; van Dijk, 1980). We will discuss declarative versus procedural knowledge again in a subsequent section of this chapter and in great depth in chapter 8. However, the distinction is also useful to the discussion here.

Declarative knowledge can be thought of as "information" and usually involves component parts. For example, knowledge of the concept of "democracy" includes an understanding that decisions are made by the people, that each person has a single vote, that votes are weighted equally, and so on. The declarative knowledge in the sample dance benchmarks are benchmarks *a* and *d*. Both involve an understanding of terms and concepts basic to dance.

The sample dance benchmarks also contain procedural knowledge. Procedural knowledge consists of skills, strategies, and processes. Benchmarks *b* and *c* both involve dance skills.

This declarative/procedural distinction is not explicitly marked in most standards documents. For example, the NCTM document *Curriculum and Evaluation Standards for School Mathematics* (1989) mixes declarative and procedural benchmarks as do the example dance benchmarks. The following two NCTM benchmarks are found under "Standard 9, Algebra," for grades 5-8:

Students can

a. understand the concepts of variable, expression, and equation.

b. apply algebraic methods to solve a variety of real-world and mathematical problems.

Benchmark *a* is certainly more declarative in nature. It involves understanding information about variables, expressions, and equations. Benchmark *b* is more procedural in nature. It involves a number of algebraic processes that can be used in solving a variety of problems. The distinction between these two types of benchmarks is not noted or marked in any way in the NCTM document.

In contrast, the document *Benchmarks for Science Literacy* (Project 2061, 1993) uses different language to express declarative versus procedural benchmarks. Declarative benchmarks are expressed in the following way:

By the end of the 5th grade, students should **know that** [emphasis added]:

- some likenesses between children and parents, such as eye color in human beings, or fruit or flower color in plants, are inherited. Other likenesses, such as people's table manners or carpentry skills, are learned. (p. 107)

Procedural benchmarks are stated differently:

By the end of the 5th grade, students **should** [emphasis added]:

- keep records of their investigations and observations and not change the records later. (p. 286)

The words "know that" cue the reader that what follows are declarative benchmarks; the word "should" followed by an action verb (e.g., "keep") cues the reader to procedural benchmarks.

The declarative/procedural distinction provides an interesting perspective on the nature of the different subject areas. Specifically, the benchmarks that comprise various subject areas have different distributions of declarative and procedural knowledge. Table 3.1 shows the percentages of declarative and procedural knowledge in the subjects of science, mathematics, geography, language arts, and history, based on our analysis of the national documents.

Table 3.1 Distribution of Declarative and Procedural Benchmarks

Subject Area	Declarative Benchmarks	Procedural Benchmarks
Science	92%	8%
Mathematics	49%	51%
Geography	98%	2%
Language Arts	24%	76%
History	97%	3%

As Table 3.1 illustrates, the vast majority of benchmarks in history are declarative in nature, whereas the benchmarks in mathematics are much more evenly distributed. The structural difference between subject areas has implications for differences in the way subjects are taught and the way they are assessed. Some of these differences are described in chapters 5 and 8. (For a detailed discussion of how these two types of knowledge should be addressed in the classroom, see Marzano, 1992.)

Benchmarks As Performance Activities

One format in which benchmarks can be written is as statements of specific information and skills, that is, as declarative and procedural knowledge. A second format that can be used to construct benchmarks is performance activities. This format is compared in Exhibit 3.1 with the information/skills format.

Exhibit 3.1 Comparison of Information/Skills Format with Performance Activity Format

Information/Skills Format	Performance Activity Format
• understands the basic characteristics of day and night and their relationship to the rotation of Earth on its axis	• compare night and day in terms of similarities and differences as they relate to the rotation of Earth on its axis
• understands the basic characteristics of the four seasons and their relationship to the tilt of Earth's axis	• construct a display or physical model representing the defining characteristics of the four seasons with specific reference to the tilt of the Earth's axis
• understands the basic characteristics of the various phases of the moon	• use a ball, globe, and light source to illustrate the phases of the moon
• understands the relationship of time of day, the Sun's position in the sky, and the size and shape of shadows	• draw a shadow of a classmate or common object specifying direction and length at different times of day and different seasons
	• use a sundial to determine the relationship between time and the changing of the Sun's position in the sky

Performance activities can be thought of as applications of benchmarks that have been stated in the information and skills format. That is, performance activities demonstrate ways that declarative and procedural knowledge can be applied. For example, the last performance activity in Exhibit 3.1, involving the sundial, is an application of the declarative knowledge about the relationship of the time of day, the Sun's position, and the characteristics of shadows.

Some national standards documents make use of the performance activity format. For example, the three standards documents published by the National Center for History in the Schools (1994a, 1994b, 1994c) make extensive use of performance activities. To illustrate, consider the activities in Exhibit 3.2 from *National Standards for United States History* (1994b).

The activities in Exhibit 3.2 are offered as ways that students might demonstrate their ability to apply the information embedded in the following benchmark (which is referred to as a "historical understanding"):

1A Demonstrate understanding of how the North and South differed and how politics and ideologies led to the Civil War.

Exhibit 3.2 Sample Performance Activities from U.S. History Standards

Identifying and explaining the economic, social, and cultural differences between the North and the South. (**Compare and contrast differing values and institutions**)

Analyzing the reasons for the disruption of the second American party system in the 1850s and explaining how they led to the ascent of the Republican party. (**Analyze multiple causation**)

Explaining how events after the Compromise of 1850 contributed to increasing sectional polarization. (**Analyze cause-and-effect relationships**)

Analyzing the importance of the "free labor" ideology in the North and its appeal in preventing the further extension of slavery in the new territories. (**Examine the influence of ideas**)

Explaining the causes of the Civil War and evaluating the importance of slavery as a principal cause of the conflict. (**Compare competing historical narratives**)

Charting the secession of the southern states, explaining the process and reasons for secession. (**Analyze cause-and-effect relationships**)

Note: From *National Standards for United States History: Exploring the American Experience* (p. 122), by the National Center for History in the Schools, 1994, Los Angeles: Author. Emphases in original.

The history standards illustrate an interesting point about performance activities—namely, that they can be thought of as the combination of thinking and reasoning skills and content knowledge. Note that each performance activity in Exhibit 3.2 is coded as to the type of thinking and reasoning skills it requires: compare and contrast, cause and effect, and so on.

The history standards documents rely heavily on the integration of thinking and reasoning with specific historical content. In fact, the history standards contain two distinct types of standards—historical thinking standards and historical understanding standards. As described by the National Center for History in the Schools (1994b), activities such as those shown in Exhibit 3.2 are a product of marrying a historical thinking standard to a historical understanding standard:

> As illustrated, the five skills in historical thinking . . . and the three historical understandings a student should acquire . . . are integrated . . . in order to define . . . what students should be able to do to demonstrate their understanding. (p. 8)

The five history thinking standards articulated in the history standards documents (1994a, 1994b, 1994c) are

1. chronological thinking
2. historical comprehension
3. historical analysis and interpretation
4. historical research
5. historical issues-analysis and decision-making

Researchers Robert Marzano, Debra Pickering, and Jay McTighe (1993) offer another set of thinking and reasoning skills that can be combined with subject-matter content to generate performance activities. These are listed in Table 3.2.

Table 3.2 Reasoning Processes That Can Be Used to Generate Performance Activities

Stimulus Question	Reasoning Process
Do you want to determine how certain things are similar and different?	Comparing
Do you want to organize things into groups? Do you want to identify the rules or characteristics that have been used to form groups?	Classifying
Are there specific pieces of information that you want to draw conclusions about?	Induction
Are there specific rules you see operating here? Are there things that you know must happen?	Deduction
Are there errors in reasoning you want to describe? Are there errors being performed in a process?	Error Analysis
Is there a position you want to defend on a particular issue?	Constructing Support
Do you see a relationship that no one else has seen? What is the abstract pattern or theme that is at the heart of the relationship?	Abstracting
Are there differing perspectives on an issue you want to explore?	Analyzing Perspectives
Is there an important decision that should be studied or made?	Decision Making
Is there some new idea or new theory that should be described in detail?	Definitional Investigation
Is there something that happened in the past that should be studied?	Historical Investigation
Is there a possible or hypothetical event that should be studied?	Projective Investigation
Do you want to describe how some obstacle can be overcome?	Problem Solving
Is there a prediction you want to make and then test?	Experimental Inquiry
Is there something you want to improve upon? Is there something new you want to create?	Invention

Note: From *Assessing Student Outcome*s (p. 33), by R. J. Marzano, D. J. Pickering, and J. McTighe, 1993, Reston, VA: Association for Supervision and Curriculum Development. Copyright © 1993 by McREL Institute.

The stimulus questions in Table 3.2 are particularly helpful in generating performance activities. One simply applies one or more of these stimulus questions to a specific statement of content knowledge to develop an activity. To illustrate, reconsider the history information above about understanding how the North and South differed and how politics and ideologies led to the Civil War. To generate performance activities relative to one's historical understanding of this information, one might simply ask a stimulus question in Table 3.2 about this historical content. This process might generate a number of performance activities like those in Exhibit 3.3.

Exhibit 3.3 Sample Performance Activities Generated Using Stimulus Questions

Comparing	Compare the key aspects of the ideologies that formed the basis of the North's perspective on slavery versus the South's perspective.
Deducing	Describe some of the rules of conduct that people in the South operated from in terms of their behavior toward slaves.
Constructing Support	Develop an argument for or against the North's treatment of the South immediately prior to the outbreak of the Civil War.
Decision Making	Describe the alternative actions Lincoln most likely was considering immediately prior to the outbreak of the Civil War.

Harvard psychologist David Perkins (1992) provides another list of reasoning processes that can be used to generate performance activities. These are described in Exhibit 3.4.

Exhibit 3.4 Perkins's Reasoning Processes

- *Explanation.* Explain in your own words what it means to go at a constant speed in the same direction and what sorts of forces might divert an object.
- *Exemplification.* Give fresh examples of the law at work. For instance, identify what forces divert the paths of objects in sports, in steering cars, in walking.
- *Application.* Use the law to explain a phenomenon not yet studied. For instance, what forces might make a curve ball curve?
- *Justification.* Offer evidence in defense of the law; formulate an experiment to test it. For instance, to see the law at work, how can you set up a situation as little influenced by friction and gravity as possible?
- *Comparison and Contrast.* Note the form of the law and relate it to other laws. What other laws can you think of that say that something stays constant unless such-and-such?
- *Contextualization.* Explore the relationship of this law to the larger tapestry of physics; how does it fit into the rest of Newton's laws, for example? Why is it important? What role does it play?
- *Generalization.* Does the form of this law disclose any more general principles about physical relationships, principles also manifested in other laws of physics? For instance, do all laws of physics say in one way or another that something stays constant unless such-and-such?

Note: Adapted with the permission of The Free Press, a division of Simon & Schuster from *Smart Schools: From Training Memories to Educating Minds* by David Perkins. Copyright © 1992 by David Perkins.

Perkins explains that each of these processes demands that students demonstrate a deep understanding of the content to which the processes are applied.

In summary, performance activities are a second format in which benchmarks can be written. Benchmarks written as declarative and procedural knowledge can be translated into performance activities by linking them to one or more thinking and reasoning processes.

Benchmarks As Performance Tasks

Performance tasks are the third format in which benchmarks can be stated. Perhaps the best way to think of performance tasks is as highly contextualized versions of performance activities. To illustrate, consider the performance task in Exhibit 3.5 from *Assessing Student Outcomes* (Marzano, Pickering, & McTighe, 1993).

Exhibit 3.5 Sample Performance Task

The accumulation of waste materials is a world-wide problem. Waste materials can be toxic, non-toxic, hard to get rid of, bulky, smelly, and so on. Imagine that your group of four has been selected to prepare a report for a task force of the federal government that classifies the various types of waste materials and proposes plans to address the problems. Using information gathered from our lessons and from sources on reserve in the school library, classify the various types of waste materials. Then select one category of waste materials and present a plan for dealing with it. Your plan should be prepared as a research report to the government and should include the following elements:

1. Your classification of all waste materials and how you determined the categories.

2. An explanation of the effect your selected category of waste material has on the environment.

3. Your plan to deal with the waste material. This plan should contain references to the information sources you used and graphs and tables where appropriate.

4. The expected effect of your plan.

Note: Adapted from *Assessing Student Outcomes* (p. 51), by R. J. Marzano, D. J. Pickering, and J. McTighe, 1993, Alexandria, VA: Association for Supervision and Curriculum Development. Copyright © 1993 by McREL Institute.

Compared to performance activities, the task in Exhibit 3.5 is relatively specific. In fact, it specifies how students are to report their findings (as a written plan), how they are to work (in groups), and what sources they are to use (lessons and reserve items in the school library). Additionally, the task is highly situationalized. We might say, then, that there are a number of defining characteristics of a performance task:

1. It puts the knowledge to be applied into a specific situation that mirrors real-world environments and episodes.

2. It provides the necessary information to complete the task or provides guidance in the general resources necessary to complete the task.

3. It specifies whether students should work independently, in pairs, or in small groups and provides guidance as to the nature of those instructions.

4. It specifies how students should report their conclusions or demonstrate their findings.

Almost from their inception, standards and benchmarks have been associated with performance tasks. In fact, some researchers and theorists have assumed that performance tasks are a necessary aspect of setting standards. For example, Perkins (1992) asserts that one of the most significant changes that we can make in education is to conceptualize learning objectives as performances: "In reconsidering what we try to teach, the single most helpful move may be to redescribe educational objectives in terms of performance rather than knowledge possessed" (p. 71).

Some of the national documents use performance tasks as a way of providing specific examples of how the knowledge inherent in their benchmarks can be applied. For example, Exhibit 3.6 depicts performance tasks that are found in *Geography for Life* within the geography benchmark entitled "Compare the causes and effects of human migration."

Exhibit 3.6 Geography Performance Tasks

Read narratives describing a variety of migrations in different regions of the world and then discuss the reasons for each migration (e.g., a voluntary move such as the move of a family to a larger apartment closer to school, landless Easterners pulled to homesteads in the Great Plains, or an involuntary move such as Africans being transported to North and South America or refugees from the potato famine fleeing starvation in Ireland)
Write a diary entry or short play describing the reasons why an individual or family would be involved in a voluntary or involuntary migration (e.g., a family deciding to leave Europe to settle in the United States in the 1890s, a man in China deciding to go to the United States to work in railroad construction in the 1860s, or a Turk deciding to go to Germany to seek employment in the 1980s)
Write an account and draw a sketch map to suggest ways in which physical geography affects the routes, flows, and destinations of migrations (e.g., rivers channeling migrating people along valleys, mountains acting as barriers, mountain passes acting as funnels, long distances impeding the flow of information about destinations)

Note. From Geography for Life: National Geography Standards (p. 123), by Geography Education Standards Project, 1994, Washington, DC: National Geographic Research and Exploration.

Performance tasks, then, can be thought of as relatively specific and contextualized versions of performance activities. They provide clear guidance on how specific declarative and procedural knowledge can be applied in situations that mirror or approach real-world contexts.

Choosing Among The Formats

A district or school developing its own benchmarks should carefully consider which of the three formats it will use. Each of the three approaches has its own advantages and disadvantages. The first approach, benchmarks stated as information and skills, has the advantage of providing maximum flexibility for teachers in terms of how content benchmarks will be approached in the classroom. Given a list of specific declarative and procedural knowledge, a teacher can decide how the information and skills will be presented to students, what students will be expected to do with the information and skills, and how they will be assessed on the information and skills. The disadvantage of this approach is that it provides no safeguards that the information and skills listed in the benchmark will not be treated as bits of knowledge that are isolated and not applied in any meaningful context. In other words, stating benchmarks as a list of information and skills does not provide teachers with guidance regarding how to present the pieces as a unified whole or how to elicit knowledge application from students.

The second format, stating benchmarks as performance activities, has the advantage of couching the important information and skills in terms of application and demonstration. That is, this format provides explicit guidance for teachers as to how students will be expected to use the declarative and procedural knowledge and demonstrate their expertise. However, there is still no explicit guidance for teachers regarding the integration of the information and skills into more holistic chunks. Another disadvantage to this approach is that it is somewhat prescriptive in terms of what teachers must do in the classroom. If a performance activity benchmark states that students must "classify objects using characteristics of composition and physical objects," then every student in the school or district must classify objects using characteristics of composition even though there might be other ways to demonstrate an understanding of the composition of objects.

The third approach, stating benchmarks as performance tasks, has the advantage of being holistic, highly integrative, and oriented to knowledge application and integration. To perform a task like the waste material example, students must obviously be able to integrate and apply information. However, it is common for a school or district to write a single performance task as representative of the knowledge students should have at a certain benchmark level. One strong disadvantage to this approach, however, is that it frequently provides limited "coverage" of the content considered important at a given level. For example, the waste material performance task certainly would not cover all of the important science content at a given benchmark level. This weakness in the use of performance tasks as benchmarks has been described in many technical reports that address their lack of "generalizability" (e.g., Shavelson & Baxter, 1992; Shavelson, Gao, & Baxter, 1993). A second major problem inherent in the use of performance tasks as the format in which benchmarks are articulated is that, like performance activities, they are highly prescriptive relative to classroom activities and place severe demands on classroom resources. For example, if the waste material task was stated as a benchmark at a specific level within a standard (most likely a science standard), then all students in the school or district at that benchmark level would have to perform this task, which, no doubt, would consume a considerable amount of time and resources in the classroom.

We have concluded that the most effective way to deal with the inherent problems of the three formats is to use the first format—information and skills—as the "official" way of stating benchmarks, but to provide sample performance activities and sample performance tasks. This is illustrated in Exhibit 3.7.

Exhibit 3.7 Recommended Format for Writing Benchmarks

Benchmark	Sample Performance Activities	Sample Performance Task
Understands the basic characteristics of the various phases of the moon	• Use everyday objects to illustrate the phases of the moon • Compare the phases of the moon in terms of their influence on the earth • Identify other cycles of phases in nature that are similar to the phase of the moon	Your aunt, uncle and two young cousins are visiting from out of town. Your parents have asked you to organize a camp-out in the backyard for yourself and your cousins. After dark, your six-year-old cousin Michael points to the sliver of the moon and asks you why the moon changes shape, sometimes appearing to be a circle and at then "shrinking" a few nights later to just a sliver. While you are tempted to answer his question with a scary story about a giant in the sky who eats pieces of the moon—and six-year-old boys—when he gets hungry, you decide to stay out of trouble and to show Michael the phases that the moon goes through during its cycle. Using the your camping supplies, set up a demonstration for Michael that will illustrate the various phases of the moon. Write your explanation, including a list of the objects you would use and the procedure you would follow in your demonstration.

Column 1 in Exhibit 3.7 lists the actual benchmarks in information and skills terms; columns 2 and 3, respectively, list one or more sample performance activities and one or more sample performance tasks for each benchmark. This approach does not prescribe the performance activities or performance tasks teachers must use; rather, it provides clear examples and guidance regarding the performance activities and tasks teachers are encouraged to use.

The Problem Of Performance Standards

One of the most misunderstood aspects of setting standards and benchmarks is the concept of *performance standards*. Even a casual reading of the literature on standards illustrates that this term is an integral part of virtually all discussions of standards. The term was formalized, or at least legitimized, in the 1993 report to the National Education Goals Panel (NEGP, 1993b) by the Goals 3 and 4 Standards Review Technical Planning Group. Commonly referred to as the Malcom Report in deference to Shirley M. Malcom, chair of the planning group, the report makes a clear distinction between content standards and performance standards:

> Content standards specify "what students should know and be able to do." They indicate the knowledge and skills—the ways of thinking, working, communicating, reasoning, and investigating, and the most important and enduring ideas, concepts, issues, dilemmas, and knowledge essential to the discipline—that should be taught and learned in school. . . .

> Performance standards specify "how good is good enough." They relate to issues of assessment that gauge the degree to which content standards have been attained. While others use the term differently, in this report "performance standards" are not the skills, modes of reasoning, and habits mentioned above [in the description of content standards] that assessments attempt to measure. Instead, they are the indices of quality that specify how adept or competent a student demonstration must be. (pp. ii-iii)

The Malcom Report (NEGP, 1993b) further attests to the integral relationship between the two types of standards: "The Technical Planning Group believes that performance standards are essential to gauging whether content standards are met" (p. iii). Additionally, reports from the National Academy of Education Panel on the Evaluation of the NAEP Trial State Assessment (Shepard, 1993) and the National Council on Education Standards and Testing (1992) attest to the importance of both types of standards.

The confusion over performance standards lies in the fact that many of the descriptions of performance standards imply or explicitly state that performance standards are synonymous with performance tasks. For example, the Malcom Report (NEGP, 1993b) notes:

> A performance standard indicates both the *nature of the evidence* (such as an essay, mathematical proof, scientific experiment, project, exam, or combination of these) required to demonstrate that the content standard has been met and the *quality of student performance* that will be deemed acceptable (that merits a passing or "A" grade). (p. iii)

The references in the Malcom Report to the "nature of the evidence" and the specific mention of essays and projects are strikingly similar to the criteria previously mentioned as the defining characteristics of performance tasks (see pages 60 to 61). Marc Tucker (1992), codirector of the New Standards Project, also makes an explicit link between performance tasks and performance standards:

You can't assess kids' performance unless you give them the tasks, and you can't assess their degree of achievement unless they actually perform the tasks.

But first you must be clear about what you want kids to know and be able to do, or what we call "content standards." Those content standards become the target for creating the assessment. (p. S3)

We believe that creating a necessary relationship between performance tasks and performance standards is a critical mistake. This is not to say that performance tasks are unimportant. Indeed, in chapter 5 we discuss the key role of performance tasks in assessing students' competence on all types of standards. However, the concept of performance standards should be distinguished from the concept of performance tasks. The reason lies in the distinction between declarative and procedural knowledge previously discussed in this chapter. To reiterate, declarative knowledge consists of information, whereas procedural knowledge consists of processes, strategies, or skills. The inherent differences between these two types of knowledge call for inherent differences between declarative and procedural performance standards.

Performance standards for procedural benchmarks deal with the fluency with which the learner performs a process, strategy, or skill. For example, assume that a language arts standard that deals with the writing process contains the following benchmark at the high school level:

- edits a variety of types of compositions for overall logic

This benchmark involves using a mental process or a set of mental processes that monitor the overall logic of composition. This set of mental processes has been shown to be a key component of the writing process (Bereiter & Scardamalia, 1982, 1985; Flower & Hayes, 1980a, 1980b, 1981a, 1981b; Hillocks, 1987; Marzano & Paynter, 1994). The various levels of competence or performance in this process might be described as shown in Exhibit 3.8.

Exhibit 3.8 Performance Levels for Example Writing Benchmark

Advanced performance	Carries out the major processes and skills inherent in editing for overall logic with relative ease and automaticity
Proficient performance	Carries out the major processes and skills inherent in editing for overall logic without significant error, but not necessarily at an automatic level
Basic performance	Makes a number of errors when carrying out the skills and processes important to editing for overall logic, but still accomplishes the basic purpose of the editing
Novice performance	Makes so many errors when carrying out the skills and processes important to editing for overall logic that the editing fails to accomplish its purpose

A common convention is to refer to a set of performance levels such as those shown in Exhibit 3.8 as a *rubric*. One of the levels of performance can be identified as the criterion, or acceptable, level of performance; this is the level of performance that a district or school expects students to meet. This criterion, or acceptable, level of performance is the performance standard. For example, a district or school might decide that the proficient level in Exhibit 3.8 is the performance standard or it might decide that the basic level is the performance standard.

A performance standard, then, can be operationally defined as an acceptable level of performance embedded within a description of various levels (a rubric). The reason that the type of knowledge that is being addressed—declarative versus procedural—plays a key role in setting performance standards is that the levels of performance for declarative knowledge are quite different in nature from the levels of performance for procedural knowledge. For example, Exhibit 3.9 shows the generic levels of performance for procedural knowledge. (Note that the performance levels described in Exhibit 3.8 for the process of editing for overall logic were modeled after this generic form.)

Exhibit 3.9 Generic Performance Levels for Procedural Benchmarks

Advanced performance	Carries out the major processes and skills inherent in the procedure with relative ease and automaticity
Proficient performance	Carries out the major processes and skills inherent in the procedure without significant error, but not necessarily at an automatic level
Basic performance	Makes a number of errors when carrying out the processes and skills important to the procedure, but still accomplishes the basic purpose of the procedure
Novice performance	Makes so many errors when carrying out the processes and skills important to the procedure that it fails to accomplish its purpose

As the generic descriptions of performance levels in Exhibit 3.9 illustrate, the syntax, or innate structure, of the performance levels for procedural benchmarks involves tracking the extent to which the skills and processes inherent in the procedures can be carried out without significant error and with relative ease, or even at the level of automaticity. In contrast, as described in Exhibit 3.10, the performance levels for benchmarks that are declarative in nature have a different generic structure.

Exhibit 3.10 Generic Performance Levels for Declarative Benchmarks

Advanced performance	Demonstrates a thorough understanding of the important information; is able to exemplify that information in detail and articulate complex relationships and distinctions
Proficient performance	Demonstrates an understanding of the important information; is able to exemplify that information in some detail
Basic performance	Demonstrates an incomplete understanding of the important information, but does not have severe misconceptions
Novice performance	Demonstrates an incomplete understanding of the important information along with severe misconceptions

Whereas the performance levels for procedural knowledge deal with the ease and automaticity with which skills and processes are carried out, the performance levels for declarative knowledge address the extent to which examples are provided, relationships and distinctions are articulated, and misconceptions are avoided. Again, a district or school could identify any performance level as the performance standard, although the basic and proficient levels are the two most commonly chosen.

To illustrate how this generic format applies to specific declarative content, assume that a district or school had identified the following as a benchmark within civics: "Students will understand the nature of limited and unlimited government." Using the generic format above, the performance levels in Exhibit 3.11 might be constructed.

Exhibit 3.11 Performance Levels for Example Civics Declarative Benchmarks

Advanced performance	Demonstrates a thorough understanding of the important information relative to limited or unlimited government; is able to exemplify that information in detail and articulate complex relationships and distinctions regarding limited and unlimited government
Proficient performance	Demonstrates an understanding of the important information; is able to exemplify the information in some detail
Basic performance	Demonstrates an incomplete understanding of the important information, but does not have severe misconceptions
Novice performance	Demonstrates an incomplete understanding of the important information along with severe misconceptions

When creating performance levels for declarative knowledge, a useful convention is to identify the important information along with the key examples, relationships, and distinctions for each level. For example, *National Standards for Civics and Government* (Center for Civic Education, 1994) identifies the information in Exhibit 3.12 as indicative of performance at the proficient level for the concepts of limited and unlimited governments.

Exhibit 3.12 Information Indicative of Proficient Understanding of Limited and Unlimited Governments

Limited Governments	Unlimited Governments
MAJOR CHARACTERISTICS	
Constitutional Governments	Non-constitutional Governments

• Institutional devices used to limit powers, e.g.,
  • written or unwritten constitutions
  • independent judiciaries
  • checks and balances
  • separation of powers
  • bill of rights
  • regular, free, and fair elections
  • powers are limited to the purposes specified in a constitution, e.g., the protection of individual rights and promotion of the common good
	Authoritarian systems
	• unlimited authority exercised by an individual or group
	• individual rights subordinated to state
	• no regularized and effective restraints on powers of government, e.g.,
	  • no popularly elected assembly
	  • no free elections
	  • no independent judiciary
	
	Totalitarian systems
	• government attempts to control every aspect of the lives of individuals and prohibits independent associations
	• government use of intimidation and terror

HISTORICAL EXAMPLES	
• Canada • Australia • New Zealand • United States	*Authoritarian systems* • Russia under the Czars • Japan under the military in the 1930s *Totalitarian systems* • Soviet Union under Stalin • Germany under Hitler • China under Mao • Romania under Ceausescu • Cambodia under Pol Pot • North Korea under Kim-Il-sung
CONTEMPORARY EXAMPLES	
• Japan • Denmark • Venezuela • United States	*Authoritarian systems* • Kenya • Myanmar (Burma) *Totalitarian systems* • Cuba under Castro • Iraq under Saddam Hussein

Note: From *National Standards for Civics and Government* (p. 149), by the Center for Civic Education, 1994, Calabasas, CA: Author. Copyright © 1994, Center for Civic Education. Reprinted with permission.

In summary, performance levels and, consequently, performance standards for declarative and procedural benchmarks have very different structures. Herein lies the basic problem with mandating that performance standards be embedded in specific performance tasks. Although performance tasks are very useful as assessment and instructional tools, they tend to mix and confound the two types of knowledge. To illustrate, reconsider the waste material performance task, which is reprinted in Exhibit 3.13.

Exhibit 3.13 Sample Performance Task

The accumulation of waste materials is a world-wide problem. Waste materials can be toxic, non-toxic, hard to get rid of, bulky, smelly, and so on. Imagine that your group of four has been selected to prepare a report for a task force of the federal government that classifies the various types of waste materials and proposes plans to address the problems. Using information gathered from our lessons and from sources on reserve in the school library, classify the various types of waste materials. Then select one category of waste materials and present a plan for dealing with it. Your plan should be prepared as a research report to the government and should include the following elements:

1. Your classification of all waste materials and how you determined the categories.

2. An explanation of the effect your selected category of waste material has on the environment.

3. Your plan to deal with the waste material. This plan should contain references to the information sources you used and graphs and tables where appropriate.

4. The expected effect of your plan.

Note: Adapted from *Assessing Student Outcomes* (p. 51), by R. J. Marzano, D. J. Pickering, and J. McTighe, 1993, Alexandria, VA: Association for Supervision and Curriculum Development. Copyright © 1993 by McREL Institute.

If this task were used to articulate a performance standard, a single set of performance levels would be constructed. However, those performance levels would necessarily mix somewhat independent components of declarative and procedural knowledge. Specifically, this task includes the following components:

    a. The declarative knowledge important to understanding the different types of toxic materials

    b. The procedural knowledge involved in the process of classifying

    c. The procedural knowledge involved in developing a plan

    d. The procedural knowledge involved in writing a research report

The performance levels for this performance task would necessarily include all four elements. In fact, the generic form of the performance levels for this task might be conceptualized as shown in Exhibit 3.14 (see next page).

This approach to designing performance levels is commonly referred to as the "holistic" approach. In this approach, the individual performance levels across each of the components are collapsed into a single set of performance levels. As the generic format in Exhibit 3.14 illustrates, the holistic approach also assumes a specific profile on the performance levels of the individual components. Specifically, this approach assumes that if the student is advanced (proficient, basic, or novice) in one component, then he or she is also assumed to be advanced (proficient, basic, or novice) in all of the other components.

Exhibit 3.14 Holistic Approach to Performance Levels

Advanced performance	• advanced performance on component *a*; • advanced performance on component *b*; • advanced performance on component *c*; • advanced performance on component *d*.
Proficient performance	• proficient performance on component *a*; • proficient performance on component *b*; • proficient performance on component *c*; • proficient performance on component *d*.
Basic performance	• basic performance on component *a*; • basic performance on component *b*; • basic performance on component *c*; • basic performance on component *d*.
Novice performance	• novice performance on component *a*; • novice performance on component *b*; • novice performance on component *c*; • novice performance on component *d*.

The logical problem with the holistic approach occurs when a student has a highly uneven profile on the components assessed by the task. For example, assume that a student exhibited the following profile on the four components, *a*, *b*, *c*, and *d*:

Component *a*: proficient level

Component *b*: proficient level

Component *c*: proficient level

Component *d*: novice level

Using the holistic approach in a strictly logical fashion, the student would receive a score of "novice" even though he had exhibited proficient performance on three out of the four components. The logic of holistic performance levels demands that all components at a given performance level be executed at least at that level. Stated in negative terms, a student's score on a holistically designed set of performance levels must always devolve to the performance level that represents the student's lowest level of performance on the multiple components assessed. To illustrate using a content example, consider the holistically designed performance levels for writing, which are shown in Exhibit 3.15.

Exhibit 3.15 Sample Performance Levels for Writing Using Holistic Approach

Advanced performance	• writing demonstrates precision in word choice • writing has a logical organizational pattern • verb and noun forms are correct • writing demonstrates well-developed supporting ideas
Proficient performance	• writing demonstrates adequate word choice • writing has an organizational pattern, although a few lapses may occur • occasional errors in verb and noun forms • writing has ample development of supporting ideas
Basic performance	• word choice is adequate but limited and occasionally vague • writing has an organizational pattern, although lapses may occur • writing has errors in verb and noun forms • writing has adequate development of supporting ideas
Novice performance	• word choice is limited and immature • writing demonstrates little evidence of an organizational pattern • writing has frequent errors in verb and noun forms • writing has minimal development of supporting ideas

Here it is assumed that if the student is proficient in word choice, he is also proficient in producing writing that has an organizational pattern, only occasional errors in verb and noun forms, and ample development of supporting ideas. These assumptions can cause problems because students rarely perform all skills at the same level.

Logical problems with holistic performance levels have led some researchers like classroom assessment expert Richard Stiggins (1994) to articulate strong warnings against their use:

> As a personal aside, I must say that I am minimizing my own use of holistic scoring . . . I see few applications for such a score in the classroom. Besides, I have begun to question the meaning of such scores. I have participated in some writing assessments in which students whose analytic profiles of performance . . . . were remarkably different ended up with the same holistic score. That gives me pause to wonder about the real meaning and interpretability of holistic scores. I have begun to think holistic scores mask the kind of more detailed information needed to promote classroom-level student growth. (p. 196)

Given the inherent problems with holistic performance levels, we recommend against their use and, consequently, against defining performance standards in terms of specific performance tasks. Unfortunately, from our perspective, defining performance standards in terms of specific performance tasks and holistically designed performance levels is still the norm. As we have seen, documents as influential as the Malcom Report (NEGP, 1993b) make explicit reference to performance tasks, and researchers and theorists as noted as Marc Tucker (1992) assert that performance standards cannot be articulated outside the context of specific performance tasks. Our recommendation is to construct performance levels around the unique characteristics of declarative and procedural knowledge within specific benchmarks. In chapters 4 and 6, we consider how performance standards for individual benchmarks can be combined when reporting student progress on standards.

Summary And Recommendations

In this chapter we have discussed the rather arbitrary nature of standards as general categories of knowledge and skill. Our conclusion is that benchmarks, not standards per se, are the critical elements in determining what students should know and be able to do. We have considered three formats in which benchmarks can be written: (1) as statements of information and skill, that is, declarative and procedural knowledge, (2) as performance activities, and (3) as performance tasks. We have recommended that benchmarks be written as statements of declarative and procedural knowledge but be accompanied by example performance activities and performance tasks. Finally, we have discussed the confusion over the concept of performance standards and recommended against tying performance standards to specific performance tasks and against collapsing declarative and procedural benchmarks into holistic performance levels.

Chapter 4

At What Levels Will Benchmarks Be Articulated?

As described in chapter 3, benchmarks are specific statements of information and skill at developmentally appropriate levels that add definition and detail to the general statements articulated at the standards level. For the most part, the national standards documents are written at three or four levels. For example, the benchmarks in Project 2061's *Benchmarks for Science Literacy* (1993) are written at four levels: K-2, 3-5, 6-8, and 9-12. Geography standards found in *Geography for Life: National Geography Standards* (Geography Education Standards Project, 1994) include benchmarks at three levels: K-4, 5-8, and 9-12. This same pattern seems to hold true for state documents. For example, the Michigan framework lists four levels, the Minnesota standards are written at four levels, and standards for the state of Florida are written at four levels. Colorado standards are written at three levels as are the standards from Arkansas and Idaho. (At least two states, Virginia and Mississippi, however, identify content at each grade level from kindergarten through at least grade 8.)

As parsimonious as the use of only three or four levels is, this approach presents some inherent problems for districts and schools. The most severe problem is that it places a heavy assessment and reporting load on a few grade levels. For example, assume that a district used the four levels explicit in *Benchmarks for Science Literacy*. If a district wished to report student progress on individual standards, it would necessarily have to assess students at each of these four levels. It would also have to report student progress on each of the standards. This would place a great strain on four particular grade levels—2nd, 5th, 8th, and 12th. In effect, these four grade levels would bear all the burden of assessing and reporting student progress on standards. One option for overcoming the disadvantages of writing benchmarks at a few grade levels only is to write benchmarks at all grade levels.

Grade-Level Benchmarks

Most districts and schools that wish to write grade-level benchmarks primarily refer to national or state documents that have benchmarks written at three or four levels only. Fortunately, these sources can be easily recast in grade-level formats if it is assumed that the benchmarks in the national and state documents represent expectations about what students should know and be able to do at the top end of each grade-level interval for which the benchmarks are written. Fortunately, this assumption is validated in many resource documents. For example, *Benchmarks for Science Literacy* (Project 2061, 1993) explicitly notes that its science benchmarks are expectations about what students should know at the end of each grade-level interval. To illustrate, the following is a benchmark at the 3-5 interval:

By the end of the 5th grade, students should know that

- The earth's gravity pulls any object toward it without touching it.
- Without touching them, a magnet pulls on all things made of iron and either pushes or pulls on other magnets.
- Without touching them, material that has been electrically charged pulls on all other materials and may either push or pull other charged materials. (p. 94)

Similarly, the three levels of benchmarks in *Geography for Life: National Geography Standards* (Geography Education Standards Project, 1994)—K-4, 5-8, 9-12—make overt reference to the fact that they are expectations for the upper end of each interval:

By the end of the fourth grade, the student knows and understands:

1. The components of ecosystems
2. The distribution and patterns of ecosystems
3. How humans interact with ecosystems

Some documents, however, do not clarify the grade-level expectations regarding benchmarks. Consider, for example, the following benchmarks from *National Health Education Standards* (Joint Committee on National Health Education Standards, 1995):

As a result of health instruction in Grades 5-8, students will

1. describe the influence of cultural beliefs on health behaviors and the use of health services.
2. analyze how messages from media and other sources influence health behaviors.
3. analyze the influence of technology on personal and family health.
4. analyze how information from peers influences health.

Districts or schools can use one of two approaches to create grade-level benchmarks. They either (1) can assume that interval benchmarks represent end-of-interval expectations and break these down to create grade-level benchmarks or (2) distribute interval benchmarks throughout the grade levels. We first consider the technique of breaking down end-of-interval benchmarks.

The most straightforward method of generating grade-level benchmarks is to assume that the interval benchmarks are end-of-interval expectations and then create grade-level benchmarks by altering each benchmark to coincide with developmental differences from grade level to grade level. To illustrate, below are the science benchmarks listed for the interval K-2 in the McREL database within the science standard "Understands essential ideas about the composition and structure of the universe and the Earth's place in it" (see Kendall & Marzano, 1996):

- Knows that the stars are innumerable, unevenly dispersed, and of unequal brightness
- Knows that the Sun can be seen only in the day time, whereas the Moon is out sometimes at night and sometimes during the day
- Knows that the Moon looks a little different every day, but looks the same again about every four weeks (pp. 79-80)

To translate these interval benchmarks into grade-level benchmarks, a school or district need only identify which elements would be deleted or altered at lower grade levels. For example, first-grade teachers might decide that the benchmarks above should be restated in the following way to be developmentally appropriate for first-grade students:

- Knows that there are many stars scattered all over the sky
- Knows that the Sun is seen during the day and the moon can be seen at night and sometimes during the day
- Knows that the Moon changes in appearance

Similarly, kindergarten teachers might conclude that the benchmarks should be written in the following way to be developmentally appropriate for kindergarten students:

- Knows that stars are seen in the sky at night
- Knows that the Sun is seen during the day and the Moon is usually seen at night

We should note that this "interval technique" has at least one critical characteristic that differentiates it from the "design down" principle we cautioned against in chapter 3. The design down principle always begins with expectations about twelfth graders; this is why the standards identified using this principle are frequently referred to as "exit standards" or "exit outcomes." Implicit in the design down principle is the assumption that all subject areas have a hierarchic structure that runs from kindergarten through twelfth grade. As we have seen, this assumption is not necessarily true. The interval technique described here does not rely on any assumptions about the K-12 structure of subject-area content. It does assume, however, that benchmarks stated as expectations regarding understanding and skill at the upper end of a grade-level interval can and should be described at all the grade levels within the interval.

Both the design down principle described in chapter 3 and the interval technique described here have roots in the concept of a spiral curriculum first popularized by curriculum reformer Hilda Taba (1967) and elaborated in later years by theorists such as Jerome Bruner (1960) and Patricia Murphy (1974). The fundamental principle underlying the concept of a spiral curriculum is that students should first be introduced to new information in its basic form. The next time students encounter the information or skill, more detail, more relationships, and more complexity should be added. In the example above, kindergartners first learn that stars are seen at night. First graders add to this knowledge by learning that there are many stars scattered all over the sky. Second graders add more complexity by learning that stars are innumerable, unevenly dispersed, and of unequal brightness.

Thus, benchmarks written at three or four intervals can be easily recast as grade-level benchmarks under the assumption that benchmarks written in intervals are expectations for what students should know and be able to do by the end of the intervals. If benchmarks stated in interval form cannot be considered end-of-interval expectations, then they might be distributed through the grades in the interval. For example, the four health benchmarks listed previously for grades 5-8 (see page 74) might be distributed throughout that interval in the following manner:

Grade 5: Analyze how information from peers influences health

Grade 6: Analyze how messages from media and other sources influence health behavior

Grade 7: Analyze the influence of technology on personal and family health

Grade 8: Describe the influence of cultural beliefs on health behaviors and the use of health services

To use this approach, a district or school must assume that one exposure to the knowledge identified in the benchmark is sufficient. In other words, the district or school must conclude that it is not necessary to teach and reinforce the knowledge within the benchmark at more than one grade level.

A combination of these two methods of writing benchmarks is frequently used by districts and schools. Some benchmarks are broken down using the interval approach, whereas others are distributed throughout the grades. Again, to determine which benchmarks should be broken down by grade level versus which benchmarks should be assigned to specific grade levels, a school or district must determine whether the skill and information in the benchmark can be adequately addressed by exposure at one grade level. If the determination is that exposure at one grade level will suffice, then there might be no need to alter the information or skill for other grade levels. Using the science benchmarks previously discussed (see page 74), a school or district might decide that students can easily acquire through exposure at one grade level only the information that the patterns of stars in the sky stay the same, although they appear to move across the sky nightly, and different stars can be seen in different seasons. Given this determination, there would be no need to identify less complex versions of this information at developmentally appropriate grade levels. The school or district would simply identify a grade level at which students would be exposed to this information.

The Problem With High School Benchmarks

Grade-level benchmarks generally work quite well up until high school. At that point, the assumption of a hierarchic arrangement of benchmarks usually breaks down. That is, the assumption that the content covered at one grade level is more complex and abstract than that covered at the preceding grade level does not necessarily hold up. This is because some courses at the high school level are considered introductory, whereas others are considered advanced. For example, an introductory course usually does not require prerequisites, whereas advanced courses do. Consequently, a course in Introductory Eastern Literature offered at the 11th-grade level might be conceptually less difficult than Algebra II offered at the 10th-grade level. There are three ways that the problem of high school benchmarks can be addressed: (1) upper and lower division benchmarks, (2) literacy versus expert benchmarks, and (3) course descriptions.

Upper and Lower Division Benchmarks

One approach to overcoming the inherent problem of grade-level benchmarks in high school is to break high school benchmarks into two broad categories—upper and lower division. In effect, two, as opposed to four, levels of benchmarks are identified for high school. The lower division benchmarks are generally meant for freshman and sophomore years; the upper division benchmarks are intended for junior and senior years. Although this does not solve all the conceptual problems, it addresses many of them because upper division courses usually address content that is more abstract and complex than lower division courses.

The "official" national arts standards document, *What Every Young American Should Know and Be Able to Do in the Arts* (Consortium of National Arts Education Associations, 1994) uses this basic convention. It refers to the lower division standards as the "proficient level" and the upper division standards as the "advanced level." Paul Lehman (1995), chair of the task force that developed the national arts standards, describes the difference between the proficient and advanced levels:

> Because the arts are elective in most high schools, two levels of achievement standards—proficient and advanced—are provided for grades 9-12. The proficient level is intended for students who have completed courses of study involving relevant skills and knowledge in that discipline for one to two years beyond grade eight. The advanced level is intended for students who have completed courses of study involving relevant skills and knowledge in that discipline for three to four years beyond grade eight. Every student is expected to achieve at the proficient level in at least one arts discipline by the time he or she graduates from high school. (p. 61)

Exhibit 4.1 provides an example of the advanced and proficient levels from the dance standard entitled "Identifying and demonstrating movement elements and skills in performing dance."

Exhibit 4.1 Dance Standards: Proficient and Advanced Levels

Proficient	Advanced
Students:	Students:
demonstrate appropriate skeletal alignment, body-part articulation, strength, flexibility, agility, and coordination in locomotor and nonlocomotor/axial movements	demonstrate a high level of consistency and reliability in performing technical skills
identify and demonstrate longer and more complex steps and patterns from two different dance styles/traditions	
demonstrate rhythmic acuity	perform technical skills with artistic expression, demonstrating clarity, musicality, and stylistic nuance
demonstrate projection while performing dance skills	

Note: From "What Students Should Learn in the Arts" (p. 8), by P. R. Lehman, 1995, in A. A. Glatthorn (Ed.), *Content of the Curriculum* (2nd ed., pp. 1-22), Alexandria, VA: Association for Supervision and Curriculum Development. Copyright © 1995 by ASCD. All rights reserved.

The upper and lower division format has also been effectively used by Central Park East Secondary School in Harlem. As described by researchers Linda Darling-Hammond and Jacqueline Ancess (1994), this school encompasses grades 7-12. Grades 7-10 are divided into Division I and II; grades 11 and 12 are referred to as the Senior Institute. The standards in Division I and II are considered prerequisites for the Senior Institute.

Finally, the upper and lower division format is quite consistent with the notion of the Certificate of Initial Mastery (the CIM) and the Certificate of Advanced Mastery (the CAM). The Certificate of Initial Mastery (CIM) was first proposed by the Commission on the Skills of the American Work Force in its 1990 report entitled *America's Choice: High Skills or Low Wages* (in Rothman, 1995b). According to researcher Robert Rothman (1995b), seven states are currently working toward implementing a CIM (i.e., Indiana, Maine, Massachusetts, New York, Oregon, Texas, and Washington). In general, the CIM represents expectations of what 16-year-olds should know and be able to do. In other words, a CIM specifies 10th-grade standards in essential content areas. In some states, another level of standards is set for 12th grade. In Oregon, this set of advanced standards is referred to as the Certificate of Advanced Mastery (CAM). The basic idea behind the CIM and CAM is that one set of standards is a prerequisite for the other. That is, a student cannot advance to the CAM without first obtaining the CIM. Conversely, a student might decide to exit the general public school system after obtaining the CIM to pursue training in a specialized technical area.

Literacy Versus Expert Standards

Closely related to the convention of articulating upper and lower division benchmarks is that of articulating literacy standards and expert standards within a subject area. We discussed the issue of literacy standards in chapter 2. To recapitulate, literacy standards (and their related benchmarks) articulate what students should know and be able to do to function well within the general population. At a higher level are standards that are sometimes referred to as expert standards, or world-class standards. Given the confusion over the term "world class" (see Resnick & Nolan, 1995 and Gandal, 1995b for discussions), we prefer to use the term *expert standards*. Whereas literacy standards are intended for the general public, expert standards are intended for those who wish to pursue advanced work in a subject area. The basic difference between expert standards and upper division benchmarks (described in the previous section) is that expert standards are not tied to specific grade levels, whereas upper division benchmarks are. For example, a student cannot progress to the advanced standards in the arts unless he has taken two years of prerequisite study in grades 9 and 10. Expert standards do not include this restriction. The mathematics standards, developed and published by the National Council of Teachers of Mathematics (1989), identify what we would refer to as expert standards but do not tie them to specific grade levels. Exhibit 4.2 (see next page) presents the NCTM standards for probability and discrete mathematics.

NCTM (1989) notes that element *f* in Standard 11 and elements *k* and *l* in Standard 12 are designed for students who want to study mathematics at the college level. These elements could be organized under their own unique standards, which would be somehow tagged as being advanced:

Advanced Concepts in Probability

f. Apply the concept of a random variable to generate and interpret probability distributions including binomial, uniform, normal, and chi square.

Advanced Concepts in Discrete Mathematics

k. Represent and solve problems using linear programming and difference equations;

l. Investigate problem situations that arise in connection with computer validation and the application of algorithms.

These advanced standards might be available to students in the same courses as the other more literacy-based standards. Hence, identifying expert and advanced standards does not carry the constraint that these standards be addressed at different grade levels as does the upper and lower division approach.

Exhibit 4.2 NCTM Standards for Probability and Discrete Mathematics

---

Standard 11: Probability

In grades 9-12, the mathematics curriculum should include the continued study of probability so that all students can:

    a. Use experimental or theoretical probability, as appropriate, to represent and solve problems involving uncertainty;

    b. Use simulations to estimate probabilities;

    c. Understand the concept of a random variable;

    d. Create and interpret discrete probability distributions;

    e. Describe, in general terms, the normal curve and use its properties to answer questions about sets of data that are assumed to be normally distributed; and so that, in addition, college-intending students can:

    f. Apply the concept of a random variable to generate and interpret probability distributions including binomial, uniform, normal, and chi square.

Standard 12: Discrete Mathematics

In grades 9-12, the mathematics curriculum should include topics from discrete mathematics so that all students can:

    g. Represent problem situations using discrete structures such as finite graphs, matrices, sequences, and recurrence relations;

    h. Represent and analyze finite graphs using matrices;

    I. Develop and analyze algorithms;

    j. Solve enumeration and finite probability problems; and so that, in addition, college-intending students can:

    k. Represent and solve problems using linear programming and difference equations;

    l. Investigate problem situations that arise in connection with computer validation and the application of algorithms.

Note: From *Curriculum and Evaluation Standards for School Mathematics* (p. 171, 176), by National Council of Teachers of Mathematics, 1989, Reston, VA: Author.

Course Descriptions

A final option for high schools is to express standards as course descriptions. This is the approach taken by the state of Virginia. As described in the document *Standards of Learning for Virginia Public Schools* (Board of Education, Commonwealth of Virginia, 1995), benchmarks for six mathematics standards are articulated for kindergarten through grade eight. However, at the high school level, mathematics standards are packaged as required information and skill specific to eight courses: Algebra I, Geometry, Algebra II, Trigonometry, Algebra II and Trigonometry, Mathematical Analysis, Advanced Placement Calculus, and Computer Mathematics. For example, the Virginia State Department lists the knowledge in Exhibit 4.3 as important to a one-year course in Algebra I.

Exhibit 4.3 Commonwealth of Virginia Standards for One-Year Course in Algebra I

A.1   The student will solve linear equations and inequalities in one variable, solve literal equations (formulas) for a given variable and apply these skills to solve practical problems. Graphing calculators will be used to confirm algebraic solutions.

A.2   The student will represent verbal quantitative situations algebraically and evaluate these expressions for given replacement values of the variables. Students will choose an appropriate computational technique, such as mental mathematics, calculator, or paper and pencil.

A.3   The student will justify steps used in simplifying expressions and solving equations and inequalities. Justifications will include the use of concrete objects, pictorial representations, and the properties of real numbers.

A.4   The student will use matrices to organize and manipulate data, including matrix addition, subtraction, and scalar multiplication. Data will arise from business, industrial, and consumer situations.

A.5   The student will analyze a given set of data for the existence of a pattern, represent the pattern algebraically and graphically, if possible, and determine if the relation is a function.

A.6   The student will select, justify, and apply an appropriate technique to graph a linear function in two variables. Techniques will include slope-intercept, x- and y-intercepts, graphing by transformation, and the use of the graphing calculator.

A.7   The student will determine the slope of a line when given an equation of the line, the graph of the line, or two points on the line. Slope will be described as rate of change and will be positive, negative, zero, or undefined. The graphing calculator will be used to investigate the effect of changes in the slope on the graph of the line.

A.8   The student will write an equation of a line when given the graph of the line, two points on the line, or the slope and a point on the line.

A.9   The student will solve systems of two linear equations in two variables, both algebraically and graphically, and apply these techniques to solve practical problems. Graphing calculators will be used as both a primary tool of solution and to confirm an algebraic solution.

A.10 The student will apply the laws of exponents to perform operations on expressions with integral exponents, using scientific notation when appropriate.

A.11 The student will add, subtract, and multiply polynomials and divide polynomials with monomial divisors, using concrete objects, pictorial representations, and algebraic manipulations.

A.12 The student will factor completely first- and second-degree binomials and trinomials in one or two variables. The graphing calculator will be used as both a primary tool for factoring and for confirming an algebraic factorization.

A.13 The student will estimate square roots to the nearest tenth and use a calculator to compute decimal approximations of radicals.

A.14 The student will solve quadratic equations in one variable both algebraically and graphically. Graphing calculators will be used both as a primary tool in solving problems and to verify algebraic solutions.

A.15 The student will determine the domain and range of a relation given a graph or a set of ordered pairs and will identify the relations that are functions.

A.16 The student will, given a rule, find the values of a function for elements in its domain and locate the zeros of the function both algebraically and with a graphing calculator. The value of f(x) will be related to the ordinate on the graph.

A.17 The student will, given a set of data points, write an equation for a line of best fit, using the median fit method, and use the equation to make predictions.

A.18 The student will compare multiple one-variable data sets, using statistical techniques that include measures of central tendency, range, stem-and-leaf plots, and box-and-whisker graphs.

A.19 The student will analyze a relation to determine whether a direct or inverse variation exists and represent it algebraically and graphically, if possible.

Note: From *Standards of Learning for Virginia Public Schools* (pp. 18-19), by Board of Education, Commonwealth of Virginia, June 1995, Richmond, VA: Author. Copyright © 1995. Reprinted with permission.

Although certainly a viable option, the course description approach has one major drawback: It does not lend itself to reporting student progress on individual standards or benchmarks. Exhibit 4.3 lists the 19 different elements that students should know and be able to do as a result of taking Algebra I. Because these 19 elements are not organized as standards, each individual teacher will have to decide the relationship between how well students perform on the 19 components and the overall grade they will receive for the course. Do students have to master all 19 elements to receive an A for the course? Can they do well on 15 elements and receive an A? If so, which 15 elements? We will discuss in depth the problem of using a single letter grade to report progress on standards in chapter 6.

The Stages-Of-Development Format

An alternative to the grade-level approach is what we refer to as the *stages-of-development approach*. Wiggins (1996) describes this approach in the following way:

> Each stage represents a cluster of skills that are linked to each other such that level 1 must be learned before level 2, level 2 before level 3 and so on. Stages are not the same as grade levels, but, rather, overlap a span of grades. Progress is measured by movement through stages, not grade levels. (p. 168)

This approach has strong intuitive appeal and is quite consistent with research and theory in developmentally appropriate practice (Case, 1985; Fischer, 1980; Flavell, 1977; Sulzby, 1986).

Fundamentally, developing benchmarks that represent stages of development involves ignoring the 13 grade levels (i.e., K-12). Instead, the focus is on the natural developmental levels a student goes through as he or she masters the information and skill within a standard. A key point here is not to assume that all standards have the same number of stages. For example, a school or district might decide that a standard that relates to the reading process involves six stages, a standard that relates to writing involves seven stages, understanding probability involves four stages, reading maps involves three stages, and scientific inquiry involves five stages. This is depicted in Figure 4.1.

Figure 4.1 Stages-of-Development Approach: Sample Stages Using Varying Stages of Development

Reading	Writing	Probability	Maps	Scientific Inquiry
Stage 6	Stage 7	Stage 4	Stage 3	Stage 5
Stage 5	Stage 6			Stage 4
Stage 4	Stage 5	Stage 3	Stage 2	
	Stage 4			Stage 3
Stage 3	Stage 3	Stage 2		
Stage 2	Stage 2			Stage 2
Stage 1	Stage 1	Stage 1	Stage 1	Stage 1

As Figure 4.1 illustrates, this approach—albeit quite logical from a cognitive perspective—generates a system that might be difficult to explain to parents and community members. For example, it might be difficult to explain why a score of 6 is the highest a student can receive in the reading standard, whereas a score of 7 is the highest a student can receive in the writing standard, and so on.

Some districts have attempted to establish a uniform number of levels for all standards. For example, Wiggins (1996) provides an illustration of a district that uses eight levels for every standard. The general design of the stages-of-development approach using a uniform number of stages is depicted in Figure 4.2.

Figure 4.2 Stages-of-Development Approach: General Design Using Uniform Number of Stages

Reading	Writing	Probability	Maps	Scientific Inquiry
Stage 8	Stage 8	Stage 8	Stage 8	Stage 8
Stage 7	Stage 7	Stage 7	Stage 7	Stage 7
Stage 6	Stage 6	Stage 6	Stage 6	Stage 6
Stage 5	Stage 5	Stage 5	Stage 5	Stage 5
Stage 4	Stage 4	Stage 4	Stage 4	Stage 4
Stage 3	Stage 3	Stage 3	Stage 3	Stage 3
Stage 2	Stage 2	Stage 2	Stage 2	Stage 2
Stage 1	Stage 1	Stage 1	Stage 1	Stage 1

Although this is a cleaner approach from a reporting perspective, we believe it violates the basic intent of the stages-of-development approach: to have benchmarks reflect natural stages of development as opposed to artificial levels. To say that all standards must have eight (or seven or six) benchmark levels is conceptually no different from saying that standards should have benchmarks at every grade.

The Performance Levels Format

In chapter 3, we introduced the concept of performance levels. This concept can be integrated into the format for writing benchmarks. This is depicted in Figure 4.3.

In Figure 4.3, benchmarks are written at four levels: K-2, 3-5, 6-8, and 9-12. However, for each benchmark, four levels of performance are also described. In effect, then, this format creates 16 levels—four at each of the four levels of benchmarks.

Figure 4.3 Relationship Between Benchmarks and Performance Levels Using Four Levels for Each Set of Benchmarks at K-2, 3-5, 6-8, and 9-12.

Standard #1		Standard #2	
Benchmarks for grades 9-12	Advanced Proficient Basic Novice	Benchmarks for grades 9-12	Advanced Proficient Basic Novice
Benchmarks for grades 6-8	Advanced Proficient Basic Novice	Benchmarks for grades 6-8	Advanced Proficient Basic Novice
Benchmarks for grades 3-5	Advanced Proficient Basic Novice	Benchmarks for grades 3-5	Advanced Proficient Basic Novice
Benchmarks for grades K-2	Advanced Proficient Basic Novice	Benchmarks for grades K-2	Advanced Proficient Basic Novice

The most difficult aspect of this approach is defining what is meant by the novice, basic, proficient, and advanced levels for each grade-level band. This is difficult because each grade-level band contains multiple benchmarks. Does the advanced level at a particular grade-level band mean that students demonstrate advanced understanding or skill for all benchmark elements? Does the basic level of performance signify basic performance for all benchmarks within an interval? Measurement experts Richard Jaeger, Ronald Hambelton, and Barbara Plake (1995) offer a scheme for addressing this issue. Using a four-point system, they recommend the following scheme:

Level 4 The top level—indicates general competence in all benchmarks within a standard and exceptional performance in a few.

Level 3 Commonly the performance standard—indicates general competence in all benchmarks within a standard.

Level 2 Indicates general competence in most benchmarks within a standard with difficulties in some of the benchmarks.

Level 1 Indicates difficulties in a majority of benchmarks within a standard.

Another way of conceptualizing this issue is that each benchmark within a standard has performance levels. Performance levels for a standard, then, are made up of sets of performance levels for the benchmarks that comprise the standards. If we refer to Jaeger, Hambelton, and Plake's four levels as advanced, proficient, basic, and novice (as we did for the levels of performance for individual benchmarks) then the levels of performance for a standard can be described in the following way:

Advanced performance for a standard: Advanced performance in some of the benchmarks and proficient performance in the others

Proficient performance for a standard: Proficient performance in the vast majority of all benchmarks

Basic performance for a standard: Basic or higher performance in most benchmarks with novice performance in the rest

Novice performance for a standard: Novice performance in the majority of benchmarks within the standard

We should note that this approach is somewhat similar to the holistic approach we so strongly recommended against in chapter 3. Both approaches collapse performance on multiple benchmarks into a single set of performance levels. However, the approach described here, which we will refer to as the multiple profile approach, does not have the debilitating assumptions of an even profile on all benchmarks as does the holistic performance levels approach. This is best illustrated by direct comparison of the two systems, as shown in Table 4.1.

Table 4.1 Comparison of Multiple Profile Approach and Holistic Approach

Level	Multiple Profile Approach	Holistic Approach
Advanced Performance	Advanced performance in some of the benchmarks and proficient performance in the others	Advanced performance in all benchmarks
Proficient Performance	Proficient performance in the vast majority of all benchmarks	Proficient performance in all benchmarks
Basic Performance	Basic or higher performance in most benchmarks with novice performance in the rest	Basic performance in all benchmarks
Novice Performance	Novice performance in the majority of benchmarks	Novice performance in all benchmarks

As the comparison in Table 4.1 illustrates, to make sense, the holistic approach requires a specific profile on the benchmarks within a standard, whereas the multiple profile approach does not.

Certainly there are disadvantages to the multiple profile approach; perhaps the primary disadvantage is the lack of exact specificity in terms of the profiles that are commensurate with each performance level. However, within the inherently messy world of summarizing performance on multiple benchmarks, we have found that this approach provides a nice balance between rigor and flexibility without sacrificing too much to subjectivity.

How Many Standards And Benchmarks Should We Identify?

A critical issue when articulating standards and benchmarks is how many should be identified. In fact, this issue is so important that the standards-setting efforts within a district or school can be easily subverted if the number of standards or benchmarks identified becomes too large. By our reasoning this is precisely what occurred within the mastery learning movement and the competency-based education movement. Specifically, in some implementations of mastery learning (see e.g., Jones, Friedman, & Tinzmann, & Cox, 1985; Menahem & Weisman, 1985) and competency-based education (see e.g., Clark & Thomson, 1976), schools and districts identified as many as 1,500 benchmarks within each content area.[1] In some districts, over 10,000 benchmarks were identified across all content areas. The sheer problem of record keeping for such large numbers of benchmarks is enough to render a system impractical. Keeping the number of benchmarks down to a manageable set, then, is a critical consideration.

[1]Note: Mastery learning was commonly built on a unit of content description called the "objective." For a comparison of the objective and benchmark, see Kendall & Marzano, 1996, p. 24.

There are at least three ways to safeguard against the problem of too many benchmarks. First, as we have just seen, a school or district can summarize student standing on multiple benchmarks within a single set of performance levels for an individual standard. This greatly reduces the reporting load because the standard, as opposed to the benchmark, is the level at which records are kept. Second, a school or district can and should keep the number of benchmarks small by thinking in terms of essential information and skill. If one continually asks the question, Do students really need to know this? then the number of benchmarks at a particular grade level or a particular grade-level interval probably will be kept to a minimum. Third, a district or school can adopt the position that standards and benchmarks should identify only a portion of the content that teachers will address in a particular course or at a particular grade level. In other words, a district or school can consciously keep the number of benchmarks down to allow individual teachers to add content they believe will be meaningful to a particular group of students at a particular point in time. Matthew Gandal (1995b), author of the American Federation of Teachers study of state standards (see pp.25-28), notes that standards and benchmarks should cover 60 to 80 percent of the curriculum. Similarly, the Core Knowledge Sequence designed by E. D. Hirsch, Jr., author of *Cultural Literacy* (1987), recommends that standards and benchmarks constitute 50 percent of the curriculum only (see Core Knowledge Foundation, 1992).

With these three principles in mind, it appears to us that a reasonable number of standards to have across all content areas would be 50 to 100, or an average of 75. A reasonable number of benchmarks to have per standard would be 2 to 4, or an average of 3. If a school or district identified benchmarks for grades 1 through 8, and two levels of benchmarks (i.e., lower and upper division) for grades 9 through 12, the total number of levels would be ten with an average of 75 standards at each level. If there is an average of three benchmarks per standard, then each level would involve an average of 225 benchmarks and there would be 2,250 benchmarks across grades 1 to 12. Additionally, these benchmarks would certainly not be distributed evenly across all grade levels. Specifically, the primary grades would have far fewer standards and benchmarks. Instead of 75 standards that cover 225 benchmarks, each primary grade might address 40 standards covering 120 benchmarks. As students progress through the grades and the content becomes more complex, their ability to assimilate new information and skill increases proportionately.

Having benchmarks that number 2,250 immediately frightens some educators, but it is a far cry from the 10,000 (and more) benchmarks that were addressed within the mastery learning and competency-based movements. Additionally, the very nature of content knowledge is that it involves many component parts. For example, psychologist John Anderson (1983) notes that the process of two-column addition involves over 60 component parts. Similarly, Anderson (1995) explains that the development of skill in algebra involves mastering up to 10,000 rules. The point here is that subject-area knowledge inherently involves a large number of component parts. Teachers address these myriad elements daily without being consciously aware of the large number of elements to which they are attending.

In short, learning the essential information and skill within a content area involves the acquisition of many elements. We believe that identifying 75 standards and some 2,250 benchmarks within those standards does not create unreasonable expectations for reporting, assessment, or instruction.

Summary And Recommendations

In this chapter, we have focused attention on the number of levels at which benchmarks should be written. Although the current convention in most national- and state-level documents is to articulate benchmarks in grade-level bands, articulating benchmarks at each grade level for grades 1-8 (or K-8) and at two levels, lower and upper division, for the high school grades seems to be a useful design. To facilitate this, a process was described for translating benchmarks written in grade-level bands into benchmarks written for individual grade levels. Alternative approaches include the stages-of-development format and the performance levels format.

The issue of how many standards and benchmarks should be articulated was also addressed. We recommended about 75 standards and 2,250 benchmarks in grades 1-12 as a reasonable number to handle the inherent complexity of subject-matter material without placing undue demands on reporting, assessment, or instruction.

Chapter 5

Who Will Assess Students And How Will They Be Assessed?

The issue of assessment is intimately linked to standards because assessment provides feedback to students and parents. Without accurate feedback, students and parents have no way of knowing how well students are doing on specific academic standards.

One of the basic questions relative to assessment is, Who is responsible for assessing students on standards and benchmarks? Answers to this question can be conceptualized as lying along a continuum, the basis of which is the degree of knowledge that different assessment designers have about specific students. This is depicted in Figure 5.1.

Figure 5.1 Relationship Between Level of Assessments and Knowledge of Specific Students

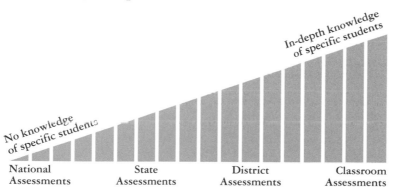

Assessments at one end of the continuum are designed by those who have little knowledge about specific students. Assessments at the other end of the continuum are designed by those who have a great deal of knowledge about specific students. We will consider assessments from each of the levels depicted in Figure 5.1—national, state, district, and classroom.

Assessments Developed At The National Level

Quite obviously, those who develop national tests have no knowledge of students in a specific school or district. Yet, some districts and schools use national tests to assess students' standings and progress on standards. For example, a district might decide to use a standardized test, such as the Iowa Test of Basic Skills, as the primary assessment of students' performance on standards. The hallmark of standardized tests is items that require students to select the correct answer from an array of options. For this reason these types of items are commonly referred to as selected response, or forced-choice response (Stiggins, 1994). In addition, nationally developed standardized tests are sometimes referred to as "off-the-shelf" tests because they can be purchased as one would purchase an item "off-the-shelf" of a store.

Off-the-shelf tests come in two basic types: criterion referenced and norm referenced. Criterion-referenced tests (CRTs) measure student performance on an agreed-upon set of skills and against an agreed-upon "cut-score," or criterion. To illustrate, if a student does not reach a specific minimum score on the subtest for mathematical computation on a criterion-referenced test, the student will be assessed as not having met the criterion—the cut-score—for that subtest. CRTs traditionally use multiple-choice item, although some CRTs are now employing performance tasks. Norm-referenced tests (NRTs) compare student test performance against that of other students, usually a national sample. NRTs usually report student performance as a percentile score and, like CRTs, traditionally rely primarily on multiple-choice items (Bond, Friedman, & van der Ploeg, 1994).

The perceived advantages of using off-the-shelf, nationally developed standardized tests are that they are easy to administer, easy to score, and relatively inexpensive. All of these perceptions are accurate. The allure of standardized tests has made them popular for decades. However, standardized tests were never designed to assess student progress on standards. A brief review of their history shows that they were designed for a specific purpose and are of limited use for making decisions about individual students.

The Problem With Standardized Tests

Few educators realize that standardized tests were initially designed for the purpose of identifying which students would most likely succeed in school and which students would most likely fail. This purpose was a direct consequence of the assumption that intelligence, or aptitude, is a fixed, unidimensional characteristic. Psychologist Howard Gardner (1992) explains that the widespread use of standardized tests in this country can be traced to the work on intelligence testing carried out in Paris at the turn of the century by psychologist Alfred Binet and his colleagues. Binet was asked by city education leaders to assist in determining which students would most likely succeed and which would most likely fail in elementary school. Gardner explains:

> [Binet] hit upon the inspired idea of administering a large set of items to
> young school children and identifying which of the items proved most

discriminating in light of his particular goal. The work carried out by the Binet team ultimately led to the first intelligence tests, and the construct of intelligence quotient or IQ.

So great was the appeal of the Binet method that it soon became a dominant feature of the American educational and assessment landscape. . . . In the United States, especially with its focus on quantitative markers and its cult of educational efficiency, there has been a virtual mania for producing tests for every possible social purpose. (p. 79)

Given how entrenched standardized tests are in our culture, it is no wonder that many educators and noneducators are calling for their use as the primary method of assessing student performance on standards. However, even a cursory review of the research and theory on testing indicates that there is little support for this approach.

One of the primary weaknesses of off-the-shelf tests is that they are severely limited in the types of knowledge they can assess. Although tests are being developed that assess students' higher level thinking and application of knowledge (see Arter & Salmon, 1987, for a discussion), it is generally agreed that standardized tests assess only surface understanding and lower level skills (see Frederiksen & Collins, 1989; Marzano, 1990; Marzano & Costa, 1988; Mitchell, 1992; Resnick, 1987a; Shepard, 1989; Stiggins, 1994; Wiggins, 1993a, 1993b; Williams, Phillips, & Yen, 1991). Researchers Lauren Resnick and Daniel Resnick (1992) explain that standardized tests are designed to assess low-level algorithmic skills and isolated pieces of factual information. To illustrate the cognitive demands of a standardized test, consider the following item, which is characteristic of items on most off-the-shelf tests:

What is the perimeter of an equilateral triangle with side 6 cm?

a. 10 cm

b. 12 cm

c. 18 cm

d. 24 cm

This item requires students to simply recall the characteristics of an equilateral triangle and then perform simple addition or multiplication—all of which is fairly low-level knowledge. In fairness to standardized-test designers, many publishers are now experimenting with "enhanced multiple-choice items." Mitchell (1992, p. 15) offers the enhanced multiple-choice item in Exhibit 5.1 as an example of such an item.

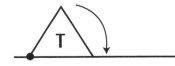

Exhibit 5.1 Example Enhanced Multiple-Choice Item

A cardboard piece shaped as an equilateral triangle with each side 6 cm long is rolled to the right a number of times. If the triangle stops so that the letter "T" is again in the upright position, which one of the following distances could it have rolled?

 °24 cm °30 cm °60 cm °90 cm

Note: From *Testing for Learning: How New Approaches to Evaluation Can Improve American Schools* (p. 15), by R. Mitchell, 1992, New York: The Free Press. Copyright © 1992 by California Department of Education. Reprinted with permission.

This task requires more of students than simple recall and computation. As Mitchell explains, it calls on students to analyze the situation and use spatial reasoning. However, even enhanced multiple-choice items fall far short of the type of knowledge found in standards. Mitchell (1992) chronicles the many weaknesses of standardized tests:

> No matter how sophisticated the techniques, however, multiple-choice tests corrupt the teaching and learning process for the following reasons:
>
> 1. Even at their best, multiple-choice tests ask students to select a response. Selection is passive; it asks students to recognize, not to construct, an answer. The students do not contribute their own thinking to the answer.
>
> 2. Multiple-choice tests promote the false impression that a right or wrong answer is available for all questions and problems. As we know, few situations in life have a correct or incorrect answer.
>
> 3. The tests tend to rely on memorization and the recall of facts or algorithms. They do not allow students to demonstrate understanding of how algorithms work.
>
> 4. The form of multiple-choice tests means that test makers select what can easily be tested rather than what is important for students to learn.
>
> 5. Multiple-choice tests do not accurately record what students know and can do, either positively or negatively, as a personal example shows. In 1974, I passed by four points over the cut score the German-language examination to qualify for the Ph.D., and I am on record somewhere as having a reading knowledge of German. But I cannot read any word of German that does not look like an English or Latin cognate. My answers were either guesses or choices based on probabilities. If the graduate examiners had really wanted to know if I could read German, I should have been required to translate a passage.
>
> 6. The tests trivialize teaching and learning. If all classroom activity—the books, the lectures, the discussions, the exercises, the homework—ends up in a few bubbles

taking no more than an hour, then what is all the fuss about? The end is incommensurate with the means. Students know that much of passing multiple-choice tests is test wisdom—how to guess productively, what items to omit—and they invest only enough effort to get by. (pp. 15-16)

The problems inherent in standardized tests have led test developers to consider a new type of assessment: performance tasks.

Performance Tasks

We introduced the concept of performance tasks in chapter 3. There we noted that performance tasks have caught the attention of American educators, some of whom have looked to them to cure the many ills effected by off-the-shelf tests. The purported benefits of performance tasks are many. Indeed, their very nature seems to support their superiority over off-the-shelf tests. For example, assessment expert Joan Baron identifies a number of characteristics of performance tasks. According to Baron (1990a, 1990b, 1991), performance tasks

- are grounded in real-world contexts
- involve sustained work and often take several days of combined in- class and out-of-class time
- deal with big ideas and major concepts within a discipline
- present non-routine, open-ended, and loosely structured problems that require students both to define the problem and to construct a strategy for solving it
- encourage group discussion and "brainstorming" in which a problem is considered from multiple perspectives
- require students to determine what data are needed, collect the data, report and portray them, and analyze them to discuss sources of error
- call upon students to make and explain their assumption
- stimulate students to make connections and generalizations that will increase their understanding of the important concepts and processes
- spur students to monitor themselves and think about their progress in order to determine how they might improve their investigational and group process skills
- necessitate that students use a variety of skills for acquiring information and for communicating their strategies, data, and conclusions.

Baron explains that tasks that meet these criteria are best used as a regular part of classroom instruction. The intent in doing so is to make instruction and assessment an integrated, seamless whole. However, when such tasks are developed at the national level and administered in controlled situations, they do not have all of the qualities listed by Baron and are, therefore, more restricted in their use (see Resnick & Resnick, 1992).

The key characteristic of performance tasks as compared to standardized tests is that they require students to construct their responses as opposed to selecting from a list of options. For this reason, performance tasks are referred to as "constructed-response" tasks. To illustrate, consider the following mathematics task designed by the National Assessment of Educational Progress (NAEP) and administered to a representative sample of eighth graders across the country:

> Treena won a 7-day scholarship worth $1,000 to the Pro Shot Basketball Camp. Round-trip travel expenses to the camp are $335 by air or $125 by train. At the camp she must choose between a week of individual instruction at $60 per day or a week of group instruction at $40 per day. Treena's food and other expenses are fixed at $45 per day. If she does not plan to spend any money other than the scholarship, what are all choices of travel and instruction plans that she could afford to make? Explain your reasoning. (Dossey, Mullis, & Jones, 1993, p. 116)

As described by researchers John Dossey, Ina Mullis, and Chancey Jones (1993), this task requires the following types of thinking and reasoning:

> The solution to this task requires students to use everyday consumer sense to determine Treena's fixed expenses and analyze the various choices she has for travel (plane or train) and instruction (individual or group). Students also must compare the total cost for each of the four alternatives to which this analysis leads to the $1,000 value of Treena's scholarship, in order to conclude which choices meet the given conditions. (p. 116)

Contrast the thinking and reasoning required in the NAEP task to the simple recall and computation required of the previously given standardized test example of calculating the perimeter of an equilateral triangle. Simply stated, constructed-response items require much more of students than do selected-response items. This trait has spawned a veritable flood of support for their use as supplements to standardized tests or as alternatives to standardized tests (see Archbald & Newmann, 1988; Baron, 1991; Baron & Kallick, 1985; Berk, 1986a, 1986b; Frederiksen & Collins, 1989; Marzano, 1990; Marzano & Costa, 1988; Mitchell, 1992; Resnick, 1987a, 1987b; Resnick & Resnick, 1992; Shepard, 1989; Stiggins, 1994; Wiggins, 1989, 1991, 1993a, 1993b; Winograd & Perkins, 1996). Unfortunately, soon after their meteoric rise to popularity, performance tasks were shown to have at least one major flaw: They were not as generalizable as originally thought.

In a series of studies (Shavelson & Baxter, 1992; Shavelson, Gao & Baxter, 1993; Shavelson & Webb, 1991; Shavelson, Webb, & Rowley, 1989), researcher Richard Shavelson and his colleagues demonstrated that a student's performance on a single performance task is not necessarily a very good indicator of the student's knowledge and skill within the subject area that the task is designed to represent. For example, when Shavelson and his co-researchers gave students the same science task in three different formats (i.e., hands on, computer simulated, and written descriptions derived from a hands-on experiment), they found that students might perform well on one format but not perform well on the other two formats. Such findings have led Shavelson and his colleagues to conclude that a single performance assessment is not a good general indicator of how well students can perform within a content area. In fact, measurement experts (e.g., Lane, Liu, Ankenmann, & Stone, 1996; Linn, 1994; Shavelson, Gao, & Baxter, 1993) now contend that anywhere from 10 to 36 performance tasks are necessary to assess accurately students' competence within a single subject area.

Another problem with performance assessments is their cost. In 1992, education reporter John O'Neil noted that assessment experts feared that performance assessments would be two to three times more expensive than their machine-scorable, multiple-choice-format counterpart. However, a study by the RAND Corporation found that performance assessments could cost as much as 20 times more than the machine-scorable tests ("Educator's Weigh," 1996, p. 1).

In summary, tests developed at the national level, whether they use selected-response or constructed-response formats, have severe limitations as assessments of student performance on standards. Assessments developed at the state level have many of the same inherent weaknesses.

Assessments Developed At The State Level

Many states are attempting to design assessments that are geared toward standards. One major advantage that assessments designed at the state level have over those designed at the national level is that state-level assessments can be focused on the standards specific to a state and are more sensitive to the unique characteristics of students in that state.

According to researchers Linda Bond, David Braskamp, and Edward Roeber (1996), 45 of the 50 states conducted some form of statewide assessment in the 1994-1995 school year. Some of these assessments were mandatory and some were voluntary. Table 5.1 (see next page) provides a comprehensive summary of state assessment efforts in 1994-1995.

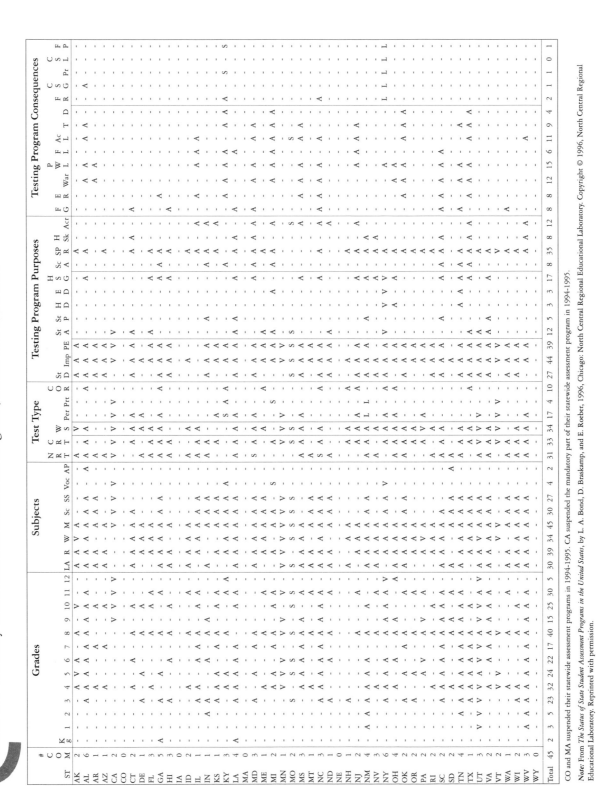

Table **5.1** Summary Table: Statewide Assessment Programs, School Year 1994-1995

CO and MA suspended their statewide assessment programs in 1994-1995. CA suspended the mandatory part of their statewide assessment program in 1994-1995.

Note: From *The Status of State Student Assessment Programs in the United States,* by L. A. Bond, D. Braskamp, and E. Roeber, 1996, Chicago: North Central Regional Educational Laboratory. Copyright © 1996, North Central Regional Educational Laboratory. Reprinted with permission.

Table 5.1 Legend

Summary Table Legend

Note: Totals are computed by adding up the number of As, Ss, and Vs in each column. In any cell, only one description is included. If multiple component descriptions were present in the same cell, then this cell was coded to match the component testing the most students. See Part III responses of the SSAP database for component names and component-level descriptions.

Cell Contents	Subjects	Test Type	Testing Program Purposes	Testing Program Consequences
Indicates at least one component where: A = All students are tested S = Students are sampled V = Inclusion is voluntary for students, schools, or school districts L = Decision is made at local level #COM = Number of assessment components	LA = Language Arts R = Reading W = Writing M = Math Sc = Science SS = Social Studies Voc = Vocational Ed Ap = Aptitudes	*Multiple-Choice Testing* NRT = Norm-Referenced Testing CRT = Criterion-Referenced Testing *Writing Assessment* WS = Writing Sample *Alternative Assessments* Per = Performance Testing Prt = Portfolio Assessment COR = Constructed, Open-Response Items	*Instructional Process* StD = Student diagnosis or placement Imp = Improvement of instruction, curriculum PE = Program evaluation *Student Accountability* StA = Student awards or recognition StP = Student promotion HD = Honors diploma ED = Endorsed diploma HSG = High school graduation (exit requirement) *School Accountability* ScA = School awards or recognition SPR = School performance reporting HSk = High school skills guarantee Acr = School accreditation	*For Schools* FG = Funding gain ER = Exemption from regulations War = Warnings PWL = Probation, watch lists FL = Funding loss AcL = Accreditation loss T = Takeover D = Dissolution *For School Staff* FR = Financial rewards CSG = Certification status gain Pr = Probation CSL = Certification status loss FP = Financial penalties

Note: From *The Status of State Student Assessment Programs in the United States*, by L. A. Bond, D. Braskamp, and E. Roeber, 1996, Chicago: North Central Regional Educational Laboratory. Copyright © 1996, North Central Regional Educational Laboratory. Reprinted with permission.

According to Bond, Braskamp, and Roeber (1996), 33 states reported using criterion-referenced, multiple-choice tests; 31 states reported using norm-referenced, multiple-choice tests; and 17 states reported using performance assessments. A few states clearly have been the vanguard in the use of performance assessments. Here we consider two of these states: Maryland and Vermont.

Maryland

Maryland's state assessment program is comprised of three basic elements: open-ended assessments, the High School Functional Graduation Test, and the Comprehensive Test of Basic Skills. Open-ended assessments (in the form of open-ended questions, essays, and performance assessments) are given in mathematics, reading, science, social studies, and writing to samples of students in grades 3, 5, and 8. The High School Functional Graduation Test, a minimum competency test that all students must pass in order to graduate, is composed of traditional, multiple-choice questions. It is first given in grade 7;

most students pass it by grade 9. A school's annual performance report shows the percentage of students who meet satisfactory or excellent standards of performance. The Comprehensive Test of Basic Skills/4 is a norm-referenced, off- the-shelf test in basic skills that is given to a sample of students in each district for use in national comparisons (see Bond, Friedman, & van der Ploeg, 1994).

As can be seen from their descriptions, the second and third elements of the Maryland system are fairly traditional in nature. The performance component of the first element is commonly referred to as the Maryland State Performance Assessment Program (MSPAP). According to an article in a popular educational newsletter entitled the *Fair Test Examiner* ("Maryland Performance," 1995), the MSPAP is designed to make classroom teachers integrate the state test into their day-to-day instruction:

> Its designers expect that "teaching to the test"—a negative phrase when it refers to multiple-choice tests—will, in this case, mean teaching that is in line with worthwhile goals for instruction and student progress. (p. 8)

To facilitate the impact of the MSPAP in the classroom, the Maryland State Department of Education provides practice tasks like that in Exhibit 5.2.

Exhibit 5.2 The Writing Portion of the Publicly Released Operational Task for Grade 5 from the Maryland School Performance Assessment Program

---

Integrated Subject Areas: Reading, Writing, Language Usage, Social Studies
Topic: Child Labor

Writing Prompt: Writing to Persuade

Suppose that it is the year 1912. The United States Congress is investigating child labor. A town meeting in your community has been called to examine the issues.

Decide whether you believe that it is right or wrong for children, like yourselves, to work. Take a firm stand.

Write a speech that you will read to citizens at the town meeting persuading them to accept your point of view on child labor. Use information from "A Letter to Hannah" and "Mill Children" to support your stand.

You will have 40 minutes to plan, write, and think about your speech on paper. Later, you will have an opportunity to share your speech with your partner before making final revisions. Only the revised speech that you write in your Student Response Book will be scored. You may begin work by yourself. As you write, you may want to do these things:

Pre-Writing: Think about what it is like to be a child who works. Think about working conditions. Think about what they have and don't have because of their jobs. Try making a list, web, or diagram to come up with ideas about whether it is right or wrong for children to work.

Drafting: Write a rough draft of your speech.

Revising: Read your draft and think about what you have written. Imagine that you are a citizen at the town meeting listening to the speech.

Think about the questions below:

1. Does this speech make sense?
2. Does the speech include facts that support the writer's argument?
3. Does the speech persuade the reader to accept the writer's point of view?

After you have thought about how well your speech answers these questions, you will get some more information from your partner to help improve your writing.

Peer Response Form

Directions:

1. Ask your partner to listen carefully as you read your rough draft out loud.
2. Ask your partner to help you improve your writing by telling you the answers to the questions below.
3. In the space provided, jot down notes about what your partner says.

   1. What did you like about my rough draft?
   2. What did you have the hardest time understanding about my rough draft?
   3. What else can you suggest that I do to improve my rough draft?

Use the space below to write additional comments.

Writing the Revised Draft

Now that you have had the chance to think about your writing and get information from your partners, it is time to revise your speech. Remember that you are the author, and only you can decide if you want to use your partner's suggestions when you revise your writing. You will have 35 minutes to revise your draft. Make sure that you get all of your revised draft in the response book in 35 minutes, because only the material that is in the book will be scored.

Proofreading

Look over your writing. Because your speech may be printed in the newspaper, be sure your speech is clear and complete. Also, check for correct spelling, punctuation, grammar, and usage. Use the suggestions on the Proofreading Guide Sheet to check your work. Many any necessary corrections on your revised draft.

Note: From "Maryland Performance Assessment Update" (p. 9), 1995, Spring, *Fair Test Examiner, 9*(2), 8-10, 12. Reprinted with the permission of the *Fair Test Examiner* and the Maryland Department of Education.

According to the Maryland state superintendent, the MSPAP has provided valuable accountability data showing that students in Maryland are heading in the right direction. Specifically, the 1994 test showed that 35.4% of students were scoring at the satisfactory level, compared to 31.7% in 1993 ("Maryland Performance," 1995, p. 8).

Vermont

According to researchers Linda Bond, Lawrence Friedman, and Arie van der Ploeg (1994), Vermont is one of only a handful of states that has never had a statewide assessment program. Its attempt to implement a traditional, standardized test in 1989 was criticized so severely by educators that the state dropped the plan. The current state assessment is voluntary, but most districts participate. The most unique aspect of Vermont's approach is that it encompasses the use of portfolios.

From their inception, portfolios have generated great excitement among educators. Researchers and theorists, such as Denny Palmer Wolf and Jane Hansen, have been strong advocates of portfolios as the primary tool for assessment. For example, Wolf (1988, 1989) notes that portfolios are the only form of assessment that explicitly requires students to present a wide range of evidence for their performance on standards. Hansen (1991, 1992) asserts that portfolios can be used to enhance student self-assessment and self-understanding.

At a very basic level, a portfolio is a collection of a student's work, some or most of which is student selected and even student evaluated. Although education researchers define portfolios somewhat differently, their descriptions share some common elements. Resnick and Resnick (1992) describe a portfolio in the following way:

> A variant of the performance assessment is the *portfolio assessment*. In this method, frequently used in the visual and performing arts and other design fields, individuals collect their work over a period of time, select a sample of the collection that they think best represents their capabilities, and submit this portfolio of work to a jury or panel of judges. (p. 61)

Researcher Mark Reckase (1995) describes a portfolio as

> a purposeful collection of student work that exhibits to the student (and/or others) the student's efforts, progress, or achievement in (a) given area(s). This collection must include
>
> • student participation in selection of portfolio content,
> • the criteria for selection,
> • the criteria for judging merit, and
> • evidence of student self-reflection. (p. 21)

A portfolio should illustrate the various stages through which a complex project progresses. For example, a portfolio might include the initial ideas for a composition, the first draft of the composition, the draft that includes the final edits, and the final draft of the composition. In addition, the portfolio might include the student's description of the development of the essay along with a discussion of what he or she learned as a result of writing the essay.

By their very nature, portfolios are oriented to subject areas that naturally involve products, such as writing and the arts. Recently, there have been efforts to articulate the recommended contents of portfolios in subject areas that are not necessarily product oriented. For example, mathematics teacher Pam Knight (1992) delineates a number of items that a mathematics portfolio should contain, including the following:

- samples of word problems in various stages of development along with the student's description of his or her thinking during the various problem-solving stages;
- the student's self-evaluation of his or her understanding of the mathematical concepts that have been covered in class along with examples;
- the student's self-evaluation of his or her competence in the mathematical procedures, strategies, and algorithms that have been covered in class along with examples.

In Vermont, 4th and 8th graders keep portfolios in both writing and mathematics. Writing portfolios contain six to eight pieces. Mathematics portfolios contain five to seven papers; each is a "best piece" of three types: puzzles, math applications, and investigations (Herman & Winters, 1994).

A great deal of time, energy, and money has been spent in Vermont developing a system for scoring portfolios in a consistent fashion. Unfortunately, reliable scoring procedures have not, as yet, been developed. The RAND Corporation conducted an independent study of teachers' abilities to score portfolios reliably within the Vermont system. As reported by *Education Week* reporter Elizabeth Schulz (1993), "The state had planned to have teachers score portfolios and to publish the results for comparison purposes. But it was discovered that teachers' scoring is not reliable enough to compare schools fairly" (p. 38). Similarly, low reliabilities for judgment of portfolios have been reported by other researchers (Gearhart, Herman, Baker, & Whittaker, 1993; Koretz, Stecher, & Deibert, 1993). However, Reckase (1995) has demonstrated that portfolios can be scored in a reliable fashion if

1. the portfolio contains five or more entries;
2. each entry is scored independently; and
3. the independent scores for each entry are summed to obtain a total score.

Unfortunately, Reckase also notes that scoring a portfolio in this fashion will cost at least $10.00 per portfolio and possibly as much as $18.00 per portfolio. Additionally, this cost would be multiplied by the number of content areas to be assessed through portfolios. Reckase concludes that "if such a procedure were to be implemented in place of current procedures for high stakes assessment, it would be a very expensive alternative" (p. 14).

States other than Maryland and Vermont have been experimenting with performance tasks and other forms that are alternatives to NRTs and CRTs. Among those states that were the first are Arizona, California, Maine, Massachusetts, and Delaware. However, some of these efforts have already been rescinded. Specifically, concerns about the technical quality and the test content caused the innovative assessment programs in California and Arizona to be shelved in 1995 (Bond, Braskamp, & Roeber, 1996).

In summary, many states have assessments that can be used by districts and schools to assess student performance on standards. The vast majority of these assessments use forced-choice items and, therefore, are subject to many of the same limitations as off-the-shelf tests designed at the national level. Some states are experimenting with alternative types of assessments, including performance tasks and portfolios.

Assessments Developed At The District And School Levels

Individual districts and schools are obviously quite knowledgeable about students and, therefore, could design assessments that are most compatible with their local needs. However, individual districts and schools usually do not have the internal capacity to develop their own forms of NRTs and CRTs. The process of constructing sound multiple-choice items and then determining their utility is complex and time consuming. (For a discussion of this process, see Anastasi, 1982; Osterlind, 1989). However, given the seemingly straightforward nature of performance assessments, some districts and schools are constructing their own performance tasks and then using classroom teachers to score those tasks. For example, Exhibit 5.3 reports a mathematics performance task constructed by a district we worked with on designing assessments. This task was administered to 161 students in grades 9, 10, 11, and 12 and to a handful of adults. The results are reported in Table 5.2.

Exhibit 5.3 Sample Performance Task Designed at the District Level

Rodney plans to join several people on a camping trip. Each person has been asked to carry, as well as his or her own personal items, some part of the group's meals for the next few days. If conditions are right, they may want to extend their stay in the mountains, so the group hopes to bring as many meals as possible without overtaxing individuals. Each person has been asked to determine the greatest number of meals he or she can carry. Rodney plans to report to the group the number of each type of meal he could take and the total cost. Rodney was presented with the information in the table below. Although there are a number of meal types, all come in one of two package sizes and approximate weights.

	Approximate Weight	Size	Price
Meal Type A	9.25 ounces	$5 \times 6 \times 1.25"$	$3.75
Meal Type B	11 ounces	$8.75 \times 6.5 \times 1.25"$	$4.25

Rodney has determined that he's willing to carry no more than 5 additional pounds in his pack and that he has about 384 cubic inches of free space available.

Can you represent mathematically the central question Rodney should answer for the group? In addition, can you represent mathematically all the questions, constraints and limits, explicit or implied, that Rodney should consider in order to arrive at a solution?

Table 5.2 Student Results on District-Level Performance Task

			% of Students Scoring				
	Mean	% of Students Meeting Standards	Less than 1.00	1.00 or more, but less than 2.00	2.00 or more, but less than 3.00	3.00 or more, but less than 4.00	4.00
9th Grade (N = 25)	2.30	36%	12%	32%	20%	28%	8%
10th Grade (N = 52)	1.74	8%	14%	44%	35%	8%	0%
11th Grade (N = 51)	1.70	10%	14%	49%	28%	8%	2%
12th Grade (N = 33)	1.81	18%	21%	42%	18%	12%	6%
Adults (N = 8)	2.38	25%	13%	13%	50%	13%	13%

Note: R.J. Marzano and J.S. Kendall, 1992, unpublished data, Aurora, CO: Mid-continent Regional Educational Laboratory.

The results were quite useful for this district for a number of reasons. They demonstrated that district students were capable of doing complex mathematics problems. In fact, district officials were quite pleased with the results, especially in light of the fact that findings reported by NAEP indicate that students nationally do far worse on similar tasks (see Dossey et al., 1993). Of particular interest was the performance of the adults who took the task. It is important to note that the district did not overly emphasize the performance of the adults because the total number participating in the assessment was only eight. However, the findings did raise some interesting possibilities. As Table 5.2 illustrates, 25% received a satisfactory or better score. Although this was higher than the performance of the high school students, it was not dramatically higher. These results gave teachers, students, and parents a new perspective on the quality of education in the district. Specifically, these results confirmed the perception of some that American students are being asked to know more and do more than past generations. The adults who participated in the study all commented on the difficulty of the task and the fact that they did not recall being asked to solve complex, open-ended tasks such as this when they were in high school.

As useful as it is for a district or school to construct its own performance tasks, measurement experts offer a strong warning: Constructing performance assessments is a technical chore that should not be approached lightly. For example, researchers Richard Shavelson and Gail Baxter (1992) warn:

> Performance assessments are very delicate instruments. They need to be carefully crafted, each requiring a specially developed or adapted scoring method. Shortcuts taken in developing these assessments will likely produce poor measuring devices. (p. 24)

We concur with Shavelson and Baxter. In our work with well-intended district and school personnel, we have seen a number of poorly constructed performance tasks, the purposes of which were at best ambiguous. If a district or school desires to construct its own performance assessments, it should address the technical issues inherent in test instruction. Two of these technical issues are reliability and validity. Fortunately, there are many fine sources that can guide the study of reliability and validity. Among the best are *A Practical Guide to Alternative Assessment* (Herman, Aschbacher, & Winters, 1992) and *CRESST Performance Assessment Models: Assessing Content Area Explanations* (Baker et al., 1992).

Briefly, reliability means the consistency with which judgments are made. If one teacher gives a particular student a high score on a performance task and another teacher gives the student a low score on the same performance task, then scoring is unreliable. Validity means the extent to which an assessment provides accurate information given the purpose for which it is intended. Relative to the discussion in this section, validity refers to the degree to which a score on a district- or school-made performance task accurately provides information about individual students' understanding and skill relative to specific standards. Studying the reliability and validity of assessments designed by districts and schools is critical if these assessments are to be used to make decisions about students' performance on standards. Although these studies are not simple projects, they are well within the means and ability of most individual districts and schools.

District- and school-level assessments can be a useful component of standards assessments. However, like assessments designed at the national and state levels, they have many drawbacks. The most logical place within which to focus standards assessment is the classroom. In fact, we believe so strongly in the importance of classroom-level assessments that we refer to any assessment designed outside of the classroom as an *external assessment*.

The Logic Behind Classroom Assessment

Those who are closest to individual students and know them best are classroom teachers. This reason alone should justify giving classroom teachers primary responsibility for assessing students on standards and benchmarks. However, there are other reasons equally as important.

One of the most compelling reasons to use classroom teachers as the primary agents of assessment is that external assessments—those designed and administered at the national, state, or even district levels—usually only provide single scores or a small set of scores. Making decisions about students on a single score or a small set of scores is a precarious endeavor. Measurement expert Bernard Gifford (1992) explains the problem of a single score cutoff:

> Whenever people are classified on the basis of cutoff scores on standardized tests, misclassifications are bound to occur. The solution is not to avoid classifying people—such classifications are essential and inevitable in modern society. It is, rather, to avoid making decisions about anyone's future solely on the basis of one imperfect instrument. (p. 4)

Wiggins (1993a) strongly echoes Gifford's warning. He explains that those educational organizations entrusted with monitoring the use of tests have cautioned against placing too much emphasis on a single score:

> The American Psychological Association/National Council on Measurement in Education/American Educational Research Association Standards for Educational and Psychological Testing . . . are unequivocal in this matter. Standard 8.12 says that "in elementary and secondary education, a decision that will have a major impact on a test taken should not automatically be made on the basis of a single test score." (p. 19)

The technical reason that single scores or even small sets of scores should not be used to make decisions about students' performance on standards is quite revealing about the nature of assessment. Measurement theorists (e.g., Gulliksen, 1950; Lord & Novick, 1968;

Magnusson, 1966; Nunnally, 1967) represent any score on any type of assessment in the following way:

observed score = true score + error score

This formula states that any observed score—a score on a test, a score on a quiz, an observation made by a teacher—is made up of two parts: a true score and an error score. The true score is what the student "should have" received on the test. It represents his "true" understanding and skill relative to the knowledge being assessed. The error score represents that component of any score that is due to factors other than the student's true understanding and skill, for example, fatigue, confusion over what is meant by a question, or luck in guessing.

The error score can work in favor of a student or against a student. That is, the error score can have the effect of artificially raising or lowering a score. To illustrate, assume that a student receives a score of 85 points out of 100 on a test. The student's score might be five points higher than it should be because the student guessed correctly on a number of items. In other words, the student should have received a score of 80—his true score—but he had five points of error "working for him." Conversely, the student might have had five points of error "working against him" because he misread some items. Thus, he may have received a score of 75 but actually deserved a score of 80.

The amount of error one can expect on a test is reported in an index called the standard error of measurement. This index is calculated and reported for every section of every standardized test. For example, Table 5.3 reports the standard errors of measurement that are typical for various sections of a norm-referenced, standardized test like the Iowa Test of Basic Skills. We should note that Table 5.3 does not report the exact standard errors for the various subtests of the Iowa Test of Basic Skills. Rather, Table 5.3 should be considered as representative of the standard errors of measurement that generally will be found in norm-referenced standardized tests. For specific standard errors for the Iowa Test of Basic Skills, the reader should consult the *Manual for School Administrators: Levels 5-14: ITBS, Forms G/H* (Hieronymous & Hoover, 1986).

These standard errors are reported in grade equivalency units. Educators can use these indices to estimate how much error they can expect in a single score. To illustrate, consider the standard error for the problem-solving subtest at the 6th-grade level and assume that a student had received a grade equivalency score of 5.0. To be 68% sure of the range of scores in which the student's true score would fall, one would add and subtract the standard error of measurement (i.e., the score of .5) from the student's observed score. Thus, the 68% "confidence interval" for the student would be 4.5 to 5.5. One could be 68% sure that the student's true score fell somewhere in this range. To calculate a range of scores within which one would be 95% sure the student's true score falls, one would add and subtract two standard errors form the observed score. Thus, the 95% confidence interval for the student is 4.0 to 6.0.

Table 5.3 Representative Standard Errors of Measurement in Grade Equivalency Units for Sections of Norm-Referenced Standardized Tests

	Grade		
Subtest	6	7	8
Vocabulary	.6	.5	.7
Reading	.6	.5	.6
Spelling	.6	.7	.8
Capitalization	.7	.8	1.0
Punctuation	.6	.9	.8
Usage	.7	.7	.8
Visual Materials	.6	.7	.7
References	.6	.7	.7
Math Concepts	.5	.6	.6
Problem Solving	.5	6	.8
Computation	.4	.6	.5

Most educators are shocked when they realize how unreliable a single score is even when it comes from a standardized test. Yet, even the most respected tests have relatively large standard errors. For example, the Scholastic Aptitude Test (SAT) has a standard error of 33.5 points. This implies that an individual student's score on the SAT is highly unreliable if it is to be used to make decisions about the student's future. As reported by measurement expert Amy Allina (1991):

> According to ETS, the SAT has a margin of error of 67 points [i.e., the 68% confidence interval] and two test-taker's scores must differ by at least 134* points [i.e., the 95% confidence interval] before it's sure that their abilities differ. Yet, colleges and agencies such as the National Merit Scholarship Corporation routinely use cutoff scores, whereas even ten points—just one question—can mean the difference between acceptance and rejection. (p. 17)

*Note: The original text contained a transposition error and reported this number as 143.

According to an educational newsletter put out by the National Center for Fair and Open Testing in Cambridge, Massachusetts, the Graduate Record Examination (GRE) also has a relatively large standard error of measurement:

> The GRE's standard error of measurement (SEM)—which determines the point spread that must separate two individuals' scores in order to say with "reasonable confidence" that they are truly different—ranged from 96 to 118 points (depending on the section) in 1994-95. So while it cannot be said with "reasonable confidence" that 420 and 530 represent different levels of whatever is measured by the GRE Analytic section (SEM 118), a 420 scorer would nonetheless be shut out from a school or scholarship with a 500 cutoff. ("ETS Loses," 1995-1996, p. 13)

Error score is the bane of single assessments. No matter how well constructed an assessment is by a national publisher, a state department of education, or a school district, it will always contain a significant amount of error in the individual scores it generates for students. The remedy to the problem surrounding a single score or set of scores obtained at a specific point in time is to use multiple assessments obtained over an extended period of time. This is because the error scores for a single student tend to cancel each other out; error might inflate a particular student's score one time, yet deflate that same student's score the next time. Thus, the most effective way of assessing students on standards and benchmarks is to make multiple observations over time. Again, the classroom teacher is the best (and perhaps only) educator capable of doing this because he or she interacts with students on a daily basis. Tests developed at the national, state, or district level are of limited use because they are administered at a single point in time.

Another reason that national-, state-, or even district-level tests are not the appropriate primary vehicle for assessing student performance on standards and benchmarks is that they are simply too time consuming. This is particularly true if the external assessments are performance based. For example, education reporter John O'Neil (1992) notes that Maryland's performance assessments—as useful as they have been—have taken a significant amount of time away from classroom instruction.

Even the machine-scorable tests that can be administered in a relatively short period of time consume much more time than is immediately apparent. In a study of the effects of external tests in the classroom, it was found that teachers spend up to three weeks preparing students for a standardized test, at an actual cost of close to $100.00 per student (Office of Technology Assessment [OTA], 1992).

A final reason that external tests are not appropriate primary measures of student performance on standards and benchmarks is that educators are already overdependent on them—particularly standardized tests. As reported by the Office of Technology Assessment (OTA, 1992):

The United States is unique in the extensive use of standardized tests for young children. Current proposals for testing all American elementary school children with a commonly administered and graded examination would make the United States the only industrialized country to adopt this practice. (p. 31)

Clearly, relying on assessments external to the classroom is not the optimum way of organizing schools around standards. Like it or not, we must rely on classroom teachers if we wish to raise student performance on content standards. As measurement expert George Madaus (1993) notes:

The nation cannot test its way out of its educational problems . . . it is the teachers, not tests or assessments, that must be the cornerstone of reform efforts. (p. 10)

In spite of the many reasons that external assessments should not be the primary vehicle for standards-based reform, there is still a tendency to rely on them. This is evidenced by President Clinton's comments on March 27, 1996, in Palisades, New York, when speaking to the National Governors Association at the second Education Summit:

I believe every state, if you're going to have meaningful standards, must require a test for children to move, let's say, from elementary to middle school, or from middle school to high school, or to have a full-meaning high school diploma. And I don't think they should measure just minimum competency. You should measure what you expect these standards to measure. (pp. 6-7)

Tools For The Classroom Teacher

For the many reasons cited above, our conclusion is that the classroom teacher is the most appropriate educator to collect assessment data regarding student performance on standards and benchmarks. This is not to say that external assessments designed at the national, state, or district levels should not be used. Indeed, they provide useful information. However, they should be considered supplemental to the assessment information produced at the classroom level by teachers.

To perform the assessment task effectively, the classroom teacher must be equipped with a wide variety of assessment techniques (Dorr-Bremme & Herman, 1986). In the next sections we consider different ways that teachers can collect assessment data for specific standards and benchmarks. First, however, it is important to note that a teacher should not confuse testing data with assessment. Scores on a multiple-choice test, a performance task, or an essay question are simply data or information that will be used to make judgments about a student's performance on standards and benchmarks. As our previous discussion of standard error of measurement indicated, no single score on any test should be considered the final indication of a student's performance on standards and benchmarks. All judgments of student competence should be considered negotiable and subject to revision. As Wiggins (1993a) notes, "All assessment should be thought of as 'formative,' to put it glibly" (p. 51).

Classroom assessment expert Richard Stiggins (1994) notes that different forms of classroom assessment are appropriate for different types of standards. Table 5.4 shows the types of assessment that can be used for different types of benchmarks.

Table 5.4 Types of Assessment for Different Types of Benchmarks

	Forced-Choice Items	Essay Questions	Performance/ Portfolios	Teacher Observation	Student Self-Assessment
Subject-specific declarative benchmarks	X	X	X	X	X
Subject-specific procedural benchmarks		X	X	X	X
Thinking and reasoning standards and benchmarks		X	X	X	X
Lifelong learning standards and benchmarks			X	X	X

As Table 5.4 illustrates, some forms of classroom assessment can be used for all types of standards and benchmarks; others are more restricted in their use. Next we consider each type.

Forced-Choice Items

Stiggins (1994) defines forced-choice items in the following way:

> This is the classic objectively scored paper and pencil test. The respondent is asked a series of questions, each of which is accompanied by a range of alternative responses. The respondent's task is to select either the correct or the best answer from among the options. The index of achievement is the number or proportion of questions answered correctly. (p. 84)

Stiggins lists four options for forced-choice tests: (1) multiple-choice items, (2) true/false items, (3) matching exercises, and (4) short answer fill-in-the-blank items.

As explained by Stiggins (1994) short answer, fill-in-the-blank items are counted in this category because they only allow for a single answer, which is counted either right or wrong. In other words, the student is forced into providing a single, correct response. Teachers commonly use forced-choice items (along with essay items) to design their quizzes, homework assignments, midterm examinations, and final examinations. Such items play a major role in classroom assessment. There are some educators who mistakenly believe that forced-choice formats should be totally discarded in favor of formats that require students to construct personal responses from what they know and understand. These educators fail to acknowledge that forced-choice tests have a valid role in the assessment process especially when they are used in conjunction with other forms of assessment. As Mitchell (1992) notes:

> Multiple-choice tests would not be so bad if they were part of a spectrum of evaluation including essays, cooperative productions, collections of work, and teachers' observations. (p. vii)

Forced-choice items are particularly useful for benchmarks that are declarative in nature. Recall from chapter 3 that declarative benchmarks address information—concepts, generalizations, abstractions, and facts about people, places, things, and events important to a given subject area. To illustrate how forced-choice items can be used to assess declarative knowledge, consider Exhibit 5.4.

Exhibit 5.4 Sample Forced-Choice Test Items for Declarative Benchmark

Declarative Benchmark Grades 3-5	Forced-Choice Item

The student knows that the Earth is layered with a thin brittle crust, hot convecting mantle, and dense metallic core; three-fourths of the Earth's surface is covered by a thin layer of water; and the entire planet is surrounded by a blanket of air.	**Multiple Choice Item**
	The Earth is layered with
	  a. a thick, sturdy crust
	  b. a convecting, sturdy crust
	  c. a thin, brittle crust
	  d. a dense, metallic crust

	True/False Item
	The Earth's surface is covered by a thick layer of water.
	  a. True
	  b. False

	Fill-in-the-Blank Item The Earth is surrounded by _____.

	Matching Item
	  1. Earth's core a. dense and metallic
	  2. Earth's mantle b. thin and brittle
	  3. Earth's crust c. hot and convecting

As Exhibit 5.4 illustrates, forced-choice items are fairly straightforward and effective ways of assessing students' understanding of declarative knowledge particularly when that knowledge is at a factual level.

Again, it is important to realize that these types of items are best used in conjunction with other formats that require students to construct their responses. For example, the National Center for Research on Evaluation Standards and Student Testing (CRESST) at UCLA recommends that students complete short-answer items in the following content prior to answering a complex essay question about the Lincoln/Douglas debate:

- Popular sovereignty
- Dred Scott
- Missouri Compromise
- Bleeding Kansas
- State's rights
- Federalism
- Underground railroad
- Abolitionists

(Baker et al., 1992, pp. 15-16)

Short-answer items that address factual information about topics such as the Dred Scott decision, the Missouri Compromise, and the like allow the essay question to address the broader aspects of this historical period.

In summary, specific elements of declarative knowledge have their place in benchmarks, and one of the most efficient ways of assessing this information is through forced-choice tests.

Essay Questions

Essay questions have long been a feature of educational assessment. They literally date back to the inception of public education (Durm, 1993). As Table 5.4 indicates, they can be effectively used to assess both declarative and procedural subject-area knowledge as well as student performance on thinking and reasoning standards and benchmarks. When used to assess declarative knowledge, they commonly are designed to test students' understanding of the big ideas—concepts and generalizations—and the relationships among those ideas.

The most effective essay questions commonly provide students with information that they react to and use to construct their responses. By providing students with information, an essay question can take the emphasis off of the strict recall of information. For example, as part of a history examination, CRESST provides students with the original transcripts from the Lincoln/Douglas debate. Excerpts from these transcripts are presented in Exhibit 5.5.

Exhibit 5.5 Excerpts from the Lincoln/Douglas Debate

Stephen A. Douglas

Mr. Lincoln tells you, in his speech made at Springfield, before the Convention which gave him his unanimous nomination, that—

"A house divided against itself cannot stand."

"I believe this government cannot endure permanently, half slave and half free."

"I do not expect the Union to be dissolved, I don't expect the house to fall; but I do expect it will cease to be divided."

"It will become all one thing or all the other."

That is the fundamental principle upon which he sets out in this campaign. Well, I do not suppose you will believe one word of it when you come to examine it carefully, and see its consequences. Although the Republic has existed from 1789 to this day, divided into Free States and Slave States, yet we are told that in the future it cannot endure unless they shall become all free or all slave. For that reason he says...

Abraham Lincoln

Judge Douglas made two points upon my recent speech at Springfield. He says they are to be the issues of this campaign. The first one of these points he bases upon the language in a speech which I delivered at Springfield which I believe I can quote correctly from memory. I said there that "we are now far into the fifth year since a policy was instituted for the avowed object, and with the confident promise, of putting an end to slavery agitation; under the operation of that policy, that agitation had not only not ceased, but had constantly augmented." "I believe it will not cease until a crisis shall have been reached and passed. 'A house divided against itself cannot stand.' I believe this Government cannot endure permanently, half slave and half free." "I do not expect the Union to be dissolved"—I am quoting from my speech—"I do not expect the house to fall, but I do expect it will cease to be divided. It will become all one thing or the other. Either the opponents of slavery will arrest the spread of it and place it where the public mind shall rest, in the belief that it is in the course of ultimate extinction, or its advocates will push it forward until it shall become alike lawful in all the States, North as well as South."...

Note: From *Political Debates Between Abraham Lincoln and Stephen A. Douglas*, by Cleveland, 1902, in *CRESST Performance Assessment Models: Assessing Content Area Explanations* (pp. 43-47), by E. L. Baker, P. R. Aschbacher, D. Niemi, and E. Sato, 1992, Los Angeles, CA: National Center for Research on Evaluation, Standards, and Student Testing (CRESST), UCLA.

With this information as a backdrop to which all students have access, the following essay item is presented:

> Imagine that it is 1858 and you are an educated citizen living in Illinois. Because you are interested in politics and always keep yourself well-informed, you make a special trip to hear Abraham Lincoln and Stephen Douglas debating during their campaigns for the Senate seat representing Illinois. After the debates you return home, where your cousin asks you about some of the problems that are facing the nation at this time.
>
> Write an essay in which you explain the most important ideas and issues your cousin should understand. Your essay should be based on two major sources: (1) the general concepts and specific facts you know about American History, and especially what you know about the history of the Civil War; (2) what you have learned from the readings yesterday. Be sure to show the relationships among your ideas and facts. (Baker et al., 1992, p. 23)

Note that the task specifically requires students to comment on general concepts and relationships among ideas—elements not easily assessed by forced-choice items. Essay questions, then, are most appropriate for assessing big ideas and relationships among ideas within declarative knowledge, whereas forced-choice items are better suited for lower level factual information.

As indicated in Table 5.4, essay tests can also be used to determine a student's proficiency with procedural knowledge. This is accomplished by asking students to explain or critique a procedure. To illustrate, consider the CRESST chemistry example below:

> Imagine you are taking a chemistry class with a teacher who has just given the demonstration of chemical analysis you read about earlier.
>
> Since the start of the year, your class has been studying the principles and procedures used in chemical analysis. One of your friends has missed several weeks of class because of illness and is worried about a major exam in chemistry that will be given in two weeks. This friend asks you to explain everything that she will need to know for the exam.
>
> Write an essay in which you explain the most important ideas and principles that your friend should understand. In your essay you should include general concepts and specific facts you know about chemistry, and especially what you know about chemical analysis or identifying unknown substances. You should also explain how the teacher's demonstration illustrates important principles of chemistry.
>
> Be sure to show the relationships among the ideas, facts, and procedures you know. (Baker et al., 1992, p. 29)

Although a more direct assessment of a student's knowledge of the procedures involved in chemical analysis would involve the student's actual demonstration of such procedural skills, this essay test will provide the teacher with useful information. In fact, research by Shavelson and his colleagues (Shavelson & Baxter, 1992; Shavelson, Gao, & Baxter, 1993; Shavelson & Webb, 1991; Shavelson, Webb, & Rowley, 1989) has shown that this indirect assessment of procedural skills correlates highly with more direct, hands-on types of assessments.

A final area that is commonly assessed using essay questions is thinking and reasoning. Recall from chapter 2 that we recommend the following thinking and reasoning standards (see Kendall & Marzano, 1996, p. 572):

1. Understands and applies basic principles of presenting an argument
2. Understands and applies basic principles of logic and reasoning
3. Effectively uses mental processes that are based on identifying similarities and dissimilarities (compares, contrasts, classifies)
4. Understands and applies basic principles of hypothesis testing and scientific inquiry
5. Applies basic trouble-shooting and problem-solving techniques
6. Applies decision-making techniques

When these processes are applied to declarative knowledge in an essay format, a student must demonstrate competence in both the declarative knowledge and the thinking and reasoning process. (This approach was briefly described in chapter 3 in our discussion of performance tasks.) For example, assume that a teacher wishes to construct an essay examination around the information in the Lincoln and Douglas debate that also utilizes a specific thinking and reasoning skill or skills. That essay question might be structured in the following way:

> Douglas and Lincoln said many things in their debate. Identify their areas of agreement as well as their areas of disagreement. Then, select one of their areas of disagreement and analyze the arguments each has presented to determine which one has presented the best case. In your analysis, look at the logic of each argument as well as the accuracy of their information.

This essay actually assesses three elements regarding the Lincoln/Douglas debate, two of which deal with thinking and reasoning and one that deals with declarative knowledge:

1. students' ability to identify similarities and differences
2. students' ability to analyze an argument
3. students' understanding of the accuracy of the information presented by Lincoln and Douglas

In summary, essay questions can provide rich assessment information across a number of types of standards and benchmarks.

Performance Tasks And Portfolios

Performance tasks and portfolios are two highly related forms of assessment that can be effectively used by the classroom teacher. Both are effective vehicles for assessing students' performance on standards and benchmarks.

Performance Tasks

As mentioned previously, performance assessments have always been considered an integral part of standards assessment. Many teachers use the terms *performance task* and *authentic task* synonymously. Although there is nothing wrong with this practice, it is useful to make a distinction between the two terms. Evaluation specialist Carol Meyer (1992) explains that performance assessments involve situations in which students must construct responses that illustrate that they can apply knowledge. Authentic assessments also involve situations in which students must construct responses that demonstrate an application of knowledge. However, in authentic assessment, the situation is more "real life." For example, a performance task might ask students to describe how they would solve the problems of inefficient wastepaper disposal around the school; an authentic task would have them physically solve the problem, developing all necessary procedures and even making necessary tools. Researchers Fred Newmann, Walter Secado, and Gary Wehlage (1995) offer the examples of authentic tasks in geometry and social studies reprinted in Exhibit 5.6.

Exhibit 5.6 Sample Authentic Assessments

| **Authentic Geometry Task** |
| Design packaging that will hold 576 cans of Campbell's Tomato Soup (net weight, 10 ¾ oz.) or packaging that will hold 144 boxes of Kellogg's Rice Krispies (net weight, 19 oz.). Use and list each individual package's real measurements; create scale drawings of front, top, and side perspectives; show the unfolded boxes/containers in a scale drawing; build a proportional, three-dimensional model. |
| **Authentic Social Studies Task** |
| Write a letter to a student living in South Central Los Angeles conveying your feeling about what happened in that area following the acquittal of police officers in the Rodney King case. Discuss the tension between our natural impulse to strike back at social injustice and the principles of nonviolence. |

Note: From *A Guide to Authentic Instruction and Assessment: Vision, Standards and Scoring* (pp. 24-25), by F. M. Newmann, W. G. Secado, G. G. & Wehlage, G. G, 1995, Madison, WI: Wisconsin Center for Educational Research, University of Wisconsin.

Quite obviously, authentic tasks take a great deal of time and effort. Consequently, there is a limit on how many of them a classroom teacher can perform. In fact, when we asked 72 teachers in grades K-12 who were experienced in designing and using performance tasks and authentic tasks how many they could use, they responded that, at most, they could utilize three performance tasks every two months (or about 1.5 per month) and only one authentic task per semester.

Another important distinction is the difference between an essay question and a performance task. In fact, a good essay test is a type of performance task. That is, whenever an essay test requires students to apply knowledge, it is, by definition, a type of performance task that has a specific format for the product that is generated—a written composition.

One of the most powerful aspects of performance tasks is that they can be used to assess standards and benchmarks of all types—declarative and procedural subject-specific standards, thinking and reasoning standards, and lifelong learning standards. To illustrate, consider the following performance task, adapted from *Assessing Student Outcomes* (Marzano, Pickering, McTighe, 1993):

> For the next two weeks we will be studying American military conflicts of the past three decades, in particular the Vietnam War. You will form teams of two and pretend that you and your partner will be featured in a newsmagazine television special about military conflict. Your team has been asked to help viewers understand the basic elements of the Vietnam War by relating them to a situation that has nothing to do with military conflict but has the same basic elements. You are free to choose any nonmilitary situation you wish. In your explanation, the two of you must describe how the nonmilitary conflict fits each of the basic elements you identified in the war. You will prepare a report, with appropriate visuals, to present to the class in the way you would actually present it if you were doing your feature on the newsmagazine special. You will be assessed on and provided rubrics for the following:

1. your understanding of the specific details of the Vietnam War;
2. your ability to identify the similarities and differences between the Vietnam War and the nonmilitary conflict you selected; and
3. your ability to work as an effective member of a team.

As the directions to the students reveal, this task is designed to measure three different types of standards and benchmarks: (1) the student's declarative knowledge regarding the Vietnam War, (2) the student's ability to use the thinking and reasoning skill of identifying similarities and differences, and (3) the student's ability to use the lifelong learning skill of working in a group.

Although the use of performance tasks and authentic tasks is not new in education, their effects are only now being studied in depth. Not surprisingly, there is mounting evidence that the use of performance tasks alters what happens in the classroom (see e.g., Borko, Flory, & Cumbo, 1993; Falk & Darling-Hammond, 1993; Kentucky Institute for Education Research, 1995; Smith et al., 1994). As described by researchers Nidhi Kattri, Michael Kane, and Alison Reeve (1995), performance assessments inspire teachers to integrate instructional practices with assessment practices so that they become more "seamless," use a wide array of instructional strategies, ask students to describe their thinking as they worked on their assessments, and ask students to evaluate their own thinking and their own skill.

In a fairly comprehensive review of the research, Newmann and his colleagues (Newmann, Secado, & Wehlage, 1995) found that performance tasks generate more engagement from students from all types of backgrounds and engender in students a deeper understanding of the content being studied.

In studies conducted at McREL, we have found that students' abilities to do performance tasks can be dramatically increased if teachers systematically use these tasks in the classroom. For example, in one elementary school, performance tasks in mathematics were first given in September to all children in first grade through fifth grade. Two skills were assessed in each performance task: the ability to problem solve and the ability to communicate mathematically. The percentage of students who provided a satisfactory or better than satisfactory score for these skills is reported in columns A and C of Table 5.5.

Table 5.5 Pretest and Posttest Results on Performance Tasks

Ethnicity	A Pretest Problem Solving	B Posttest Problem Solving	C Pretest Communication	D Posttest Communication
Asian (25)	16.0% (4)	68.0% (17)	12.0% (3)	44.0% (11)
African American (130)	8.5% (11)	50.8% (66)	12.3% (16)	32.3% (42)
Hispanic (31)	3.2% (1)	77.4% (24)	0% (0)	48.4% (15)
White (116)	29.3% (34)	78.4% (92)	24.1% (28)	62.9% (73)
Grand Total (302)	16.6%	65.6%	15.6%	46.7%

Note: From R. J. Marzano and J. S. Kendall, 1992, unpublished data, Aurora, CO: Mid-continent Regional Educational Laboratory.

In all, 16.6% of the students constructed satisfactory or better responses in the problem-solving component of the tasks and 15.6% in the communication component of the tasks given in September. During the year, classroom teachers presented students with performance tasks of their own design. As teachers interacted with students, they concentrated on asking students to explain what they did and why they did it. In other words, the teachers and students focused their attention on thinking and reasoning as opposed to simply getting the correct answers.

At the end of the year, all students were given another performance task, which again was scored for problem solving and communication. These posttest results are reported in columns B and D. The gains were dramatic: The percentage of students who achieved satisfactory or better responses in problem solving rose to 65.6% (from 16.6%). Similarly, the percentage of students who achieved a satisfactory or better rating in communicating mathematically rose to 46.7% (from 15.6%). Even more impressive were the gains in the performance of African American and Hispanic students. For example, the percentage of African-American students receiving a satisfactory or better score on problem solving rose from 8.5% to 50.8%. Results such as these indicate that performance tasks used in the classroom as combined instructional and assessment tools might provide a powerful environment in which students can enhance and demonstrate their ability to apply subject-area knowledge.

Apparently, the benefits of using performance tasks as a regular part of classroom instruction have already been discovered by Chinese and Japanese educators. In their comparison of schooling in China and Japan with that in the United States, researchers Harold Stevenson and James Stigler (1992) found that Asian educators presented students with real-world performance tasks in up to 85% of their lessons, whereas the highest percentage of comparable U.S. classes that involved real-world performance tasks was about 10% only. This is depicted in Figure 5.2.

Figure 5.2 Percent of Lessons in Which Teacher Was Observed to Present Students with a Written or Oral Real-World Problem

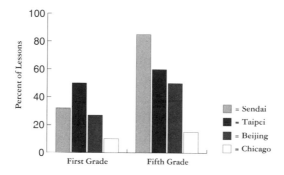

Note: Reprinted with the permission of Simon & Schuster from *The Learning Gap* by Harold W. Stevenson and James W. Stigler. Copyright © 1992 by Harold W. Stevenson and James W. Stigler.

Portfolios

As mentioned in a previous section of this chapter, portfolios can be described as a variant of performance tasks and authentic tasks. Although portfolios are probably not the best tool for large-scale assessment, they are very useful in the classroom (Winograd & Webb, 1994). A classroom portfolio commonly contains the various products from a collection of performance tasks, such as a final written report and notes from an oral report. In addition to the products themselves, a portfolio might also contain examples of the various stages of development for specific products. For example, the portfolio might contain selected drafts of the written report. Perhaps most important, the portfolio should contain the student's description of the process he or she went through for various projects and why certain decisions were made. For example, the student might include a description of why certain changes were made in the written report.

Finally, portfolios are usually accompanied by exhibitions. Simply stated, exhibitions are "presentations" of student work, or, as Wiggins notes, exhibitions call on students to present the fruits of their work (in Willis, 1996). Education reporter Scott Willis (1996) describes exhibitions in the following way:

> Typically [exhibitions are] multimedia in nature: students may have to write a paper, make an oral presentation, build a model or create computer graphics, and respond spontaneously to questions. Often, exhibitions are a "culminating"

performance. The audience for exhibitions may include teachers, classmates, younger students, parents, or other community members. (p. 1)

In summary, performance tasks, portfolios, and exhibitions represent an integrated set of assessments that can be used to assess virtually any type of standard or benchmark.

Teacher Observation

One of the most straightforward ways of collecting assessment data is through informal observation of students. Reading expert Yetta Goodman refers to this as "kid watching" (Goodman, 1978; Wilde, 1996). Researcher Robert Calfee attests to the validity of teacher observation if teachers are highly knowledgeable about the subject area they are observing (Calfee, 1994; Calfee & Hiebert, 1991).

Quite simply, with "kid watching" (which we refer to as observation) a teacher makes note of students' competence in specific benchmarks as students go about their daily business. This is the most "unobtrusive" way of collecting assessment data because the teacher does not design a special assignment or test to assess students. Stiggins (1994) provides the following example of how a teacher might observe a student relative to social interaction skills that might be part of a school or district's lifelong learning standard:

A primary-grade teacher might watch a student interacting with classmates and draw inferences about that child's level of development in social interaction skills. If the levels of achievement are clearly defined in terms the observer can easily interpret, then the teacher, observing carefully, can derive information from watching that will aid in planning strategies to promote further social development. Thus, this is not an assessment where answers are counted right or wrong. Rather, like the essay test, we rely on teacher judgment to place the student's performance somewhere on a continuum of achievement levels ranging from very low to very high. (p. 160)

To keep track of these informal observations, researchers Robert Marzano, Pat Hagerty, Sheila Valencia, and Philip DiStefano (1987) recommend the use of a daily log like that in Exhibit 5.7.

Exhibit 5.7 Sample Daily Log

Period: _2_ Date: _May 5th_

Course: _American Literature_

Student Name	Comments
Arndt, Carol	*Lifelong Learning—Reliability and Responsibility* *Came unprepared for class discussion on Gatsby, Beaufort, Bryant*
Creek, Rob	*Usage, Style, and Rhetoric* *Big improvement in use of supportive details in second draft of theme*
DeRienzo, John	*Listening & Speaking* *Questions enriched class discussion!*
Klopek, Nancy	*Literature* *Seems to have difficulty understanding Gatsby's significance to American literature*

Note that Exhibit 5.7 is simply a list of students with room to make anecdotal comments. Also note that this record is for a single day. Finally, note that only a few comments have been made. The key to the effective use of the daily log is to not force observations. If a teacher does not observe any behavior that significantly addresses standards, she records nothing. Additionally, the process of filling out a daily log should only take a few moments. At the end of a class period or while class is in progress, the teacher should make simple notes in the log.

Another prominent feature of the daily log is that it can be used to collect assessment data on any type of standard. Note that in Exhibit 5.7, the teacher has made entries about usage, style, and rhetoric standards (see Rob), listening and speaking standards (see John), literature standards (see Nancy), and lifelong learning standards (see Carol).

Student Self-Assessment

Perhaps the most useful form of assessment data is student self-assessment. As the name indicates, this type of data comes directly from the student. Wiggins (1993a) so strongly advocates student self-assessment that one of his nine postulates for a more thoughtful assessment system is "Postulate 4: An authentic education makes self-assessment central" (p. 53).

Hansen (1994) notes that self-assessment is central to the development of higher order metacognitive skills. Additionally, she postulates that self-assessment leads to the identification of individual learning goals, which are at the heart of the assessment process:

> Self-evaluation leads to the establishment of goals. That is what evaluation is for. We evaluate in order to find out what we have learned so we will know what to study next. People who self-evaluate constantly ask themselves, "Where am I going? Am I getting there? Am I getting somewhere? Am I enjoying the trip? Is this worthwhile? Do I approve of the way I'm spending my time?" (p. 37)

Researchers Sheila Valencia and Nancy Place (1994) recommend that students be given specific questions that guide their self-assessment, such as the following questions designed for reading:

- Have you changed as a reader? What are your strengths and weaknesses?
- How have you changed as a writer? What are your strengths and weaknesses?
- Having looked at your work, what grade would you set for yourself as a reader and writer? (p. 146)

Another useful tool in terms of student self-assessment is the student learning log. The student log is similar to that kept by the teacher. That is, the student keeps a record of his perception of his progress in the standards and benchmarks covered in the class. A sample student log is presented in Exhibit 5.8.

Exhibit 5.8 Sample Student Log

My evaluation of my understanding of the Lincoln/Douglas debate	My evaluation is based on the following evidence
I think I have a fairly good grasp of the Lincoln/Douglas debate. I would rate myself as very competent in this topic.	My oral report on the debate included information that neither Lincoln nor Douglas specifically said. I had to take what they actually did say and combine it with information I knew about that particular situation to come up with some new ideas about the debate.

As illustrated in Exhibit 5.8, the student is asked to provide two types of information about a specific topic—his self-evaluation and the evidence that supports his evaluation. The teacher identifies the declarative or procedural knowledge the student is asked to evaluate—in this case, declarative knowledge about the Lincoln/Douglas debate. The student then provides his self-evaluation and the evidence that supports his evaluation. Finally, this log is used by the student in an assessment conference held with the teacher during the grading period.

Some parents, and even some educators, assume that if given the chance, students will always provide inflated assessments of their understanding and skill. This fear is not supported by those who have made extensive use of student self-assessment. For example, Linda Darling-Hammond, Jacqueline Ancess, and Beverly Falk (1995) report that in their studies students have demonstrated a "clear-headed capacity" to evaluate their own work (p. 155). Middle school teachers Lyn Countryman and Merrie Schroeder (1996) report that students' candor in making self-assessments was noted by parents. After hearing her child's self-assessment, one mother remarked, "I feel our child was more honest with us than most teachers would be" (p. 68). Another parent commented, "Students seem more open and honest about their performance. I didn't get the sugar-coated reports from advisors who tend to present negative aspects in a positive manner" (p. 68).

Assessment Conferences

Ultimately, the various types of assessment data collected in a classroom must be put together. This can be done effectively in a conference between teacher and student. The purpose of this conference is for the teacher to share the assessment data she has collected on the student and for the student to share his self-assessment data. Assessment specialist Doris Sperling (1996) refers to this type of interaction as collaborative assessment, as does curriculum theorist David Hawkins (1973). Wiggins (1993a) notes that a collaborative approach to assessment is inherent in the very etymology of the word:

> The etymology of the word *assess* alerts us to this clinical—that is, client-centered—act. *Assess* is a form of the Latin verb *assidere*, to "sit with." In an assessment, one "sits with" the learner. It is something we do *with* and *for* the student, not something we do to the student. The person who "sits with you" is someone who "assigns value"—the "assessor" (hence the earliest and still current meaning of the word, which relates to tax assessors). But interestingly enough, there is an intriguing alternative meaning to that word, as we discover in *The Oxford English Dictionary*: this person who "sits beside" is one who "shares another's rank or dignity" and who is "skilled to advise on technical points." (p. 14)

We believe that Wiggins's comments capture the true spirit of effective assessment: teacher and student jointly analyzing the student's strengths and weaknesses relative to specific learning outcomes.

The specifics of conducting a student/teacher assessment conference are not complex (we describe such a conference in chapter 8) and are not new. In fact, within the whole language movement such conferences have been standard fare for at least two decades (see Atwell, 1987; Calkins, 1986; Cazden, 1986; Hansen, 1987; Staton, 1980; Thaiss, 1986; Valencia, 1987; Young & Fulwiler, 1986). Briefly, within an assessment conference, the teacher presents her evaluation of a student's performance on specific standards along with evidence she has used (e.g., quizzes, projects, and observations) to form her judgments. Similarly, the student presents his evaluation of his performance on specific standards and the evidence he has used to form his judgment. If the teacher is using a specific scale for performance levels on specific standards or benchmarks (e.g., advanced, proficient, basic, and novice), then the student evaluates herself on the same standards and benchmarks using exactly the same scale. Any discrepancies between the teacher's rating and the student's rating on specific standards or benchmarks are then discussed in depth with the intent of coming to the most accurate judgment regarding the student's understanding and skill.

Summary And Recommendations

In this chapter, we have considered various ways that students can be assessed on standards and benchmarks. When assessment is done using an external test—designed at the national level, state level, or even the district level—a great deal of confidence is being placed on the accuracy of a single assessment given at one specific point in time. Measurement theory indicates that this is a dangerous proposition because the measurement of a student's performance at any point in time will almost always have error associated with it. It is only by using repeated assessments over time that measurement error can be effectively minimized.

Given these measurement issues, the most accurate and appropriate place to assess students on standards and benchmarks appears to be the classroom. Consequently, the classroom teacher should use a variety of assessment tools that include forced-choice items, essay questions, performance tasks, portfolios, exhibitions, teacher observations, and student self-assessments. These tools should be used over time to form judgments of student performance on specific standards and benchmarks. This is not to say that national-, state-, or district-level tests given at specific points in time have no place in standards assessment. Indeed, they are valuable and, perhaps, even necessary compliments to classroom assessment. In the past, such tests have been considered the primary indicators of student performance. However, it is vital that they be considered supplements to classroom-level assessments.

Chapter 6

How Will Student Progress Be Reported?

Closely related to the question of how students will be assessed is the question of how students' performance on standards will be reported. In chapter 5, we strongly promoted the position that the classroom should be the focal point for the assessment of standards and benchmarks. However, assessments designed at the national, state, and district levels can be useful adjuncts. We referred to these types of assessments as "external assessments." In this chapter, we consider how a school or district might report performance on standards and benchmarks using assessment data from these various levels. We start with reporting data from nationally developed tests.

Reporting Data From Assessments Developed At The National Level

As mentioned in chapter 5, nationally developed, off-the-shelf standardized tests appear to have limited use for assessing students' performance on standards. Therefore, we recommend against using tests such as these as the primary means by which students' performance on standards is measured. However, nationally developed tests that are more performance oriented can provide useful information. Again, one of the best sources of nationally developed performance assessments is the National Assessment of Educational Progress, which not only provides specific performance tasks but also the necessary resources to administer, score, and interpret those tasks at the local level. To illustrate, reconsider the NAEP mathematics task that was introduced in chapter 5. This is reproduced in Exhibit 6.1.

NAEP provides the task along with a recommended solution and example responses for each of six levels of performance. To illustrate, Exhibit 6.2 reports the recommended solution for the Treena task.

Exhibit 6.1 NAEP Performance Task: The "Treena" Task

> This question requires you to show your work and explain your reasoning. You may use drawings, words, and numbers in your explanation. Your answer should be clear enough so that another person could read it and understand your thinking. It is important that you show *all* your work.
>
> > Treena won a 7-day scholarship worth $1,000 to the Pro Shot Basketball Camp. Round-trip travel expenses to the camp are $335 by air or $125 by train. At the camp she must choose between a week of individual instruction at $60 per day or a week of group instruction at $40 per day. Treena's food and other expenses are fixed at $45 per day. If she does not plan to spend any money other than the scholarship, what are *all* choices of travel and instruction plans that she could afford to make? Explain your reasoning.

Note: From *Can Students Do Mathematical Problem Solving?* (p. 116), by J. A. Dossey, I. V. S. Mullis, and C. O. Jones, 1993, Washington, DC: U.S. Department of Education, Office of Educational Research and Improvement.

Exhibit 6.2 NAEP Treena Task Recommended Solution

> Treena's fixed expenses will be $45 \times 7 = \$315$ for the seven days. Therefore, she has $\$1,000 - \$315 = \$685$ to spend on travel and instruction. Travel costs are either train ($125) or plane ($335). Instruction costs are either group ($40 \times 7 = \$280$), or individual ($60 \times 7 = \$420$).
>
> The four choices Treena has are:
>
> 1. Travel by train, group instruction, and fixed expenses: $\$125 + \$280 + \$315 = \$720$
> 2. Travel by plane, group instruction, and fixed expenses: $\$335 + \$280 + \$315 = \$930$
> 3. Travel by train, individual instruction and fixed expenses: $\$125 + \$420 + \$315 = \$860$
> 4. Travel by plane, individual instruction, and fixed expenses: $\$335 + \$420 + \$315 = \$1,070$
>
> Students must realize that Treena cannot choose the individual plan and travel by plane because the total expenses ($1,070) would be greater than the allotted scholarship. Any full credit response must clearly communicate that Treena has three options that do not exceed $1,000, what the three options are, and how the student arrived at the three options.

Note: From *Can Students Do Mathematical Problem Solving?* (pp. 116-117), by J. A. Dossey, I. V. S. Mullis, and C. O. Jones, 1993, Washington, DC: U.S. Department of Education, Office of Educational Research and Improvement.

In addition to the recommended correct answer, NAEP also describes six levels of performance for each mathematics performance task along with student responses that exemplify each level. Table 6.1 lists the levels of performance, student examples, and commentaries on the student examples for the Treena task. With this level of detail, a district or school can quite easily administer open-ended NAEP tasks to its students and score them in a reliable fashion.

Finally, NAEP provides norms of student performance for each task. For example, Table 6.2 (see page 128) presents the percentage of student responses within each of the performance levels for the national sample of eighth-grade students to whom the Treena task was administered.

Table 6.1 NAEP Treena Task: Levels of Performance, Student Examples, and Commentaries on Student Examples

Level	Description	Student Example	Commentary on Student Example
No response	0. No response		
Incorrect	1. The work is completely incorrect or irrelevant, or the response states, "I don't know."	Add everything other than scholarship and you will get 230.	This INCORRECT response appears to be somewhat on task but the work shown does not warrant credit even at the minimal level.
Minimal	2a. Student indicates one or more options only (such as group and train) with no supporting evidence, or 2b. Student work contains major mathematical errors and/or flaws in reasoning (e.g., the student does not consider Treena's fixed expenses).	She could take the train to camp, have individual instruction, and eat every day and not run out of money.	This MINIMAL response does illustrate one valid budget option, but does not show any supporting calculations.
Partial	3. The student a) indicates one or more correct options; additional supporting work beyond the minimal level must be present, but the work may contain some computational errors; or b) demonstrates correct mathematics for one or two options, but does not indicate the options that are supported by his or her mathematics.	train at $125 group at $280 $315 $720 40 45 ×7 ×7 280 315 $720 would she all spend She just took the cheapest ones of her choices, now she has money left over.	This PARTIAL response illustrates one acceptable budget alternative (group and train) and the corroborating computational work.
Satisfactory	4a. The student shows correct mathematical evidence that Treena has three options, but the supporting work is incomplete, or 4b. The student shows correct mathematical evidence for any two of Treena's three options and the supporting work is clear and complete.	125 + 420 + 315 = $860 $1,000 > $860 If $1,000 is more than $800 she has money left over so she could take private lessons, a train and her food. 325 + 315 + 280 = $930 $1,000 > $930 She could take a plane, her food and group lessons.	This SATISFACTORY response illustrates two appropriate budget options (both individual and train and group and plane) as well as the correct supporting calculations.
Extended	5. The correct solution indicates what the three possible options are and includes supporting work for each option.	1) 1000 2) 1000 3) 1000 335 -125 -125 665 875 875 -280 -280 -420 385 595 455 -315 315-315 $ 70 $280 $140 1) take air, group, food 2) train, group, food 3) train, individual, food	This outstanding EXTENDED response provides the correct calculations in terms of the excess dollars that remain from the $1,000 scholarship, for the three acceptable budget options.

Note: From *Can Students Do Mathematical Problem Solving?* (pp. 117-120), by J. A. Dossey, I. V. S. Mullis, and C. O. Jones, 1993, Washington, DC: U.S. Department of Education, Office of Educational Research and Improvement.

Table 6.2 NAEP Treena Task: Percentage of Student Responses Per Performance Level, National Sample of Eighth-Grade Students

	No Response	Incorrect	Minimal	Partial	Satisfactory	Extended	Satisfactory or Better
Nation	22	37	22	15	2	2	4
Northeast	23	37	21	14	2	2	4
Southeast	23	43	22	10	2	1	3
Central	17	34	25	18	4	2	6
West	26	34	21	17	2	1	3
White	18	34	25	18	3	2	5
Black	30	50	13	7	0	0	0
Hispanic	36	40	19	5	1	0	1
Male	28	38	19	12	1	1	2
Female	16	36	26	17	3	3	6
Advantaged Urban	10	33	35	15	3	4	7
Disadvantaged Urban	42	39	10	8	2	0	2
Extreme Rural	24	30	23	19	2	3	4
Other	21	38	22	15	2	2	4
Public	23	37	21	14	2	2	4
Catholic and Other Private	14	35	30	16	2	2	4

Note: From *Can Students Do Mathematical Problem Solving?* (p. 121), by J. A. Dossey, I. V. S. Mullis, and C. O. Jones, 1993, Washington, DC: U.S. Department of Education, Office of Educational Research and Improvement.

In addition to a wide array of performance tasks, NAEP also provides highly usable forced-choice items that are easily adapted for use in assessing performance on standards and benchmarks. Each NAEP item is assigned to a specific level of performance (referred to by NAEP as "anchor levels"). In this way, student performance on specific items can be interpreted as evidence of specific levels of understanding and skills. To illustrate, Exhibit 6.3 reports the four levels of performance for NAEP's forced-choice science items.

NAEP also provides a wide array of sample items at each performance level. Exhibits 6.4 and 6.5 show sample items for each level described in Exhibit 6.3 and the response of students at different grade levels.

Exhibit 6.3 NAEP Levels of Science Proficiency

Level 200	**Understands Simple Scientific Principles** Students at this level are developing some understanding of simple scientific principles, particularly in the life sciences. For example, they exhibit some rudimentary knowledge of the structure and function of plants and animals.
Level 250	**Applies General Scientific Information** Students at this level can interpret data from simple tables and make inferences about the outcomes of experimental procedures. They exhibit knowledge and understanding of the life sciences, including a familiarity with some aspects of animal behavior and of ecological relationships. These students also demonstrate some knowledge of basic information from the physical sciences.
Level 300	**Analyzes Scientific Procedures and Data** Students at this level can evaluate the appropriateness of the design of an experiment. They have more detailed scientific knowledge and the skill to apply their knowledge in interpreting information from text and graphs. These students also exhibit a growing understanding of principles from the physical sciences.
Level 350	**Integrates Specialized Scientific Information** Students at this level can infer relationships and draw conclusions using detailed scientific knowledge from the physical sciences, particularly chemistry. They also can apply basic principles of genetics and interpret the societal implications of research in this field.

Note: From *The 1990 Science Report Card* (p. 26), by L. R. Jones, I. V. S. Mullis, S. A. Raizen, I. R. Weiss, and E. A. Weston, E. A, 1992, Washington, DC: Department of Education, Office of Educational Research and Improvement.

Exhibit 6.4 NAEP Sample Items for Levels of Science Proficiency:
Levels 200 and 250

Example: Level 200							
Grade 4: 80% Correct Overall Percent Correct for Anchor Levels				Grade 8: 93% Correct Overall Percent Correct for Anchor Levels			
200	250	300	350	200	250	300	350
68	92	99	---	84	95	98	100

Which of the following gases must an animal breathe in order to remain alive?
- A   Helium
- B   Hydrogen
- C   Nitrogen
- D   Oxygen

Example: Level 250											
Grade 4: 50% Correct Overall Percent Correct for Anchor Levels				Grade 8: 93% Correct Overall Percent Correct for Anchor Levels				Grade 12: 87% Correct Overall Percent Correct for Anchor Levels			
200	250	300	350	200	250	300	350	200	250	300	350
28	70	97	---	38	77	97	100	39	76	96	99

Juan thinks that water will evaporate faster in a warm place than in a cool one. He has two identical bowls and a bucket of water. He wants to do an experiment to find out if he is correct. Which of the following should he do?
- A   Place two bowls with the same amount of water in a warm place.
- B   Place a bowl of water in a cool place and a bowl with twice the amount of water in a warm place.
- C   Place a bowl of water in a cool place and a bowl with half of the amount of water in a warm place.
- D   Place a bowl of water in a cool place and a bowl with the same amount of water in a warm place.

Note: From *The 1990 Science Report Card* (pp. 32, 36), by L. R. Jones, I. V. S. Mullis, S. A. Raizen, I. R. Weiss, and E. A. Weston, E. A, 1992, Washington, DC: Department of Education, Office of Educational Research and Improvement.

Exhibit 6.5 NAEP Sample Items for Levels of Science Proficiency:

Levels 300 and 350

Example: Level 300

Grade 4: 41% Correct Overall
Percent Correct for Anchor Levels

200	250	300	350
28	50	85	---

Cleo wants to conduct an experiment to find out whether an antacid seltzer fizzes longer in hot water than in cold water. In what order should she perform the following steps?

1. Place one antacid seltzer tablet in each jar.
2. Pick identical jars.
3. Time how long the antacid seltzer tablet fizzes in each jar.
4. Pour 50 milliliters (mL) of hot water into one jar and 50 mL of ice water into another jar.

A 1, 2, 3, 4

B 2, 1, 3, 4

C 2, 4, 1, 3

D 3, 2, 4, 1

Example: Level 350

Grade 12: 40% Correct Overall
Percent Correct for Anchor Levels

200	250	300	350
5	19	42	73

An antacid seltzer tablet is dropped into each of two glasses containing equal amounts of water. The temperature of the water is 50C in Glass 1 and 10C in Glass 2. In each glass, bubbles of gas are released as the tablet dissolves. It takes 30 seconds for the tablet to react completely in Glass 1 and 100 seconds for the tablet to react completely in Glass 2. From these results alone, one can conclude that

A temperature has no effect on the rate of chemical reactions

B increasing the volume of water increases the rate at which the antacid seltzer reacts with water

C the rate of all chemical reactions increases as the temperature increases

D the rate of chemical reactions doubles for every 10C increases in temperature

E the rate at which the antacid seltzer reacts with water is faster in hot water than in cold water

Note: From *The 1990 Science Report Card* (p. 41, 49), by L. R. Jones, I. V. S. Mullis, S. A. Raizen, I. R. Weiss, and E. A. Weston, E. A, 1992, Washington, DC: Department of Education, Office of Educational Research and Improvement.

In summary, NAEP provides enough sample items and information regarding those items that a school or district can design a forced-choice test geared to specific standards with items normed at a national level. The basic process would be to match the items provided by NAEP with the standards and benchmarks created by the school or district.

Another set of nationally developed performance tasks designed to be interpreted in terms of standards is being created by the New Standards Project. As described by education reporter Robert Rothman (1995a), the New Standards Project is a joint effort of the National Center on Education and the Economy, and the Learning Research and Development Center at the University of Pittsburgh. Under the direction of Lauren Resnick, one of the leading researchers in cognitive psychology, the New Standards Project has constructed performance tasks that are geared to specific standards in the subject areas of the English language arts, mathematics, science, and applied learning (New Standards Project, 1995a, 1995b, 1995c). Benchmarks are written at the elementary, middle, and high school levels. Unlike NAEP, the performance of students from across the country is not reported. In other words, no normative data are presented with the tasks that can be used for comparative purposes. However, each task is accompanied by samples of student work and extensive commentaries that can be used to score these tasks.

Reporting Data From Assessments Developed At The State Level

If a district or school is located in a state that has assessments designed to be interpreted in terms of standards, it need only use the reporting system designed by the state. As described in chapter 5, Maryland is one of the leaders in the development of state-level assessments organized around standards. Table 6.3 presents a sample report from the Maryland Department of Education for a specific school district.

Table 6.3 (see next page) reports the composite performance of students at grade 9 in a specific school district against the state-established levels of performance. The abbreviation *EX* stands for "excellent performance"; the abbreviation *SAT* stands for "satisfactory performance." The levels excellent and satisfactory indicate what percentage of students must achieve the passing score in reading, mathematics, writing, and citizenship. For example, for this district to receive a satisfactory rating in reading, 95% of the students would have to meet the passing score in the reading assessment. For the district to receive an excellent rating, 97% of the students would have to meet the passing score. In fact, 98.3% of the students met the passing score in 1995; therefore, the school district received a rating of excellent in reading for that year.

Even if a school or district is not in a state that has a test designed to assess standards, it might still use a test designed for another state. For example, Weld County School District 6 in Greeley, Colorado, utilized the Essential Skills Reading Assessment and the Essential Skills Mathematics Test, both of which were designed by the Michigan State Board of Education for Michigan students, to measure the performance of Weld County, Colorado, students (Waters, Burger, & Burger, 1995). Both of these tests report student performance on a four-point scale: 4=advanced, 3=proficient, 2=essential, and 1=in progress.

Table 6.3 Sample Composite Performance of Students, Grade 9, Maryland Department of Education

MD Functional Tests Grade 9 Status	Standard Percent		1993** Percent Passing	1994 Percent Passing	1995						
	EX	SAT			Number Taking	Number Absent	Number Exempt	Percent Passing	EX	SAT	Not Met
Reading	97	95	98.1	98.1	879	*	0	98.3	✔		
Mathematics	90	80	84.9	82.5	883	*	0	90.3	✔		
Writing	96	90	95.1	86.0	862	*	0	90.0		✔	
Citizenship	92	85	85.8	86.6	865	*	0	85.1		✔	

*Fewer than 20 students
**Indicates baseline year data

Note: From *Maryland School Performance Report* (p. 10), by Maryland State Department of Education, Kathleen Rosenberger, editor, 1995, Baltimore, MD: Maryland State Department of Education. Reprinted with permission.

Reporting results from portfolio assessments is also a possibility at the state level. As mentioned in chapter 5, Vermont is the first state to attempt to use portfolios for statewide large-scale assessment. Each portfolio in each subject area is analyzed in terms of specific constructs. For example, as reported by Mitchell (1992), when originally designed, the Vermont mathematics portfolio addressed seven different aspects of mathematics knowledge and skill:

- understanding of the task
- quality of approaches, procedures, strategies
- why the student made the choices along the way
- what decisions, findings, conclusions, observations, generalizations the student reached
- effective use of the language of mathematics
- mathematical representations
- clarity of presentation

Student performance on these seven traits was recorded on a form like that depicted in Exhibit 6.6.

Exhibit 6.6 Portfolio Profile Worksheet Like That Used in Vermont

Student Name _____
Reference No. _____ Grade _____
School _____
District _____
Evaluator _____

	Understanding of Task	How—Quality of Approaches/Procedures	Why—Decisions Along the Way	What—Outcomes of Activities	Language of Mathematics	Mathematical Representations
Assessment 1 Description						
Assessment 2 Description						
Assessment 3 Description						
Assessment 4 Description						
Assessment 5 Description						
Assessment 6 Description						
Assessment 7 Description						
Overall Scores	Final Score 1 Demonstrated severe misconceptions about the task 2 Displayed an incomplete understanding of the task 3 Displayed a complete and accurate understanding of the task 4 Demonstrated a thorough understanding of the task and provided new insights	Final Score 1 Made numerous, significant errors while developing approaches/procedures 2 Made a number of errors developing and completing approaches/procedures 3 Developed and implemented approaches/procedures without significant error 4 Developed and implemented multiple effective approaches/procedures	Final Score 1 Displayed limited range of critical thinking skills 2 Displayed adequate decision-making skills some of the time 3 Displayed reasoned decision-making much of the time 4 Effectively used a variety of complex reasoning strategies	Final Score 1 Made significant, serious errors in drawing conclusions, making inferences, and developing generalizations from the tasks at hand 2 Made a number of errors in drawing conclusions, making inferences and developing generalizations from tasks at hand 3 Demonstrated the ability to draw valid conclusions, make inferences, and develop generalizations from the tasks at hand 4 Demonstrates thoughtful, creative approaches to drawing conclusions, making inferences, and developing generalizations from tasks at hand	Final Score 1 Displayed severe misconceptions about and errors using mathematics language 2 Displayed an incomplete understanding and limited use of mathematics language 3 Displayed an accurate use and understanding of mathematics language 4 Demonstrated a thorough understanding of mathematics language and how it is used	Final Score 1 Made frequent and significant errors in mathematical representations 2 Made some errors in mathematical representations 3 Used mathematical representations accurately 4 Used mathematical representations without error and with little or no conscious effort

Comments

Note: The Vermont State Department of Education has precluded us from reprinting the exact form used inasmuch as new rubrics and a new form are being developed. The above form preserves the general intent of the Vermont form but does not contain the specific terminology or format.

Mitchell (1992) reports that in spite of the rather specific categories of mathematics skill and knowledge explicit in the information sheet depicted in Exhibit 6.6, the Vermont State Department of Education opted to report student performance in mathematics in narrative form "rather than as a set of scores" (p. 117).

Although it is certainly useful to work toward legitimizing the use of narratives to report student progress, given the problems described in chapter 5 regarding the scoring of portfolios and the public's distrust of current reform efforts that deal with student assessment (see Olson, 1995b for a discussion), it seems advisable to include some quantification of students' understanding and skill if portfolios are used. It is important to note that Vermont is in the process of totally revising the categories that will be used to assess student performance within a mathematics portfolio and the forms that will be used to record results.

Reporting Data From Assessments Designed At The District Level

If a district wishes to develop its own assessments that are designed around standards, one of its primary considerations will be to construct or select the scale with which to report student results. Virtually all scales use the convention of identifying a satisfactory level of performance—the performance standard—and levels above and below the standard. However, scales differ dramatically in their levels of generality. Some scales are specific to the tasks that are used to assess specific standards and benchmarks. Some scales relate to a specific task only; for example, below is a scale that McREL designed for a Colorado district to be used with the task in Exhibit 6.7.

4   The student chooses the Appaloosa, addresses each criterion in turn, implicitly or explicitly identifying automobiles included or excluded on the basis of selected criteria. Additionally, the student provides a clear, coherent description of the logic that resulted in the decision.

3   The student addresses all important criteria and presents a cogent argument for the decision, whether or not the student chooses the Appaloosa.

2   The student misses important criteria or has a misconception of the use or application of some criteria. The logic of the argument is difficult to follow or not present.

1   The student does not understand the problem posed but makes some attempt.

0   The student makes no attempt at an answer.

Exhibit 6.7 Performance Task:
Designed by a Colorado District to Assess Specific Standards

The box below lists information that has been gathered about various automobiles. Some information was gathered from dealers; other information was provided by the prospective buyer, a high school junior. Using this data, consider which used car might be the "best buy" for this student. The following information should be kept in mind:

- The student can buy the car only if the insurance rate can be covered by no more than a third of the student's wages from a summer job.
- Since the summer job doesn't pay much, it's important that the car does not require frequent expensive repairs.
- The car has to be reliable, since it's going to be used to get to work.

The following factors should also be taken into consideration:

- Gas mileage is not a big concern, because the job and school are not that far away (the car is needed because the student must be able to respond quickly to calls from work).
- The student has saved $2000 over the years, and has received a contribution of $500 from grandparents and $1000 from parents.
- Any money not spent on the purchase of the car can be used to offset the insurance bill or possible repairs.
- The student has rated the physical appearance of each car with a high, medium or low.

Make of Car	Year	Yearly Cost for Repairs	Trouble Index (1-5)*	Cost at Present Time	Mileage Per Gallon	Insurance as a Percentage of Wages	Physical Appearance
Rancher	1988	$133	2	$3495	30	34%	medium
Appaloosa	1986	$250	2	$3195	23	29%	high
SunFire	1987	$171	1	$3595	35	32%	high
Arapahoe	1984	$421	2	$3395	20	32%	medium
Jupiter	1985	$309	3	$2995	21	28%	high
Mark V	1980	$630	4	$1495	11	15%	high

When writing your answer:
1. List the criteria you are using to make your decision and explain why each one is important.
2. Make your selection and justify it in light of the criteria you have identified.

Your answers will be assessed based on the extent to which
- you have illustrated that you can accurately interpret the data in Figure 1;
- you have justified the criteria you use for your decision;
- you use the criteria in making your decision.

(Below and on the next page show all your work and explain your decision.)

This scale makes sense only in the context of this specific problem. Some scales are a little more general in nature and relate to a specific type of task as opposed to a specific task. To illustrate, Wiggins (1996) proposes the scale in Exhibit 6.8 (designed by a district in Toronto, Canada) for use with any task that requires students to make an oral presentation.

Exhibit 6.8 Eighth-Grade Scale for Oral Performance

LEVEL FIVE

The student is aware of the importance of both content and delivery in giving a talk. The content is powerfully focused and informative. The issue is clearly defined, and detail is judiciously selected to support the issue. The talk is delivered in a style that interests and persuades the audience. Questions, eye contact, facial expressions and gesture engage the audience. The student displays evidence of social, moral and political responsibility, and offers creative solutions. Causes and effects are elaborated. The second version of the talk reveals significant changes based on revision after viewing. The student may make effective use of cue cards. The student is confident and takes risks.

LEVEL FOUR

The student is aware of the importance of both content and delivery in giving a talk. The student's talk is well shaped and supported with pertinent information. The student supports conclusions with facts, and makes connections between cause and effect. The talk is delivered in a style that may interest and persuade the audience. Questions, eye contact, facial expressions, and gesture are used occasionally to engage the audience. Delivery is improved after viewing the first draft of the talk. The student is fairly confident and can self-evaluate.

LEVEL THREE

The student is aware of the importance of both content and delivery in giving a talk. The talk displays a noticeable order and some organization, primarily through lists. The student includes some specific information, some of which supports or focuses on the topic. The conclusion may be weak. The student may show personal involvement with topic and concern about the consequences of not dealing with the issues. There is evidence of revision as a result of viewing the first version of the talk. The student is fairly confident and can self-evaluate.

LEVEL TWO

The student's talk contains some specific information with some attempt at organization. The main idea is unclear and facts are disjointed. Some paraphrasing of text is evident. The student uses no persuasive devices, has little eye contact or voice inflection and does not take a clear stand on the issue. The delivery is hesitant and incoherent. Little improvement is shown in the talk after watching the first version. The student demonstrates little confidence.

LEVEL ONE

The student chooses one or two details to talk about but the talk lacks coherence. The talk is confused and illogical. There may be no response.

Note: In "Honesty and Fairness: Toward Better Grading and Reporting" (pp. 152-153), by G. Wiggins, 1996, in T. R. Guskey (Ed.), *ASCD Yearbook, 1996: Communicating Student Learning* (pp. 141-177). Alexandria, VA: Association for Supervision and Curriculum Development. Copyright © 1996. All rights reserved.

Another example of a scale that relates to a general type of task is offered by measurement experts Joan Herman, Pamela Aschbacher, and Lynn Winters (1992). This scale, depicted in Exhibit 6.9, can be used with any constructed-response mathematics task.

Exhibit 6.9 General Scale Designed for Mathematics Performance Tasks

EXEMPLARY RESPONSE—Rating = 6

Gives a complete response with a clear, coherent, unambiguous, and elegant explanation; includes a clear and simplified diagram; communicates effectively to the identified audience; shows understanding of the open-ended problem's mathematical ideas and processes; identifies all the important elements of the problem; may include examples and counter examples; presents strong supporting arguments.

COMPETENT RESPONSE—Rating = 5

Gives a fairly complete response with reasonably clear explanations; may include an appropriate diagram; communicates effectively to the identified audience; shows understanding of the problem's mathematical ideas and processes; identifies the most important elements of the problems; presents solid supporting arguments.

SATISFACTORY RESPONSE

Minor Flaws But Satisfactory—Rating = 4

Completes the problem satisfactorily, but the explanation may be muddled; argumentation may be incomplete; diagram may be inappropriate or unclear; understands the underlying mathematical ideas; uses mathematical ideas effectively.

SATISFACTORY RESPONSE

Serious Flaws But Nearly Satisfactory—Rating = 3

Begins the problem appropriately, but may fail to complete or may omit significant parts of the problem; may fail to show full understanding of mathematical ideas and processes; may make major computational errors; may misuse or fail to use mathematical terms; response may reflect an inappropriate strategy for solving the problem.

INADEQUATE RESPONSE

Begins, But Fails to Complete Problem—Rating = 2

Explanation is not understandable; diagram may be unclear; shows no understanding of the problem situation; may make major computational errors.

UNABLE TO BEGIN EFFECTIVELY—Rating = 1

Words do not reflect the problem; drawings misrepresent the problem situation; copies parts of the problem but without attempting a solution; fails to indicate which information is appropriate to problem.

NO ATTEMPT—Rating = 0

Note: From *A Practical Guide to Alternative Assessment* (p. 56), by J.L. Herman, P.R. Aschbacher, and L. Winters, 1992, Alexandria, VA: Association for Supervision and Curriculum Development. Copyright © 1992 by California State Department of Education. Reprinted with permission.

At the most general level are scales that can apply to tasks within any content area. For example, Clyde Miller Elementary School in Aurora, Colorado, uses the following generic scale developed by educators Evelyn Kenney and Suzanne Perry (1994):

N = No attempt

1 = Getting started

2 = Making progress

3 = Meets standard

4 = Exceeds standard

This scale quite obviously provides far less detail than the previous ones. In fact, there is so little detail that one might question its utility. However, parents commonly appreciate an easily understood, shorthand report of how their children are doing. As reported by Kenney and Perry (1994), this is precisely how parents responded to their generic scale.

> An amazing 65 percent of our parents found the new report card to be as useful or better than the previous one. As one parent put it, "The rubrics tell us more about the effort our son is putting into his work than we knew from looking at a single test score" (p. 24).

Bellingham Public Schools in Washington State uses the following generic scale (in Lake & Kafka, 1996), which is similar to that used in Aurora, Colorado:

Emergent
Beginning
Developing
Capable
Strong
Exceptional

One convention that some schools and districts have considered is to assign intermediate values to the levels of a particular scale. For example, assume that a district has designed a scale with four levels where level 4 is the highest level and level 1 is the lowest. Also, assume that each level has been described in detail as have those in Exhibits 6.8 and 6.9. When assigning a score using this scale, a basic decision that someone must make is which score will be assigned. These decisions can be difficult when a student's performance falls between levels, for example, when a student's performance is not quite as high as level 4 but not as low as level 3. One option is to assign the student a score somewhere between a 3 and a 4. This was the approach recommended by measurement experts Lee Cronbach, Norman Bradburn, and Daniel Horvitz (1994) for the California Learning Assessment System (CLAS):

> Judges scoring open-ended questions should be encouraged to report intermediate values. Unnecessary error is introduced when a judge is forced to call a borderline response either 4.0 or 3.0. Recording 3.5 as the judgment can only make [performance scores] more accurate. (p. 37)

Rather than assign intermediate numeric values as suggested by Cronbach and his colleagues, an option is to use pluses and minuses. A minus is assigned if a student's performance is not quite at a given level but is far above the next lowest level. For example, if a student's performance is not quite a 4 but well above a 3, the student would receive a score of 4−. A plus is assigned if a student's score is above a particular level but well below the next level up. For example, if a student's score was above a 3 but well below a 4, the student would receive a 3+. We have found that using this convention decreases the standard error of measurement for a particular scale by as much as one half (Marzano & Kendall, 1991).

In short, there is no single scale that a school or district should use. The major consideration should be what best meets the needs of teachers, students, and parents.

Using Letter Grades

Most districts across the country use letter grades—A, B, C, D, F—as the primary way of reporting student accomplishments in courses, particularly from the middle school level on up. A critical question, then is, Can a single letter grade be used to report student understanding and skill regarding specific standards? The answer is a qualified "yes" if, and only if, the manner in which teachers currently assign grades is drastically altered.

To illustrate how a classroom teacher might use a single grade to report performance on standards, assume that a seventh-grade mathematics teacher is responsible for assessing students on the following standards within her course:

Mathematics 1:	Effectively uses a variety of strategies in the problem-solving process.
Mathematics 2:	Understands number concepts and uses effective computational techniques.
Mathematics 3:	Understands and applies basic measurement techniques.
Mathematics 4:	Understands and applies basic concepts of geometry.
Mathematics 5:	Understands basic concepts of data analysis and distribution.
Mathematics 6:	Understands and applies basic concepts of probability and statistics.
Mathematics 7:	Understands basic properties of functions and algebra.
Reasoning:	Understands and applies basic principles of logic and reasoning.
Lifelong Learning:	Contributes to the overall effectiveness of a group.

Presumably, the decision regarding which standards are to be covered in this particular course would have been made at the school or district level. The individual teacher's job would be to teach the information and skills inherent in the seventh-grade benchmarks appropriate to these standards and then make a judgment regarding each student's understanding and skill for each standard and its related benchmarks. The teacher would assess students on each of the standards using the multiple techniques described in chapter 5. For example, the teacher might design a performance task to assess mathematics standards 1, 2, and 6, the reasoning standard, and the lifelong learning standard. Likewise, the teacher might give quizzes and unit tests using forced-choice items, essay items, and homework assignments. Taken together, the quizzes, unit tests, homework, and so on would address all nine standards. Additionally, the teacher would make informal observations of students in all standards whenever possible. Finally, the teacher would ask each student to present a self-evaluation on each standard. This student-generated information would be combined with the teacher-generated information to form a judgment about students' understanding and skill in each of the standards. These judgments about understanding and skill would then be translated into an overall grade.

This is a radically different way in which to keep grades, which challenges the basic assumption on which current grading practices are built. We describe this new method in more detail in an upcoming section. First, however, we consider the cumulative assumption, upon which the current grading method is based.

The Cumulative Assumption

At a very basic level, the *cumulative assumption* is the basic belief that learning is a matter of acquiring more and more units of knowledge; the more units of knowledge a student has accumulated in a specific subject area, the more the student knows about that subject area. As it relates to grading practices, the cumulative assumption means that the more units of knowledge a student accumulates in a course, the higher her grade will be.

The cumulative assumption clearly underlies the percentage method of grading. This method has been in place for a century. According to Durm (1993), one hundred years ago, Mount Holyoke College described letter grades in terms of specific percentages:

A: Excellent - equivalent to percents 95-100

B: Good - equivalent to percents 85-94

C: Fair - equivalent to percents 76-84

D: Passed (barely - equivalent to percent 75)

F: Failed - below 75

Apparently, perceptions have changed little in 100 years. Jane Bailey and Jay McTighe (1996) report that many districts currently associate the following percentages with letter grades:

A: 93-100

B: 86-92

C: 78-85

D: 70-77

E/F: Below 70

Teachers using the percentage method of grading commonly think in terms of assignments, tests, and activities for which they can give points. If assignments, tests, and activities sum to 100 points, grades are easy to compute. For example, below is a set of assignments, tests, and activities that might be included in a specific course and the points a teacher might assign to each:

final exam	=	20 points
midterm exam	=	10 points
homework	=	25 points
final project	=	15 points
quizzes	=	20 points
class participation	=	10 points
Total	=	100 points

On the surface, this percentage method of grading appears to work quite well. Teachers simply give a student a score on each element and then add up individual scores at the end of the grading period to obtain an overall score that is easily translated into a letter grade. It is interesting to note that the percentage method of grading, which is strongly grounded in the cumulative assumption, grew out of the need to document the performance of increasing numbers of students. Specifically, the percentage method of grading became popular in the early 1900s when the number of public high schools swelled to 10,000 from a mere 500 over a period of about 30 years (Gutek, 1986). Researcher Thomas Guskey (1996b) notes that

> subject areas in the high schools became increasingly specific; and student populations became more diverse. While elementary teachers continued to use written descriptions to document student learning, high school teachers began to employ percentages and other similar markings to certify students' accomplishments in different subject areas. . . .

> The shift to percentage grading was gradual, and few American educators questioned it. The practice seemed a natural byproduct of the increased demands on high school teachers, who now faced classrooms with growing numbers of students. (p. 14)

It is probably not coincidental that this same time period saw the wide acceptance of standardized tests. Researcher Robert Rothman (1995a) explains that standardized testing in various subjects was introduced in American schools in the period 1880-1920, when booming school enrollments and the efficiency movement in industry pressured public education to justify its effectiveness in a quantitative manner. Much of the theory that guided the development of standardized tests was developed by psychologist Edward L. Thorndike (see Anastasi, 1982; Frederiksen, Mislevy, & Bejar, 1993, for a discussion). Thorndike attempted to bring the rigors of "hard science" to educational measurement. Interestingly, Thorndike was fond of saying that whatever exists, exists in quantity (in Rothman, 1995a). In effect, Thorndike was a staunch promoter of the cumulative assumption. He reasoned that the more important a topic was within a given subject area, the more items should be dedicated to it on a test. The influence of Thorndike's reasoning can be seen today in the form of a specification table—standard fare in the development of standardized tests. In a specification table, the skills and information that are to be tested are identified along with the number of items for each skill or element of information. The more important the skill or information, the more items are allocated to it (Anastasi, 1982; Osterlind, 1989). For example, Table 6.4 shows a specification table for a science test in which the fourth topic is considered to be the most important, the second topic is considered to be the next most important, and topics one and three are considered to be equally important.

Table 6.4 Sample Specification Table, Science Test

Topics	Number of Test Items
#1 Structure and properties of matter	5
#2 Energy types, sources, and conversions	9
#3 Motion and related principles	5
#4 Magnetic, electric, gravitational forces	12

The concept of the specification table was quickly adopted as the standard approach for designing classroom assessments (Anastasi, 1982; Osterlind, 1989). Teacher preparation institutions and textbooks on classroom assessment promoted the item specification table as the basis for designing classroom assessments. This perfectly complimented the percentage method of grading—items were easily counted up and percentages were easily computed.

In summary, the percentage method of grading and the method in which tests are constructed both have strong roots in the cumulative assumption about learning. These two movements converged in the early 1900s to form the foundation of modern grading practices, a foundation that is now being challenged from at least two perspectives: (1) the structure of knowledge and (2) the variation in classroom assessments.

The Structure Of Knowledge

Even a quick examination of the nature of subject-area knowledge demonstrates that the cumulative assumption is not a good model upon which to base classroom assessment practices. As mentioned in chapter 3, subject-area knowledge can be thought of as either declarative knowledge or procedural knowledge. To some degree, declarative knowledge lends itself to the cumulative assumption, but procedural knowledge does not.

To illustrate, consider the concepts of limited and unlimited government that are included in the *National Standards for Civics and Government*, developed and published by the Center for Civic Education (1994). Competence regarding these concepts is clearly a matter of information, or declarative knowledge. In chapter 3 we saw that one of the distinctions between a basic, proficient, or advanced understanding of these concepts is the accumulation of more and more examples. For example, the basic level of understanding requires a facility with the examples shown in the upper section of Exhibit 6.10 (see next page). The proficient level requires an understanding of the examples shown in the lower part of this exhibit in addition to those specified for the basic level.

The more examples of limited and unlimited government that a student can provide, the better the student is assumed to know these concepts. Thus far, this approach fits well with the cumulative assumption. However, the recitation of more examples is not the only thing that differentiates basic from proficient from advanced performance. To illustrate, note that in the example of unlimited government, the student is expected to make the distinction between authoritarian and totalitarian systems at the proficient level, whereas at the basic level, students are not expected to make this distinction. The accumulation of information is not the key characteristic here; rather, students are expected to identify finer and finer distinctions that allow them to see differences between sets of information.

Another characteristic that is important to different levels of understanding of declarative knowledge is the identification of relationships to other information. Research and theory (e.g., deBeaugrande, 1980; Halliday & Hasan, 1976; Kintsch, 1974; Marzano, 1983; Meyer, 1975; Turner & Greene, 1977) indicate that there are a number of types of relationships that can be established between elements of declarative knowledge. The most complex relationships that can exist involve exemplifying rules and principles and identifying causality; the simplest types of relationships involve similarity and dissimilarity. For example, a student might find it relatively easy to determine how different forms of limited governments are similar and different but find it difficult to see that a specific situation is an illustration of a general rule about limited governments. Competence relative to relationships, then, is a matter of kind rather than "amount."

Exhibit 6.10 Concepts of Limited and Unlimited Government
Basic and Proficient Levels of Understanding

BASIC LEVEL OF UNDERSTANDING	
LIMITED GOVERNMENT	UNLIMITED GOVERNMENT
Historical Examples	
The United States Great Britain	Italy under Mussolini Spain under Franco
Contemporary Examples	
Israel Japan	Iraq Libya

PROFICIENT LEVEL OF UNDERSTANDING	
LIMITED GOVERNMENT	UNLIMITED GOVERNMENT
Historical Examples	
Canada Australia	**Authoritarian Systems** Russia under the Czars Japan under the military in the 1930s **Totalitarian Systems** Soviet Union under Stalin Germany under Hitler China under Mao Romania under Ceausescu Cambodia under Pol Pot North Korea under Kim Il Sung
Contemporary Examples	
Botswana Japan Denmark Venezuela United States	**Authoritarian Systems** Kenya Myanmar (Burma) **Totalitarian Systems** Cuba under Castro Iraq under Saddam Hussein

Note: From *National Standards for Civics and Government* (pp. 148-149), by Center for Civic Education, 1994, Calabasas, CA: Author. Copyright © 1994 by Center for Civic Education. Reprinted with permission.

In summary, competence or performance as it relates to declarative knowledge involves at least three elements: (1) the understanding of more information, (2) the identification of distinctions regarding different sets of information, and (3) the generation of different types of relationships. Only the first element fits well with the cumulative assumption.

Although some aspects of declarative knowledge lend themselves to the cumulative assumption, the structure of procedural knowledge has little that relates to this assumption. This is because procedural knowledge is not comprised of independent component parts. Rather, procedural knowledge is comprised of interactive processes that work together to produce a specific result. To illustrate, consider reading. Research and theory indicate that reading can be conceptualized as five interrelated processes (see Marzano & Paynter, 1994):

1. The general task processor
2. The information screener
3. The propositional network processor
4. The word processor
5. The macrostructure generator

The function of each of these is described briefly in Exhibit 6.11.

Exhibit 6.11 Processing Components of Reading

1. The general task processor: The general task processor monitors whether the reader is getting close to or further away from his general purpose for reading (e.g., to find specific information to vicariously experience an event and so on).
2. The information screener: The information screener determines whether the information in the text is reasonable given the reader's general knowledge about the topic.
3. The propositional network processor: The propositional network processor organizes the words decoded in the text into meaningful sets of interrelated clauses.
4. The word processor: The word processor uses phonetic and spelling patterns to decode words.
5. The macrostructure generator: The macrostructure generator constructs a shorthand version of the main ideas and supporting details in the text.

These processing components interrelate in the fashion depicted in Figure 6.1. This figure portrays the hierarchic interaction of the processing components: The general task processor influences the information screener, which influences the propositional network processor, and so on.

Figure 6.1 Model of Reading Process Components

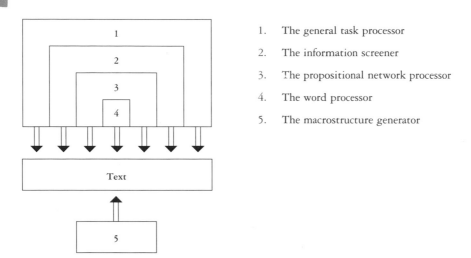

1. The general task processor
2. The information screener
3. The propositional network processor
4. The word processor
5. The macrostructure generator

Note: From *New Approaches to Literacy* (p. 29) by R. J. Marzano and D. E. Paynter, 1994, Washington, DC: American Psychological Association. Copyright © 1994 by the American Psychological Association. Reprinted with permission.

A key point of this model is that all readers use all five processing components all of the time. That is, the 2nd grader reading a story about bears uses all five components as much as does the 12th grader reading a book on physics. The difference in their ability to read is primarily a function of the fluency with which the components are executed; the 12th grader executes the processing components with greater ease and with fewer errors than does the 2nd grader. Again, this conception of procedural knowledge does not fit well with the cumulative assumption. The very structure of knowledge, then, is incompatible with the cumulative assumption.

The Variation In Classroom Assessments

Even if the structure of declarative and procedural knowledge more closely fit with the cumulative assumption, the variety of classroom assessments that teachers use does not.

Within assessment theory, the cumulative assumption is restricted to the development of standardized and classroom tests that primarily use forced-choice items. Stated differently, the cumulative assumption was never designed to address the wide variety of elements teachers now use for classroom assessments. Recall the diverse list of assignments, tests, and activities that a teacher might use to construct a grade: final examination, midterm examination, homework, final project, quizzes, class participation. Because the final exam, the midterm, and quizzes all use forced-choice items, these elements fit somewhat with the cumulative assumption—the more items a student correctly answers on the final examination, the midterm, and the quizzes, the more skill and understanding she probably has about the subject matter. The rest of these assignments and activities, however, do not fit even remotely well with the cumulative assumption. Take homework for example. Most homework assignments cannot be easily thought of as units of understanding or skill that can be added up. If students are given the assignment of reading a chapter in a textbook, summarizing the chapter, and then identifying the information about which they are clear and the information about which they have questions, how could one think about student performance on this assignment in terms of individual additive units? The assignment simply does not lend itself to this type of analysis. Class participation is also problematic. What are the equal units into which this activity could be partitioned? Similar problems exist with other elements that teachers consider when assigning grades such as handing in assignments on time, working well with others, and attendance. How does one divide "working well with others" and so on into additive units?

In summary, neither the nature of subject-area knowledge nor the wide array of activities and assignments teachers use to construct grades lend themselves well to the cumulative assumption. We might accurately conclude, then, that a new method of assigning grades might greatly improve current education practices.

A New Way Of Assigning Grades

How can teachers assign grades in a manner that is more consistent with what we know about the nature of knowledge? First and foremost, the teacher must stop thinking in terms of assignments, tests, and activities to which points are assigned and start thinking in terms of levels of performance in the declarative and procedural knowledge specific to her subject area. Recall that we began this section with the assumption that a seventh-grade mathematics teacher would be addressing seven mathematics standards, one reasoning standard, and one lifelong learning standard in her course. Each of these standards would have specific benchmarks that had been identified. These are listed below for our hypothetical teacher:

MA1. Effectively uses a variety of strategies in the problem-solving process

 MA1.1 Follows a general model for solving problems that includes making some basic assumptions about the problem; constructing a representation of the problem; choosing the appropriate strategy, operations, formula, or rule; adequately using the strategy, operations, formula, or rule; checking to see if answers make sense and if answers do not make sense; reconsidering each part of the problem-solving process (1 & 2)

 MA1.2 Breaks complex problems into simpler parts (1)

 MA1.3 Works backwards from the answer to a solution (1)

MA2. Understands number concepts and uses effective computational techniques

 MA2.1 Understands basic characteristics of fractions, ratios, proportions, decimals, and percents (1 & 2)

 MA2.2 Understands basic similarities and differences between rational numbers and irrational numbers (2)

MA2.3   Adds, subtracts, multiplies, and divides mixed numbers and fractions (1)

MA2.4   Mentally multiplies and divides basic combinations of whole numbers with reasonable accuracy (1)

MA2.5   Selects and uses appropriate types of estimation strategies (1 & 2)

MA3.   Understands and applies basic measurement techniques

MA3.1   Accurately calculates perimeter and area (2)

MA3.2   Effectively determines the level of accuracy needed in measurement situations (1)

MA3.3   Estimates distances and travel times from maps and actual size of objects from scale drawings (1)

MA4.   Understands and applies basic concepts of geometry

MA4.1   Understands the basic characteristics of the concept of symmetry (1)

MA4.2   Analyzes the effects of basic transformations on geometric shapes (2)

MA4.3   Understands the basic similarities and differences between pyramids and prisms, cubes, and rectangular prisms (2)

MA5.   Understands and applies basic concepts of data analysis and distributions

MA5.1   Understands basic characteristics of measures of central tendency (i.e., mean, median, mode) (1 & 2)

MA5.2   Understands that comparison of data from two groups involves comparing their middles and the dispersion of data around them (1 & 2)

MA5.3   Constructs, reads, and interprets data in scatter plots (2)

MA6.   Understands and applies basic concepts of probability and statistics

MA6.1   Understands the basic features of a sample and sampling error (2)

MA6.2   Understands that how probability is estimated depends on what is known about the situation (1)

MA7.   Understands basic properties of functions and algebra

MA7.1   Has a basic understanding of the concept of equations (1 & 2)

R1.   Reasoning: Understands and applies basic principles of logic and reasoning

R.1   Understands that a single example can never prove that something is true but that a single example can prove that something is not true (1 & 2)

LL1.   Contributes to the overall effectiveness of a group

LL1.1   Demonstrates respect for others in the group (2)

LL1.2   Helps the group establish goals (1)

In all, there are 23 elements (i.e., benchmarks) that the teacher will attempt to teach to and assess students on in an 18-week period of time. Assume now that there are two reporting periods within this 18-week block of time—one at the end of 9 weeks, the other at the end of 18 weeks. The teacher would first identify which benchmarks would be covered within each grading period. We've marked those elements to be covered in the first grading period with a "1" and those in the second grading period with a "2." Note that some elements will be covered and assessed in both grading periods.

The teacher would next organize her grade book around standards and make entries in the grade book regarding students' performance on each standard. The most straightforward way of thinking about a grade book organized around standards is that the columns of the grade book are dedicated to standards rather than to assignments, tests, and activities. To illustrate, consider Exhibit 6.12 (see page 151).

Note that the grade book has room for six standards. With a foldout page there is room for 12 standards. (For space considerations and ease of discussion, we have depicted in Exhibit 6.12 only six of the nine standards addressed by our hypothetical mathematics teacher.) Space is provided at the top of the grade book for the teacher to keep track of different assessments, activities, and homework assignments used for grading. Our sample grade book lists twelve items:

A. Quiz: September 10
B. Quiz: September 24
C. Performance Task: October 8
D. Homework: October 17
E. Quiz: October 24
F. Unit Test #1:   October 30
G. Performance Task: November 1
H. Quiz: November 9
I. Unit Test #2:   November 16
J. Performance Task: December 8
K. Student Self-Assessment:
L. Observations

Notice that in this marking period the teacher has given one graded homework assignment, four quizzes, three performance tasks, and two unit tests. Also note that assessment item *K* is the student's self-assessment for his or her performance on each standard. (The teacher entered this into the grade book at the time of the teacher/student assessment conference during which each student provided the teacher with his or her personal judgments on each standard and the evidence for the student's judgment.) Each box below each standard contains room for the teacher to enter a number reflecting his or her judgments about the student's performance on each standard for a specific assessment, activity, homework assignment, and so on. For example, consider Bill Aiello's scores for standard 2, number concepts and computation. This box has a number of rows, each preceded by a letter. The letter in each row represents the assignment, the test, or the event that the teacher used to make judgments about Bill's performance on standards. The number represents the teacher's judgment about Bill's performance on each of the assessments for each applicable standard. Note that most of the assessments cover more than one standard. For example, consider assessment A—the quiz given on September 10. The quiz provided assessment information for standard 1 (problem solving), standard 2 (number concepts and computation), standard 3 (measurement), and the standard on logic and reasoning.

It is important to note that some standards have far more entries than others. In fact, every assessment that was given covered information about mathematics standards 1 and 2, and the reasoning standard. This indicates that the teacher was quite consciously emphasizing problem solving (standard 1), number concepts and computation (standard 2), and reasoning in virtually everything that was done. Finally, note that row L is used to record the teacher's informal observations on each standard. For example, the teacher made two informal observations about Bill Aiello's performance on standard 1. The teacher assigned a score of 2 on one occasion and a score of 3 on the other occasion.

The use of columns in a grade book to represent standards, instead of assignments, tests, and activities, is a major shift in thinking for teachers. Under this system, when an assessment is designed, the teacher must think in terms of the standards it is intended to address. If a quiz is given that covers three standards, then the teacher makes three entries in the grade book for each student—one entry for each standard—as opposed to one overall entry for the entire quiz. Teachers who have tried this approach assert that it makes them plan their assessments much more carefully. Instead of simply assigning questions at the end of a chapter for homework or constructing a set of forced-choice items to form a quiz, the teacher must continually ask himself, About which standards am I trying to obtain assessment information? and, What's a good way to obtain that information?

Exhibit 6.12 Sample Grade Book

Assessment Key:

A.	Quiz: Sept. 10	E.	Quiz: Oct. 24	I.	Unit Test #2: Nov. 16
B.	Quiz: Sept. 24	F.	Unit Test #1: Oct. 30	J.	Perf. Task: Dec. 8
C.	Perf. Task: Oct. 8	G.	Perf. Task: Nov. 1	K.	Student Self-Assessment
D.	Homework: Oct. 17	H.	Quiz: Nov. 9	L.	Observations

Standards: / Students:		#MA1 Problem solving	#MA2 Number concepts & comp.	#MA3 Measurement	#MA4 Geometry	#R1 Logic and Reasoning	#LL1 Contrib. to groups
Bill Aiello	A	1	1	1		2	
	B	2	1		1	2	
	C	1	1		1	2	2
	D	2	2			1	
	E	1	3	3		1	
	F	1	4	3	2	2	
	G	3	4			4	3
	H	3	4			4	
	I	3	4			4	
	J	2	4	3	2	4	3
	K	3	4	3	2	4	3
	L	2 / 3 [3]	2 / 4 [4]	2 / 3 [3]	1 / 2 [2]	2 / 4 [4]	2 / 2 [2]
Marv Aronsen	A	3	3	4		2	
	B	3	2		3	2	
	C	3	2		2	3	3
	D	4	3			4	
	E	4	3	4		3	
	F	3	3	3	2	3	
	G	4	4			3	4
	H	2	4			4	
	I	3	3			4	
	J	4	3	3	3	4	4
	K	4	3	3	3	3	4
	L	3 / 4 [4]	2 / 3 [3]	3 / 3 [3]	3 / 2 [2]	3 / 3 [3]	2 / 3 [3]
Teresa Isaacs	A	3	1	2		2	
	B	2	2		2	2	
	C	2	2		2	3	3
	D	3	2			3	
	E	3	3	3		2	
	F	3	2	3	3	2	
	G	2	2			2	
	H	2	2			3	
	I	2	3			3	
	J	3	2	3	3	3	2
	K	2	2	3	3	2	3
	L	2 / 2 [2]	1 / 3 [2]	3 / 3 [3]	3 / 3 [3]	2 / 2 [2]	2 / 2 [2]

An equally radical change in grading is the use of numbers that represent levels of performance as opposed to points to total the number of correct responses. Note that in Exhibit 6.12 all entries for a given assessment are either 1, 2, 3, or 4. This is because the teacher has used four performance levels like those in Table 6.5.

Table 6.5 General Scale Summarizing Performance on Multiple Benchmarks

4	Advanced performance in some of the benchmarks within this standard and at least proficient in the others
3	Proficient performance in the vast majority of all benchmarks within the standard
2	Proficient or higher performance in some benchmarks within the standard with basic or lower performance in the rest
1	Basic or lower performance in the majority of benchmarks within the standard

Recall from the discussion in chapter 4 that this is the preferred method of combining assessments of performance on benchmarks into a single set of performance levels. This is particularly useful if a standard covers multiple benchmarks within a grading period. In our sample unit, standard 2 addresses four benchmarks in the first grading period and standard 1 addresses three benchmarks (see pages 147 to 148). Thus, the performance levels in Table 6.5 would be most appropriate. Standards 3 and 5 address two benchmarks during the first grading period and standards 4, 6, and 7 and the reasoning and lifelong learning standards address one benchmark only. For these standards it is probably more useful to use the performance levels for declarative and procedural benchmarks. For declarative knowledge, those levels are defined in the manner depicted in Table 6.6. For procedural knowledge, those levels are defined in the manner depicted in Table 6.7.

Table 6.6 General Scale for Performance on a Declarative Benchmark

4	**Advanced Performance:** Demonstrates a thorough understanding of the important information; is able to exemplify that information in detail and articulate complex relationships and distinctions
3	**Proficient Performance:** Demonstrates an understanding of the important information; is able to exemplify that information in some detail
2	**Basic Performance:** Demonstrates an incomplete understanding of the important information, but does not have severe misconceptions
1	**Novice Performance:** Demonstrates an incomplete understanding of the important information along with severe misconceptions

Table 6.7 General Scale for Performance on a Procedural Benchmark

4	**Advanced Performance:** Carries out the major processes/skills inherent in the procedure with relative ease and automaticity
3	**Proficient Performance:** Carries out the major processes/skills inherent in the procedure without significant error, but not necessarily at an automatic level
2	**Basic Performance:** Makes a number of errors when carrying out the processes and skills important to the procedure, but still accomplishes the basic purpose of the procedure
1	**Novice Performance:** Makes so many errors when carrying out the process and skills important to the procedure that it fails to accomplish its purpose

These generic performance levels for declarative and procedural knowledge are also commonly used when a standard covers more than one benchmark but a particular assessment addresses only one benchmark. For example, assume that although standard 2 above addresses five benchmarks, the teacher designs a quiz or a homework assignment that covers only one of these benchmarks. In this case, the performance levels for declarative or procedural knowledge would be a more appropriate scale to use when making entries in the grade book. In summary, the performance levels portrayed in Tables 6.5, 6.6, and 6.7 are used by the teacher as needed to assign scores on standards that cover single or multiple benchmarks.

The key feature in this approach is that the teacher makes multiple judgments over a grading period regarding each student's understanding and/or skill relative to specific benchmarks. To do this, the teacher must translate performance on a specific test, assignment, task, or activity into a judgment of the student's level of understanding or skill. If a quiz is administered, the teacher considers the set of items that deal with each standard and each benchmark within a standard and makes judgments relative to each student's level of performance; the teacher does not simply add up the number of correct items that pertain to each standard. This allows the teacher to do some "reading between the lines" in terms of the items. For example, suppose there were six quiz items pertaining to the concept of symmetry and the student missed three of them. The student answered only half of the items correctly, which might lead one to assume that the student should receive a score of 2 if the rubric for declarative benchmarks was used. However, the three items the student missed were multiple-choice items made up by the teacher. The three items the student answered correctly were short-answer items in which the student did an exceptionally good job of explaining symmetry. In this "judgment-based" system (as opposed to the traditional system based on the cumulative assumption), the teacher would be free to conclude that the student's poor performance on the multiple-choice items might be due to his or her misinterpretation when reading the items or due to poorly constructed items. Considering the strengths of the student's short-answer explanation, the teacher might conclude that the student does, in fact, understand the concept of symmetry and assign the student a score of 3 in the declarative performance levels as opposed to a score of 2. Of course, the most useful thing a teacher could do would be to query the student on a one-to-one basis regarding the student's performance on the quiz. In short, judgment-based assessment allows the teacher to use quantitative data, such as the number of correct items on a quiz, to inform his or her judgment about a student's performance without letting the quantitative data dictate the outcome of the assessment in an absolute fashion.

Some noneducators, and even some educators, react suspiciously to the role that teacher judgment plays in this system. They assume that it introduces an element of subjectivity into grading. What these critics commonly fail to realize is that the current system based on the cumulative assumption is inherently subjective. Citing the research of others (e.g., Ornstein, 1994), Guskey (1996b) notes that "regardless of the method used, assigning grades or reporting on student learning is inherently subjective" (p. 17). In a similar vein, educator Carl Glickman (1993) explains that current grading practice provides a false sense of objectivity by the sometimes complex manipulation of numbers to arrive at grades.

The extensive use of tests and the scores associated with those tests do not necessarily produce sound assessments of student understanding and skill. We assert that well-informed judgment is a much more robust and powerful tool. As Wiggins (1993a) explains:

> Judgment certainly does not involve the unthinking application of rules or algorithms—the stock in trade of all conventional tests. Dewey uses the words "knack, tact, cleverness, insight, and discernment" to remind us that judgment concerns "horse sense"; someone with good judgment is someone with the capacity to "estimate, appraise and evaluate." (Dewey adds, not coincidentally, "with tact and discernment.") The effective performer, like the good judge, never loses sight of either relative importance or the difference between the "spirit" and the "letter" of the law or rules that apply. Neither ability is testable by one-dimensional items, because to use judgment one must ask questions of foreground and background as well as perceive the limits of what one "knows." (pp. 219-220)

Guskey (1996b) adds further evidence for the validity and utility of teacher judgment. Citing the research of others (e.g., Brookhart, 1993; O'Donnell & Woolfolk, 1991), Guskey concludes:

> Because teachers know their students, understand various dimensions of students' work, and have clear notions of the progress made, their subjective perceptions may yield very accurate descriptions of what students have learned. (pp. 17-18)

The final judgment a teacher must make during a grading period is to assign an overall score representing a student's understanding and skill for each standard addressed during the grading period. This is entered into the white box in the lower portion of each column (see Exhibit 6.12) of the grade book. Again, this should not be a matter of adding up the individual scores and coming up with an average. The teacher can mentally weight some entries higher than others. We assert that the teacher should consider heavily the student's self-assessment (entry *K* for each standard in the grade book). In addition, many researchers and theorists (e.g., Conley, 1996; Fitzpatrick, Kulieke, Hillary, & Begitschke, 1996; Guskey, 1996b; Herman, 1996; Marzano, Pickering, & McTighe, 1993; McTighe & Ferrera, 1996; Mitchell, 1992; Mitchell & Neill, 1992; Spady, 1988, 1995; Wiggins, 1993a, 1993b, 1994) recommend placing heavy emphasis on the most recent information. Guskey (1996b) explains:

> The key question is, "what information provides the most accurate depiction of students' learning at this time?" In nearly all cases, the answer is "The most current information." If students demonstrate that past assessment information no longer accurately reflects their learning, that information must be dropped and replaced by new information. (p. 21)

Once a teacher has assigned a final performance level for each standard being assessed, then she must combine these in some way to construct an overall grade. At this stage, weight can be applied to the various standards. To illustrate, the seventh-grade mathematics teacher might assign the weights depicted in Table 6.8.

Table 6.8 Weights Applied to Various Standards

Standard	Weight
1. Problem solving	2
2. Number sense and computation	1
3. Measurement	2
4. Geometry	1
5. Data analysis and distribution	2
6. Probability and statistics	1
7. Algebra	1
8. Reasoning	1
9. Contributions to groups	1

Here the teacher has given a weight of 2 to standards 1, 3, and 5, thus giving these standards more quantitative influence in the final grade. These weights would be assigned to standards prior to the beginning of the grading period and communicated to students at the very beginning of the grading period. Upon assigning summary scores for each student on each standard, the teacher would then apply the weights to each standard. This is depicted in Table 6.9 for the student Carmen Walker.

Table 6.9 Computation of Total Quality Points for a Sample Student

Student Name: Carmen Walker			
Standard	Student Score	Weight	Quality Points
1	3	2	6
2	3	1	3
3	3	2	6
4	1	1	1
5	3	2	6
6	2	1	2
7	2	1	2
8	3	1	3
9	4	1	4
	Totals	12	33

Note that the quality points for Carmen have been calculated by multiplying her score on a standard by the weight assigned to the standard. An average score can be calculated for each student at the end of the grading period by using the following formula:

$$\frac{\text{Total Quality Points}}{\text{Total of Weights}}$$

In Carmen's case, her total quality points are 33. The total weights applied to the nine standards are 12. (This is the sum of column 3 in Table 6.9.) To determine Carmen's average score on the weighted standards, the teacher would divide Carmen's total quality points (33) by the total weight (12), for an average of 2.75. This is the average score, based on a scale of 1 through 4, that Carmen received in the nine standards addressed where some standards were weighted more heavily than others.

The next step is to convert each student's average score into an overall grade. The teacher might decide on the following conversion system:

3.26 – 4.00   =   A
2.76 – 3.25   =   B
2.01 – 2.75   =   C
1.50 – 2.00   =   D
1.49 or below =   F

In this system, Carmen's average score of 2.75 would be assigned the grade of C.

The reader might have the reaction that the cutoff points for the various grades appear arbitrary. In fact, they are. This is one of the greatest weaknesses of using overall letter grades. Guskey (1996b) explains that the arbitrary nature of cutoff points is a built-in flaw of overall grades:

> The cutoff between grade categories is always arbitrary and difficult to justify. If the scores for a grade of B range from 80-89 for example, a student with a score of 89 receives the same grade as the student with a score of 80 even though there is a 9-point difference in their scores. But the student with a score of 79—a 1-point difference—receives a grade of C because the cutoff for a B grade is 80. (p. 17)

Guskey's comments also apply to the conversion system above. For example, a student who had a score of 2.08 (compared to Carmen's 2.75) and only 25 quality points (compared to Carmen's 33) would receive the same grade that Carman received. A student could receive 25 quality points by having summary rubric scores that were a full point less than Carmen's on as many as six standards.

From this discussion, it should be obvious that using overall grades to report students' progress on standards is not our preferred method. As measurement expert Richard Stiggins (1994) notes, a single symbol—a single letter grade—simply cannot adequately summarize all of the complex learning involved in a course of study. Unfortunately, overall letter grades are used in almost every district from the middle school level on up and they are probably here to stay for quite some time. Consequently, if a school or district has no option but to use overall letter grades to report students' performance on standards at the classroom level, then we recommend the following guidelines:

1. Use well-informed teacher judgment to assign scores that represent levels of understanding and skill for specific standards as opposed to assigning scores to homework, quizzes, midterms, final tests, and so on, and then simply combining these scores.

2. Have a written grading policy for each course which clearly describes how scores on standards are to be weighted.
3. Clearly communicate to students and parents which standards are included in the computation of grades and how standards are weighted.

These guidelines will help make overall letter grades more representative of students' performance on specific standards. However, this approach is a compromise solution at best. The preferred method is to report performance on individual standards in lieu of a single letter grade.

Reporting Out By Standards At The Classroom Level

The use of a single letter grade to report students' performances on specific standards has little merit. It simply makes more sense to report separately on the varied components of understanding and skill that are addressed in most courses. As Wiggins (1994) notes, "Using a single grade with no clear and stable meaning to summarize all aspects of performance is the problem. We need more, not fewer grades, and more efficient kinds of grades and comments if the parent is to be informed" [emphases in original] (p. 29).

Unfortunately, when a school or district begins to alter grading practices, it runs the risk of significant opposition. Giving overall grades is something that parents and the public at large have grown to expect from schools (Glickman, 1993; Payne, 1974). Education reporter Lynn Olson (1995b) documents what can happen when a school district attempts to change the traditional practice of using a single letter grade. She details the case of a district in Rhode Island in which teachers and administrators began questioning the practice of using single letter grades at the elementary level. Parents, administrators, and volunteer community members worked for two years to develop a report card that evaluated students on relatively specific information and skills. To the surprise of those on the report card committee, there was strong negative reaction to the new approach even though it had undergone extensive study and testing. Olson (1995b) dramatizes the opposition:

> The three women seated around Dona LeBouef's butcher-block kitchen table look more like a bevy of P.T.A. moms than a rebel army. Dressed in coordinated shirts and pants and denim jumpers, they're articulate and polite. Classical music plays softly in the background as they sip their coffee and review the weapons in their campaign: a large sheaf of photocopied newspaper articles and editorials, old report cards, and petitions.
>
> Their target are pilot report cards introduced by the public school system here last fall that eliminated traditional letter grades in the elementary schools. The new format, tested citywide, was designed to more accurately reflect the teaching going on in the classroom and to provide families with more detailed information about their children. School officials thought parents would be pleased. They were wrong. (p. 23)

In general, parents were upset because they were used to 30 years of the A-B-C format and the new report cards did not look enough like what they had grown accustomed to. Even in the face of evidence that the new grading system format was much more accurate and informative, a relatively small group of parents was able to marshall support from some 1,300 community members in the form of a petition. As Olson (1995b) notes:

> At issue is one of the most sacred traditions in American education: the use of letter grades to denote student achievement. The truth is that letter grades have acquired an almost cult-like importance in American schools. They are the primary shorthand tool for communicating to parents how children are faring. (p. 24)

In spite of the opposition that a district or school might encounter by reporting by individual standards, we believe it is worth the struggle and effort it might take.

Reporting out by individual standards dramatically changes the type of report card a school or district issues. Exhibit 6.13 (see pages 160 and 161) shows an example of a report card that might be used in the school in which the seventh-grade mathematics teacher might teach.

Note that each standard in each subject area is scored on a four-point scale. This would be the same summary scale described in the previous section—that used by individual teachers to make judgments about students' performance in class on standards with multiple benchmarks (see Table 6.5 on page 152). A score of 4 indicates advanced performance on some of the benchmarks within a standard and proficient performance in all others; a score of 3 indicates proficient performance in the vast majority of all benchmarks within a standard; and so on. In other words, teachers would use the record keeping system just described. However, they would not collapse summary scores for standards into a single grade. Rather, they would simply turn in the scores on each individual standard for each student. Report cards would then be constructed from these standard scores.

Wiggins (1996) offers a useful alternative to this approach. He notes that if a district or school has constructed benchmarks using the stages-of-development format (see chapter 4), then the report card might simply contain a description of the various stages of development for each standard within each subject area. Exhibit 6.14 (see page 162) provides an example from Rialto Unified School District in California.

Exhibit 6.13 Sample Report Card: Reporting Student Performance by Standard

Standards Ratings				
Mathematics				
	Novice (1)	Basic (2)	Proficient (3)	Advanced (4)
Mathematics Standard 1: Numeric Prob. Solving	------(1)			
Mathematics Standard 2: Computation	------(1)			
Mathematics Standard 3: Measurement	----------------------(2)			
Mathematics Standard 4: Geometry	----------------------(2)			
Mathematics Standard 5: Probability & Statistics	----------------------(2)			
Mathematics Standard 6: Algebra	------(1)			
Mathematics Standard 7: Data Analysis	----------------------(2)			
Overall Mathematics 1.57				
Science				
	Novice (1)	Basic (2)	Proficient (3)	Advanced (4)
Science Standard 1: Earth and Space	---(4)			
Science Standard 2: Life Sciences	---(3)			
Science Standard 3: Physical Sciences	---(4)			
Science Standard 4: Science and Technology	---(4)			
Overall Science: 3.75				
History				
	Novice (1)	Basic (2)	Proficient (3)	Advanced (4)
History Standard 1: Civilization and Society	----------------------(2)			
History Standard 2: Exploration and Colonization	---(3)			
History Standard 3: Revolution and Conflict	---(4)			
History Standard 4: Industry and Commerce	----------------------(2)			
History Standard 5: Forms of Government	----------------------(2)			
Overall History: 2.6				
Language Arts				
	Novice (1)	Basic (2)	Proficient (3)	Advanced (4)
Lang. Arts Standard 1: The Writing Process	----------------------(2)			
Lang. Arts Standard 2: Usage, Style, and Rhetoric	---(3)			
Lang. Arts Standard 3: Research: Process & Product	---(3)			
Lang. Arts Standard 4: The Reading Process	----------------------(2)			
Lang. Arts Standard 5: Reading Comprehension	---(3)			
Lang. Arts Standard 6: Literary/Text Analysis	----------------------(2)			
Lang. Arts Standard 7: Listening and Speaking	----------------------(2)			
Lang. Arts Standard 8: The Nature of Language	----------------------(2)			
Lang. Arts Standard 9: Literature	------(1)			
Overall Lang. Arts: 2.2				

Exhibit 6.13 Sample Report Card: Reporting Student Performance by Standard

Standards Ratings		Novice (1)	Basic (2)	Proficient (3)	Advanced (4)
Physical Education					
Phys. Ed. Standard 1:	Movement Forms: Theory and Practice		(2)		
Phys. Ed. Standard 2:	Motor Skill Development			(3)	
Phys. Ed. Standard 3:	Physical Fitness: Appreciation			(3)	
Phys. Ed. Standard 4:	Physical Fitness: Application		(2)		
Overall Phys. Ed.:	**2.5**				
Music					
Music Standard 1:	Vocal Music			(3)	
Music Standard 2:	Instrumental Music			(3)	
Music Standard 3:	Music Composition			(3)	
Music Standard 4:	Music Theory		(2)		
Music Standard 5:	Music Appreciation				(4)
Overall Music:	**3.0**				
Geography					
Geography Standard 1:	Places and Regions		(2)		
Geography Standard 2:	Human Systems			(3)	
Geography Standard 3:	Physical Systems			(3)	
Geography Standard 4:	Uses of Geography		(2)		
Geography Standard 5:	Environment and Society			(3)	
Geography Standard 6:	The World in Spatial Terms		(2)		
Overall Geography:	**2.5**				
Reasoning					
Reasoning Standard 1:	The Principles of Argument				(4)
Reasoning Standard 2:	Logic and Reasoning			(3)	
Reasoning Standard 3:	Identifying Similarities and Differences			(3)	
Reasoning Standard 4:	Principles of Scientific Inquiry				(4)
Reasoning Standard 5:	Techniques of Problem Solving				(4)
Reasoning Standard 6:	Techniques of Decision Making			(3)	
Overall Reasoning:	**3.0**				
Lifelong Learning Skills					
Lifelong Learning Standard 1:	Working with Groups			(3)	
Lifelong Learning Standard 2:	Working with Individuals			(3)	
Lifelong Learning Standard 3:	Leadership Skills		(2)		
Lifelong Learning Standard 4:	Self-regulation		(2)		
Lifelong Learning Standard 5:	Reliability and Responsibility			(3)	
Overall Lifelong Learning Skills: 2.6					

Exhibit 6.14 Rialto Unified School District Pupil Progress Report K-6 Stages of Development (Partial Report)

Subject	1	2	3	4	5	6	7	8
Behavioral	Begins to take turns and shares.	Practices self-responsibility for expected behavior/safety.	Begins to take responsibility for choices. Begins to accept and appreciate differences in others.	Works well independently. Accepts the feelings resulting from challenges and successes in daily activities/outline.	Follows rules consistently and works in groups toward a common goal. Accepts responsibility for choices.	Willingness to be flexible to achieve fairness with the group/class.	Displays consistent cooperative effort toward a common goal.	Capable role model/leader. Respected by peers.
Health	Recognizes foods from plants or animals. Knows personal information: name, address, phone number, etc. Communicates daily needs to an adult.	Recognizes food groups. Identifies potentially dangerous situations. Seeks help from adults. Takes care of daily needs (food/hygiene).	Recognizes differences between food groups and other food types. Understands safety rules. Shows respect for others. Expresses feelings.	Makes healthy choices regarding food, sleep, and exercise. Describes major factors which influence growth. Makes responsible choices with friends. Demonstrates appropriate outlets for anger, disappointment, and disagreement.	Recognizes connection between dietary, sleep, and exercise habits. Describes how to protect themselves from environmental hazards. Describes feelings related to body changes. Shows respect for feelings of others.	Examines own eating, sleep, and exercise habits. Recognizes emergency situations and responds appropriately. Makes decisions about feelings, friends, and safety issues. Recognizes strategies to cope with changes.	Understands connection between healthy mind and body. Analyzes potentially dangerous situations and responds appropriately. Demonstrates positive, realistic body image appropriate to individual differences. Applies appropriate strategies to cope with change.	Uses universal precautions consistently. Analyzes situations to prevent and/or avoid potentially dangerous situations. Practices steps that promote healthy personal hygiene. Recognizes and manages fluctuations in emotions and feelings.
Reading	ONLY with individual adult support: Attends to pictures in books. Demonstrates an interest in books or stories.	With guidance: Listens to books. Uses pictures to predict a story. Begins to look at words and letters.	Independently shows reading behavior. Independently uses pictures to gain meaning from reading material. Memorizes reading material to re-read. Knows some letter/sound relationships.	Reads with instruction. Describes and predicts story sequence. Begins to self-correct to make sense of reading material. Recognizes some frequently used words. Uses letter/sound relationships.	Reads grade-level texts with minimal assistance. Understands reading material. Self-corrects to make sense of reading material. Recognizes frequently used words.	Reads grade-level texts independently. Predicts and summarizes reading material. Self-corrects consistently to make sense of reading material. Uses a variety of strategies to read new words.	Reads independently. Has insights about reading material. Questions, predicts, summarizes, draws conclusions from reading. Reads and understands a variety of increasingly difficult material.	Reads independently for a variety of purposes. Has in-depth insights about multiple perspectives on advanced reading material.
Writing	Uses pictures to create meaning. Orally assigns meaning to their pictures.	Uses scribble writing or letter-like forms. Orally assigns meaning to own writing. Writing is clearly not pictorial.	Writes words in a left-to-right, top/bottom progression. Uses letters placed in random order to write text. May copy print without comprehension. Orally assigns meaning to text. Reads own writing sequentially and logically.	Uses sound/symbol relationships to invent spellings. Writes simple sentences. Reads writing to others.	Continues to invent spelling with close approximations. Many commonly used words appear correctly in writing. Begins to use punctuation, mechanics, and grammar. Begins to include details and expand thoughts in writing.	Most words are spelled correctly. Writing reflects logical sequence and meaning. Uses punctuation/mechanics of writing regularly. Includes details and thoughts in writing. Uses a variety of of resources to enhance the written product.	Begins to use a variety of writing styles accurately. Writes with examples to support topic. Writer's voice is appropriate to the written task. Uses an expanded vocabulary in writing.	Consistently uses correct mechanics and grammar. Consistently includes relevant reasons or concrete examples to support topic. The target audience is always clear. Uses an expanded vocabulary with fluency.

Note: From "Honesty and Fairness: Toward Better Grading and Reporting," (p. 165), by G. Wiggins, 1996, in T. R. Guskey (Ed.), *ASCD Yearbook, 1996: Communicating Student Learning* (pp. 141-177). Alexandria, VA: Association for Supervision and Curriculum Development. Copyright © 1996 by ASCD. All rights reserved.

The major problem with the approach depicted in Exhibit 6.14 is that report cards can become quite long and, consequently, somewhat cumbersome. However, these descriptions of performance levels provide parents and students with a great deal of information.

A report card that reports students' performance on individual standards calls for a transcript that does the same. Exhibit 6.15 (next two pages) contains a sample transcript that is based on standards.

Note that in the first column scores on standards represent an average. This assumes that students have been assessed on individual standards more then once. The number of times each standard has been assessed is shown in the column to the right of the average score. For example, mathematics standard 5 on probability has been assessed three times; the average score is 1.7. The transcript also shows the lowest score received on this standard (1), the highest score (3), and the most recent score (3). Of particular interest to some are the most recent scores. (For a discussion, see Guskey 1996a.) As the name describes, this represents the classroom assessment of the student's most recent performance on standards. One policy decision a school or district should make is whether to compute overall performance on a set of standards using the most recent scores or using all of the scores. The transcript in Exhibit 6.15 does both. As mentioned previously, some educators believe that the most recent scores should be the only ones considered because they take into account the possibility that the student did not catch on to a new skill or new idea at first but, over time, finally mastered it. Conversely, there are those who propose that all scores on a given standard be taken into account because all scores are the products of individual teachers making a multitude of informed judgments. Because each judgment might contain errors (see the discussion of standard error of measurement in chapter 5), the most accurate representation of the student's true ability is the composite of all the available judgments.

Both of these perspectives have merit. Unfortunately, they can produce very different conclusions about students. Consider, for example, the student's overall performance in mathematics using the average of all scores in Exhibit 6.15: 1.84. Now contrast this with the student's overall performance in mathematics using the average of his most recent ratings only: 2.28. The differences in interpretation between an overall mathematics score of 2.28 and 1.84 are not trivial. A close examination of Exhibit 6.15 indicates that the largest difference in overall rating based on the average of all scores, versus the average of most recent scores, occurs in the area of reasoning. The overall score using the average of most recent scores is 4.0; the overall score using the average of all scores is 3.4.

This system of reporting scores on standards using a four-point scale has some powerful advantages. Perhaps its biggest advantage is that it bears a striking resemblance to grade point averages, which provides a sense of familiarity to parents, community members, and, perhaps most important, admissions officers in colleges and universities. However, it is critically important to remember that these scores are derived from teacher judgments regarding students' levels of performance on specific benchmarks within specific standards. They are not derived from single letter grades that have been assigned in highly idiosyncratic ways by individual teachers.

Exhibit 6.15 Sample Transcript: Reporting Student Performance by Standard

Subject and Standards Rated Average	Average Rating	Number of Ratings	Most Recent Rating	Highest Rating	Lowest Rating
Subject: MATHEMATICS					
Standard 1: Numeric Problem Solving	1.7	3	3	3	1
Standard 2: Computation	1.3	3	2	2	1
Standard 3: Measurement	2.7	3	2	3	2
Standard 4: Geometry	1.5	2	2	2	1
Standard 5: Probability	1.7	3	3	3	1
Standard 6: Algebra	1.0	2	1	1	1
Standard 7: Data Analysis	3.0	1	3	3	3
Overall Mathematics	**1.84**	17	2.28	**3**	1
Subject: SCIENCE					
Standard 1: Earth and Space	4.0	4	4	4	4
Standard 2: Life Sciences	3.5	2	4	4	3
Standard 3: Physical Sciences	3.5	4	4	4	2
Standard 4: Science and Technology	3.75	4	4	4	3
Overall Science	**3.69**	14	4.0	4	2
Subject: HISTORY					
Standard 1: Civilization & Hmn. Society	2.75	4	3	3	2
Standard 2: Exploration and Colonization	3.0	3	3	3	3
Standard 3: Revolution and Conflict	3.75	3	3	4	3
Standard 4: Industry and Commerce	2.3	3	3	3	1
Standard 5: Forms of Government	3.0	2	2	4	2
Overall History	**2.96**	15	2.8	4	1
Subject: GEOGRAPHY					
Standard 1: Places and Regions	2.0	2	1	3	1
Standard 2: Human Systems	3.75	4	3	4	3
Standard 3: Physical Systems	2.5	4	3	3	2
Standard 4: Uses of Geography	3.5	2	4	4	3
Standard 5: Environment and Society	3.0	3	4	4	2
Standard 6: The World in Spatial Terms	2.5	2	3	3	2
Overall Geography	**2.88**	17	3.0	4	1
Subject: LANGUAGE ARTS					
Standard 1: The Writing Process	2.6	7	3	3	2
Standard 2: Usage, Style and Rhetoric	3.0	9	4	4	2
Standard 3: Research: Process and Product	2.8	5	4	4	2
Standard 4: The Reading Process	2.6	5	2	3	2
Standard 5: Reading Comprehension	3.6	9	2	4	2
Standard 6: Literary/Text Analysis	2.8	6	3	3	2
Standard 7: Listening and Speaking	3.5	10	4	4	3
Standard 8: The Nature of Language	3.0	3	4	4	2
Standard 9: Literature	2.0	3	2	2	2
Overall Language Arts	**2.88**	57	3.1	4	2

Exhibit 6.15 Sample Transcript: Reporting Student Performance by Standard

Subject and Standards Rated Average	Average Rating	Number of Ratings	Most Recent Rating	Highest Rating	Lowest Rating
Subject: THE ARTS/MUSIC					
Standard 1: Vocal Music	2.0	2	3	3	1
Standard 2: Instrumental Music	3.3	3	3	4	3
Standard 3: Music Composition	2.0	2	2	2	2
Standard 4: Music Theory	3.0	2	2	4	2
Standard 5: Music Appreciation	4.0	3	4	4	4
Overall Music	2.86	12	2.8	4	1
Subject: PHYSICAL EDUCATION					
Standard 1: Movement Forms: Theory & Practice	2.3	3	2	3	2
Standard 2: Motor Skill Development	2.0	4	3	3	1
Standard 3: Physical Fitness: Appreciation	3.75	4	4	4	3
Standard 4: Physical Fitness: Application	2.0	4	3	3	1
Overall Physical Education	2.5	15	3.0	4	1
Subject: REASONING					
Standard 1: The Principles of Argument	3.7	10	4	4	2
Standard 2: Logic and Reasoning	3.0	10	4	4	2
Standard 3: Identifying Similarities & Differences	3.0	12	4	4	2
Standard 4: Principles of Scientific Inquiry	3.6	3	4	4	3
Standard 5: Techniques of Problem Solving	3.8	13	4	4	3
Standard 6: Techniques of Decision Making	3.2	13	4	4	2
Overall Reasoning	3.4	61	4.0	4	2
Subject: LIFELONG LEARNING SKILLS					
Standard 1: Working with Groups	2.8	17	3	3	2
Standard 2: Working with Individuals	3.01	17	4	4	2
Standard 3: Leadership Skills	2.7	14	3	3	2
Standard 4: Self-regulation	2.6	13	3	3	1
Standard 5: Reliability and Responsibility	3.0	17	3	3	3
Overall Lifelong Learning Skills	2.82	78	3.2	4	1
All subject areas combined	2.87	286	3.1	4	1

Reporting Out By Individual Benchmarks

Rather than report scores on standards, a school or district may choose to report scores on individual benchmarks. From a measurement perspective, there are many advantages to this approach. First, there is no need to use the summary performance levels in Table 6.5 (see page 152) in which the various levels represent performance over a number of benchmarks. Whenever you summarize performance across benchmarks into a single score, you introduce error into the assessment process. If performance on individual benchmarks is reported, then the levels can be interpreted in a much more specific way using the performance levels in Table 6.6 and 6.7 (see pages 152 and 153).

The major problem with reporting out by individual benchmarks is the number of elements that are involved. Specifically, instead of reporting on 9 standards, the teacher for our sample unit in mathematics would have to report on the 23 benchmarks embedded in those nine standards. It is fairly easy to see that the number of benchmarks involved could quickly make such a system prohibitive in terms of reporting. The only way to make reporting by benchmark a viable option is to severely limit the number of benchmarks within each standard. This can be done if a school or district is vigilant about its standards and benchmarks. To illustrate, consider Table 6.10.

Table 6.10 K-2 Sample Distribution of Benchmarks

Subject Area	Language Arts	Math	Science	Social Studies	Other	Total
K-2 Total Benchmarks	30	30	30	30	24	144
Total 1st Grade	20	10	10	10	8	58
1st Quarter	10	5	2	3	2	22
2nd Quarter	10	5	3	2	2	22
3rd Quarter	10	5	2	3	2	22
4th Quarter	10	5	3	2	2	22

Table 6.10 represents the possible distribution of benchmarks in grades K-2 for the subjects of language arts, mathematics, science, and social studies. There is also a category of benchmarks called "other," which accounts for relatively small sets of benchmarks in subjects such as physical education and art. In all there are 144 benchmarks—30 benchmarks in language arts, 30 in mathematics, 30 in science, and so on. Twenty of the benchmarks in language arts are covered in 1st grade. This implies that the other ten are covered somewhere in kindergarten and 2nd grade. Of the 20 covered in first grade, ten are covered in each of the four quarters of the second year. This implies that some or all of these 20 would be covered in more than one quarter. Some benchmarks might be addressed in all four quarters. In all, 58 benchmarks will be addressed in first grade, 22 benchmarks in each quarter. A teacher might use the following scheme to systematically record assessments on benchmarks:

- Twice per week teachers would record an assessment entry (i.e., a rubric score of 1-4) for each student for a benchmark on science, social studies, or "other."

- Three times during the week each teacher would record an entry for each student on either a language arts benchmark or a mathematics benchmark.

Assuming a class size of 30 students, a teacher would make about 150 entries in the grade book each week or about 30 entries per day. This would provide more than enough assessment entries to make overall judgments on each benchmark.

Although 30 entries in a grade book each day may sound like a lot, it is well within the limit of what most elementary teachers are used to. Specifically, many elementary teachers are quite comfortable with record-keeping techniques, such as "running records" (Clay, 1979, 1991) and the Reading Miscue Inventory (Goodman & Burke, 1972), that require literally hundreds of entries in a week's period of time.

Although the approach of reporting out by benchmarks does not present severe problems for classroom teachers, it does present difficult problems when it comes to the design of report cards and transcripts. If we assume that on the average a school or district will have 75 standards and 225 benchmarks per grade level (see chapter 4 for a discussion of how we arrived at these estimates), it is easy to see that report cards and transcripts might become inordinately long. However, if a district or school is willing to address the complexities of designing report cards and transcripts that have up to 225 elements, there is no substantive reason that benchmarks as opposed to standards cannot be the primary unit of assessment and reporting. In short, reporting out by benchmarks can be done, but the number of benchmarks must be severely limited and the management of information well planned.

Combined Course Grades And Standards

Given the cult status that single letter grades have achieved in our society, a useful compromise is to report course grades and progress on individual standards. Exhibit 6.16 provides an example of a report card that combines both course grades and scores on standards.

Here, each teacher has provided an overall grade for each student as well as scores on individual standards. Also note that teachers have used the four-point, novice, basic, proficient, and advanced scale we have exemplified throughout this chapter. This dual-purpose report card provides students and parents with the overall letter grade with which they are so familiar, yet it also provides them with ratings on specific standards. Note that with this approach, there will probably be some repetition of standards from course to course. This commonly occurs with reasoning and lifelong learning standards that cut across all content areas. For example, in Exhibit 6.16 (next two pages) both of the courses in mathematics and science have addressed logic and reasoning.

The main disadvantage to this approach is the unarticulated relationship between the overall grade and the ratings on specific standards. If a student receives top ratings in all standards, does the student automatically receive a grade of A? If not, what are the additional criteria that teachers use to assign grades? Teachers and administrators should be prepared to answer questions such as these in a logical, systematic fashion if they adopt this reporting format.

Exhibit 6.16 Sample Report Card: Reporting Student Performance
by Grade and by Standard

Nobel County School District 1: George Washington High School Student Progress Report

Name: Al Einstein
Address: 1111 E. McSquare Dr.
City: Relativity, Colorado 80000
Grade Level: 11

Course Title	Grade
Algebra II and Trigonometry	C-
Advanced Placement Physics	A+
U.S. History	B-
American Literature	C+
Physical Education	B-
Chorus	B+
Geography	B-

Current GPA:	2.81
Cumulative GPA:	3.23

Standards Ratings

Algebra II and Trigonometry

		Novice (1)	Basic (2)	Proficient (3)	Advanced (4)
Mathematics Standard 1:	Numeric Problem Solving	------(1)			
Mathematics Standard 2:	Computation	------(1)			
Mathematics Standard 3:	Measurement		-----------------------(2)		
Mathematics Standard 4:	Geometry		-----------------------(2)		
Mathematics Standard 5:	Probability		-----------------------(2)		
Mathematics Standard 6:	Algebra	------(1)			
Mathematics Standard 7:	Data Analysis		-----------------------(2)		
Reasoning Standard 5:	Decision Making		-----------------------(2)		
Lifelong Learning Standard 4:	Self-regulation	------(1)			
Overall Mathematics:	1.6				

Advanced Placement Physics

		Novice (1)	Basic (2)	Proficient (3)	Advanced (4)
Science Standard 1:	Earth and Space				--(4)
Science Standard 2:	Life Sciences			---(3)	
Science Standard 3:	Physical Sciences				--(4)
Science Standard 4:	Science and Technology				--(4)
Reasoning Standard 4:	Princ. of Scientific Inquiry				--(4)
Lifelong Learning Standard 1:	Working with Groups			---(3)	
Overall Science:	3.7				

U.S. History

		Novice (1)	Basic (2)	Proficient (3)	Advanced (4)
History Standard 1:	Civilization and Society		-----------------------(2)		
History Standard 2:	Exploration and Colonization			---(3)	
History Standard 3:	Revolution and Conflict				--(4)
History Standard 4:	Industry and Commerce		-----------------------(2)		
History Standard 5:	Forms of Government		-----------------------(2)		
Reasoning Standard 3:	Identifying Similarities & Differences			---(3)	
Lifelong Lrng. Stand. 3:	Leadership Skills			---(3)	
Overall History:	2.7				

Exhibit 6.16 Sample Report Card: Reporting Student Performance by Grade and by Standard

Nobel County School District 1: George Washington High School Student Progress Report

Name: Al Einstein

Standards Ratings					
American Literature					
		Novice (1)	Basic (2)	Proficient (3)	Advanced (4)
Lang. Arts Standard 1:	The Writing Process	-----------------------(2)			
Lang. Arts Standard 2:	Usage, Style, and Rhetoric			------------------------------------(3)	
Lang. Arts Standard 3:	Research: Process & Product			------------------------------------(3)	
Lang. Arts Standard 4:	The Reading Process	-----------------------(2)			
Lang. Arts Standard 5:	Reading Comprehension			------------------------------------(3)	
Lang. Arts Standard 6:	Literary/Text Analysis	-----------------------(2)			
Lang. Arts Standard 7:	Listening and Speaking	-----------------------(2)			
Lang. Arts Standard 8:	The Nature of Language	-----------------------(2)			
Lang. Arts Standard 9:	Literature	------(1)			
Reasoning Standard 1:	Principles of Argument				--(4)
Lifelong Learning Stand. 5:	Reliability & Responsibility	-----------------------(2)			
Overall Lang. Arts:	**2.4**				
Physical Education					
		Novice (1)	Basic (2)	Proficient (3)	Advanced (4)
Phys. Ed. Standard 1:	Movement Forms: Theory and Practice	-----------------------(2)			
Phys. Ed. Standard 2:	Motor Skill Development			------------------------------------(3)	
Phys. Ed. Standard 3:	Physical Fitness: Appreciation			------------------------------------(3)	
Phys. Ed. Standard 4:	Physical Fitness: Application	-----------------------(2)			
Reasoning Standard 6:	Decision Making			------------------------------------(3)	
Lifelong Lrng. Stand.1:	Working with Groups	-----------------------(2)			
Overall Phys. Ed.:	**2.5**				
Chorus					
		Novice (1)	Basic (2)	Proficient (3)	Advanced (4)
Music Standard 1:	Vocal Music			------------------------------------(3)	
Music Standard 2:	Instrumental Music			------------------------------------(3)	
Music Standard 3:	Music Composition			------------------------------------(3)	
Music Standard 4:	Music Theory	-----------------------(2)			
Music Standard 5:	Music Appreciation				--(4)
Reasoning Stand. 3:	Identifying Similarities and Differences			------------------------------------(3)	
Lifelong Lrng. Stand. 2:	Working with Individuals			(3)	
Overall Music:	**3.0**				
Geography					
		Novice (1)	Basic (2)	Proficient (3)	Advanced (4)
Geography Standard 1:	Places and Regions	-----------------------(2)			
Geography Standard 2:	Human Systems			------------------------------------(3)	
Geography Standard 3:	Physical Systems			------------------------------------(3)	
Geography Standard 4:	Uses of Geography	-----------------------(2)			
Geography Standard 5:	Environment and Society			------------------------------------(3)	
Geography Standard 6:	The World in Spatial Terms	-----------------------(2)			
Reasoning Standard 2:	Logic and Reasoning			------------------------------------(3)	
Lifelong Lrng. Stand. 5:	Working with Groups	-----------------------(2)			
Overall Geography:	**2.5**				

The Power Of Narrative Comments

Regardless of which system of reporting a district or school decides to use, narrative comments are always a useful addition. Researchers Jane Bailey and Jay McTighe (1996) describe the power of narrative comments in the following way:

> Written comments and narrative reports can be effective communication methods because they enable teachers to clearly and directly connect student effort and performance to elements of quality and standards of performance. They also allow for more individualized feedback than do other communication methods. Regrettably, the time-consuming nature of these methods often limits their use, especially for teachers at the secondary level because of the greater student-to-teacher ratio. (pp. 126, 130)

As evidence of the utility of narrative, Bailey and McTighe (1996) offer the report card designed by Edmonton Public Schools in Alberta, Canada. They explain that the Edmonton school district has the advantage of a large computerized database of teacher comments. The district even has the ability to include scanned photographs of students and their teachers. This allows the district to generate highly personalized report cards.

Exhibit 6.17 depicts some sample comments for a high school student named Mander.

Exhibit 6.17 Narrative Comments for Sample Student, Mander

Mathematics
This term Mander has studied the basic skills of algebra. In particular, he has studied units on the operations of polynomials, equation solving and factoring polynomials. Class time is used wisely. He organizes work effectively. He aims for excellence. Keep up the good work Mander!

Spanish
In our Spanish class we have been studying basic concepts of grammar and syntax. We have continued working on building a basic vocabulary to be used for meaningful oral and written expression. We have researched and discussed some cultural traits of various Spanish speaking countries. Mander has had the opportunity to participate in a variety of activities designed to enhance his appreciation and ability to communicate in Spanish. He makes a positive contribution to the class. Mander is always willing to participate and help his peers in class. Caramba, hombre, que bien!

Art
In Art 10, Mander developed techniques in watercolor and acrylic painting. He applied knowledge of color theory and painting techniques in several compositions. We also had a guest artist visit us. Next term's projects will include stretching a canvas and creating a composition in acrylics. Mander is improving in the area of acrylic color blending and should concentrate on brush technique and careful attention to assignment requirements and problem solving. Mander is a talented artist and is enjoyable to have in class.

Note: From "Reporting Achievement at the Secondary Level: What and How" (pp. 132-133), by J. Bailey and J. McTighe in T. R. Guskey (Ed.), 1996, *ASCD Yearbook, 1996: Communicating Student Learning.* Alexandria, VA: Association for Supervision and Curriculum Development. Copyright © 1996 by ASCD. All rights reserved.

Narrative comments put "meat on the bones" of letter grades and descriptions of levels of performance. They can describe the nature of projects and activities and the student's interactions with those projects and activities, whereas the abstract symbols cannot. As the example from Edmonton Public Schools illustrates, narrative comments can personalize report cards.

Student-Led Conferences

Perhaps the ultimate form of a personalized reporting system is student-led conferences. As the name implies, a student-led conference is a conference led by a student in which she reports her standing and progress on various standards and benchmarks. Commonly, during such a conference, the student provides evidence to support the evaluations of her progress on specific standards—projects, portfolio entries, homework assignments, and the like. Ideally, the evaluations of student performance on specific standards should be arrived at cooperatively via an assessment conference between teacher and student (see chapter 5 for a discussion).

The benefits of student-led conferences have been extolled by many educators (see e.g., Guyton & Fielstein, 1989; Hubert, 1989; Little & Allan, 1989). Many educators who have worked with this approach recommend that the conference be highly structured. Countryman and Schroeder (1996) found that providing students with a script of what they should say to parents and how they should interact lessened student apprehension and significantly increased the quality of the conferences. Students even practiced using the script a number of times before the actual conference. Countryman and Schroeder's script is reprinted in Exhibit 6.18 (see next page).

Countryman and Schroeder (1996) report that the results of the student-led conferences were immediately apparent. One parent wrote, "I felt my son understood better what he was doing in the classroom, and I was impressed with his base knowledge" (p. 67). Perhaps the most telling comments came from students, reported by Countryman and Schroeder:

One student summed it up when he wrote,
"I liked the positive comments my parents gave me and it was great to see the look on my parents' faces when they saw my good work."

Another student commented,
"That's the longest time my parent has ever sat down and listened to me."

Another said,
"Yeah, my mother doesn't usually say much to me about school, but, since conferences, she is still saying nice things and how proud she is of me and this is nice."

A usually silent girl wrote,
"I liked being able to talk in my conference."

This potential for increased parent-student communication is an unexpected bonus of student-led conferences. (p. 66)

Exhibit 6.18 Student-Led Conference Script

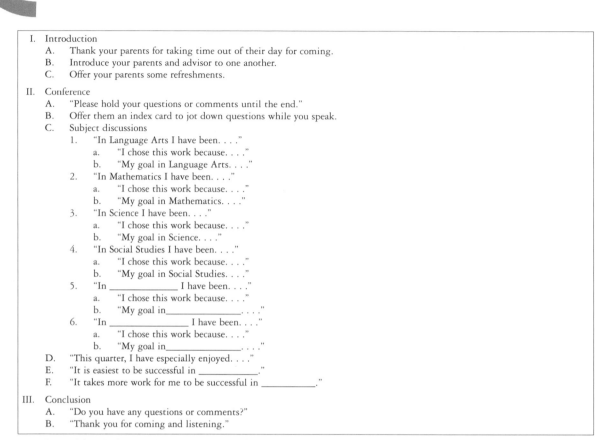

> I. Introduction
>   A. Thank your parents for taking time out of their day for coming.
>   B. Introduce your parents and advisor to one another.
>   C. Offer your parents some refreshments.
>
> II. Conference
>   A. "Please hold your questions or comments until the end."
>   B. Offer them an index card to jot down questions while you speak.
>   C. Subject discussions
>   1. "In Language Arts I have been. . . ."
>   a. "I chose this work because. . . ."
>   b. "My goal in Language Arts. . . ."
>   2. "In Mathematics I have been. . . ."
>   a. "I chose this work because. . . ."
>   b. "My goal in Mathematics. . . ."
>   3. "In Science I have been. . . ."
>   a. "I chose this work because. . . ."
>   b. "My goal in Science. . . ."
>   4. "In Social Studies I have been. . . ."
>   a. "I chose this work because. . . ."
>   b. "My goal in Social Studies. . . ."
>   5. "In _____ I have been. . . ."
>   a. "I chose this work because. . . ."
>   b. "My goal in_____. . . ."
>   6. "In _____ I have been. . . ."
>   a. "I chose this work because. . . ."
>   b. "My goal in_____. . . ."
>   D. "This quarter, I have especially enjoyed. . . ."
>   E. "It is easiest to be successful in _____."
>   F. "It takes more work for me to be successful in _____."
>
> III. Conclusion
>   A. "Do you have any questions or comments?"
>   B. "Thank you for coming and listening."

Note: From "When Students Lead Parent-Teacher Conferences," by L. L. Countryman and M. Schroeder, 1996, in *Educational Leadership*, 53(7), 64-68. Copyright © 1996 ASCD. All rights reserved.

Summary And Recommendations

In this chapter we have considered the question, How will student progress on standards be reported? If national-, state-, or district-level assessments are used, then a district should report scores on these tests in such a way that they can be interpreted relative to performance on specific standards. However, at best, these types of assessments should be considered a supplement to classroom-based assessment. If a single letter grade is used to report progress on standards at the classroom level, then the "cumulative" approach to assigning grades must be replaced by an informed-judgment approach. Although single letter grades are firmly entrenched in the culture of education, the best way to report student progress is by individual scores on individual standards. Ideally, this should be done in lieu of overall letter grades. However, as a transition strategy, a school or district might use overall grades and report by individual standards. Additionally, narrative comments, although labor intensive, are always a useful complement to any reporting system. Finally, student-led conferences appear to have great benefit both for students and parents.

172

Chapter 7

Who Will Be Held Accountable And For What Will They Be Held Accountable?

The question of who will be held accountable is one that is commonly overlooked. Most districts and schools automatically think in terms of holding individual students accountable for meeting standards. However, a viable option is to hold individual schools accountable. In this chapter we consider this option first and then describe the option of holding students accountable. We then address the question of what types of standards individual schools or individual students should be held accountable for meeting.

Holding Schools Accountable: The Kentucky Model

Rather than hold individual students accountable for meeting specific standards, individual schools can be the unit of accountability. This is the approach used in Kentucky. As described by Guskey (1994), the Kentucky school reform effort began in June of 1989 when the Kentucky Supreme Court ruled that the public school system in the Commonwealth was "unconstitutional" because children were not being provided with an equal opportunity to have an adequate education. This ruling provided the impetus for the Kentucky Educational Reform Act (KERA). Guskey (1994) notes that KERA is one of the most comprehensive pieces of education reform legislation ever enacted in the United States:

> It addresses nearly every aspect of public education in the Commonwealth, including administration, governance and finance, school organizations, accountability, personal development, curriculum, and assessment. (p. 1)

To enact this revolutionary legislation, the Kentucky Instructional Results Information System (KIRIS) was established. It had two primary functions: "developing a statewide method for ensuring local school accountability for student achievement . . . [and] helping local schools enhance their ability to use ongoing assessment to improve instruction" (Winograd & Webb, 1994, p. 21).

For the purposes of this discussion, a key aspect of the KIRIS initiative is that it holds individual schools, as opposed to individual students, accountable for obtaining certain levels of achievement. As described by researcher C. Scott Trimble (1994): "According to the statute, the school is to be the "basic unit" of accountability" (p. 40).

Trimble explains that the state accountability system for schools is based on the computation of an "accountability index" for each school. This is done by establishing a "baseline" score using the results from assessments administered in the spring of the 1991-1992 school year. The Kentucky State Board for Elementary and Secondary Education then established a "threshold" score for each school, which represents the minimum gain a school is expected to exhibit by the end of the following biennium. Threshold scores are computed by using a combination of cognitive and noncognitive measures. The cognitive measures include traditional forced-choice tests, performance tasks, and portfolio assessments that are given to a representative sample of students in a school. The noncognitive factors include measures of attendance, dropout, retention rate (failure to promote to next grade), and successful transition to adult life.

Schools that exceed the threshold score by one point or more within a two-year period are given a financial reward. Schools that do not meet the threshold score must engage in a number of compensatory activities depending on how much below the threshold they are. These activities include (1) developing a school improvement plan detailing how it will raise specific scores used in calculating the threshold score, (2) receiving extra funds to implement the plan, and (3) being visited by a "distinguished educator," a state-appointed consultant who is trained in evaluating a school's strengths and weaknesses relative to meeting the threshold score.

The most severe situation a school can face is to be classified as a school "in crisis." This occurs when a school's index falls significantly below the threshold score (i.e., declines five or more points). Trimble (1994) explains that the consequences of such a decline are severe:

> Some of the consequences of being declared a school in crisis include the requirement to develop a school improvement plan and the assignment of a Kentucky Distinguished Educator. In this case, however, the Distinguished Educator must evaluate the staff at the school within 6 months and determine the disposition of all full- and part-time certified staff members, including such options as continued employment, transfer to another site, or dismissal. The principal of the affected school must notify all parents of students in the school of its classification and of their right to transfer their child to a school that is not considered "in crisis." (p. 41)

The success of the Kentucky model illustrates that the school, as opposed to the individual student, can be an effective unit of accountability.

Holding Students Accountable

When individual students are held personally accountable for meeting specific standards, the model is commonly thought of as being outcome based. Unfortunately, this term can elicit strong negative reactions in educators and noneducators alike. We recommend a *standards-based model*, which has significant similarities and differences when compared to outcome-based education; these are described in the latter part of this chapter. However, given the notoriety of outcome-based education and its strong relationship to standards-based education, it is important to consider the nature of outcome-based education in some detail.

Outcome-Based Education

One of the problems with outcome-based education is that it means different things to different people. Education reporter John O'Neil (1994) notes, "At one level, outcome-based education is the simple principle that decisions about curriculum and instruction should be driven by the outcomes we'd like children to display at the end of their educational experiences" (p. 6). Wiggins explains that outcome-based education is "a simple matter of making sure that you're clear on what teaching should accomplish. . . . and adjusting your teaching and assessing as necessary to accomplish what you set out to accomplish" (in O'Neil, 1994, pp. 6-7). At a general level, then, outcome-based education can be described as the process of identifying what students should learn and then making sure that curriculum, teaching, and assessment are designed to support these learning goals (i.e., the intended outcomes). At a more specific level, outcome-based education has a very precise meaning and a strong rationale.

Outcome-based education has a strong underlying logic and an interesting history that includes at least two other education reform efforts: *competency-based education* and *mastery learning*. Researcher Gwennis McNeir (1993) notes that although outcome-based education is considered to be a relatively new reform initiative, its roots date back to the early 1960s when educators began to realize that little attention was being paid to the actual learning outcomes of education. The emphasis instead was on educational "inputs," such as the amount of time allocated for a course of study, the number of books in the library, the physical facilities, and the like. As discussed in chapter 1, the Coleman Report released in 1966 was highly instrumental in demonstrating the need for a shift in emphasis from educational inputs to educational outputs, or learning outcomes. Some educators reasoned that outputs should be stated in terms of minimum competencies. This reasoning spawned the competency-based movement, which focused on determining the extent to which students demonstrated minimum understanding and skills in core content areas. A 1992 report by the U.S. Congress Office of Technology Assessment (OTA) explains the rationale of the minimum competency movement:

- All or almost all students in designated grades take paper-and-pencil tests designed to measure a set of skills deemed essential for future life and work.

- The State or locality has established a passing score or acceptable standard of performance on these tests.
- The State or locality may use test results to: a) make decisions about grade-level promotion, high school graduation, or the awarding of diplomas; b) classify students for remedial or other special services; c) allocate certain funds to school districts; or d) evaluate or certify school districts, schools, or teachers. (p. 59)

The cornerstone of the minimum competency movement was testing at the end of specific grade levels. Students who did not pass a grade-level test could be denied promotion to the next level (Burns & Klingstedt, 1973). The use of minimum competency testing increased greatly in the late 1970s and early 1980s. Prior to 1975, only a few states mandated minimum competency testing. By 1980, 29 states had implemented legislation that required students to pass minimum competency tests, and eight more states had legislation pending. Eleven of the states with legislation in place required that students pass a minimum competency test prior to graduation from high school (see Berk, 1986a).

By the mid 1980s, minimum competency testing was on the decline, primarily because of its heavy reliance on end-of-level testing. Educators using end-of-level testing assumed that the barrier of passing a test would provide all of the necessary incentives to improve achievement. This assumption was simply not accurate; student achievement was not significantly improved by the heavy emphasis on testing (Office of Technology Assessment [OTA], 1992).

With the perceived failure of the minimum competency movement, some educators turned their attention to making instruction, as opposed to testing, the cornerstone of schooling. It was in this environment that the mastery learning movement reached its peak. (We should note here that many of the issues we address about mastery learning are now being reconciled through a new model currently in development [Guskey, 1996c]. Therefore, the following comments should be considered to apply to the original model only.)

Guskey (1995) explains that Benjamin Bloom of the University of Chicago was the architect of mastery learning. According to Guskey, Bloom was motivated by a desire to make group instruction as effective as one-on-one tutoring. Bloom's research (1984) and that of others (Block, 1971, 1974; Block & Burns, 1976; Block, Efthim, & Burns, 1989; Burns, 1987; Guskey, 1980, 1985, 1987; Guskey & Gates, 1986; Levine & Associates, 1985) had shown that with tutoring, virtually any student, regardless of socioeconomic status or natural aptitude, could master even the most complex content. Bloom posited that the great variation found in levels of achievement among students could be largely eliminated by adhering to the basic operating principles of one-to-one tutoring, which research consistently had shown would enhance the achievement of virtually any student. Bloom observed that most large-group instruction involved the presentation of information (usually organized around a textbook) for a set interval of time. The interval ended with a test to determine how well students had learned what the teacher had taught. Under these conditions, the distribution of achievement in a classroom looked like the bell-shaped curve with which educators are so familiar (see Figure 7.1).

Figure 7.1 Distribution of Achievement in Most Traditional Classrooms

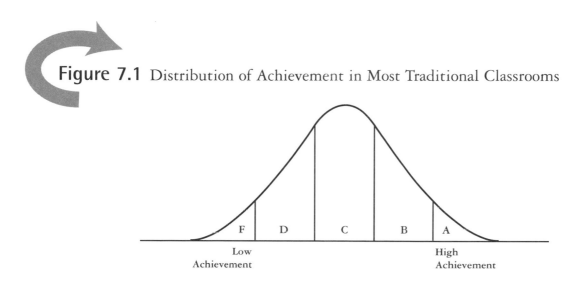

Note: From "Mastery Learning" (p. 93), by T. R. Guskey, 1995, in J. H. Block, S. T. Everson, and T. R. Guskey (Eds.), *School Improvement Programs: A Handbook for Educational Leaders*, New York: Scholastic. Reprinted with permission of J. H. Block.

Guskey (1995) explains that Bloom conceived of a much more useful relationship between instruction and testing:

> Bloom saw dividing the material to be learned into units and checking on students' learning with a test at the end of each unit as useful instructional techniques. He believed, however, that the tests used by most teachers did little more than show for whom the initial instruction was or was not appropriate. If, on the other hand, these tests were accompanied by a *feedback and corrective* procedure, they could serve as valuable learning tools. That is, instead of using these tests solely as evaluation devices marking the end of each unit, Bloom recommended they be used to diagnose individual learning difficulties (feedback) and to prescribe specific remediation procedures (correctives). (p. 94)

In the Bloom model, then, testing occurred at the beginning of a unit of instruction. This testing provided valuable information for both teacher and students, identifying which students had mastered the content even before instruction began and what type of instruction those who had not mastered the content must receive. Bloom posited that it is precisely this type of corrective feedback that takes place when an individual student works with a tutor. If the student makes an error, the tutor provides feedback and then helps the student correct the error.

Research found that this method of instruction—dubbed *mastery learning* in 1968 by Bloom—produced a distribution of achievement that was significantly different from the distribution of achievement found in most traditional classrooms. This distribution is depicted in Figure 7.2.

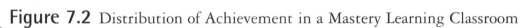

Figure 7.2 Distribution of Achievement in a Mastery Learning Classroom

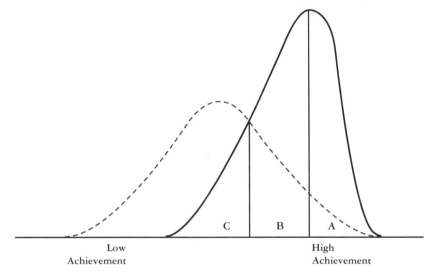

Note: From "Mastery Learning" (p. 97), by T. R. Guskey, 1995, in J. H. Block, S. T. Everson, and T. R. Guskey (Eds.), *School Improvement Programs: A Handbook for Educational Leaders*, New York: Scholastic. Reprinted with permission of J. H. Block.

Guskey (1995) explains that under mastery learning conditions, 80 percent of students reach the same high level of success that only about 20 or 30 percent do under traditional approaches to instruction. Although mastery learning has been criticized (see e.g., Slavin, 1987), its effectiveness has a strong research base (see Guskey, 1990a, 1990b).

In spite of its rather impressive research record, mastery learning has not taken hold as a major vehicle for reform in American education. There are two probable reasons for this. First, most schools and districts that implemented mastery learning identified far too many highly specific learning objectives. For example, the Chicago Mastery Learning Project identified 1,400 learning objectives for kindergarten through grade eight for a single subject area, language arts. An individual teacher was held accountable for 271 objectives covering such discrete skills as syllabication, the use of guide words in a dictionary, and alphabetizing. This level of detail became so cumbersome that many teachers rejected the basic concept of mastery learning simply because of the amount of work involved (Jones, Friedman, Tinzmann & Cox, 1985).

Another problem with mastery learning was the relatively explicit and somewhat restrictive instructional process necessary to implement the model. This process is depicted in Figure 7.3.

Figure 7.3 The Mastery Learning Instructional Process

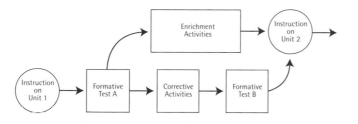

Note: From "Mastery Learning" (p. 100), by T. R. Guskey, 1995, in J. H. Block, S. T. Everson, and T. R. Guskey (Eds.), *School Improvement Programs: A Handbook for Educational Leaders*, New York: Scholastic. Reprinted with permission of J. H. Block.

As powerful as the mastery learning model was in some ways, it still required that all units of instruction begin with a formative test, employ correctives and feedback for those students who did not meet the criterion score on the formative test, use enrichment activities for those who did meet the criterion on the test, and so on. To provide more instructional flexibility to mastery learning, researcher Beau Jones and her colleagues (Jones, Friedman, Tinzmann, & Cox, 1985) developed "instruction-enriched mastery learning." However, this also proved too restrictive for teachers who were used to a great deal of academic freedom.

As Spady (1995) notes, the instructional model explicit in mastery learning was simply too radical for modern American education:

> Mastery learning as an instructional strategy could not address or overcome the myriad organizational factors in schools that militated against its widespread and full blown use. It was very much like putting a large, round peg (mastery) into a small square hole (the inertia of a time-defined system). The two were inherently incompatible, and the hole represented the stronger force by far. (p. 392)

The demise of mastery learning set the stage for *outcome-based education* (OBE). Chief architect Spady wished to capitalize on the strengths of mastery learning while improving on its weaknesses.

In a series of works (Spady, 1988, 1995; Spady & Marshall, 1991), Spady defined the underlying tenets of OBE. He credited the early work of psychologist John Carroll as the basis for OBE's unique perspective on the use of time. Carroll (1963) observed that schools were tremendously tolerant of individual differences in student achievement but tremendously intolerant of differences in the amount of time it took for students to learn. Carroll reasoned that if schools were willing to tolerate differences in the amount of time it takes students to learn, drastic reductions in the variation in achievement among students would result. Spady asserted that mastery learning did not go far enough in providing students flexibility in the amount of time they could take to master a learning objective because most mastery learning models still were tied to the notion of entire classes of students moving through a set of learning objectives within a given interval of time. The enrichment loop depicted in Figure 7.3 was basically the only vehicle mastery learning had for dealing with students who moved quickly through the learning objectives. During a unit of instruction, those students who initially demonstrate competence in the learning objectives were directed to engage in enrichment activities. Guskey (1995) describes the nature and function of enrichment activities in the following way:

> In most group-based applications of mastery learning, correctives are accompanied by enrichment or extension activities for students who attain mastery from the initial teaching. Enrichment activities provide these students with exciting opportunities to broaden and expand their learning. To be effective, these enrichments must be both *rewarding* and *challenging*. In general, they are related to the subject area being studied, but need not be tied directly to the content of a particular unit. Hence, enrichment offers an excellent means of involving students in challenging, higher-level activities such as those designed for the gifted and talented. (p. 99)

According to the theory of enrichment activities, while the teacher works with those students who need correctives, the other students work on self-selected enrichment activities. Unfortunately, in some situations in which mastery learning was used, these enrichment activities were less than challenging and, in some cases, devolved into "time fillers" to occupy those students who have exhibited mastery over the content while those who had not, caught up.

Seeing the potential pitfalls of enrichment, Spady attempted to devise a system in which the traditional structure of courses would neither slow students down nor rush their development. To aid those students who might take longer to learn a subject, some schools and districts that follow Spady's model have adopted an A, B, I grading approach. Students receive a grade of A, B, or I (Incomplete) in courses. Students who do not master the content of a course are expected to make up the Incomplete grade through compensatory activities that are negotiated with the teacher.

To meet the needs of students who can demonstrate mastery of content before a course is over or even before it starts, some districts and schools that use OBE have instituted the practice of "on demand" assessment: Students can demand to be assessed on content when they believe they are ready. If a student believes she can demonstrate competence in the content of a course one week after the course begins, then she can demand to be assessed. Conversely, if the student believes she cannot demonstrate competence in the content until two months after the course is over, then she can demand to be assessed at this later date.

Rather than place the decision regarding testing solely in the hands of students, some schools and districts have made this a joint decision involving the student and the teacher. As described by educators Tim Waters, Don Burger, and Susan Burger (1995), on-demand assessments have the following characteristics:

> Students may elect to pass up the scheduled test or take it over if and when they and the teacher decide they are ready to demonstrate mastery. (p. 39)

Spady's model, then, breaks the potentially restrictive education practice of expecting all students to progress through course content at about the same pace. In this respect, Spady's model differs substantially from mastery learning.

Perhaps Spady's biggest digression from the mastery learning model was in the area of the nature of outcomes. Spady posited a particular view of the nature of outcomes. In fact, those using an OBE approach must write outcomes in a very specific way. This approach to outcomes contrasts sharply with the mastery learning approach, which simply noted that teachers should consciously set learning outcomes. Guskey's comments (1995) illustrate the somewhat loose approach mastery learning took toward the design of learning outcomes:

> Admittedly, identifying the desired learning goals requires teachers to make some very crucial decisions. They must decide, for example, what concepts or skills are most important for students to learn and most central to students' understanding of the subject. But, it is also important for all teachers to recognize that they are already making these decisions. Every time a test is administered, a paper is graded, or any evaluation of learning is made, teachers communicate to their students what they consider to be most important. The use of mastery learning simply compels teachers to confront these decisions more carefully and more thoughtfully than usual. (p. 103)

For Spady (1992), an outcome has specific and necessary characteristics. First, an outcome is "a demonstration of learning that occurs at the END of a learning experience" (p. 6). It is not a grade or test score but an actual demonstration of competence in an authentic context. Second, an outcome must represent significant learning. In fact, Spady (1994) wrote, content knowledge in and of itself could not be considered an outcome: "Content alone . . . cannot be an outcome because it is inherently inert" (p. 18). In his landmark article "Choosing Outcomes of Significance" (1994), Spady explained that the most noteworthy educational outcomes are those that focus on ten complex role performances:

- team members and partners
- supporters and contributors

- teachers and mentors
- creators and producers
- planners
- problem finders and solvers
- implementers and performers
- leaders and organizers
- listeners and communicators
- learners and thinkers

Spady asserted that these role performances occur as people carry out their day-to-day responsibilities. Because these performances involve a high degree of generalizability across time and situation, they should be the basis for developing exit outcomes.

Influenced by Spady's ideas, a number of states began constructing outcomes designed directly or indirectly around the ten role performances. For example, under the Oregon Education Act for the 21st Century, the Oregon Department of Education (1994) identified, among others, the following outcomes:

- deliberate on public issues
- interpret human experiences
- think
- collaborate

As a result of revising their state graduation rule, the state of Minnesota (see Minnesota Department of Education, 1993) identified the following outcomes:

- acts responsibly as a citizen
- makes lifework decisions
- communicates effectively
- directs own learning
- thinks purposefully
- works productively with others

Similarly, as a consequence of Wisconsin Act 269, the Wisconsin Department of Public Instruction (1994) identified the following outcomes:

- makes informed decisions by examining options and anticipating consequences of actions
- responds to the aesthetic and intellectual aspects of an event, performance, or product
- identifies personal interests and goals and pursues them

The movement to identify very generalizable, real-world outcomes was also embraced by individual school districts. For example, Exhibit 7.1 shows the five general outcomes and more specific indicators identified by one district in Colorado.

Exhibit 7.1 General Outcomes Identified by a Colorado School District

---

Outcome 1: A Self-Directed Learner

- Sets priorities and achievable goals
- Monitors and evaluates progress
- Creates options for self
- Assumes responsibility for actions
- Creates a positive vision for self

Outcome 2: A Collaborative Worker

- Monitors own behavior as a group member
- Assesses and manages group functioning
- Demonstrates interactive communication
- Demonstrates consideration for individual differences

Outcome 3: A Complex Thinker

- Uses a wide variety of strategies for managing complex issues
- Selects strategies appropriate to the resolution of complex issues and applies the strategies with accuracy and thoroughness
- Accesses and uses topic-relevant knowledge

Outcome 4: A Quality Producer

- Creates products that achieve their purpose
- Creates products appropriate to their intended audience
- Creates products that reflect craftsmanship
- Uses appropriate resources/technology

Outcome 5: A Community Contributor

- Demonstrates knowledge about his or her diverse communities
- Takes action
- Reflects on role as a community contributor

Note: From "Assessing the Big Outcomes," by N. Redding, 1991, in *Educational Leadership*, 49(8), 49-53. Copyright © 1991 by ASCD. All rights reserved.

In summary, OBE differs from mastery learning in at least two significant ways. First, mastery learning does little to break the convention of students moving at a relatively similar pace through subject matter, whereas OBE requires that students be allowed to progress toward learning outcomes at their own individual rates regardless of the constraints imposed by schedules and course structures. Second, mastery learning does not place constraints on the format or nature of learning outcomes, whereas OBE mandates that exit outcomes be designed as demonstrations that illustrate competence in broad life-role skills as opposed to specific subject-area content. We might also add that mastery learning has an explicit model of instruction, whereas OBE does not. (Spady is somewhat silent on instructional practices in his writings.)

Another difference between mastery learning and OBE is the research base on their effectiveness. Research demonstrating the effectiveness of mastery learning is extensive, whereas research demonstrating the underlying effectiveness of OBE is rather sparse. As examples of the effectiveness of the OBE approach, Spady (1995) offers Glendale Union High School District in Glendale, Arizona, and Oak Park River-Forest High School in Oak Park, Illinois, both of which sport impressive academic accomplishments. In both schools, after the OBE approach was implemented, students from all socioeconomic levels exhibited gains in academic achievement as measured by classroom assessments and standardized tests. In spite of the number of districts and schools that have attempted to implement OBE, there is relatively little research to support it. Researchers Karen Evans and Jean King (1994), for example, concluded after reviewing the research on OBE that OBE is an unproven entity.

Recently, OBE has met with severe criticisms from a number of quarters. As reported by researchers Barbara Gaddy, T. William Hall, and Robert Marzano (1996), it has become so prominent a target for criticism that two of the largest education journals devoted entire issues in 1994 to the controversy. Specifically, the March 1994, issue of *Educational Leadership*, with a circulation of over 200,000, was entitled "The Challenge of Outcome-Based Education." Similarly, the September 1994, issue of the journal *School Administrator* was entitled "Outcomes: The Dirtiest Word in School Reform."

Many of the attacks on OBE have come from groups that claim to represent conservative Christian values. One such group is Beverly LaHaye's Concerned Women for America. LaHaye (1994) notes that Spady's conception of OBE is highly objectionable "because it completely restructures education as we know it" (p. 28). To her credit, LaHaye is quite specific about her objections to OBE. Specifically, she finds fault with the highly general nature of its exit outcomes and the lack of emphasis it places on traditional subject matter.

Others are less discriminating in their criticisms. For example, Phyllis Schlafly, founder of the Eagle Forum, levels the following charges at all OBE efforts:

1. OBE is packaged in a deceptive language that appears to be mischievously chosen to mislead parents. . . .

2. OBE uses students as guinea pigs in a vast social experiment. . . .

3. OBE is a dumbed-down egalitarian scheme that stifles individual potential for excellence and achievement. . . .

4. OBE sets up a computer file on each child. . . . The computer records how the child responds to behavioral modifications . . . and whether he develops positive attitudes toward the mandated outcomes. ("What's Wrong," 1993, pp. 1-3)

As broad and extreme as Schlafly's accusations are, they are mild when compared with some others. For example, education researchers Ann-Maureen Pliska and Judith McQuade (1994) report:

> Typically, the criticisms have been emotionally charged, well organized, and well publicized. Among the more inflammatory anti-OBE materials is *The New World Order*, a videotape widely circulated by Citizens for Excellence in Education (CEE), a national Fundamentalist Christian coalition. The video depicts a Christian student who is declared "at risk" and targeted for special services in the public schools. In one scene, the child is taken away as uniformed guards restrain the parent, who struggles to save her daughter from the clutches of the state. (pp. 66-67)

Still other organizations define anything they are against as OBE. In a 1994 article for *Educational Leadership*, education reporter Linda Chion-Kenney reports:

> The Michigan Alliance of Families takes it a step further. In its report, "The ABC's of OBE: Does Your School Have OBE?" the alliance lists 26 ways to tell whether your school is doing OBE. Among them: site-based management, inclusive education, team teaching, individualized education plans, professional development programs in consensus building and collaboration, cooperative learning, peer tutoring, thematic teaching, year-round schooling, portfolios, continual assessment of growth and development, multi-age level grouping, and multi-year improvement plans.
>
> According to the Michigan group, your school also is pursuing OBE if "you hear reference to mastery learning, performance-based education, Glasser's Reality Therapy, management by objectives, planning programming budgeting systems, Total Quality Management, Accelerated Schools, Effective Schools, Comer Schools, Johnson City Schools, Schools for the 21st Century, Sizer's Coalition of Essential Schools, Professional Development Schools, and outcomes-driven development model, all of which are outcome-based education." (p. 14)

Certainly, many of the criticisms of OBE are outlandish. However, legitimate concerns about OBE are its lack of a strong research base and the questionable nature of the broad outcomes it advocates. As education reformer Bruno Manno (1994) explains, "Spady-type outcomes are so broad as to be value laden and so vague as to make it impossible to measure whether students are achieving them in any useful way" (p. 25).

Standards-Based Education

In this book we attempt to describe a new structure for school reform entitled standards-based education. Our intent is to draw from the best ideas contained in mastery learning and OBE. Table 7.1 highlights some of the similarities and differences between standards-based education, mastery learning, and OBE. As we conceive of it, standards-based education has eight basic tenets. We should note that these tenets represent our conceptualization of standards-based education with our preferences and biases. No doubt others would articulate different tenets representing different conceptualizations of standards-based education.

1. *Standards-based education holds students accountable for specific schoolwide or districtwide content standards that have accompanying benchmarks.* Mastery learning sometimes leaves the identification of outcomes to individual teachers, whereas standards-based education makes the identification of learning standards a school-wide or district-wide endeavor. This is similar to OBE's emphasis on the school-wide or district-wide construction of outcomes. However, unlike OBE, which has general outcomes that deal with life roles, standards-based education and mastery learning hold students accountable for specific content knowledge. Unlike mastery learning, which involves thousands of outcomes, standards-based education involves scores of standards.

2. *Standards-based education holds students accountable for specific thinking and reasoning standards.* The thinking and reasoning standards described in chapter 2 represent a type of information and skill that a district or school ideally should hold students accountable for learning. Neither mastery learning nor OBE places explicit emphasis on this type of information and skill, although neither model precludes teaching and reinforcing thinking and reasoning. Because of their importance to learning, we include them as a critical aspect of our definition of standards-based education. The thinking and reasoning standards may either be set apart as a separate category of standards or embedded in specific subject areas. Our preference is to establish a separate category of standards so that they might be addressed in a wide variety of subject areas.

3. *Standards-based education separates out lifelong learning standards.* Like OBE, standards-based education identifies lifelong learning standards as a unique category. However, unlike OBE, these standards are not superordinate to the other types of standards. Also unlike OBE, standards-based education does not necessarily hold students accountable for these standards. In fact, given the current criticism of these types of standards, it is perhaps advisable to report students' progress on such standards but not to hold students to specific performance levels.

Table 7.1 Comparison of Standards-Based Education with Mastery Learning and OBE

	Research base	Nature and format of outcomes	Identification of outcomes	Student progress through outcomes	Number of outcomes	Instructional model	How students will be asked to apply knowledge	Thinking and reasoning	Reporting emphasis	Assessment
Mastery Learning	Extensive	No constraint on format or nature. Students are held accountable to specific content knowledge	Commonly left to teachers who consult textbooks and curriculum guides	Students move at similar pace	Thousands	Explicit model	Does not prescribe how students will be asked to apply knowledge	No explicit emphasis on T&R	Students' standings on specific outcomes	At beginning of unit. Teachers are primary assessors of whether students have met specific outcomes. Commonly traditional forms of assessment are used
OBE	Sparse	General outcomes. LLL standards are unique category, superordinate to others. Students held accountable for LLL standards	Schoolwide or districtwide process based on life-role descriptions	At their own rate	Commonly 10 or less	No explicit model	Format in which students will apply knowledge "institutionalized" by mandating exit outcomes be written as performance tasks	No explicit emphasis on T&R	Students' standing on specific outcomes	Use of performance tasks as exit requirements
Standards Based	Emerging	Students are held accountable for specific content knowledge. LLL standards are unique category, not superordinate to others. Students not necessarily held accountable for LLL standards	Schoolwide or districtwide process usually informed by national subject-area documents	Varies depending on approach (see chapter 9)	Scores	No explicit model	Does not prescribe how students will be asked to apply knowledge. Encourages application of knowledge through use of performance tasks in class and as external forms of assessment	T&R are critical aspect of	Students' standing on specific standards	Individual classroom teachers. External assessments supplement classroom assessments. Student self-assessment encouraged

Note: OBE = Outcome-based education; LLL = Lifelong learning (standards)

4. *Standards-based education has no explicit, mandatory instructional model.* Unlike mastery learning and like OBE, standards-based education has no mandatory instructional model. Teachers are free to organize instruction in any manner they see fit. However, they are still accountable for students effectively learning necessary knowledge and skills.

5. *Standards-based education emphasizes the application of knowledge.* Standards-based education emphasizes students' application of knowledge; this is similar to OBE's emphasis on demonstrations and exhibitions. However, like mastery learning, standards-based education does not prescribe the manner in which students will be asked to apply knowledge. OBE, on the other hand, institutionalizes the format in which students will apply knowledge by mandating that exit outcomes be written as performance tasks. Standards-based education encourages the application of knowledge through the use of performance tasks in the classroom and through the use of performance tasks as external forms of assessment.

6. *Standards-based education provides direct feedback to students on their standings relative to standards.* Whether reporting is done by specific standards (the preferred method) or by overall letter grades, students within a standards-based system can interpret report cards and transcripts in terms of understanding and skill relative to specific standards. If overall letter grades are used, then a written policy describes the relationship of specific grades to performance on specific standards. This reporting emphasis on specific standards is similar to OBE's emphasis on reporting students' standing on specific outcomes.

7. *Standards-based education relies heavily on classroom teachers for assessment data.* Because student performance on standards is best evaluated by assessing performance multiple times in a variety of ways, individual classroom teachers are the primary source of assessment data in a standards-based system. This is reminiscent of the mastery learning approach within which classroom teachers are the primary determiners of whether students have met specific learner outcomes. Additionally, a standards-based school or district will commonly use external assessments (i.e., assessments designed and administered externally to the classroom) as supplements to classroom assessments.

8. *Standards-based education emphasizes student self-assessment.* Although the classroom teacher is the primary source of assessment data, individual students are also a key source of information. Students are asked to self-assess and provide evidence for their self-assessments on all standards.

These eight tenets form the parameters within which many different versions of a standards-based system can be built. Within these parameters there are still many issues that a district or school must address. The manner in which a district or school addresses these issues can drastically affect the type of standards-based system that it designs. Here we consider four basic issues: (1) the issue of levels, (2) the option of being standards referenced, (3) conjunctive versus compensatory systems, and (4) the issue of students with special needs.

The Issue Of Levels

The issue of levels refers to the grade levels at which a district or school will hold students accountable for meeting specific standards. At one end of the continuum, a district or school could be standards based at every grade level. Within this approach, students are not able to pass from one grade to another without demonstrating competence in the standards and benchmarks specified at that level. At the other end of the continuum, a district or school could be standards based at high school graduation only. Here, students progress from grade level to grade level regardless of their performance on specific standards up until the 12th grade. At that point, students must demonstrate competence on specific standards to receive their diploma. Somewhere in the middle of the continuum is to be standards based at the major transition points with the K-12 sequence of grades. Probably the most logical transition points are

1. between the primary and upper elementary grades;
2. between the upper elementary grades and middle school or junior high school;
3. between middle school or junior high and high school; and
4. at high school graduation.

Within this approach, students must meet the performance standard on specific standards before they can pass from the primary level to the upper elementary level, from the upper elementary level to the middle school level, and so on.

Obviously, the approach with the "lowest stakes" is to be standards based only at high school graduation and the approach with the "highest stakes" is to be standards based at each grade level. This latter position—being standards based at every grade level—seems extreme, particularly when one considers the research on grade-level retention.

There is a common sense belief among noneducators and educators alike that retaining students is advantageous if a student has not demonstrated mastery over the information and skills at his current grade level. As researchers Lorrie Shepard and Mary Lee Smith (1990) note:

> The assumption is that by catching up on prerequisite skills, students should be less at risk for failure when they go on to the next grade. Strict enforcement of academic standards at every grade is expected both to ensure the competence of high school graduates and lower the dropout rate because learning deficiencies would never be allowed to accumulate. (p. 84)

Unfortunately, this common-sense notion is simply not true. In fact, it has been contradicted by virtually all of the research on retention (see Holmes, 1989; Grissom &

Shepard, 1989; Shepard & Smith, 1989, 1990). That research can be summarized in the following way:

- Students who are retained actually perform worse on average at the next grade level than those with similar academic failing who have been promoted to the next grade.

- Dropouts are five times more likely to have repeated a grade than are high school graduates.

- Sending a student to summer school to enhance academic deficiencies costs only about one-fourth of the cost of retaining a student.

- Students perceive retention as a punishment and it generates a level of stress and a sense of failure that takes years to overcome.

Being standards based at every grade level carries the risk of producing an inordinate number of retentions. Indeed, the research against retention is so strong that a district or school should also be cautious about being standards based at major transition points, although we believe that this latter approach could be designed to work well.

The Option Of Being Standards Referenced

Given the dangers of holding students back because they do not meet standards, a viable option is to be *standards referenced*. In a standards-based system, students must demonstrate that they have met the standards at one level before they are allowed to pass on to the next level. In a standards-referenced system, students' standings relative to specific standards are documented and reported; however, students are not held back if they do not meet the required performance levels for the standards. This provides students and parents with highly specific information about students' standing relative to standards but allows students to progress through the system even if they have not met specific standards.

Wiggins (1993a, 1996) was perhaps the first modern-day reformer to recognize the utility of a standards-referenced approach. He explains that it is unrealistic to expect all students to meet high standards in all content areas. For Wiggins, being standards referenced represents a powerful alternative to the sometimes precarious endeavor of being standards based. It represents a major shift in perspectives. Rather than viewing themselves as "gate-keepers" who decide who is permitted to pass from one level to the next, Wiggins suggests that educators might see one of their major roles as providing information; specifically, they should provide students with highly accurate information regarding their standing in terms of standards. Wiggins posits that this type of nonthreatening "referencing" in and of itself may provide students with the motivation to reach levels of achievement to which they would otherwise not aspire. This is based on the assumption that if students are presented with a goal (i.e., a specific performance standard) along with accurate information as to where they stand relative to the goals (i.e., their level of performance), they quite naturally may be motivated to improve their performance. This assumption is supported by much of the research on feedback (e.g., Glasser, 1981; Powers, 1973).

In effect, if a district or school chooses to be standards based at the high school graduation level only, it could be standards referenced at all other levels. That is, students' progress on standards would be reported at each grade level, but it would be only at the level of high school graduation that students would be held responsible for meeting specific standards only. Similarly, if a district was standards based at the four transition points described above, it could be standards referenced at the other grade levels. This is depicted in Figure 7.4.

Figure 7.4 Options for Combining Standards-Based and Standards-Referenced Approaches

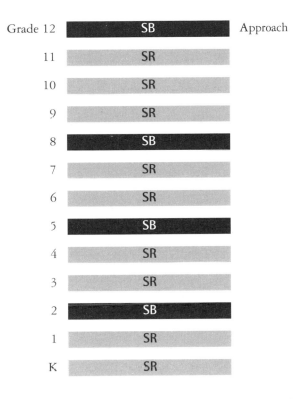

SB = *Standards Based* (students are held accountable for meeting standards)
SR = *Standards Referenced* (students' progress is reported out at each grade level)

Mixing standards-based and standards-referenced approaches provides districts and schools with a wide range of options that can retain the inherent power in holding students accountable for meeting certain standards but alleviate the dangers inherent in retaining students at inappropriate levels.

Compensatory Versus Conjunctive Approaches

One important yet technical consideration a district or school should address is whether to use a *conjunctive* or a *compensatory* approach to standards. In a conjunctive approach students must reach the minimum performance level on all standards (Plake, Hambelton, & Jaeger, 1995). To illustrate, consider the following science standards:

1. Understands the nature of scientific inquiry and makes effective use of the scientific method.

2. Understands the basic features of earth and earth processes.

3. Understands essential ideas about the composition and structure of the universe and the Earth's place in it.

4. Knows about the diversity and unity that characterize life.

5. Understands the genetic basis for the transfer of biological characteristics from one generation to the next.

6. Understands the cycling of matter and flow of energy through the living environment.

7. Understands basic concepts about the structure and properties of matter.

8. Understands energy types, sources and conversions, and their relationship to heat and temperature.

If these standards are approached using a conjunctive system, a student's performance on each standard is considered individually. For example, a student's performance on science standard 2 is considered in isolation of her performance on the other seven standards. The student might do quite well on standards 2, 3, 4, and 8, yet do quite poorly on standards 1, 5, 6, and 7. Performance on one standard has no bearing on performance on other standards.

In a compensatory approach, performance on one standard affects performance on others (Kifer, 1994). More specifically, performance on one standard can "compensate" for performance on another. To illustrate, assume that a student received the following scores (on a four-point scale) on the eight science standards:

Standard 1: 1

Standard 2: 3

Standard 3: 3

Standard 4: 4

Standard 5: 2

Standard 6: 1

Standard 7: 1

Standard 8: 4

In a compensatory approach, the student's strong performance on standards 2, 3, 4, and 8 would compensate for her weak performance on standards 1, 5, 6, and 7. Usually the compensation is accomplished by averaging the scores on specific standards within a domain. In the example above, the student's average score on the eight science standards would be 2.38. Other approaches include excluding the lowest scores from the average, weighting some standards higher than others in the calculation of the average, and considering the most common score (the mode) as the most representative score.

What About Students With Special Needs?

Since the passage of Public Law 94-142 in 1975, school districts have been required to provide a continuum of services for handicapped students ranging from special schools, to special classes within regular schools, to various part-time placements (Slavin, 1989). That bill generated a great deal of activity in three basic areas: (1) getting children with disabilities who were not in school into school, (2) ensuring that children with handicaps who were in school were receiving the proper services, and (3) guaranteeing a fair process in designing programs for individual students (Roach, 1991).

One of the negative consequences of that bill is that Individual Education Plans (IEP) tended to focus on minimal skills and broad process goals. This emphasis did little to enhance the achievement and aptitude of students with special needs (Braven, O'Reilly, & Moore, 1994; Roach, 1991). The standards movement challenges the tacit assumption that special education students cannot meet high standards. Indeed, this expectation was made explicit by the National Education Goals Panel (1993b):

> The purpose of standards-based reform is to include everyone in deeper understanding of the most important and enduring knowledge and skills. To succeed, the nation must raise achievement at all levels—among the most able as well as the disabled. . . . The standards discussed in this report would apply directly to all students except those, like the severely mentally retarded, whose diagnosis implies a judgment that the student cannot meet them. (p. 27)

How to accomplish the goal laid out by the National Education Goals Panel is the subject of much discussion. One option commonly proposed is to lower the expected level of performance for students with special needs (Braven, O'Reilly, & Moore, 1994; Roach, 1991). Recall from the discussion in chapter 6 that various levels of performance can be associated with each benchmark within a standard. Those levels of performance are commonly labeled advanced, proficient, basic, and novice. Whereas regular education students might be held to the proficient level of performance, special education students might be held to the basic level of performance.

Another option is to increase the amount of time students need to meet specific standards (McLaughlin & Warren, 1992). Here special education students are held to the same level of performance as are regular education students; however, they are simply given significantly more time to attain those performance levels.

A third option is to provide instructional services for special education services above and beyond those provided for regular education students (Braven, O'Reilly, & Moore, 1994). These "extraordinary" services would, no doubt, be similar to those currently provided within compensatory programs (see Slavin, Karweit, & Madden, 1989, for a discussion).

What Will We Hold Students Accountable For Learning?

Ultimately, the most critical question a district or school must answer is, What will we hold students accountable for learning? In general, there are four options to consider when answering this question.

Option 1: Hold students accountable for all standards in all content areas. One option is to hold students accountable for all standards in all content areas. For example, assume that a district or school identified some 75 standards in mathematics, science, language arts, history, foreign language, the arts, health education, and physical education. Under this option, students would be held accountable for meeting all 75 standards. This option has a strong intuitive, but unfortunately naive, appeal. There is a surface-level appeal to the notion that requiring students to meet standards in all subject areas will increase their achievement somewhat uniformly across all domains. However, current research and theory on the nature of intelligence and aptitude do not support this. For example, Gardner (1983, 1991) has posited seven different types of intelligence: language, logical mathematical analysis, spatial representation, musical thinking, the use of the body to solve problems or make things, an understanding of other individuals, and an understanding of ourselves. Competence in one type of intelligence does not necessarily transfer well to competence in another type of intelligence. In fact, according to Gardner's theory, people tend to have highly uneven profiles relative to their competence across these domains; they may be strong in some areas, weak in others, and have moderate competence in still others. This multitrait conception of intelligence and aptitude has been supported by a number of researchers and theorists (Carroll, 1982; Feuerstein, 1980; Fischer, 1980; Gagne, 1977; Guilford, 1967; Meeker, 1969; Perkins, 1981, 1986, 1992; Presseisen, 1987; Sternberg, 1979, 1984, 1991). If this theory is accurate, requiring students to meet standards across all content areas flies in the face of natural learning tendencies. In fact, research and theory support the assertion that forcing students to excel in all areas might detrimentally affect their development in their natural areas of competence.

Option 2: Hold students accountable for standards in the core subjects only. By "core subjects" we mean those that have traditionally formed the basis of what most Americans would consider a "basic" education. Although there is no official list of core subjects, there does appear to be some agreement regarding those subjects that most educators and noneducators consider the basis of a general understanding of our culture. These subjects are

- reading
- writing
- mathematics
- science
- history
- geography

The validity of this list is supported by the fact that these subjects were identified by the governors in the first Education Summit in 1989. Specifically, Goal 3 of the six goals mentions that American students will master complex content in the areas of English (i.e., reading and writing), mathematics, science, history, and geography (National Education Goals Panel [NEGP], 1993b). These are also the areas identified by E. D. Hirsch, Jr. as central to a well-rounded education (Hirsch, 1993a, 1993b, 1993c, 1993d, 1993e, 1993f).

This option is obviously less demanding than the first, yet requires a great deal more of students than is currently the case. In fact, geography is rarely required for high school graduation, and most districts and schools place only moderate expectations on students regarding mathematics, science, and history.

Option 3: Hold students accountable for minimum competencies only. Again, there is no official list of subject areas considered minimal, but there seems to be agreement that reading, writing, and rudimentary aspects of mathematics (i.e., computation and number sense) are essential to success in academic as well as nonacademic endeavors. Evidence for the importance of these subjects can be found in federally funded programs for students at risk. As researchers Robert Slavin, Nancy Karweit, and Nancy Madden (1989) note, the vast majority of Chapter 1 programs for students at risk focus on reading, writing, and mathematics (see also Madden & Slavin, 1989; Slavin & Madden, 1989). Evidence for the rudimentary nature of these domains is also found in the world of work. For example, both the SCANS report (Secretary's Commission, *What Work Requires of Schools: A SCANS Report for America 2000*, 1991) and *Workplace Basics* (Carnevale, Gainer, & Meltzer, 1990) specifically mention reading, writing, and basic mathematics as skill areas that are essential for an effective work force. Finally, these three areas formed the basis of the minimum competency movement of the 1970s (OTA, 1992).

The major problem with this option is that it is minimalistic; it tends to focus on minimum standards as opposed to those that would raise the overall level of understanding and skill for American students.

Option 4: Let students identify the standards for which they will be held accountable. Another option is to have students identify the specific standards they will meet within a limited set of choices. This is in keeping with the current thinking on student-centered learning and self-regulated learning (see Covington, 1983, 1985; McCombs, 1984, 1989; McCombs & Marzano, 1990; Zimmerman, 1990). This theory asserts that students learn best the content that they select based on their interests and aptitude. Additionally, this theory asserts that over time, students will quite naturally see the need for competence in areas to which they might not initially be drawn. This approach is also consistent with what Darling-Hammond and her colleagues (Darling-Hammond, Ancess, & Falk, 1995) refer to as achieving standards without standardization. In other words, students strive for high standards within various subject areas, but the subject area on which students must focus is not standardized.

One drawback to this approach is that it appears to run counter to some strongly held beliefs about the purpose of education. E. D. Hirsch, Jr. (1987), for example, states that "the basic goal of education in a human community is acculturation, the transmission to children of the specific information shared by the adults of the group or polis" (p. xvi). The selection of such "specific information" seems to rule out the possibility that students could be permitted to personally select the content they will cover. Another criticism to this option is that students are not knowledgeable or experienced enough to make decisions concerning which standards they should meet (Frost, 1996).

The Price And Promise Of Standards-Based Education

From the previous discussion, it is reasonable to infer that standards-based education can place extreme demands on a district or a school. Perhaps the most difficult issue standards-based education raises is what to do with students who do not meet the standards at identified transition points. The current system has no obligation to help those who are failing, and apparently many districts and schools opt not to provide any extraordinary support for such students. This was dramatically illustrated in Jonathan Kozol's *Savage Inequalities* (1991). After studying public schools across the country, Kozol concluded that America has two public education systems. One system provides both implicit and explicit support for those who do not demonstrate competence quickly; the other system does not. Unfortunately, the ability and willingness of a school or district to provide such support is a direct function of the level of financial support available. Not surprisingly, districts and schools that serve students from low socioeconomic backgrounds have lower funding available and consequently provide less extraordinary support for those students who need it the most. Within a standards-based system, extraordinary support is mandatory; it is built into the system. Those students who initially do not meet required performance levels must be provided the opportunity and resources to do so at later dates. This approach to schooling would obviously place great demands on the time, energy, and financial resources that are available, which is no small price to pay. Consequently, a district or school should not enter into standards-based reform lightly. It takes a great resolve to effectively design and implement a standards-based system. However, those few districts that have succeeded report that the results justified the effort. One of those districts is Weld County District 6 in Greeley, Colorado.

As reported by educators Waters, Burger, and Burger (1995), the Greeley district serves 13,500 K-12 students, 65% of whom are Anglo, 33% of whom are Hispanic, and 2% are of other ethnicities. One of the primary motivations for designing a standards-based system was not only to increase the achievement of all students in the district but to narrow the gap in achievement among different ethnic and socioeconomic (SES) groups. As in most large districts, middle and high SES groups consistently and significantly outperformed low SES groups, and Anglos consistently and significantly outperformed Hispanics and African Americans. In 1988, the district introduced a standards-based system that focused on reading, writing, and mathematics. As described by Waters, Burger, and Burger (1995):

> We introduced a system that is based, not on grade levels, but on evaluations at various junctures in a student's schooling. Before students can proceed to the next level (for example, middle school), they must demonstrate their mastery of certain concepts and skills in writing, reading, and mathematics that are important for everyone to know. In short, it is no longer acceptable to send students from one level of the system to the next knowing they have not met minimum standards. (p. 35)

The results of their effort were most promising. Figure 7.5 reports the results in writing.

Figure 7.5 District 6 Writing Assessment
Gap Reduction Between Race/Ethnicity and Socioeconomic Groups

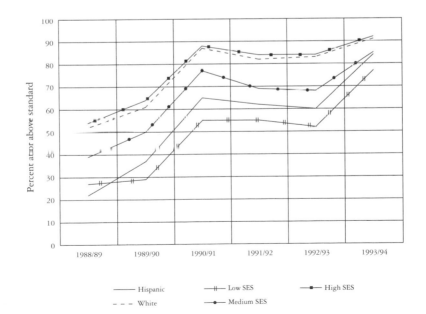

Note: Composite adapted from "Moving Up Before Moving On," by T. Waters, D. Burger, and S. Burger, 1995, *Educational Leadership, 52*(6), 35-40.

The key feature of Figure 7.5 is that there is not only a gradual increase in overall student achievement, but there is a dramatic decrease in the variance among socioeconomic and ethnic groups. Waters, Burger, and Burger (1995) describe this achievement in the following way:

> Since the introduction of the standards-based measures for writing, reading, and mathematics, there has been a dramatic increase in the percentage of students who have met or exceeded the performance standards (the Essential level or higher) in each assessment area.
>
> In 1991-92 and 1992-93, there was a slight decrease, which we believe was a consequence of introducing the new reading test. As teachers concentrated on reading skills, they paid less attention to writing skills than they had in previous years. Performance on the reading assessment improved dramatically in 1991-92, however, and again in 1992-93.
>
> In 1992-93, the new math tests were introduced. Although they, too, required additional time and attention of teachers, we were better prepared this time and so did not lose our focus on writing and reading. By 1993-94, both teachers and students were familiar with the standards and the expectations of the reading, writing, and math assessments.
>
> Overall, our progress has been encouraging and exciting. Each year, more and more students are moving to the next level with the skills required to be successful. Teachers report that new classes of students are better prepared than ever. And as student performance continues to improve, teachers expect more of all students. (p. 38)

Perhaps what is most impressive is that the standards-based emphasis in reading, writing, and mathematics apparently produced positive results on a very general measure of aptitude—namely the ACT (American College Test). There was an overall increase in the achievement of all students as well as a narrowing of the gap between various ethnic and socioeconomic groups.

The success of Weld County District 6 does not appear to be unique. As a result of an effort to collect data on the effectiveness of standards-based education, the Education Commission of the States (ECS) concludes that reform efforts designed around standards are developing an impressive track record. For example, ECS (1996) reports the following results in Colorado:

- In Colorado's San Luis Valley, a district began working to define specific student proficiencies in language arts in 1987. The percentage of high school students passing Adams State College's English Proficiency Examination (an exam used to measure the writing skills of first-year college students) rose from 33% in 1987 to 72% in 1994.

- In a Colorado Springs district, work on standards began in 1989. The percentage of 11th grade students scoring "proficient" or "advanced" on a locally developed writing exam climbed from 60% in 1989 to over 90% in 1994. For 8th grade students, the proportion rose from 30% to 60% over the same period. (p. 12)

ECS (1996) reports the following results in Maryland:

The state expects that 70% of its students will perform at the "satisfactory" level on the Maryland School Performance Assessment Program (MSPAP) by the year 2000. The percentage of schools already reaching that goal climbed from 31.7% in 1993 to 39.7% in 1995. At grades 3, 5 and 8, there have been increases each year in the number of schools that meet or approach the standards in at least one of the assessment categories. In addition:

- In 1993, 158 schools (or 20% of all schools tested) were, in the state's estimation, "far" from meeting the standards in 3rd grade mathematics. By 1995 only 7.7% were "far" from the standard.
- In 1993, 113 schools approached or met the 3rd grade mathematics standards. The total reached nearly 300 in 1995.
- In 1995, elementary school attendance reached the state objective of 95% in 23 out of 24 school systems. (p. 13)

Certainly it is true that standards-based education is difficult to design and implement. However, as evidenced by the discussion above, the rewards appear to be worth the effort. According to Waters, Burger, and Burger (1995), the formula underlying its success appears quite simple:

Students know exactly what is expected of them and where they stand in relationship to standards, which help them focus on continuous improvement. Teachers get accurate feedback on their instruction, and they know what each student needs to do to meet or exceed the next standard. In other words, they can base teaching decisions on solid data rather than on assumptions, and they can make adjustments early on to avoid the downward spiral of remediation. (p. 39)

Summary And Recommendations

In this chapter we have considered the questions of who will be held accountable and what will they be held accountable for learning. One viable unit of accountability is individual schools as opposed to individual students. This is the basic approach used in the state of Kentucky under the Kentucky Educational Reform Act. However, the most common approach is to consider the student as the basic unit of accountability.

This chapter also described the basic characteristics of standards-based education as we define it. To establish a context for this approach, we considered in depth the important distinctions between mastery learning and outcome-based education. Standards-based education attempts to draw from the strengths of both of these reform efforts. If a district or school chooses to be standards based, it must decide whether it will hold students accountable for all standards, for core standards, for minimum standards, or allow students to personally identify those standards for which they will be held accountable. A viable option is to be standards referenced, as opposed to standards based, about some or all standards. Finally, this chapter addressed the power and potential benefits of a standards-based approach.

Chapter 8

What Can I Do By Myself?

Thus far, we have focused our discussion on the issues a single school or entire school district must address if it wishes to organize itself around standards. In this chapter, we consider what an individual teacher can do if he or she wishes to focus on standards. In other words, even if a teacher is in a school or district that is highly traditional and requires that overall letter grades be assigned to all students, he can still organize his curriculum, instruction, and assessment around standards.

Quite obviously, a standards-based or standards-referenced approach to schooling is most effective when implemented at the level of the entire school or, even better, at the level of the entire district. However, an individual teacher can focus on standards in her classroom and still remain within the confines of a traditional grading system. We describe how this can be done in nine steps.

Step 1: Organize Content Into Standards

The first step a teacher must take when organizing her classroom around standards is to think of her course content in terms of standards and benchmarks. This process is greatly enhanced if the teacher utilizes the distinction between declarative and procedural knowledge discussed in chapter 3. Declarative knowledge consists of information—concepts, generalizations, facts, and so on. Procedural knowledge consists of skills and processes. A great deal of research has been conducted on these two types of knowledge (see Anderson, 1983, 1993; Bransford & Franks, 1976; Carroll, 1964; Clark & Clark, 1977; Fitts, 1964; C. H. Frederiksen, 1977; Johnson, 1967, 1969; Klausmeier, 1980, 1985; Lindsay & Norman, 1977; Marzano, 1983; Tennyson & Cocchiarella, 1986; Tennyson & Park, 1980). The more a teacher knows about these two types of knowledge, the more adept she will be at translating her course content into standards and benchmarks. Next we consider both types of knowledge in some depth.

Declarative Standards

Declarative knowledge can be thought of as hierarchic in nature. The most basic way of thinking about organizing declarative knowledge is as vocabulary terms. The most general way is as concepts. Between these two extremes are facts, time sequences, causal networks, episodes, generalizations, and principles. Here we consider these levels in some detail.

Vocabulary Terms

At the most specific level of declarative knowledge are vocabulary terms. In this system, knowing a vocabulary term means understanding the meaning of a word at a very general level. For example, when a student understands declarative knowledge at the level of a vocabulary term, he has a general idea what the word means and no serious misconceptions about its meaning. To organize classroom content as vocabulary terms is to organize it as independent words. The expectation is that students have an accurate, but somewhat surface-level, understanding of the meaning of these terms.

Facts

Facts are a very specific type of declarative content. Facts convey information about specific persons, places, living and nonliving things, and events. They commonly articulate information such as the following:

- The characteristics of a specific person (e.g., The fictitious character Robin Hood first appeared in English literature in the early 1800s).
- The characteristics of a specific place (e.g., Denver is in the state of Colorado).
- The characteristics of specific living and nonliving things (e.g., My dog, Tuffy, is a golden retriever; the Empire State Building is over 100 stories high.).
- The characteristics of a specific event (e.g., Construction began on the leaning tower of Pisa in 1174).

Time Sequences

Time sequences include important events that occurred between two points in time. For example, the events that occurred between President Kennedy's assassination on November 22, 1963, and his burial on November 25, 1963, are organized as a time sequence in most people's memories. First one thing happened, then another, then another.

Cause/Effect Sequences

Cause/effect sequences involve events that produce a product or an effect. A causal sequence can be as simple as a single cause for a single effect. For example, the fact that the game was lost because a certain player dropped the ball in the end zone can be organized as a causal sequence. More commonly, however, effects have complex networks of causes; one event affects another that combines with a third event to affect a fourth that then affects another and so on. For example, the events leading up to the Civil War can be organized as a causal sequence.

Episodes

Episodes are specific events that have (1) a setting (e.g., a particular time and place), (2) specific participants, (3) a particular duration, (4) a specific sequence of events, and (5) a particular cause and effect. For example, the events of Watergate could be organized as an episode: The episode occurred at a particular time and place; it had specific participants; it lasted for a specific duration of time; it involved a specific sequence of events; it was caused by specific events; and it had a specific effect on the country.

Generalizations

Generalizations are statements for which examples can be provided. For example, the statement, "U.S. presidents often come from families that have great wealth or influence" is a generalization, for which examples can be provided. It is easy to confuse some generalizations with some facts. Facts identify characteristics of specific persons, places, living and nonliving things, and events, whereas generalizations identify characteristics about *classes or categories* of persons, places, living and nonliving things, and events. For example, the statement, "My dog, Tuffy, is a golden retriever" is a fact. However, the statement, "Golden retrievers are good hunters" is a generalization. In addition, generalizations identify characteristics about abstractions. Specifically, information about abstractions is always stated in the form of generalizations. Below are examples of the various types of generalizations:

- Characteristics of classes of persons (e.g., It takes at least two years of training to become a fireman).
- Characteristics of classes of places (e.g., Large cities have high crime rates).
- Characteristics of classes of living and nonliving things (e.g., Golden retrievers are good hunting dogs; Firearms are the subject of great debate).
- Characteristics of classes of events (e.g., The Super Bowl is the premier sporting event each year).
- Characteristics of abstractions (e.g., Love is one of the most powerful human emotions).

Principles

Principles are specific types of generalizations that deal with relationships. In general, there are two types of principles found in school-related declarative knowledge: *cause/effect principles* and *correlational principles*.

Cause/effect principles. Cause/effect principles articulate causal relationships. For example, the sentence, "Tuberculosis is caused by the tubercle bacillus" is a cause/effect principle. Although not stated here, understanding a cause/effect principle includes knowledge of the specific elements within the cause/effect system and the exact relationships those elements have to one another. That is, to understand the cause/effect principle regarding tuberculosis and the bacterium, one would have to understand the sequence of events that occur, the elements involved, and the type and strength of relationships between those elements. In short, understanding a cause/effect principle involves a great deal of information.

Correlational principles. Correlational principles describe relationships that are not necessarily causal in nature, but in which a change in one factor is associated with a change in another factor. For example, the following is a correlational principle: "The increase in lung cancer among women is directly proportional to the increase in the number of women who smoke." Again, to understand this principle, a student would have to know the specific details about this relationship. Specifically, a student would have to know the general pattern of this relationship, that is, the number of women who have lung cancer changes at the same rate as the number of women who smoke changes.

These two types of principles are sometimes confused with cause/effect sequences. A cause/effect sequence applies to a specific situation, whereas a principle applies to many situations. The causes of the Civil War taken together represent a cause/effect sequence. They apply to the Civil War only. However, the cause/effect principle linking tuberculosis and the tubercle bacillus can be applied to many different situations and many different people. Physicians use this principle to make judgments about a variety of situations and a variety of people. The key distinction between principles and cause/effect sequences is that principles can be exemplified in a number of situations, whereas cause/effect sequences cannot—they apply to a single situation only.

Concepts

Concepts are the most general way of thinking about knowledge in that virtually all ways of thinking about knowledge can be subsumed under them. That is, a concept can be the general category under which fall a number of principles and generalizations, a time sequence, a cause/effect sequence, an episode, and a number of vocabulary terms. Concepts are commonly represented by a single word or a phrase. For example, the word *dictatorship* can represent a concept. An important question here is, What is the difference between a vocabulary term and a concept inasmuch as both can be represented by a single word? For the most part, the difference lies in how the word is approached. If *dictatorship* were approached as a simple vocabulary term, students would be expected to have a general understanding of the term only—a general, but accurate, sense of what the word means. However, if the word were approached as a concept, students would be expected to know specific principles and generalizations about *dictatorships,* along with facts, episodes, and the like. At the level of concept, then, the word *dictatorship* would function as an organizer for all of the other types of declarative knowledge. Thus, concepts encompass much more information than the narrow range encompassed by a vocabulary term.

One final noteworthy difference between concepts and vocabulary terms is that all words can be addressed as vocabulary terms, but not all words can be addressed as concepts. Rather, only those words that represent broad categories of information qualify as concepts.

To illustrate how this hierarchy of declarative knowledge might be used to organize a unit of instruction around standards, assume that a teacher is planning a unit on soils. The teacher might begin her deliberations about the unit by identifying the essential declarative knowledge she would like students to know as a result of the unit. At first, this is done in a fairly unorganized fashion. For example, the teacher planning the unit on soils might identify the following information as important to the unit:

a. Soil is composed of solid particles and spaces.

b. Liquids and gasses are able to move through the spaces between soil particles.

c. Clay and sand have different-sized particles. Clay has much larger particles than sand.

d. Liquids and gases move more quickly through larger spaces between soil particles than they do between smaller spaces.

e. Terms:

soil:	The portion of the earth's surface consisting of humus and disintegrated rock
clay:	A type of soil that is plastic when wet
sand:	A type of soil consisting of small, loose grains of disintegrated rock
percolation:	Liquids or gases moving through a porous substance
humus:	The dark matter in soil produced by the decomposition of vegetables or animals

Using her knowledge of the hierarchic structure of declarative knowledge, the teacher would then try to organize the content in a more meaningful way. She might decide that the following represents the best way of organizing the content:

- *Major concept:* percolation
- *Principle regarding percolation:* The rate of percolation of a liquid or a gas through soil is a direct function of how porous the soil is. The more porous the soil, the higher the rate of percolation.
- *Facts about clay:* Clay is not very porous. The spaces between particles are relatively small.
- *Facts about sand:* Sand is very porous. The spaces between particles are relatively large.

- *Vocabulary terms:*
  - soil
  - clay
  - sand
  - humus

None of the content has changed, just the manner in which the content is organized. Percolation is now considered a concept under which all the other declarative knowledge in the unit falls. There is one major principle about percolation and some facts about two types of soil. Finally, there are some vocabulary terms about which students will have a general understanding. The unit now has shifted its focus from a general unit on soil to a relatively specific unit on the concept of percolation as it relates to soil.

The teacher now can write this information as standards. Recall from the discussion in chapter 2 that standards are somewhat arbitrary ways of organizing knowledge. The teacher might decide to organize this knowledge as a single standard or as two or three standards. For illustrative purposes, assume that the teacher chooses to organize this content as two standards.

Standard 1: Students will understand the basic concept of percolation as it relates to soil.

Standard 2: Students will understand basic facts and terms regarding the nature of soil and specific types of soil.

Procedural Standards

Like declarative knowledge, procedural knowledge can also be organized in a hierarchic fashion. The various levels of the procedural hierarchy are algorithms, strategies, and macroprocesses.

Algorithms

Algorithms are the most specific type of procedural knowledge. They are usually comprised of steps that are performed in a fairly strict order. For example, when you divide one number into another, you are performing an algorithm, the steps of which must be performed in a set order. An important feature of algorithms is that to be effective they should be performed without much conscious effort. For example, the process of dividing 2756 by 21 will be severely inhibited if you continually have to stop to remember which step to perform next. Examples of processing that tend to be algorithmic in nature include

- performing addition, subtraction, multiplication, and division,
- balancing an equation,
- diagraming a sentence, and
- performing different functions on a word processor (e.g., moving paragraphs around).

Strategies

Strategies commonly involve the application of basic rules. However, these rules are not necessarily applied in any specific order. In effect, strategies are much "fuzzier" processes than algorithms. The job can be accomplished in a wide variety of ways. For example, when you read a graph, there are some steps involved, such as reading the title of the graph, identifying what is reported on one of the axes, identifying what is reported in the other axis, and so on. However, there is no set order in which the steps must be performed. Additionally, strategies are not performed as automatically as algorithms. They take some thought to determine the best rule to be applied at any given time. Examples of processes that involve strategies include reading a chart or graph; editing an essay for logic, diction, or mechanics; determining the meaning of an unknown word; and analyzing a presentation for errors.

Macroprocesses

Macroprocesses are the most general type of procedural knowledge. As the name implies, they are "big" processes with many interactive components. For example, we saw in chapter 6 that the macroprocess of reading is comprised of five interactive components:

1. The general task processor
2. The information screener
3. The idea network processor
4. The word processor
5. The macrostructure generator

Each of these components represents separate lines of cognitive processing, which commonly occur simultaneously (Marzano & Paynter, 1994). For example, while reading a chapter in a book, a student must keep thinking of his purpose for reading (the job of the general task processor); he must also determine if the information he is reading makes sense given what he knows about the topic (the job of the information screener) while he tries to connect ideas in a logical manner (the task of the idea network processor) and so on. Because of this complex interaction of processing components, macroprocesses characteristically take a great deal of conscious thought because you are constantly determining which is the most appropriate action to take next. Examples of macroprocesses include reading for comprehension; writing different types of expository and narrative texts; driving a car; problem solving in various situations; and giving a speech.

One problem that teachers have relative to procedural knowledge is that they usually identify the macroprocesses they want students to master but do not identify the component parts on which they will focus. For example, a teacher might easily determine that she wishes to enhance students' reading ability. However, she might not identify which of the five processing components she wishes to highlight in the unit. Does she want to focus on the effective functioning of the general information processor, providing strategies that help students set goals for their reading and monitor their progress toward those goals, or does she want to focus on the idea network processor and provide techniques to help students organize their thoughts in meaningful ways?

Another aspect of identifying the procedural knowledge within a unit of study is to determine the declarative knowledge associated with the procedures that have been identified. Researchers and theorists in cognitive psychology (e.g., Anderson, 1983, 1995; Fitts, 1964; Fitts & Posner, 1967) explain that all algorithms, strategies, and macroprocessors have declarative knowledge associated with them. To illustrate, consider the strategy of editing a composition for subject/verb agreement. The rules involved in this strategy might be stated in the following way:

For each clause in every sentence you have written

1. find the subject of the clause,
2. find the verb in the clause,
3. say the subject and verb aloud or in your head,
4. listen to hear whether the subject agrees with the verb, and
5. if they do not agree, change the subject or verb so that they do.

To implement this rather straightforward strategy, students must know more than just the steps. Rather, they must also know

1. the concepts of subject and verb,
2. the rules for agreement between subject and verb, and
3. the concept of a clause.

Without a thorough understanding of this information, the steps in the strategy are of little use to a student.

In the unit on percolation, the teacher might decide that she wishes to teach and reinforce the process of constructing a bar graph that represents the findings in various trials of an experiment. Her first task is to identify the steps she considers important to process. She might identify the following steps:

1. Select an appropriate unit of measurement to represent the intervals or increments that have been measured.
2. Draw a vertical axis with the units of measurement noted.
3. Draw a horizontal axis with each of the trials of the experiment appropriately labeled.
4. Accurately draw bars on the vertical axis that represent the measurement for each trial in the experiment.

The teacher would next identify the declarative knowledge students must understand to perform the steps in the strategy. For the strategy above, the teacher might conclude that she must teach students the following information:

- the terms *vertical axis* and *horizontal axis*
- the terms *increment* and *interval*

Note that the teacher has decided to approach this information as vocabulary terms. That is, she has determined that in order to perform the strategy for constructing a bar graph, students must have only a general understanding of these terms, as opposed to understanding at the level of detail that would be required if the terms were approached as concepts.

In summary, after considering the procedural knowledge important to her unit on percolation, the teacher now has identified a third standard that will be important within the unit. The teacher might articulate that standard in the following way:

> **Standard 3:** Students will understand and effectively apply the basic strategy of constructing a bar graph.

Step 2: Identify Thinking And Reasoning Standards

In chapters 2 and 7 we articulated our bias that thinking and reasoning standards should be an overt part of schooling. Therefore, we recommend that individual teachers identify specific thinking and reasoning standards that they wish to teach and reinforce in specific units of instruction. Recall that we have identified the following thinking and reasoning standards:

1. Understands and applies basic principles of presenting an argument
2. Understands and applies basic principles of logic and reasoning
3. Effectively uses mental processes that are based on identifying similarities and dissimilarities (compares, contrasts, classifies)
4. Understands and applies basic principles of hypothesis testing and scientific inquiry
5. Applies basic trouble-shooting and problem-solving techniques
6. Applies decision-making techniques

The teacher in our sample unit on percolation might identify the standard on hypothesis testing and the scientific method as important to the unit. She would also identify the specific aspects of this thinking and reasoning process that she wishes to teach and reinforce. In this case, she might identify the following elements:

- generating a specific hypothesis regarding what will occur under specific conditions
- explaining the underlying rationale for the hypothesis
- reevaluating the hypothesis in light of the results of an experiment

Because thinking and reasoning standards are basically procedural in nature, the teacher would also identify the declarative knowledge she might have to teach so that students can utilize the thinking and reasoning process. In this case, the teacher might determine that she should address the term *hypothesis* as a vocabulary item.

As a result of this step in the planning process, the teacher has now identified a fourth standard that will be included in her unit on percolation. She might state this standard in the following way:

> Standard 4: Students will understand and apply the basic processes of generating, testing, and evaluating hypotheses.

Step 3: Identify Lifelong Learning Standards (If Any)

In chapter 2 we identified a number of lifelong learning standards that a district or school might adopt. These include the following:

Working with Others

1. Contributes to the overall effort of a group
2. Uses conflict-resolution techniques
3. Works well with diverse individuals and in diverse situations
4. Displays effective interpersonal communication skills
5. Demonstrates leadership skills

Self-Regulation

1. Sets and manages goals
2. Performs self-appraisal
3. Considers risks
4. Demonstrates perseverance
5. Maintains a healthy self-concept
6. Restrains impulsivity

An individual teacher might decide to incorporate one or more of these into her unit of instruction. For illustrative purposes, assume that the teacher identifies standard 1 under the general category of working with others, which deals with contributing to the overall effectiveness of a group. Again, the teacher would also identify the specific aspects of the standard that will be addressed. These might include

- identifying specific goals for the group,
- helping the group stay on track, and
- helping group members identify effective roles for individual members.

After this step, the teacher has identified a fifth standard that will be addressed in her unit.

> Standard 5: Students will contribute to the overall effectiveness of a group.

Step 4: Identify Major Performance Tasks And Exhibitions

A number of times throughout this book, we have commented on the importance of performance tasks and exhibitions. These should be a central part of any classroom that is designed around standards because of the many positive benefits of performance tasks and exhibitions. A good time to design a performance task is immediately after standards have been identified. This helps the teacher design the task so that it addresses one or more of the standards. In this unit, the teacher might design the performance task in Exhibit 8.1.

Exhibit 8.1 Sample Unit: Performance Task

How can you tell if a soil sample is composed of larger particles or it is made up of something different, something smaller? Complete your own percolation test:

You will need the following:

- ✔ 3 8- or 9-ounce paper cups, each labeled #1, #2, or #3
- ✔ a protractor
- ✔ 3 clean coffee filters
- ✔ 3 glass or metal pans, such as pie pans, each labeled #1, #2, or #3
- ✔ 3 soil samples: one-quarter cup each of sand, clay and soil from your yard or neighborhood
- ✔ a 2-cup (16 ounce) liquid measure filled with 1fi cups of water
- ✔ a timer or stop watch
- ✔ paper and pencil

First, using a sharp object such as a protractor, poke 5 holes in the bottoms of 5 different 8-ounce paper cups. Place a clean coffee filter inside of each cup. Fill each coffee filter with a quarter-cup of one of the following: clay, sand, and 3 different soil samples from your neighborhood. Next, set each cup into its similarly numbered metal or glass pan. Before going any further, generate specific hypotheses about what will happen when you pour the water through each of the soil samples. Write out each hypothesis and explain the reasoning behind your hypothesis.

Set a timer for one minute. Immediately pour one-half cup of water into each cup. At the end of one minute, remove the cups from the pie pans, saving the water that has drained into each pan.

Pour the liquid from the first pan back into the measuring cup. How much water percolated through the soil in cup #1? Mark down the exact amount on your notepaper. Repeat this measuring and note-taking with the water in pan #2, pan #3, and so on.

What conclusions can you draw about the size of the particles—and spaces—in each sample?

Finally, chart your observations in the form of a bar graph. Select an appropriate unit of measurement to represent ounces of water.

When you are done, you will be asked to make a presentation on your hypotheses and your findings.

This performance task addresses at least three of the five standards the teacher has generated. Specifically, the performance task addresses Standard 1 on the nature of percolation. It addresses Standard 3 on the basic strategy for constructing a bar graph, and it addresses Standard 4 on hypothesis testing.

Step 5: Identify Content Not Taught But Used

Not all information and skill that is important to a unit is necessarily introduced within the unit. Rather, teachers will frequently utilize information and skills that they assume students have already acquired. This usually becomes evident once a performance task has been designed. In terms of the performance task in Exhibit 8.1, the teacher is asking students to make an oral presentation; yet, she has not previously identified this as a skill to be taught and reinforced. This is because she is assuming that students have acquired this skill previously (perhaps in another of her units). However, she wishes to highlight this skill in her unit and build it into her grading. Therefore, she should construct a standard for it.

> **Standard 6:** Students will be able to make effective oral presentations.

Step 6: Assign A Weight To Each Standard

If a teacher is in a school that utilizes a traditional grading system, he or she will have to collapse all information about performance on individual standards into a single grade. In chapter 6, we discussed the disadvantages in doing this; however, in a traditional school setting, a teacher will have no choice. In chapter 6, we described a process for relating standards to an overall letter grade. A key step in this process is to determine how much of the grade each standard will account for. This can be done by assigning percentages to standards. Using our sample unit on percolation, the teacher might assign the percentages shown in Table 8.1.

Table 8.1 Sample Unit: Percentages Assigned to Standards

Standard	Weight
1. Students will understand the basic concept of percolation as it relates to soil.	25%
2. Students will understand basic facts and terms regarding the nature of soil and specific types of soil.	25%
3. Students will understand and effectively apply the basic strategy for constructing a bar graph.	10%
4. Students will understand and apply the basic processes of generating, testing, and reevaluating hypotheses.	20%
5. Students will contribute to the overall effectiveness of a group.	10%
6. Students will be able to make effective oral presentations.	10%

The weights that have been identified for each standard should be reported to students and parents as soon as possible, preferably at the beginning of the course or unit. Exhibit 8.2 shows a sample letter that might be given to parents communicating the different standards that will be addressed in the course.

Exhibit 8.2 Sample Unit: Letter to Parents

Dear Parents:

In this unit we will be studying an important concept called percolation. To master this topic, students will have to know and be able to do a number of things. Specifically, each student will have to

Standard 1:   Understand the basic characteristics of percolation.
Standard 2:   Understand basic information about soil and different types of soil.

In addition, each student will have to show competence in a number of general skills and abilities. These include

Standard 3:   Effectively design a bar graph depicting the results of an experiment.
Standard 4:   Effectively generate and test hypothesis.
Standard 5:   Contribute to the overall effectiveness of a group.
Standard 6:   Make an effective oral presentation

To calculate your student's letter grade for the unit, I will use the following scheme:

Standard 1:   25% of grade
Standard 2:   25% of grade
Standard 3:   10% of grade
Standard 4:   20% of grade
Standard 5:   10% of grade
Standard 6:   10% of grade

Unit activities will include readings from the science text, quizzes, homework assignments, a lab experiment and report, demonstrations, and group work. Your son's or daughter's performance in these activities will provide the information that will be used to make judgment about his or her performance on these six standards.

Communication like this at the very beginning of a course or unit of study provides parents and students with clear learning goals. They do not have to guess at the expectations of the teacher.

Step 7: Identify Learning Experiences

Once standards have been identified, the teacher then turns her attention to the question of how students will first experience the knowledge and skill identified within the standards. This is a particularly important step if students have had no prior knowledge of the knowledge and skill in the standards.

In a very general sense, there are two ways a student can experience new knowledge and skill—directly and indirectly. These are depicted in Figure 8.1.

Figure 8.1 Ways to Experience Declarative Information

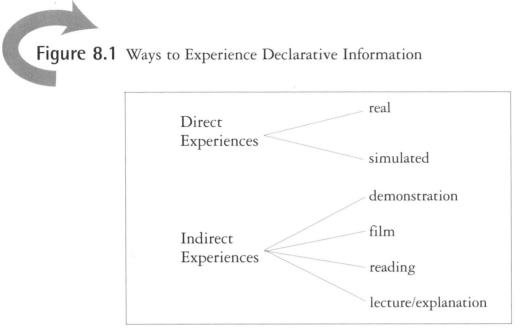

Note: From *Dimensions of Learning Teacher's Manual* (p. 59), by R. J. Marzano, D. J. Pickering, D. E. Arredondo, G. J. Blackburn, R. S. Brandt, and C. A. Moffett, 1992, Alexandria, VA: Association for Supervision and Curriculum Development.

A direct experience, as the name implies, involves physical activity by students. This physical involvement can be real or simulated. For instance, students cannot learn about hibernation by experiencing it directly because hibernation is physically impossible for human beings. They can simulate the experience, however, by lying very still for ten minutes and consciously trying to slow their heartbeat and their breathing.

Indirect experiences are those in which students are not physically involved. Demonstrations, films, readings, and lectures are all indirect experiences. Some indirect ways of learning about hibernation would be observing a classroom pet that goes into hibernation for the winter, watching a film on hibernation, reading about hibernation, or listening to an oral presentation about hibernation.

In our sample unit, the teacher might decide that she does not have the time or resources to provide direct experiences about percolation and the nature of soil. However, she can provide students with a number of indirect experiences that include demonstrations, video tapes, guest lectures, and the like.

The examples above are all declarative in nature. When procedural knowledge is the subject of instruction, direct experiences are the only types of experiences that make any sense. That is, students must have a hands-on experience of the new skill or process. Initially, this involves learning the basic steps in the skill or process. Teachers can provide students with an initial experience of the steps in a variety of ways that include

1. demonstrating the skill or process in a step-by-step fashion,
2. presenting students with a written set of steps, and
3. presenting students with, or having students develop, a flow chart for the steps.

(For a detailed discussion of these and other techniques, see Marzano, et al., 1992.)

Once students have had an initial experience with new declarative and procedural knowledge, this learning should be reinforced. For declarative knowledge, reinforcement involves students making connections with what they already know and then organizing and representing information in meaningful ways. Some of the many instructional strategies that can be used to help students reinforce declarative knowledge include

1. the K-W-L strategy,
2. reciprocal teaching,
3. using graphic representations,
4. outlining, and
5. using pictographic and physical representations.

Reinforcing procedural knowledge involves helping students "shape" the new skill or process so that they can use it in different situations and have ownership of the process. It also involves practicing the process to such an extent that it can be performed with relative ease. Instructional techniques that aid in reinforcing procedural knowledge include

1. demonstrating variations in the skill or process,
2. pointing out common pitfalls and errors in the skill or process,
3. setting up a practice schedule and
4. having students chart their speed and accuracy regarding the new skill or process.

(Again, for a more detailed discussion of instructional activities that reinforce procedural knowledge, see Marzano, et al., 1992).

This level of planning is obviously quite detailed, but it provides teachers with a comprehensive picture of the instructional activities that will be used to initially expose students to the new declarative and procedural knowledge and then to reinforce that new knowledge.

Step 8: Identify How Standards Will Be Assessed

With the standards and learning experience identified, the next step for the teacher is to determine the manner in which assessment data will be collected. In chapter 6, we described a number of ways that teachers can obtain assessment data. These include

- forced-choice items,
- essays,
- performance tasks and exhibitions,
- kid watching, and
- student self-assessment.

Usually the first two types of assessment techniques are used with activities such as homework, quizzes, and tests.

One useful technique when determining the various types of assessments that should be used to gather information on standards is to fill out a matrix like that in Table 8.2.

Table 8.2 Sample Unit: Assessment Matrix

	Performance Task	Observation	Homework	Quizzes/Tests	Self-Assessment
Standard 1	X	X	X	X	X
Standard 2		X	X	X	X
Standard 3	X	X	X	X	X
Standard 4		X			X
Standard 5		X			X
Standard 6	X	X			X

Recall from the discussion in chapter 6 that these activities should be considered information to be used by teachers to make "informed judgments." This is why we recommend the use of the generic performance levels shown in Table 8.3 to translate the students' performance on quizzes, homework, performance tasks, and so on into a common scale that represents levels of understanding and performance as opposed to simply tallying up points.

Table 8.3 Performance Levels: Multiple Profile Approach

Advanced performance for a standard	Advanced performance in some of the benchmarks and proficient performance in the others
Proficient performance for a standard	Proficient performance in the vast majority of all benchmarks
Basic performance for a standard	Basic or higher performance in most benchmarks with novice performance in the rest
Novice performance for a standard	Novice performance in the majority of benchmarks

It is also important to remember that some teachers prefer to use the generic performance levels in Table 8.4 when standards are comprised of single benchmarks or when an assessment covers one benchmark only.

Table 8.4 General Scales for Declarative and Procedural Benchmarks

Generic Performance Level for Declarative Knowledge	Generic Performance Level for Procedural Knowledge
Advanced performance: Demonstrates a thorough understanding of the important information; is able to exemplify that information in detail and articulate complex relationships and distinctions	Carries out the major processes/skills inherent in the procedure with relative ease and automaticity
Proficient performance: Demonstrates an understanding of the important information; is able to exemplify that information in some detail	Carries out the major processes/skills inherent in the procedure without significant error, but not necessarily at an automatic level
Basic performance: Demonstrates an incomplete understanding of the important information, but does not have severe misconceptions	Makes a number of errors when carrying out the processes and skills important to the procedure, but still accomplishes the basic purpose of the procedure
Novice performance: Demonstrates an incomplete understanding of the important information along with severe misconceptions	Makes so many errors when carrying out the processes and skills important to the procedure that it fails to accomplish its purpose

Of course, these generic rubrics would be modified to be more specific to each standard that the teacher has identified.

Note that at this point in the planning process, teachers would only need to identify assessment activities for each standard. Exhibit 8.3 (next page) shows how the grade book would be filled out by the end of the unit based on our discussion in chapter 6.

Exhibit 8.3 Sample Unit: Grade Book

Grade Book						

Assessment Key:

A. *Homework: Sept 7*　　　　E. *Homework: Sept 21*　　　　I. _____

B. *Quiz: Sept 9*　　　　　　　F. *Perf. Task: Sept 23*　　　　J. _____

C. *Perf. Task: Sept 14*　　　 G. *Unit Test: Sept 25*　　　　K. Student Self-Assessment

D. *Quiz: Sept 16*　　　　　　H. _____　　　　　　　L. Observations

Standards: / Students:		#1 Understands percolation	#2 Understands soil information	#3 Designs and uses bar graph	#4 Generates and tests a hypothesis	#5 Contributes to groups	#6 Makes an oral presentation
Carmen Adams	A	4	4				
	B	3	4	4			
	C	4					
	D	4	4	3			
	E	4	3	4			
	F	3		4			4
	G	4	4	4			
	H						
	I						
	J						
	K	4	4	4	3	3	4
	L	4 / 3 [4]	4 / 4 [4]	4 / 4 [4]	4 / 4 [4]	4 / 4 [4]	4 [4]
James Barton	A	2	2				
	B	2	3	2			
	C	3					
	D	2	2	2			
	E	2	3	2			
	F	1		3			1
	G	2	3	2			
	H						
	I						
	J						
	K	3	3	3	3	3	3
	L	1 / 2 [2]	2 / 3 [3]	2 / 3 [2]	1 / 1 [2]	2 / 2 [2]	2 [2]
Michael Caruso	A	3	3				
	B	3	3	3			
	C	4					
	D	2	2	4			
	E	3	3	4			
	F	3		4			4
	G	3	3	3			
	H						
	I						
	J						
	K	3	4	3	3	4	3
	L	3 / 4 [3]	3 / 3 [3]	4 / 4 [4]	3 / 3 [3]	4 / 3 [4]	4 [4]

Step 9: Sequence Instructional Activities

One of the more artistic aspects of creating a unit of instruction is to sequence the activities that will occur in the unit. For the sample unit, this has been done in Table 8.5.

Table 8.5 Arrangement of Classes for the Percolation Unit

	Monday	Tuesday	Wednesday	Thursday	Friday
Week #1	P—Marbles-in-the-jar demonstrating percolation K-W-L on soil composition	P—Textbook, pp. 45-49 Pairs read activity Add new learnings to K-W-L worksheet	P—Videotape: *The Ever-Changing Sahara*	P—Guest speaker from the Rock Shop	P—Group work: Venn diagram comparing and contrasting soil samples Essay homework on soil samples
Week #2	P—Anticipation Guide to textbook assignment Pairs Read Activity for textbook pp. 50-55	W—Present steps to creating bar graphs Using statistics from newspaper articles, students develop and share their own bar graphs.	W—I demonstrate set-up and procedures for performance activity: percolation experiment I explain components needed in lab report.	W—Performance Activity: Pairs set up and perform percolation test Pairs work on lab reports. I conference.	W—Pairs work on lab reports and bar graphs. Quiz on soil samples and percolation
Week #3	W—Pairs continue to work on lab reports and bar graphs. I conference.	P— Field trip to exhibit on soils, rocks, and physical weathering at the Natural History Museum	P—I present graphic organizer format. Students complete graphic organizer on information gleaned from field trip.	P—Community Circle review W—Pairs finish final copies of lab reports and bar graphs	W—Students prepare oral reports.
Week #4	P—Students present oral reports. W—Assessment conferences	P—Students present oral reports. W—Assessment conferences	P—Students present oral reports. W—Assessment conferences	P—Students present oral reports. W—Assessment conferences	Final examinations

Note: P = presentation classes
         W = workshop classes

Here the teacher has decided to present information on the topic of soil composition first. However, the very first activity in the unit—the marbles-in-a-jar demonstration is a demonstration of percolation. This demonstration ideally will establish an overall purpose for the entire unit. Also note that the teacher has decided to present the performance task relatively early in the unit, that is, in the middle of week #2. The purpose of using an engaging demonstration such as "marbles in a jar" is to provide students with a motivation for studying about soil and the process of percolation.

Another important distinction in Table 8.5 is the difference between the classes coded with the letter *W* and the classes coded with the letter *P*. The letter *P* stands for presentation classes; the letter *W* stands for workshop classes. They represent two basic ways that classes should be structured if one wishes to organize instruction around standards.

Presentation Classes

The purpose of presentation classes is to have students experience and reinforce new declarative and procedural knowledge. It is important that presentation classes not be associated with a didactic approach to instruction. Although the focus of learning in this kind of class is directed by the teacher, the act of learning is still highly constructive and learner centered.

A typical presentation class has some, but not all, of the characteristics of the methodologies described by Hunter (1969, 1976, 1982, 1984) and Rosenshine (1983, 1986). For example, a presentation class might begin with some type of anticipatory set: an activity that helps students develop interest in the learning experience. Similarly, a presentation class commonly ends with some type of closure activity in which students summarize what they have learned.

Workshop Classes

The workshop approach is firmly established within what might be loosely called the "writing process" and the "whole language" movements. Atwell (1987) and Hansen (1987) have detailed the uses of writing and reading workshops across a variety of grade levels. Marzano and his colleagues have described how workshop classes can be used in a variety of subject areas (Marzano, 1991, 1992; Marzano, Paynter, Kendall, Pickering, & Marzano, 1991; Marzano, et al., 1992).

Within a classroom organized around standards, the primary purpose of workshop classes is to provide students with opportunities to work on their performance tasks and exhibitions. Generally, a workshop class has three parts: a mini-lesson, an activity period, and a sharing period. Each of the components of the workshop has a specific function.

The Mini-Lesson

As its name implies, the mini-lesson is short (five to ten minutes). For the most part, it is a time for the teacher to provide guidance and assistance as students work on their performance tasks and exhibitions. At first a teacher might use the mini-lesson to help students work on their performance tasks and exhibitions.

For example, the teacher in the sample unit might present students with techniques for analyzing their soil sample so that they can generate effective hypotheses within their performance tasks. The mini-lesson, then, is a vehicle for teachers to provide guidance to the entire class about performance tasks and exhibitions.

The Activity Period

The activity period is a block of time (20-45 minutes) in which students work on their projects individually, in pairs, or in small groups. While students work on their projects, the teacher's main function is to "conference" with individual students. It is useful to think in terms of two different types of conferences: the performance task conference and the assessment conference.

Performance Task Conference. When a conference focuses on performance tasks, its purpose is to provide individual students or groups of students with highly specific guidance that can be used to enhance their performance tasks and exhibitions. The teacher and student discuss progress on the task and any problems the student might be having. Then they jointly plan next steps for the project. The conference is also used to provide guidance about what resources are necessary to complete the project. The teacher might point the student to a particular book or person who can help her with the next phase of the project. Within the framework of the conference, teacher and student become partners in pursuit of a shared goal.

Assessment Conference. The purpose of a conference with an assessment is for the student to provide the teacher with self-assessment information on the standards covered in the course or the unit. The basic dynamic of this interaction is that students answer the question, "If I had to evaluate my level of understanding or performance right now on standard _____, I would give myself a _____." This is invaluable information for the teacher. If a student reports that she has low understanding or performance in a given standard, the teacher and student can jointly identify problem areas and brainstorm ways that the student can increase her understanding or performance.

If conferences are kept short (five to ten minutes per student), a teacher can move efficiently through the class. For example, assuming workshop activity periods last an average of 25 minutes and conferences an average of five minutes, during each workshop a teacher can meet with five students. Assuming that there are 30 students in a class, a teacher can see more students in a workshop by reducing the amount of time for each conference or by increasing the amount of time for the activity period. And if students are working on a performance task as a cooperative group, a teacher might meet with the entire group, thus significantly decreasing the average per-pupil conference time.

The Sharing Period

The sharing period of a workshop is quite short, usually only five to ten minutes. During this time, students discuss a variety of topics, ranging from insights to problems to strategies. For example, one student might describe how his awareness of a topic has grown as a result of his performance task. Another student might describe a problem he is having on his performance task and ask for help. The hallmark of sharing period is that the students and teacher freely discuss their learning as students work on their performance tasks and exhibitions.

Summary And Recommendations

In this chapter we have outlined a process by which a teacher can organize a class around standards—even though her school has not embraced standards—to assign overall letter grades. The process outlined involves nine steps within which a teacher organizes her content into standards, identifies instructional and assessment activities, and sequences these activities. Performance tasks and exhibitions should be a key component of a classroom organized around standards as should teacher/student conferences.

Chapter 9

How Will It Look When We Are Done?

Ultimately, a district or school must determine the overall design that its approach to standards-based or standards-referenced education will take. As mentioned in chapter 1, we believe that designing a school or district organized around standards is not a cookie-cutter process—one size does not fit all. There are many ways that a school or district can design a standards-based or standards-referenced system. However, these many and varied ways tend to fall into four basic approaches. The critical attributes of these four approaches are briefly summarized in Exhibit 9.1. It is important to note that these approaches are not mutually exclusive. That is, it is common (even advisable) to combine aspects of one approach with those of another to design a system that is unique to a specific school or district.

Exhibit 9.1 Four Approaches to Designing Standards-Based or Standards-Referenced Systems

---

Approaches that rely on external assessments:

Students must meet or exceed a specific cut-score on assessments that are external to the classroom. Assessments can use traditional forced-choice items and/or performance tasks.

Approaches that use core courses:

General standards that cut across a number of subject areas are embedded in specific, required courses. Students' grades in these courses represent their performance on these standards.

Approaches that rely on projects, exhibitions, and portfolios:

Students complete performance tasks, exhibitions, and portfolios that demonstrate their knowledge of specific standards or a combination of standards.

Approaches that report performance on individual standards:

Individual teachers report students' performance on specific standards.

Approach I: Relying On External Assessments

In chapter 5 we defined external assessments as those that are designed independent of the classroom level and, therefore, independent of knowledge of specific students. We also stated our strong bias that classroom assessment should be central to a standards-based approach. However, it is our belief that external assessments should not be the only, or even the primary, means by which standards are assessed. Nevertheless, there are some districts and schools that design their entire system around external assessments. In such cases, the external assessments are usually performance tasks augmented by some forced-choice items that cover specific subject areas. As described in chapter 5, many states are currently designing assessments with this configuration (see Table 5.1 in chapter 5). These external tests are usually given at specific transition points in the K-12 sequence and are limited to core subject areas (e.g., reading, writing, mathematics, science and social studies or history). For example, a district might require students to take external tests in core subject areas at the end of elementary school, at the end of middle school, and at the end of high school.

A district that relies on external assessments is typically standards based about these tests. Students must exhibit a specific performance level (i.e., they must perform at or above the level of a specific cut-score) on all tests before they can progress to the next level. If a district adopts this approach, the majority of its energies necessarily go into the construction of its external assessments. In fact, the entire success of this approach is dependent on the strength of the external assessments.

The main advantage to this approach is that it is straightforward. External assessments are designed at specific transition points for specific subject areas. Students must obtain specific scores on the external assessments in order to progress to the next level. The external assessments are the focal point of the system. Virtually everything else in the system—courses, scheduling, and record keeping, for example—remains unchanged.

The biggest drawback to this approach is its lack of connection to daily life in the classroom. Because the external assessments are given at a few grades only and because, by definition, these assessments are external to the classroom, teachers might tend to ignore them as they plan and carry out instruction. This is particularly true for teachers at grade levels that are not transition points.

Approach II: Relying On A Core Course Or Courses

Using this approach, a district or school identifies a single course or a set of courses that focus on standards. All students in the school are required to take these core courses as part of their course of study. Commonly, the core courses focus on a combination of reasoning standards, lifelong learning standards, and other types of standards that cut across a variety of content areas. For example, a high school might design the four core courses depicted in Exhibit 9.2. Students would be required to take one course each year of high school.

Exhibit 9.2 Sample of Standards Covered in Core Courses at the High School Level

---

Course #1: Basics 1 (Grade 9)

Standards
Reasoning 1:	Decision making
Reasoning 2:	General problem solving
Communication 1:	Comprehending complex expository information
Communication 2:	Presenting information in an organized manner
Lifelong Learning 1:	Working with others
Lifelong Learning 2:	Managing resources

Course #2: Basics 2 (Grade 10)

Standards
Reasoning 2:	General problem solving
Reasoning 3:	Generating and testing hypotheses
Communication 2:	Presenting information in an organized manner
Communication 3:	Analyzing the effectiveness of how information is presented
Lifelong Learning 2:	Managing resources
Lifelong Learning 3:	Setting and working toward goals

Course #3: Basics 3 (Grade 11)

Standards
Reasoning 3:	Generating and testing hypotheses
Reasoning 4:	Analyzing and presenting arguments
Communication 3:	Analyzing the effectiveness of how information is presented
Communication 4:	Displaying data in a variety of formats
Lifelong Learning 3:	Setting and working toward goals
Lifelong Learning 4:	Managing conflict

Course #4: Basics 4 (Grade 12)

Standards
Reasoning 4:	Analyzing and presenting arguments
Reasoning 5:	Using logical reasoning
Communication 4:	Displaying data in a variety of formats
Communication 5:	Using computer-based data bases
Lifelong Learning 4:	Managing conflict
Lifelong Learning 5:	Taking a leadership role

Note that core courses depicted in Exhibit 9.2 deal with three types of standards: reasoning, communication, and lifelong learning. Five standards have been identified in each area and sequenced in such a way that most standards are addressed twice in the four-year sequence. Presumably, these standards were selected because the school identified them as critical learnings for all students. That is, those who designed the courses felt that all students could benefit from instruction and feedback in the skills of decision making, working with others, and the like. Mandatory core courses are a vehicle for ensuring that all students are taught the information and skills important to these standards.

In addition to specifying the standards that core courses will address, a school must identify the manner in which grades will be assigned. Specifically, in order to effectively use this approach, the school must determine the weights that will be applied to each standard in

Exhibit 9.2 in the assignment of grades for those courses. If the school is standards based relative to the core courses, then it will commonly employ an A, B, C, I (or A, B, I) grading policy. If students do not obtain a grade of A, B, or C, then they receive an I (Incomplete). The work necessary to change a grade of I to an A, B, or C must be completed before the student matriculates to the next grade. If the school is standards referenced relative to the core courses, then the grade simply communicates the student's standing relative to the standards.

The major advantage of this approach is that the core courses present a highly visible vehicle for the standards. The very existence of the core showcases specific standards. An additional advantage to this is that it is easily integrated into current scheduling and reporting procedures. It is relatively easy to schedule core courses so that all students have access to them, and the report cards and transcripts can be easily modified to meet the demands of A, B, C, and I grading.

The primary disadvantage of this approach is that it does not accommodate many standards. Because standards are explicitly addressed in a single course or a small set of courses only, educators are forced to consider only a few very general standards like those in Exhibit 9.2.

Approach III: Relying On Performance Tasks, Exhibitions, And Portfolios

In chapter 6 we discussed the power and utility of performance tasks, exhibitions, and portfolios. Performance tasks require students to apply their knowledge; exhibitions are the vehicle by which students display what they have learned from their performance tasks; and portfolios are collections of performance tasks.

Using this approach, districts and schools require students to complete performance tasks (which they commonly refer to as *projects*), exhibitions, and portfolios before they pass on to the next level. Commonly, districts and schools are standards based about these mandatory projects, exhibitions, and portfolios. A useful comparison to make here is between this approach and the first approach—external assessments—because both involve assessments at key transition points. Using the first approach, students must "pass" some type of external assessment to matriculate from one level to the next. In this sense, the first approach and the third approach are similar: Both utilize some form of "exit assessment" to pass students on to the next level. However, within the external assessment approach, the exit assessments occur at a specific point in time. In effect, students take a test to pass from one level to the next. Even though that test may include or be totally comprised of performance tasks, it is, nevertheless, a test that is administered within a relatively short interval of time at a specific point in time (e.g., a couple of hours on a specific day or week devoted to the administration of the external tests). As discussed in the previous section of this chapter, these assessments are not directly tied to the daily life of the classroom—hence the name external assessments. The difference between this approach and the performance task, exhibition, and portfolio

226

approach is that the latter occurs over an extended period of time and is frequently linked to the daily life of the classroom. In fact, students commonly work on their performance tasks and portfolios for years before they actually perform their exhibitions. Both approaches involve exit assessments at three transition points: the end of elementary school, the end of middle school, and the end of high school. However, the performance tasks and portfolios are a central part of each student's academic life for a number of years leading up to the actual exhibitions.

The performance task, exhibition, and portfolio approach is perhaps the most popular model in current use. Indeed, much of the literature on standards-based education assumes the use of this approach. For example, researcher Joseph McDonald and his colleagues (McDonald, Smith, Turner, Finney, & Barton, 1993) highlight this approach in their discussion of the innovations engendered through Theodore Sizers's Coalition of Essential Schools. The coalition grew out of the studies that Sizer and his colleagues conducted between 1979 and 1984 (Sizer, 1985; Powell, Farrar, & Cohen, 1985; Hampel, 1986). One of the key aspects of the Coalition philosophy is that diplomas should be awarded only after students have demonstrated their competence. In most Coalition schools, this principle manifests as an emphasis on performance tasks, exhibitions, and portfolios.

McDonald et al. (1993) provide two examples of Coalition schools that utilize this approach. English High School in Boston utilizes a single project that is organized around a position paper. Specifically, all graduates must complete a paper stating and defending a point of view on some provocative issue. The paper is read, critiqued, and approved by a panel of teachers (McDonald et al., 1993). Walbrook High School in Baltimore requires students to complete multiple projects that are compiled into a portfolio. The entire portfolio is then presented as evidence that the student has mastered a variety of subject areas and general skills. To a great extent, this approach is modeled after that developed at Central Park East Secondary School (CPESS), which is perhaps the prototypical example of the performance task, exhibition, and portfolio approach.

Central Park East Secondary School was founded in 1985 in East Harlem, New York. As described by Linda Darling-Hammond and Jacqueline Ancess (1994), its 450 students in grades 7-12 are drawn largely from the local community. About 85 percent of the students are from Latino and African American families, 60 percent quality for free or reduced-price lunch, and 25 percent are eligible for special education services. The success of the CPESS model is well known. As described by Darling-Hammond and Ancess:

> Visited by over 2,000 educators and others each year, the school has set a standard for urban education that works for young people. In a city with a graduation rate of only 55 percent in five years, CPESS graduates well over 90 percent of its ninth-graders within five years and does so to much more demanding standards than most schools. The school also sends more than 90 percent of its graduates on to college right after graduation, with others entering college after working a year or two. (p. 3)

According to Darling-Hammond and Ancess (1994), the core of the CPESS approach is the completion of 14 projects organized into a portfolio. These are

1. A postgraduate plan
2. An autobiography
3. A report on school/community internship
4. A demonstration of an awareness of ethics and social issues
5. A demonstration of an appreciation of fine arts and ethics
6. A demonstration of an awareness of mass media
7. A demonstration of the importance and utility of "practical" skill areas such as medical care, independent living, legal rights, and securing a driver's license
8. A demonstration of an understanding of geography
9. A demonstration of competence to work in a language, other than English, as a speaker, listener, reader, or writer.
10. A demonstration of facility with the scientific method
11. A demonstration of competence in mathematics
12. A demonstration of an understanding and appreciation of a broad array of literature
13. A demonstration of an understanding of history and how it affects our lives today
14. A demonstration of participating in any team or individual, competitive or non-competitive sport or activity (pp. 14-15)

Darling-Hammond and Ancess explain that there is no one way to complete these projects or present them. A student might use a single project to fulfill a number of the 14 areas described above. For example, in her internship portfolio, one student (Marlena) described and documented three different internships in science that she took over a two-year period at Brookhaven National Laboratory, Hunter College, and Columbia University. Her mathematics portfolio included mathematical models of rainfall developed under differing assumptions. Marlena's media project included a sophisticated, evidence-based analysis of race, gender, and class stereotyping in prime-time television. Her history project traced the history of segregated education in the United States and applied it to current debates about Afrocentric schools. This was also used as Marlena's entry for ethics and social issues (see #4 above).

Teachers evaluate each project on a 20-point grid scoring system. This numeric scale is then translated to a more qualitative descriptive scale: distinguished (18-20), satisfactory (15-17), and minimally satisfactory (12-14). Below a score of twelve, students must resubmit their projects.

Scores on the projects are recorded in a special section of the transcripts. Figure 9.1 depicts the portfolio section of Marlena's transcripts.

Figure 9.1 Portion of Transcript Devoted to Projects at Central Park East
Secondary School

Central Park East Secondary School 1573 Madison Avenue, New York, NY 10029		(212) 860-8936

TRANSCRIPT OF PORTFOLIOS

Please refer to the Curriculum Bulletin for Portfolio requirements. A Portfolio is graded on the basis of all items within it as well as knowledge and skill defended before the student's Graduation Committee. Listed below is the title of the student's major work in each area as well as the cumulative grade. Individual portfolio items are available on request.

Dist = Distinguished work   Sat = Satisfactorily met requirements

MinSat = Minimally met requirements   FP = Final project (in-depth study)

THE PORTFOLIO

	Grade	Date (completed project)
Post Graduate Plan	Sat	12-90
Autobiography	Sat	12-13-91
Practical Skills & Knowledge (Life Skills)	Dist	3 1 92
Internship (Brookhaven National Lab and Hunter College, NY)	Dist	1-3-91
Ethics, Social Issues, & Philosophy (Controversy of Afrocentric schools)	Dist	2-28-92
Literature (Influences on Malcolm X's life)	Sat+	3-92
History (Events affecting the controversy of Afrocentric schools)	Sat	2-28-92
Geography (Geography of the West Indies)	Sat+	6-5-92
Language other than English (Spanish: English only vs. dual language)	Sat+	1-3-92
Mathematics (Mathematical models: lines and sines)	Dist	3-16-92
Science & Technology (Construction of Expression vectors with Phosphatases 1 & 2A)	Dist	4-92
Fine Arts & Aesthetics (Opera: "Die Fliedermaus" and "The Marriage of Figaro")	Sat	12-13-91
Mass Media (Entertainment or News? Our Children's Education)	Sat+	2-24-91
Physical Challenge (Aerobics)	MinSat	6-17-92
Review Date:		

Note: From *Graduation by Portfolio at Central Park East Secondary School* (p. 20), by L. Darling-Hammond and J. Ancess, 1994, New York: National Center for Restructuring Education, Schools, and Teaching, Columbia University. Reprinted with permission from The National Center for Restructuring Education, Schools, and Teaching (NCREST).

The success of CPESS approaches legend. Darling-Hammond and Ancess (1994) attest to the success of the approach using the words of the first graduates:

> As one of the first graduates, Steve concurs that the CPESS approach has allowed him to develop his own evidence that he can and will succeed: "This environment gives us more standards. It makes us stand up straight. . . . It makes us look at ourselves in the mirror and feel proud of our accomplishments." His experience has given him a sense of self, an entitlement to be somebody, in contrast with kids he describes feeling sorry for in his neighborhood, "who hang around wasting their lives." And he, like his classmates, has his work tested against his own and the community's standards to testify to the fact that his accomplishments are real and will stand up in the "Court of the World." (p. 52)

Clearly, CPESS is one of the stellar examples of the utility of the performance task, exhibition, and portfolio approach. Of its many advantages, the most obvious of this approach is its visibility. Like external assessments (see Approach I), performance tasks, exhibitions, and portfolios are concrete representations of student performance on standards. One of the main drawbacks to this approach is that performance tasks, exhibitions, and portfolios simply cannot address all of the standards important to a given content area. As discussed in chapter 5, performance tasks (and consequently exhibitions, and portfolios) simply are not as generalizable as they were once thought to be. To cover the variety of standards within a subject area, it would be necessary to have multiple projects, exhibitions, and portfolios in each subject area. Given the time it takes to complete a single performance task (see discussion in chapter 5), this is impractical. Another potential problem with the performance task, exhibition, and portfolio approach is its potential lack of connection with the daily life of the classroom. If performance tasks, exhibitions, and portfolios are not related to courses, then they become extra work that students must accomplish outside of their regular classroom instruction their regular classroom work. If these tasks are totally embedded within courses, then there is a risk that they will be subsumed into the course work and, consequently, lose some of their distinctiveness. Teachers should strive for a balance between these two extreme positions. They should help students design and carry out their performance tasks, exhibitions, and portfolios as a regular part of classroom instruction. However, some aspects of these endeavors should be conducted outside of regular classroom instruction. The work outside of class should be done under the tutelage of a teacher who acts as a mentor to the student. CPESS accomplishes this by scheduling teachers to teach courses only 12 hours per week. Five hours a week, each teacher meets with one or more of his or her advisees to provide guidance in their performance tasks, exhibitions, and portfolios (Darling-Hammond & Ancess, 1994).

Approach IV: Reporting on Individual Standards

The major difference between this approach and the previous three approaches is that all models within this approach provide information on individual standards. In contrast, the models in Approach I utilize a score or scores on tests as the indication of how well students are performing on a set of standards. The models in Approach II utilize course grades as the indicator of how well students are performing on specific standards. The models in Approach III utilize scores on performance tasks, exhibitions, and portfolios as the indication of how well students are performing on specific standards. All three of these approaches aggregate or "collapse" a great deal of information. In Approach I, performance on standards is collapsed into a score or scores on external assessments; in Approach II, performance on standards is collapsed into a traditional grade within a course; in Approach III, performance on standards is collapsed into scores on projects, exhibitions, and portfolios. In Approach IV, there is far less collapsing of information. Performance on each standard is reported for each student.

There are four models within this approach: combined course grades and standards; multiple validations, grade-level models, and the nongraded standards-based model.

Combined Course Grades and Standards

Using this model, each teacher assigns a letter grade to each student representing overall performance in a course. In addition, each teacher provides scores on individual standards representing student performance on those standards within the context of the course. We discussed this model in chapter 6. A sample report card is presented in Exhibit 6.16 of chapter 6.

Along with a report card that reports grades in courses and performance on standards, this model employs a transcript that reports both grades and scores on standards. A sample transcript is depicted in Exhibit 9.3 (on next page).

The transcript in Exhibit 9.3 provides students and teachers with a great deal of information. Courses are listed along with other information traditionally found on a transcript: letter grades, credits, and a grade point average. Additionally, performance in individual standards and groups of standards (e.g., composite scores for mathematics standards, science standards, and so on) are reported in a separate section of the transcript. Here the cumulative performance of a student is addressed in terms of standards as opposed to courses. This dual reporting method provides multiple perspectives on student progress.

Note: Due to space considerations, only part of the transcript is depicted here.

CENTRAL HIGH SCHOOL TRANSCRIPT						

Name:	Gregory Weber			ID #:	2334	
Address:	8742 Elm					
City:	Jordan, MI					

Key to Letter Grades

A	4.0	C	2.0	
A-	3.7	C-	1.7	
B+	3.3	D+	1.3	
B	3.0	D	1.0	
B-	2.7	D-	.7	
C+	2.3			

Fall Semester, 1996

Course	Grade	Credits Earned		
Algebra I	A-	3		
World History	B-	3		
Accelerated English	A	4		
Spanish I	B+	3		
Biology	A-	3	Semester GPA:	3.5
Phys. Ed.	B+	3	Overall GPA:	3.5
			Total Credits:	19

Spring Semester, 1997

Course	Grade	Credits Earned		
Algebra I	A	3		
Geography	B	3		
Accelerated English	A-	4		
Spanish II	B	3	Semester GPA:	3.6
Biology	A	3	Overall GPA:	3.57
Health	A	3	Total Credits:	38

Key to Performance Ratings

1: Novice
2: Basic
3: Proficient
4: Advanced

Subject and Standards Rated	Average Rating	# of Ratings	Most Recent Rating	Highest Rating	Lowest Rating
Subject: MATHEMATICS					
• Standard 1: Numeric Problem Solving	4	1	4	4	4
• Standard 2: Computation	4	1	4	4	4
• Standard 3: Measurement	3	1	3	3	3
• Standard 4: Geometry	4	1	4	4	4
• Standard 5: Probability	4	1	4	4	4
• Standard 6: Algebra	4	1	4	4	4
• Standard 7: Data Analysis	3	1	3	3	3
Overall Mathematics:	3.7	1	3.7	3.7	3.7
Subject: SCIENCE					
• Standard 1: Earth and Space	4	1	4	4	4
• Standard 2: Life Sciences	4	1	4	4	4
• Standard 3: Physical Sciences	4	1	4	4	4
• Standard 4: Science and Technology	4	1	4	4	4
Overall Science:	4	1	4	4	4
	3.7	3.7	3.7	3.7	3.7

If a school or district opted for this model, it would probably select to be standards referenced relative to individual standards—although it could simultaneously be standards based about individual courses. The reason it might not be standards based about individual standards is that it is very difficult to hold students to a specific level of performance on an individual standard when performance on a set of standards is combined to form an overall grade. The fact that the overall grade is comprised of a combination of scores on individual standards mandates a compensatory approach (see discussion of the compensatory versus conjunctive approaches in chapter 7), which, by definition, does not allow for setting minimum performance levels for individual standards.

The main advantage to this model is that it does not present a jarring change to current grading practices. Parents and students still receive overall course grades and grade point averages. However, in addition, student performance is reported on individual standards. This ensures that standards have a prominent role in the day-to-day life of the class. Finally, this model does not restrict the number of standards that can be addressed as does the core course method described in Approach II and the performance task, exhibition, and portfolio method described in Approach III.

The main disadvantage to this model is that it requires teachers to keep records in a manner that tracks students' performance on individual standards as opposed to their performance on tests, activities, and assignments. However, in chapters 6 and 8 we described how this might be done without placing a significant record-keeping burden on teachers.

Multiple Validations

With the multiple validations model, students must meet the performance standard (i.e., attain a specific level of performance) on each standard multiple times. Each time a student meets the performance standard for a particular standard, he is said to have received a "validation." More than one validation must be received for each standard. To illustrate, assume that a school has decided to employ a four-point scale like the generic scales described in chapter 6 to report student performance on standards. Also assume that the school has identified level 3 as the performance standard (the minimum acceptable level of performance) for each standard.

Before graduation from high school, each student would have to obtain a specific number of validations (i.e., a score of at least 3) on each standard. That is, each teacher would make judgments regarding each student on each standard covered in the teacher's course. If a student received a judgment of 3 on a specific standard, the student would receive a validation on that standard. The student would be said to have met a standard when he or she received the requisite number of validations on the standard.

The report card for this model might look like that in Exhibit 9.4 on the following page.

Exhibit 9.4 Report Card for a Sophomore Student With Validations Noted

CENTRAL HIGH SCHOOL REPORT CARD
Fall, 1996

Name: Jonathan Starek   **ID#:** 463650
Address: 459 Lexington   **Grade:** 10
City: Harmony, IL

	Algebra II	Biology	English II	Geography	Spanish II	Phys. Ed.
COURSE GRADE	B+	B	B-	B	B-	C+
Thinking and Reasoning						
Understands and applies basic principles of presenting an argument			2			
Understands and applies basic principles of logic and reasoning	2	4-V	2	3-V	2	
Effectively uses mental processes that are based on identifying similarities and differences	3-V	2	3-V		2	
Understands and applies basic principles of hypothesis testing and scientific inquiry		3-V				
Applies basic trouble-shooting and problem-solving techniques	4-V					3-V
Applies decision-making techniques			3-V			2
Communication and Information Processing						
Effectively interprets and synthesizes information	2	2	2			
Effectively uses a variety of information-gathering techniques and information resources		2	3-V			
Accurately assesses the value of information	3-V	2	2			2
Expresses ideas clearly	3-V	2	2	4-V	4-V	2
Effectively communicates with diverse audiences and for diverse purposes			2	2	2	
Effectively communicates through a variety of media			1	2	2	
Self-Regulation						
Seeks different perspectives and considers choices before acting				1	3-V	
Generates and pursues personal standards of performance	2	2	3-V		2	2
Evaluates effectiveness of own actions	2	2	2		2	2
Restrains impulsivity	2	2			2	2
Working with Others						
Works toward the achievement of group goals		2			2	2
Demonstrates effective interpersonal skills	2	2	1	3-V	2	
Takes a position when the situation warrants		2	2			

Note that the student has received traditional grades for the courses he took: Algebra II, Biology, and so on. However, each course also addresses a number of standards from the general categories of thinking and reasoning, communication and information processing, self-regulation and working well with others. The student received a score of 1-4 on these standards. Any score of 3 or higher is coded with the letter "v" indicating that the student has received a validation for that standard as addressed in that particular course.

Under this model, a transcript would indicate the number of validations that have been obtained for each standard. This is depicted in Exhibit 9.5 on the next two pages. Note that no entry is made for a standard if a student has not received a judgment of 3 or 4. Standards on which three or more validations have been recorded are coded with a checkmark indicating that the requisite number of validations have been obtained.

The multiple validations model was designed and popularized by Alverno College in Milwaukee, Wisconsin. Alverno is a small liberal arts college that has been using the multiple validation model for almost two decades (Alverno College Faculty, 1985). The actual course offerings at Alverno look fairly traditional when listed. However, in addition to "passing" the required general courses and specific courses for their major, each student must receive validations in eight general standards:

1. Effective communication ability
2. Analytic capability
3. Problem-solving ability
4. Valuing in a decision-making context
5. Effective social interactions
6. Taking responsibility for the global environment
7. Effective citizenship
8. Aesthetic responsiveness

(Alverno College Faculty, 1985, p. 5)

Each of these general standards is evaluated on a specific four-point scale. For example, the four performance levels for the problem-solving standard, standard 3, are

Level 4: Integrates approach
Level 3: Resolves problems
Level 2: Formulates problem
Level 1: Discerns problem

(Alverno College Faculty, 1985, p. 5)

Exhibit 9.5 Transcript for a Sophomore Student With Validations Noted

CENTRAL HIGH SCHOOL REPORT CARD
Fall, 1996

Name: Jonathan Starek
ID#: 463650

	Grade 9						Grade 10						Validations met
	Algebra I	Earth Science	English I	Spanish I	World History	Phys. Ed.	Algebra II	Biology	English II	Spanish II	Geography	Phys. Ed.	
Thinking and Reasoning													
Understands and applies basic principles of presenting an argument			3		3								
Understands and applies basic principles of logic and reasoning		3					3	4	3	3			✓
Effectively uses mental processes that are based on identifying similarities and differences			3						3				✓
Understands and applies basic principles of hypothesis testing and scientific inquiry								3					
Applies basic trouble-shooting and problem-solving techniques	3						4		3			3	✓
Applies decision-making techniques													
Communication and Information Processing													
Effectively interprets and synthesizes information											3		
Effectively uses a variety of information-gathering techniques and information resources													
Accurately assesses the value of information							3						
Expresses ideas clearly							3			4	4		✓
Effectively communicates with diverse audiences and for diverse purposes													
Effectively communicates through a variety of media													

Exhibit 9.5 Transcript for a Sophomore Student With Validations Noted (continued)

CENTRAL HIGH SCHOOL REPORT CARD
Fall, 1996

| | Grade 9 | | | | | | Grade 10 | | | | | | |
	Algebra I	Earth Science	English I	Spanish I	World History	Phys. Ed.	Algebra II	Biology	English II	Spanish II	Geography	Phys. Ed.	Validations met
Name: Jonathan Starek													
ID#: 463650													
Self-Regulation													
Seeks different perspectives and considers choices before acting											3		
Generates and pursues personal standards of performance									3				
Evaluates effectiveness of own actions													
Restrains impulsivity													
Working with Others													
Works toward the achievement of group goals													
Demonstrates effective interpersonal skills									3				
Takes a position when the situation warrants													

237

Of course, these levels are articulated in much finer detail for actual classroom use. In fact, a great amount of training on how to define these performance levels within the context of specific courses is a prerequisite to obtaining faculty status at Alverno.

At the core of the Alverno model is the principle that students must demonstrate competence in the eight general standards in a variety of situations. This is referred to as "multiplicity." As described by the Alverno College Faculty (1985), multiplicity is

> [built] into a student's experience of assessment by requiring demonstration of an ability in several settings, by introducing variety of modes into their assessment design, and by constantly providing multiple viewpoints— co-assessment with faculty, off-campus assessors, peers, and self-assessment.

> In practice, a student must demonstrate each level of an ability in a variety of contexts in order to achieve validation for that level. For example, she might show her powers of observing (analysis, level 1) at a microscope in her science course, in a drawing in her art class, and in a report of observed behavior for her psychology class. (p. 9)

In effect, the concept of multiplicity is at the core of the multiple validation model. Multiple validations provide an opportunity for students to demonstrate their skill on a given standard within a variety of contexts.

By definition, the multiple validation model is standards-based—students must receive a specific number of validations on standards. The advantage to this model is the power of multiplicity: Each standard is approached in a variety of settings. The major disadvantage to this model is scheduling. Each student's schedule must be planned in such a way that the student is ensured the opportunity to receive the required number of validations on each standard. Another disadvantage to this approach is that it is usually restricted to standards that cut across all content areas, such as thinking and reasoning standards, general communication standards, self-regulation standards, and standards related to working with others.

Grade-Level Approaches

Using the grade-level model, performance on standards is reported in lieu of grades at each grade level. That is, no overall grades are given, only scores on standards that represent various performance levels. Theoretically, a district or school can be standards based or standards referenced relative to this model. If a school is standards referenced, it would simply report student performance on each standard but not retain students if they did not meet a specific level of achievement.

This is the basic approach taken by Clyde Miller Elementary School in Aurora, Colorado (Kenney & Perry, 1994). Students receive scores on a highly general four-point scale like that below:

Level 4   Advanced performance: exceeds expectations

Level 3   Proficient performance: meets expectations

Level 2   Basic performance: exhibits some minor problems

Level 1   Novice performance: does not meet expectations

This highly general scale can be applied to virtually any type of standard. Clyde Miller Elementary applies its scale to both content standards (which it refers to as "content outcomes") and to lifelong learning standards (which it refers to as "learner outcomes"). Exhibit 9.6 depicts a portion of the report card dedicated to content standards. Exhibit 9.7 (next page) depicts a portion of the report card dedicated to the lifelong learning standards.

Exhibit 9.6 Portion of Report Card on Content Standards (Outcomes): Sample Standards for Three of Twelve Content Outcomes

AURORA PUBLIC SCHOOLS, CLYDE MILLER ELEMENTARY, STUDENT PROGRESS REPORT

Student Name	Student Number	Year	Quarter	Track	Teacher	Grade
		1994-95				

Content Outcomes	Quarter	I	II	III	IV
Science Literacy					
Knows how systems work					
Creates models					
Interprets patterns					
Uses the scientific method					
Arts and Humanities--Literature					
Evaluates literature					
Uses information from literature					
Mathematics Proficiency					
Solves Problems (a proficiency that is scored every quarter)					
Uses mathematical language					
Uses number sense					
Recognizes and creates patterns					
Develops concepts of geometry					
Uses probability and statistics					

Note: From "Talking With Parents About Performance-Based Report Cards," by E. Kenney and S. Perry, in *Educational Leadership*, 52(2), 24-27. Copyright © 1994 by ASCD. All rights reserved.

Exhibit 9.7 Portion of Report Card on Lifelong Learning Standards (Outcomes): Sample Standards for Two of Five Learner Outcomes

Student Name _____

Content Outcomes Quarter	I	II	III	IV
Collaborative Worker				
Takes charge of his/her behavior in group				
Works with group to reach goal				
Communicates well with others				
Shows respect for others				
Quality Producer				
Makes a product that meets a purpose				
Makes a product for an audience				
Makes a product that is well done				
Uses resources/technology				

Note: From "Talking With Parents About Performance-Based Report Cards," by E. Kenney and S. Perry, in *Educational Leadership*, 52(2), 24-27. Copyright © 1994 by ASCD. All rights reserved.

As students progress through the grades, they receive continual feedback on their performance relative to specific standards.

This model works quite well until the high school years. As discussed in chapter 4, this is where the concept of grade-level benchmarks breaks down. However, at the high school level, options exist such as the use of upper and lower division benchmarks.

A school or district can also utilize this design in a standards-based mode. Here, students are not allowed to pass from grade level to grade level without meeting specific performance levels on all standards or on selected standards. This standards-based, grade-level model is reminiscent of the competency-based movement of the 1970s (see Burns & Klingstedt, 1973; Thompson, 1977; Clark & Thomson, 1976).

As described in chapter 7, the "high stakes" nature of the grade-level, standards-based model is a debilitating drawback. Simply stated, holding a student back from matriculating to the next grade because he or she does not meet the required performance level for a standard is a serious endeavor with extreme consequences for students, parents, and teachers. Consequently, we strongly caution against the use of this model, although some districts we have worked with are giving it serious consideration.

One way to "soften" the "high stakes" nature of this grade-level model is to be standards based at selected levels as opposed to every grade level. This was discussed in chapter 7. For example, a district might be standards-based at the following transition points:

Level 1: from end of primary to the beginning of upper-elementary

Level 2: from the end of upper-elementary to the beginning of middle school or junior high

Level 3: from the end of middle school or junior high to the beginning of lower division high school

Level 4: from the end of lower division high school to the beginning of upper division high school

Level 5: from the end of upper division high school to college or entry into the world of work

However, within each level, the district would be standards referenced. As students move from first grade to second grade, for example, their performance on specific standards would be reported, but students would not be held back if they did not meet specific performance levels on specific standards.

The Nongraded, Standards-Based Approach

This model is a logical extension of the transition point model just described. Here the school or district is standards-based at specific transition points. Additionally, there are no formal grade levels and no benchmarks within intervals. Rather, all benchmarks are written as end-of-interval expectations. For example, the upper elementary benchmarks are written as expectations regarding student understanding and skill at the end of the upper elementary level; the middle school benchmarks are written as expectations of students' understanding and skill at the upper elementary level, and so on. A key feature of this model is that within an interval students work on benchmarks at their own pace. When a student has mastered the benchmarks in a particular subject area at a particular interval, he or she is free to move on to the benchmarks at the next level. Theoretically, then, a student could be working on the mathematics benchmarks at the upper high school level and, at the same time, be working on the history benchmarks at the upper elementary level. The reporting system for this approach necessarily documents the level at which students were functioning for each subject area. Exhibit 9.8 presents a transcript that might be used in this nongraded, standards-based model.

Exhibit 9.8 Transcript Using Non-Graded, Standards-Based Approach

JEFFERSON MIDDLE SCHOOL

Name _____   ID# _____

Address _____

Key: Performance   Approximate Grade Level
        N: Novice   Level 1: Early Elementary
        B: Basic   Level 2: Late Elementary
        P: Proficient   Level 3: Middle School
        A: Advanced   Level 4: High School

Subject	Level	Standards	Performance
MATH	4	Uses a variety of strategies in the problem-solving process	N
		Understands and applies properties of the concept of numbers	B
		Uses computation procedures effectively	N
		Understands and applies properties of the concept of measurement	B
		Understands and applies properties of the concept of geometry	N
		Understands and applies properties of the concept of algebra	N
		Understands and applies properties of the concept of probability and statistics	N
SCIENCE	2	Understands essential ideas about the universe and the Earth's place in it	P
		Understands the genetic basis for the transfer of biological characteristics from one generation to the next	A
		Understands motion and the principles that explain it	A
		Understands energy types, sources, and conversion, and their relationship to heat and temperature	A
		Understands the nature of scientific knowledge and inquiry	A
LANG ARTS	3	Demonstrates competence in the writing process	P
		Writes with a command of grammar and mechanics	P
		Applies the reading process to specific types of texts	B
		Demonstrates competence in the skills and strategies of the reading process	B
		Demonstrates an understanding of the nature and function of the English language	P
		Gathers and uses information for research purposes	P
		Demonstrates competence in speaking and listening as tools for learning	A
		Familiarity with literary works of enduring quality	B

The great advantage to this model is that students are not held back from working on advanced standards simply because they are not a certain age or at a certain grade level. Conversely, they are not pushed into working on standards that are too difficult for them simply because they are a certain age or are at a certain grade level. The entire model is designed to allow for the natural developmental differences that will exist in a student across subject areas. Specifically, current theory in learning theory asserts that any individual will be highly developed in some areas, yet underdeveloped in other areas (see Case, 1985;

Fischer, 1980; Gardner, 1983, 1991; Guilford, 1967; Meeker, 1969). This model highlights the natural abilities and interests of individual students.

Although the logic of this model is strong, it is very difficult to implement because of the massive changes it requires in scheduling, assessment, reporting, and resource allocations. It is probably for this reason that no school or district we are aware of has seriously attempted to implement this model. Conversely, the vast majority of districts and schools we have worked with have commented on the intuitive appeal of this model and have expressed an interest in working toward implementing it at some future date.

Designing Your Own Model

It is important to recognize that the four approaches described in this chapter are not mutually exclusive. It is legitimate, even advisable, to combine elements from two or more approaches to construct a model that fits the particular needs of a school or district. For example, a district might use externally developed, forced-choice tests and performance tasks (Approach I) at key transition points (e.g., end of elementary, end of middle school, end of high school). Additionally, the district might require students to complete performance tasks, exhibitions, and portfolios (Approach III) at those same transition points. The district might also report overall grades in each subject area in addition to scores on individual standards (Approach IV). Finally, the district might choose to be standards based regarding the external assessments and performance tasks, exhibitions, and portfolios at the transition points, but be standards referenced regarding the scores on individual standards reported at each grade level. Stated differently, the district would not hold students back if they did not receive specific scores on the standards addressed in individual courses, but it would not allow students to matriculate from one level to the next if they did not obtain specific scores on the external assessments and on the performance tasks, exhibitions, and portfolios. The working principle behind designing a system is that it should meet the individual goals and aspirations of the school or district doing the designing.

Summary And Recommendations

In this chapter, we have described four approaches to organizing a district or school around standards. Models in the first approach utilize external assessments that might be comprised of traditional, forced-choice items or, more preferably, performance tasks. Models in the second approach embed standards in a specific course or courses referred to as core courses. Performance tasks, exhibitions, and portfolios are the focus of the third approach. Commonly, students take a number of years to construct these complex assignments and then present them at the end of key transition grades. The key characteristic of the fourth approach is that performance on individual standards is reported for each student. The primary recommendation made in this chapter is that districts and schools should combine elements from all four approaches to design a system that is unique to their particular needs and desires.

Chapter 10

How Do We Proceed?

Even the casual reader of this book will likely grasp the message that designing a district or school around standards is a complex endeavor fraught with many hazards. As a result of reading this book some may conclude that standards-based or standards-referenced education is not for them. This is a legitimate, and even advisable, option that we commonly recommend to schools and districts that do not have the energy and resources necessary to design and implement a standards-based or standards-referenced system. However, our purpose in writing this book was to encourage districts and schools to reorganize curriculum, instruction, assessment, and reporting systems around standards and to provide specific options and guidance in that endeavor.

A district or school that chooses to embark on the path of such reform might legitimately ask the question, How do we proceed? Unfortunately, we can offer no simple answer. Districts and schools approach standards-based and standards-referenced reform in a variety of ways. As a result of working with a variety of districts and schools, however, we have noticed that there are certain practices that seem to enhance and facilitate the design and implementation of standards-based or standards-referenced reform. Here we describe four of those practices. We have also produced a vignette describing an approach one district took. This is presented in Appendix E.

Study Standards-Based Reform

One of the most important practices a district or school can engage in is to study the nature of standards-based or standards-referenced education in detail. Many districts and schools with which we have worked jump into standards-based or standards-referenced reform without realizing the consequences of the various decisions they have made. For example, more than one district we have worked with has spent a considerable amount of time and energy articulating highly specific grade-level benchmarks without realizing that the approach they were taking implied a drastic change in their curriculum and the textbooks they were using. When they realized the probable consequences of their efforts, they discontinued the project until they studied the feasibility of buying new textbooks. Obviously, it would have been better if they had realized the implication of what they were doing from the outset. This is only one example of many in which the failure to consider the full implications of standards-based or standards-referenced reform has caused a school or district to expend a great deal of time and energy on a project that was ultimately discontinued.

It is our hope that this book will become a valuable tool for districts and schools as they undertake standards-based and standards-referenced reform. Although sometimes relatively technical and perhaps even tedious, the discussions in this text were intended to provide educators with a firm grasp of standards-based and standards-referenced reform. We also highly recommend that educators immerse themselves in the writings of other researchers and theorists currently engaged in designing models of standards-based and standards-referenced reform. Among those researchers and theorists leading the field are Grant Wiggins, Richard Stiggins, Jay McTighe, Thomas Guskey, William Spady, and Ruth Mitchell. A review of the references section in this book will provide the reader with a preliminary set of works by each of these individuals.

Do Not Write Anything In Stone

A district or school frequently begins the process of organizing schooling around standards by developing documents that articulate a specific direction in terms of standards, reporting systems, graduation requirements, and the like. After these documents have been published and, all too frequently, widely disseminated, the district or school identifies an error in its initial reasoning or it simply concludes that it would be better to take a slightly different approach from the one originally designed. This is quite common in the design and implementation of any complex endeavor. The final product rarely looks precisely the way it was originally conceptualized.

In our experience, however, all too often districts and schools are reticent or even unwilling to make the desired modifications simply because the original documents are viewed as products that cannot be altered. Yet, frequently when we have queried members of the writing teams that produced these initial documents, we found that they believed that their work was intended as a beginning point only. In addition, they had every expectation that their work would be changed. Some were quite surprised that the document they produced had taken on such a revered and prescriptive status. One of the healthiest perspectives a district or school can take is to view all plans and documents as drafts that will most likely be altered until the standards-based or standards-referenced system is actually implemented.

Involve The Classroom Teacher From The Outset

A common practice when designing a standards-based or standards-referenced system is to ignore the classroom teacher until very late in the design process. For example, districts and schools will initially spend their time and energy writing standards and their related assessments. This is usually done by groups of teachers, administrators, and community members. However, the work of these groups rarely affects the daily life of the classroom teachers. Consequently, the efforts of the district or school to design a standards-based or standards-referenced system commonly lives as an abstract idea to most teachers—an abstract idea that might, but most likely will not, manifest at some future date. We believe that ignoring the classroom level is a costly and unnecessary practice. It is costly in the sense that the very individuals who will be primarily responsible for carrying out the standards-based or standards-referenced system once implemented—the classroom teachers—do not share in the initial excitement that constructing such a system can generate. It is unnecessary in the sense that there are at least two activities that classroom teachers can be engaged in from the outset even if they are not involved in the decision-making process regarding standards, assessment and record keeping.

The first activity is performance tasks. In chapters 5 and 8, we described in detail how performance tasks might be used in the classroom for instructional purposes as well as assessment purposes. It is fairly safe to assume that no matter what specific model the district or school designs, performance tasks will be a useful activity at every grade level in every subject area. Consequently, it is highly advisable to offer staff development programs for classroom teachers that depict how performance tasks can be utilized in the classroom. We have found that districts and schools that involve classroom teachers in the use of performance tasks from the outset create an environment of positive expectations about the district or school initiatives around standards.

A second activity in which all teachers can engage is to alter their grading practices from a dependence on the cumulative assumption to a focus on standards. This, of course, demands more time and effort. As described in chapter 8, this can be done even before the district or school has articulated standards and benchmarks. Following the nine steps outlined in chapter 8, teachers organize the content within their units of instruction into meaningful categories (i.e., "teacher-developed" standards) and then use multiple forms of assessment to gather information on student performance on these categories of information and skill. Overall grades are then computed using a combination of the scores on the various categories. This type of activity by teachers within a district or school can truly establish the groundwork for a standards-based or standards-referenced system, particularly if the district or school wishes to report student performance on individual standards (see discussion of Approach IV in chapter 9).

Make Standards Reform The Overarching Initiative

Once a district or school is ready to implement its model of standards-based or standards-referenced education, it should be the only reform initiative or, at least, the overarching reform initiative. Standards-based or standards-referenced reform, if designed properly, is such a comprehensive endeavor that it should subsume every other reform initiative in the district or school. This does not imply that a district or school cannot or should not engage in the pursuit of new ideas and new practices. If new techniques are available for assessing students, teaching content, motivating students, and the like, these promising practices should be presented to teachers. However, every new practice should be presented within the context of the standards-based or standards-referenced model that is being implemented. If a new method of instruction is to be presented to teachers, it should be tied directly to the improvement of student performance on standards; if a new method of assessment is to be presented to teachers, it should be directly linked to teacher judgment of student performance on standards and so on.

If a district or school views standards-based or standards-referenced reform as just another practice that is parallel to such fine, but less comprehensive, initiatives as cooperative learning, the teaching of thinking, and the like, then that district or school probably does not have a firm understanding of standards-based and standards-referenced reform.

A Word Of Encouragement

In this book, we have attempted to describe in adequate detail the many characteristics and options involved in standards-based and standards-referenced reform. We have also tried to be candid in our appraisal of the time, energy and resources necessary to design and implement such reform. In doing so, we realize that we run the risk of "scaring off" some would be reformers. If this is the case, we would like to conclude with the strong assertion that standards-based and standards-referenced education represents the single most promising and systematic reform of at least the last two decades. No other endeavor, in our opinion, has the potential of generating as many positive effects at the district, school, and classroom levels. We encourage readers to accept the challenges of such reform with confidence that the rewards will justify the efforts.

Documents to Consult for Comprehensive Review of Subject Areas

Arts

California Department of Education. (1989). *Visual and Performing Arts Framework For California Public Schools: Kindergarten Through Grade Twelve*. Sacramento, CA: Author.

California Department of Education. (1991). *Model Curriculum Standards: Grades Nine Through Twelve*. Sacramento, CA: Author.

Consortium of National Arts Education Associations. (1994). *National Standards for Arts Education: What Every Young American Should Know and Be Able to Do in the Arts*. Reston, VA: Music Educators National Conference.

Music Educators National Conference. (1986). *The School Music Program: Description and Standards*. Reston, VA: Author.

National Assessment of Educational Progress Arts Education Consensus Project. (1994). *Arts Education Assessment Framework*. Washington, DC: National Assessment Governing Board.

Civics

Carnevale, A. P., Gainer, L. J., & Meltzer, A. S. (1990). *Workplace Basics: The Essential Skills Employers Want*. San Francisco: Jossey-Bass.

Center for Civic Education. (1994). *National Standards for Civics and Government*. Calabasas, CA: Author.

Center for Occupational Research and Development. (1995). *National Voluntary Skills Standard: Hazardous Materials Management Technology*. Waco, TX: Author.

College Board. (1983). *Academic Preparation for College: What Students Need to Know and Be Able to Do*. New York: College Entrance Examination Board.

Law in a Free Society. (1977). *Authority I (Elementary): A Civic Education Unit* (Teacher's Ed.). Calabasas, CA: Author.

Law in a Free Society. (1977). *Privacy I (Elementary): A Civic Education Unit* (Teacher's Ed.). Calabasas, CA: Author.

Law in a Free Society. (1977). *Privacy II (Elementary): A Civic Education Unit* (Teacher's Ed.). Calabasas, CA: Author.

Law in a Free Society. (1979). *Justice I (Elementary): A Civic Education Unit* (Teacher's Ed.). Calabasas, CA: Author.

Law in a Free Society. (1983). *Responsibility I (Elementary): A Civic Education Unit* (Teacher's Ed.). Calabasas, CA: Author.

National Council for the Social Studies. (1994). *Expectations of Excellence: Curriculum Standards for Social Studies*. Washington, DC: Author.

Quigley, C. N., & Bahmmeller, C. F. (Eds.). (1991). *Civitas: A Framework for Civic Education*. (National Council for Social Studies, Bulletin No. 86). Calabasas, CA: Center for Civic Education.

Economics

Colorado Council on Economic Education. (1994). *Economics: Conceptual Content Standards, Grades K-12*. (Draft). Denver: Colorado Council on Economic Education.

Gilliard, J. V., Caldwell, J. Dalgaard, B. R., Highsmith, R. J., Reinke, R., & Watts, M. (with Leet, D. R., Malone, M. G., & Ellington, L.). (1989). *Economics, What and When: Scope and Sequence Guidelines, K-12*. New York: Joint Council on Economic Education.

National Council for the Social Studies. (1994). *Expectations of Excellence: Curriculum Standards for Social Studies*. Washington, DC: Author.

National Council on Economic Education. (1996, August). *Content Statements for State Standards in Economics, K-12* (Draft). New York: Author.

Saunders, P., & Gilliard, J. (Eds.). (1995). *A Framework for Teaching Basic Economic Concepts With Scope and Sequence Guidelines, K-12*. New York: National Council on Economic Education.

English Language Arts

Australian Education Council. (1994). *English: A Curriculum Profile for Australian Schools.* Commonwealth of Australia: Curriculum Corporation.

California Department of Education. (1989). *Recommended Literature, Grades Nine Through Twelve.* Sacramento, CA: Author.

California Department of Education. (1990). *Recommended Readings in Literature, Kindergarten Through Grade Eight.* Sacramento, CA: Author.

California Department of Education. (1993). *The Writing Assessment Handbook: High School.* Sacramento, CA: Author.

California Department of Education. (1994). *1994 Elementary Performance Assessments: Integrated English-Language Arts Illustrative Material, Grade 4.* Sacramento, CA: Author.

California Department of Education. (1994). *1994 Middle Grades Performance Assessments: Integrated English-Language Arts Illustrative Material, Grade 8.* Sacramento, CA: Author.

Committee on the Junior High and Middle School Booklist of the National Council of Teachers of English & Nilsen, A.P. (Ed.). (1991). *Your Reading: A Booklist for Junior High and Middle School Students* (8th Ed.). Urbana, IL: National Council of Teachers of English.

Committee on the Senior High School Booklist of the National Council of Teachers of English & Wurth, S. (Ed.). (1992). *Books for You: A Booklist for Senior High Students* (11th Ed.). Urbana, IL: National Council of Teachers of English.

Edison Project. (1994). *Student Standards for the Elementary Academy.* New York: Author.

Edison Project. (1994). *Student Standards for the Junior Academy.* New York: Author.

Edison Project. (1994). *Student Standards for the Primary Academy.* New York: Author.

Gillespie, J. T. (Ed.). (1991). *Best Books for Junior High Readers.* New Providence, NJ: Bowker.

Gillespie, J. T. (Ed.). (1991). *Best Books for Senior High Readers.* New Providence, NJ: Bowker.

Hirsch, E. D., Jr. (1987). *Cultural Literacy: What Every American Needs to Know.* Boston: Houghton Mifflin Company.

Hirsch, E.D., Jr. (Ed.). (1993). *What Your 1st Grader Needs to Know: Fundamentals of a Good First-Grade Education. The Core Knowledge Series: Resource Books for Grades One Through Six, Book I.* New York: Delta.

Hirsch, E.D., Jr. (Ed.). (1993). *What Your 2nd Grader Needs to Know: Fundamentals of a Good Second-Grade Education. The Core Knowledge Series: Resource Books for Grades One Through Six, Book II.* New York: Delta.

Hirsch, E.D., Jr. (Ed.). (1993). *What Your 3rd Grader Needs to Know: Fundamentals of a Good Third-Grade Education. The Core Knowledge Series: Resource Books for Grades One Through Six, Book III.* New York: Delta.

Hirsch, E.D., Jr. (Ed.). (1993). *What Your 4th Grader Needs to Know: Fundamentals of a Good Fourth-Grade Education. The Core Knowledge Series: Resource Books for Grades One Through Six, Book IV.* New York: Delta.

Hirsch, E.D., Jr. (Ed.). (1993). *What Your 5th Grader Needs to Know: Fundamentals of a Good Fifth-Grade Education. The Core Knowledge Series: Resource Books for Grades One Through Six, Book V.* New York: Delta.

Hirsch, E.D., Jr. (Ed.). (1993). *What Your 6th Grader Needs to Know: Fundamentals of a Good Sixth-Grade Education. The Core Knowledge Series: Resource Books for Grades One Through Six, Book VI.* New York: Delta.

National Assessment of Educational Progress. (1992). *Description of Writing Achievement Levels-Setting Process and Proposed Achievement Level Definitions.* Iowa City, IA: American College Testing Program.

National Assessment of Educational Progress Reading Consensus Project. (1990). *Assessment and Exercise Specifications: 1992 NAEP Reading Assessment.* Washington, DC: National Assessment Governing Board.

National Assessment of Educational Progress Reading Consensus Project. (1990). *Reading Assessment Framework for the 1992 National Assessment of Educational Progress.* Washington, DC: National Assessment Governing Board.

National Council of Teachers of English. (1982). *Essentials of English: A Document for Reflection and Dialogue.* Urbana, IL: Author.

National Council of Teachers of English. (1989). *The English Coalition Conference: Democracy Through Language.* Urbana, IL: Author.

National Council of Teachers of English and the International Reading Association. (1996). *Standards for the English Language Arts.* Urbana, IL: National Council of Teachers of English.

New Standards. (1995, June). *Draft Performance Standards for English Language Arts.* Washington, DC: Author.

New York State Education Department. (1994). *Curriculum, Instruction, and Assessment: Preliminary Draft Framework for English Language Arts.* Albany: Author.

Stotsky, S., Anderson, P., & Beierl, D. (1989). *Variety and Individualism in the English Class: Teacher-Recommended Lists of Reading for Grades 7-12.* Boston: New England Association of Teachers of English.

Foreign Language

Colorado Department of Education. (1996, June). *Content Standards for Foreign Language.* (Draft). Denver, CO: Author.

National Standards in Foreign Language Education Project. (1996). *Standards for Foreign Language Learning: Preparing for the 21st Century.* Lawrence, KS: Allen Press, Inc.

Geography

Geographic Education National Implementations Project. (1987). *K-6 Geography: Themes, Key Ideas, and Learning Opportunities.* Washington, DC: Author.

Geography Education Standards Project. (1994). *Geography for Life: National Geography Standards.* Washington, DC: National Geographic Research and Exploration.

Joint Committee on Geographic Education. (1984). *Guidelines for Geographic Education: Elementary and Secondary Schools.* Washington, DC: Association of American Geographers.

National Assessment of Educational Progress. (1992). *Item Specifications: 1994 National Assessment of Educational Progress in Geography.* Washington, DC: National Assessment Governing Board.

National Assessment of Educational Progress Geography Consensus Project. (1992). *Geography Assessment Framework for the 1994 National Assessment of Educational Progress.* (Draft). Washington, DC: National Assessment Governing Board.

Health

California Department of Education. (1994). *Health Framework for California Public Schools: Kindergarten Through Grade Twelve.* Sacramento, CA: Author.

Joint Committee on Health Education Terminology. (1991). Report of the 1990 Joint Committee on Health Education Terminology. *Journal of Health Education, 22,* (2), 97-107.

Joint Committee on National Health Education Standards. (1995). *National Health Education Standards: Achieving Health Literacy.* Reston, VA: Association for the Advancement of Health Education.

Michigan State Board of Education. (1988). *Michigan Essential Goals and Objectives for Health Education.* Lansing, MI: Author.

History

Bradley Commission on History in the Schools. (1988). *Building a History Curriculum: Guidelines for Teaching History in the Schools.* Washington, DC: Educational Excellence Network.

California Department of Education. (1989). *Recommended Literature, Grades Nine Through Twelve.* Sacramento, CA: Author.

Crabtree, C., Nash, G. B., Gagnon, P., & Waugh, S. (Eds.). (1992). *Lessons From History: Essential Understandings and Historical Perspectives Students Should Acquire.* Los Angeles: National Center for History in the Schools.

Gagnon, P., & Bradley Commission on History in the Schools (Eds.). (1989). *Historical Literacy: The Case for History in American Education.* Boston: Houghton Mifflin Company.

National Assessment of Educational Progress. (n.d.). *Framework for the 1994 National Assessment of Educational Progress U.S. History Assessment.* Washington, DC: Author.

National Assessment of Educational Progress. (1992). *Provisional Item Specifications: 1994 National Assessment of Educational Progress in U.S. History.* Washington, DC: National Assessment Governing Board.

National Assessment of Educational Progress in U.S. History. (1994). *Provisional Item Specifications.* Washington, DC: Council of Chief State School Officers.

National Center for History in the Schools. (1994). *National Standards for History for Grades K-4: Expanding Children's World in Time and Space.* Los Angeles: Author.

National Center for History in the Schools. (1994). *National Standards for United States History: Exploring the American Experience.* Los Angeles: Author.

National Center for History in the Schools. (1994). *National Standards for World History: Exploring Paths to the Present.* Los Angeles: Author.

National Center for History in the Schools. (1996). *National Standards for History: Basic Edition.* Los Angeles: Author.

National Council for the Social Studies. (1994). *Expectations of Excellence: Curriculum Standards for Social Studies.* Washington, DC: Author.

Mathematics

National Assessment of Educational Progress. (1992, March 26). *Content Specifications for the 1994 National Assessment of Educational Progress Mathematics Assessment.* Washington, DC: Author.

National Assessment of Educational Progress. (1992, March 31). *Framework for the 1994 National Assessment of Educational Progress Mathematics Assessment.* Washington, DC: Author.

National Council of Teachers of Mathematics. (1989). *Curriculum and Evaluation Standards for School Mathematics.* Reston, VA: Author.

New Standards. (1995, June). *Draft Performance Standards for Mathematics.* Washington, DC: Author.

Physical Education

Michigan Department of Education. (1995, September). *Physical Education: Working Draft Content Standards and Benchmarks.* (Draft). Lansing: Author.

National Association for Sport and Physical Education. (1992). *Outcomes of Quality Physical Education Programs.* Reston, VA: Author.

National Association for Sport and Physical Education. (1995). *Moving Into the Future, National Standards for Physical Education: A Guide to Content and Assessment.* St. Louis: Mosby.

Science

Aldridge, B. G. (Ed). (1995). *Scope, Sequence, and Coordination of Secondary School Science: Vol. 3. A High School Framework for National Science Education Standards.* Arlington, VA: National Science Teachers Association.

Aldridge, B. G., & Strassenburg, A. A. (Eds.). (1995). *Scope, Sequence, and Coordination of National Science Education Content Standards: An Addendum to the Content Core Based on the 1994 Draft National Science Education Standards.* Arlington, VA: National Science Teachers Association.

California Department of Education. (1990). *Science Framework for California Public Schools: Kindergarten Through Grade 12.* Sacramento, CA: Author.

National Assessment of Educational Progress. (1989). *Science Objectives: 1990 Assessment.* Princeton, NJ: Educational Testing Service.

National Assessment of Educational Progress Science Consensus Project. (1993). *Science Assessment and Exercise Specifications for the 1994 National Assessment of Educational Progress.* Washington, DC: National Assessment Governing Board.

National Research Council. (1996). *National Science Education Standards.* Washington, DC: National Academy Press.

National Science Board Commission on Precollege Education in Mathematics, Science and Technology. (1983). *Educating Americans for the 21st Century.* Washington, DC: National Science Board Commission.

Pearsall, M. K. (Ed). (1993). *Scope, Sequence, and Coordination of Secondary School Science. Vol. 1. The Content Core: A Guide for Curriculum Designers.* Washington, DC: National Science Teachers Association.

Project 2061, American Association for the Advancement of Science. (1989). *Science for All Americans.* Washington, DC: Author.

Project 2061, American Association for the Advancement of Science. (1993). *Benchmarks for Science Literacy.* New York: Oxford University Press.

Social Studies

National Council for the Social Studies. (1994). *Expectations of Excellence: Curriculum Standards for Social Studies.* Washington, DC: Author.

Standards Setting: State By State

State	Content Organization	Grade Range	AFT	Degree of Local Control	Timeline	Current or recently completed work
Alabama	The Alabama Course of Study in Science, recently adopted, uses content standards. Earlier courses of study organize outcomes for grades K-6 under topics or sub-goals and organize outcomes for grades 7-12 courses under instructional objectives.	Varies by subject area. Mathematics, as an example, provides content descriptions for each grade level K-8, and by course for grades 9-12.	Y	The courses of study describe the minimum course content for Alabama public schools. Schools are required to implement the courses of study in a number of subject areas, including science, language arts, and social studies. School systems may include additional content, as well as implementation guidelines, resources and/or activities.	Subject areas are on a 6-year update cycle. Courses of study are currently being updated for mathematics, physical education, and health education.	The course of study in science was published in 1995; English language arts in 1993; social studies in 1992; visual arts, music, and foreign language in 1991; agribusiness, business, trade and industrial education, home economics, and marketing in 1990.
Alaska	Standards	No grade-specific standards	N	Standards are voluntary.	Frameworks, which are based on the standards, are in the publishing stage for English/language arts, math/science, and social studies. These frameworks will be made available on the Alaska Department of Education Homepage by fall 1996 (http://www.educ.state.ak.us). Frameworks for world languages and the arts should be completed in summer, 1997.	Standards in the following areas were adopted by the Alaska State Board of Education in 1994 and 1995: • English/language arts • mathematics • science • government and citizenship • geography • history • skills for a healthy life • the arts • world languages • and technology
Arizona	Standards	PreK-K, 1-4, 5-8, 9-12, honors	Y	Mandatory. The Arizona Student Achievement Program (ASAP) Assessment will be implemented to test students' achievement of standards in mathematics, language arts (reading and writing), and skills relevant to the workplace.	Academic standards are now in revision. Standards for mathematics and writing are up for board approval on August 7, 1996. Standards for social studies and the arts are still in process.	The reading standards have recently been approved. Standards for foreign language, workplace skills, comprehensive health (including physical education), science, and technology are in draft form.

Standards Setting: State By State

State	Content Organization	Grade Range	AFT	Degree of Local Control	Timeline	Current or recently completed work
Arkansas	Strands organize content standards, which organize student learning expectations.	K-4, 5-8, 9-12	N	State-level assessments are to measure students' ability to apply core concepts and skills.	Health and physical education will be completed by fall, 1996.	English language, foreign language, mathematics, music, reading, social studies, science, and visual arts are in near-final draft form.
California	Strands organize standards, which change at each grade level; examples of student performance are provided for each standard.	Varies by subject area. By completion of the current project, standards will be provided for each grade level.	N	Adoption of the standards is currently voluntary.	History/social science, science, and math will be completed by fall, 1997. All other subject areas will be completed by fall, 1998.	English/language arts will be completed by fall, 1996. Draft standards are available for English/language arts, mathematics, science, social studies, health, physical education, the arts, foreign language, applied learning, service-learning, career preparation, industrial and technology education, health careers, and home economics.
Colorado	Standards are frequently divided into two or more separate components; these are followed by statements of what students should know and be able to do to meet the standard at each grade level.	K-4, 5-8, 9-12	Y	Local school boards grant diplomas and set graduation requirements; legislation requires districts to meet or exceed state model content standards in math, science, history, geography, reading, and writing by 1997.	Standards in visual arts, civics, economics, foreign language, music, and physical education have been adopted as working drafts. These standards should be adopted in final form in spring, 1997.	Standards in geography, history, mathematics, reading and writing, and science were adopted by the State Board of Education in fall, 1995.
Connecticut	Current work is being done on guides to curriculum development.	Content for all subject areas except science will be divided into 3 grade-level clusters: K-4, 5-8, 9-12; science will use 4 grade-level clusters: K-2, 3-5, 6-8, 9-12.	N	Voluntary. Connecticut has no state-mandated curriculum.	Guides to curriculum development should be available in draft form by late fall, 1996, for the following subject areas: mathematics, science, reading/language arts, social studies, geography, the arts, health, physical education, world language, and learning resources (including library media).	Draft guides are not yet available.

Appendix B

Standards Setting: State By State

State	Content Organization	Grade Range	AFT	Degree of Local Control	Timeline	Current or recently completed work
Delaware	Subject content standards and student performance standards	Science and social studies are divided into K-3, 4-5, 6-8, 9-12; English/language arts and mathematics are divided into K-3, 4-5, 6-8, 9-10.	Y	Standards will eventually be mandatory when they are aligned with the performance-based, statewide assessment system.	Standards in mathematics, science, English language arts, and social studies (civics, economics, geography, and history) were completed in 1995.	Standards in progress include the arts, foreign languages, and vocational education.
Florida	Benchmarks are organized under content standards, which in turn are organized by strand.	K-2, 3-5, 6-8, 9-12	Y	The standards and benchmarks in the curriculum frameworks identify the essential knowledge and skills that students should learn for which the state will hold schools accountable.	Curriculum frameworks, which include standards, vignettes, and guidelines for instruction, were approved by the State Board of Education on May 29, 1996.	Curriculum frameworks are available for language arts, mathematics, science, social studies, the arts (dance, music, theatre, visual arts), health education and physical education, and foreign languages.
Georgia	Mastery objectives are organized under topics or concepts in a "quality core curriculum."	K, 1, 2, 3, 4, 5, 6, 7, 8, and 9-12	Y	Mandatory. Legislation states that the State Board of Education "shall establish competencies that each student is expected to master prior to completion of his public school education" and adopt a uniformly sequenced core curriculum for K-12. "All local units of administration shall include this uniformly sequenced core curriculum as the basis for their own curriculum, although they may expand and enrich this curriculum to the extent they deem necessary and appropriate for their students and their	The curriculum was completed in fall, 1995. Curriculum for each subject area will be reviewed on a four-year cycle.	Quality core curricula were developed for dance, drama, foreign language (including Latin), health and safety, mathematics, physical education, science, social studies, vocational arts, English language arts, music, and visual arts.
Hawaii	Performance standards describe, by grade-range, the content of the overarching content standards.	K-3, 4-6, 7-8, 9-12	Y	Mandatory. Student performance standards are the basis for designing curriculum and instructional programs.	The content and performance standards document containing standards for eight areas, was completed in June, 1994. Standards will be updated as deemed necessary.	Standards in eight areas: language arts, mathematics, science, social studies, fine arts, health and fitness, world languages, and home and work skills.

Standards Setting: State By State

State	Content Organization	Grade Range	AFT	Degree of Local Control	Timeline	Current or recently completed work
Idaho	Each skills-based curriculum guide organizes standards, which in turn organize skills to be taught and learned.	Content is provided at each grade K-12.	Y	Idaho identifies itself as a strong local control state. Skills-based curriculum guides and the assessments that will be based upon them are recommended but not required.	If the K-6 curriculum guides are approved they will be implemented in the fall of 1997. The 7-12 curriculum guides are slated for implementation in fall, 1998.	Draft standards for language arts, humanities, foreign languages, fine arts, health education, mathematics, physical education, science, social studies, and vocational and technical education
Illinois	Goals organize academic standards which organize learning benchmarks.	Early elementary, late elementary, middle school, early high school, late high school	N	There will be mandatory assessments based on the standards. Legislation has been proposed that would require high school assessments to be tied to graduation requirements.	The standards drafts are in the revision process; target date for completion is November 1996.	Currently under review: draft standards in fine arts, English language arts, math, physical development and health, science and social science. A draft of advisory goals and standards for foreign languages is also under review.
Indiana	Content standards and performance standards*	The grades are not uniformly grouped across subject areas. Most of the subjects cluster grades as K-2, 3-5, 6-8, 9-12.*	N	Standards are for the most part voluntary but are tied to the state assessment system and used as guides to establish expectations for the schools. *	The content standards are to be re-evaluated every six years.*	Math and language art standards have been recently revised; content standards have been developed in fine arts, foreign languages, health, language arts, physical education, science, social studies and vocational education.*
Iowa	The math and science curriculum guides organize content differently.	The math and science curriculum guides group grades differently.		Iowa is a strong local control state; districts are required to develop their own student achievement goals and assessment systems.*	In fall, 1996, a content design team will develop exemplary models for math, language arts, and science and a resource guide, which schools can use if they wish.	The math curriculum guide was completed in 1987 and Science was revised in 1991.
Kansas	How curriculum standards organize information varies by subject area.	Varies by subject. For example, social studies describes outcomes for K-5, K-8, and K-12; math describes outcomes at grades 4, 8 and 10.	N	Kansas identifies itself as a local control state. The state assessments cover some of the information in the standards, but schools are not specifically required to teach the state's standards. The state has assessments for math, reading, social studies, and science.	The communication standards are expected to receive approval by January 1997.	Mathematics standards were completed in July 1993, science standards in June 1995, and social studies standards in February 1996.

Standards Setting: State By State

State	Content Organization	Grade Range	AFT	Degree of Local Control	Timeline	Current or recently completed work
Kentucky	Expectations organize demonstrators; each expectation also has sample activities and applications across the curriculum.	Demonstrators are identified for elementary, middle school, and high school.	N	Kentucky has student assessments aligned to the expectations, which are mandatory. Schools are held accountable for their students' performance on the assessments. The grade levels at which the subjects are assessed varies, but all subjects are assessed at grade 11. The assessments are not tied to graduation requirements.	Kentucky has recently developed core content for assessment, which serves as a supplement to the academic expectations. Core content for assessment exists for all subject areas except for the arts and humanities, which are in progress.	Subject areas completed include mathematics, the sciences, the arts, language arts/communications, the humanities, social studies, practical living studies, and vocational studies.*
Louisiana	Curriculum guides	Varies by subject. Most subjects are organized into elementary, secondary, and high school levels.*	N	Louisiana administers tests based on the curriculum guides at grades 3, 5 and 7. At grades 10-12 students take exit exams in math, language arts, writing, social studies, and science. All of these tests must be passed in order for a student to graduate.	None of the curriculum guides are under revision at this time.	English, mathematics, science, social studies, health education, physical education and electives such as the arts, vocational education, and foreign languages*
Maine	Learning results are comprised of three parts: guiding principles (goals of education generally), content standards, and their related performance indicators	Performance indicators are written at levels PreK-2, 3-4, 5-8, and 9-12.	N	Although local school units may establish additional diploma requirements, all graduating students must demonstrate achievement of the learning results through a combination of state and local assessments.	By January 1, 1997 the Maine Legislature will have approved and/or made recommended changes to the learning results for the eight approved subject areas.	Eight areas: career preparation, English language arts, mathematics, health and physical education, social studies, visual and performing arts, foreign languages, and science
Maryland	Learning outcomes organize performance indicators.	K-3, 4-5, 6-8	N	The state outcomes at grades 3, 5, and 8 are mandatory. Students are not required to master the outcomes in order to advance, but schools are evaluated on their students' performance. Currently, area competency tests, which are not based on learning outcomes, must be passed for graduation.	Assessments based on the essential core learning goals will be available in five to seven years.	Maryland has developed essential core learning goals at the high school level for English, science, social studies, and math.

Appendix B

Standards Setting: State By State

State	Content Organization	Grade Range	AFT	Degree of Local Control	Timeline	Current or recently completed work
Massachusetts	Curriculum frameworks include strands that organize learning standards.	PreK-4, 5-8, 9-10, and 11-12	N	Frameworks are voluntary for districts, but eventually students will have to meet the standards in certain subject areas to graduate. There will be mandatory assessments based on the curriculum frameworks.	English language arts and social studies curriculum frameworks are currently under revision and are scheduled to be submitted for approval in the fall of 1996. The pilot for their assessment program will be in the 1997-98 school year.	World languages, mathematics, science and technology, the arts, and health were revised in October 1995 and approved in January 1996.
Michigan	Content standards organize benchmarks.	Early elementary, later elementary, middle school, and high school	Y	Districts are required to have a core academic curriculum in math, science, English language arts (which includes reading and writing), and social studies (which includes geography, history, American government and economics), but districts are not strictly required to adopt the state's content standards.	The state plans to implement the Michigan Education Assessment Program (MEAP) based on the content standards in the year 2000.	In addition to model content standards for the core curriculum, Michigan has also created a draft of model content standards in arts education, career and employability skills, health education, life-management education, physical education, technology, and world languages. These standards have not yet been submitted for approval.
Minnesota	Content standards organize declarative and procedural knowledge; in the state's profile of learning, over 60 standards are organized under 10 elements, which are broad descriptions of skills and knowledge.	K-3, 4-5, 6-8, and graduation standards for 9-12	N	Beginning with the graduating class of 2000, all Minnesota public schools will phase in statewide standards for earning a high school diploma.	Students graduating in the year 2000 will have to pass a Basic Standards Test in reading and mathematics and in 2001 a writing component will be added. Students must pass these tests in order to graduate.	The Profile of Learning is being phased in over three years starting with the 1996-97 school year. The Profile of Learning will be reviewed yearly and updated if necessary.
Mississippi	Varies by subject area	Varies, but content is commonly written at each grade for K-8, and by course for 9-12.	Y	The curriculum frameworks are voluntary. Performance-based assessments are aligned with these frameworks, incorporating national standards into content areas. These assessments are used statewide.	The science curriculum framework will be fully implemented in the 1996-97 school year.	Frameworks have been completed for language arts, mathematics, fine arts, foreign languages, science, and social studies.

Standards Setting: State By State

State	Content Organization	Grade Range	AFT	Degree of Local Control	Timeline	Current or recently completed work
Missouri	Knowledge standards describe content; performance standards describe general skills.	Knowledge standards and performance standards are not written at levels. Drafts of curriculum frameworks are written at K-4, 5-8, and 9-12 grade ranges.	N	The Outstanding Schools Act of 1993 states that the state board of education will adopt performance standards, develop voluntary curriculum frameworks for use by local school districts, and develop a statewide assessment system that is flexible for local school districts. The standards function as a blueprint from which local school districts might develop curriculum; Missouri law assures local control of education. Each school district will determine how its curriculum will be structured and the best methods to implement that curriculum in the classroom.	A pilot test of math was conducted during the spring of 1996. The objective is to conduct a statewide assessment for use in the spring of 1997 for grades 4, 8, and 10. Tests in other areas will be introduced in subsequent years.	Knowledge standards have been completed for communication arts, fine arts, health/physical education, mathematics, science, and social studies. It is expected that the curriculum frameworks will be approved in September 1996.
Montana	Program area standards organize model learner goals. Model learner goals organize focus statements that organize more specific student focus statements.	The program area standards are not organized by grade levels. The model learner goals are written for the primary, intermediate, and graduation levels.	N	Accreditation standards require local districts to develop learner goals in nine program areas (communication arts, health, mathematics, science, social studies, vocational practical arts, guidance, fine arts, and library media) and to assess student progress toward achieving the learner goals. State model learner goals can be used by districts in the development of their own goals.	The Montana Office of Public Instruction is planning to present a proposal to the legislature, which convenes in January, to acquire funding for the revision of the model learner goals.	Program area standards have been written for each of the nine program areas (communication arts, health, mathematics, science, social studies, vocational practical arts, guidance, fine arts, and library media). Model learner goals have been written for communication arts, which include thinking, English, reading, writing, listening, literature, media, speaking, and second language.

Standards Setting: State By State

State	Content Organization	Grade Range	AFT	Degree of Local Control	Timeline	Current or recently completed work
Nebraska	Standards will be derived from curriculum frameworks.	Curriculum frameworks provide descriptions of content at primary, upper elementary, middle school, and secondary levels. Grade ranges will vary by individual school district.	N	Nebraska is a local control state. Frameworks function as guidance tools for local districts but are not mandatory.	A Goals 2000 panel is extracting standards that will be presented to the state school board in September 1996 for approval. These, however, will be voluntary.	Frameworks have been developed for social studies, math, science, business education, industrial technology, family/consumer science, the arts, and foreign language. Frameworks in reading, writing, and health are under way and should be completed in about a year.
Nevada	Frameworks, currently in development, will provide content and performance standards, assessments, and sample projects.	Current proposals call for content descriptions at K, 1-3, 4-6, 7-8, 9-10, and 11-12.*	N	Plans call for the content standards to be written into state statute and to be mandatory for each school district.	Nevada is in the process of developing frameworks in science, social studies, foreign languages, and geography. State assessments will ultimately be aligned with the frameworks.	Nevada plans to complete its English language framework by late spring, 1996.
New Hampshire	Curriculum frameworks contain strands that organize 1) curriculum standards, which in turn describe content, and 2) proficiency standards that identify specific expectations for assessment of cumulative learning.	Grade range of curriculum standards vary by subject area, commonly K-3, 4-6, 7-12, or K-12; Proficiency standards are found at end of grades 3, 6, and 10 for mathematics and language arts; grades 6 and 10 for science and social studies.	Y	Use of the frameworks is voluntary; state assessments are designed to reflect student academic achievement based on the standards set forth in the frameworks and to help school districts design and implement educational improvement activities.	There are no immediate plans to develop frameworks for subjects other than those just completed.	Curriculum frameworks have been developed in English language arts, mathematics, science, and social studies.
New Jersey	Content standards are further defined by cumulative progress indicators.	Content is described for end of grade at 4, 8, and 12, except for the cross-content workplace readiness standards, which do not have specified grade levels.	N	Content standards will be mandatory, but curriculum frameworks will not. Frameworks are guides for local districts, consisting of a statement of each standard, vignettes, activities, and resource materials for use in implementing standards.	Frameworks in science and language arts will be completed in about a year. The arts and social studies frameworks will be started in the next 18 months with the remaining subject areas following soon thereafter. Over the next 2 to $2\frac{1}{2}$ years, frameworks in all subject areas should be developed. The math frameworks have been distributed to districts in draft form.	The core curriculum content standards in the areas of arts, comprehensive health and physical education, language arts, literacy, mathematics, science, social studies, and world languages were adopted by the State Board of Education on May 1, 1996. These were accompanied by a set of workplace readiness standards that address skills across these subject areas.

Standards Setting: State By State

State	Content Organization	Grade Range	AFT	Degree of Local Control	Timeline	Current or recently completed work
New Mexico	Content Standards with benchmarks and performance standards	K-4, 5-8, 9-12	N	Standards will be mandatory, once approved. Currently, curriculum frameworks, which reflect exit-level competencies, are mandatory, but they will ultimately be phased out.	Over the next year, draft standards will be written for other discipline areas.	Draft standards in science, math, and language arts are expected to be approved by the State Board of Education in August 1996. The arts and social studies are expected to be approved in fall, 1996. Health, physical education, modern/classical languages, and employability/life skills are expected to be approved in spring, 1997.
New York	Learning standards organize key ideas and performance indicators, or checkpoints, and sample tasks.	Performance indicators are written at elementary, intermediate, and commencement, except for foreign language standards which are written as checkpoints, which vary according to the age when students begin language study.	N	Standards, like the frameworks from which they were taken and revised, are not mandatory and serve as guides for local curriculum and assessment.	The state assessment system is under revision. Regents Competency Tests are being phased out over the next five years. Regents Examinations are being revised as part of graduation guidelines. New assessments will be phased in by 2001 and will replace current assessments in various grades and subject areas. Assessments are to be aligned with the recently approved standards.	In July, 1996, Regents approved standards in the seven subject areas: mathematics; science, and technology; English language arts; social studies; the arts; languages other than English; health, physical education, and home economics; career development and occupational studies.
North Carolina	Competency goals organize objectives in computers, healthful living, information skills, mathematics, science, social studies, second languages, and vocational education. In guidance and the arts there is no specific language to describe goals or objectives, although the format is similar to the other subject areas.	Grade levels vary. For example, in math, science, and social studies, content is provided at each grade of K-8 with courses at the high school level. Computers and healthful living provide content for each grade of K-8 and 9-12 as a whole. Vocational education has courses for middle grades and 9-12. Information Skills has no specified grade levels.	N	Goals and objectives are mandated by the state. Local school districts develop their own curriculum frameworks based on these standards.	Material for each subject area is reviewed under a continuous cycle.	Content in the arts, computers, math, science, social studies, guidance, second languages, and healthful living has been revised within the last six years.

Standards Setting: State By State

State	Content Organization	Grade Range	AFT	Degree of Local Control	Timeline	Current or recently completed work
North Dakota	Standards organize benchmarks along with examples of specific knowledge and performance activities that support the benchmarks.	Content is described at grades 4, 8, and 12.	N	Neither the standards nor the curriculum frameworks are mandated.	North Dakota's English Language Arts Curriculum Framework was revised in 1996.	Curriculum frameworks for library media, science, and social studies were completed in January 1993; frameworks in arts education, business education, foreign language, health, and physical education were completed in July 1993.
Ohio	Strands organize instructional or subject objectives, which indicate what students should know and be able to do at a given level in their education; performance objectives describe skills necessary for advancement.	Grade levels vary by subject. For example, objectives are written at each grade PreK-12 for social studies and science. Language arts and mathematics content is written for each grade K-12 with additional courses at the high school level.	N	Ohio's frameworks are known as Model Competency Based Education (MCBE) programs. These consist of curricula, subject and performance objectives, assessments and intervention services or strategies. These programs are approved by the state but are not mandated. Local school districts are expected to design competency-based education programs that "compare satisfactorily" with those produced by the state.	Ohio is in the process of revising school standards K-12, which may result in a revision of both proficiency tests and MCBE programs.	There are currently Model Competency Based Education programs for foreign language, the arts, math, science, social studies, and language arts.
Oklahoma	Priority academic student skills make up the state's core curriculum.	Each subject area is organized differently.	N	Schools are required to include the state's core curriculum, but districts can choose how to implement the academic student skills. States have criterion-based assessments at grades 5, 8, and 11 which are developed from the core curriculum. Currently, math, science, reading and writing are assessed.	Legislation calls for review and revision of curriculum in the target areas every three years.	Math, science, technology, and information services have recently been reviewed. Social studies was field tested and reviewed by curriculum committees in 1995-96 and will be implemented in 1996-97.

Appendix B

Standards Setting: State By State

State	Content Organization	Grade Range	AFT	Degree of Local Control	Timeline	Current or recently completed work
Oregon	Content standards organize benchmarks.	Draft benchmarks for grades 3, 5, 8, 10, and 12	N	Content will be mandatory, but districts and schools will have control over implementation and curriculum decisions.	Academic standards will be sent to the State Board of Education in September 1996 for revision and adoption. English and math will be assessed in 1996-97 for Certificate of Initial Mastery; science will be added in 1998-99, and social sciences in 1998-99.	English, math, science, social sciences, second languages and the arts for grades 3, 5, 8 and 10 are in public draft. Benchmarks for grade 12 are being written currently.
Pennsylvania	Goal areas organize standards.	Draft standards are being referenced to national documents, so their organization may vary by subject area.	N	Curriculum will not be mandated.	The standards initiative is under way while awaiting legislative authorization. Ten task forces are working to write standards in the academic goal areas.	Revision of the 1994 math framework to develop model content standards will serve to guide similar efforts in other subject areas.
Rhode Island	The common core of learning includes those competencies that all students should achieve at all grade levels and subject areas. Content area frameworks describe how the competencies are demonstrated in particular areas of the curriculum. Organization of individual frameworks varies by subject.	Subject areas are organized differently. For example, science content is written for K-2, 3-5, 6-8, and 9-12; mathematics is written for end of grade at 4, 8, and 10. Language arts does not specify grade levels.	N	Neither the frameworks nor the common core of learning are mandated. However, state assessments in math, health, and language arts are closely tied to the frameworks.	Frameworks for the arts and social studies are currently being developed.	Frameworks are available in health, mathematics, science, and language arts. Mathematics and science were completed in October 1995. Language arts was completed in June 1996.
South Carolina	Strands organize content standards, which are broad statements of what students are expected to know and be able to do and which organize academic achievement standards, which describe the evidence a student must provide to demonstrate attainment of the content standard. Companion curriculum frameworks describe academic content more generally.	Academic achievement standards are organized in levels PreK-3, 4-6, 7-8, and 9-12. Curriculum frameworks in each subject area organize content differently.	N	The curriculum frameworks are not mandates of what should be taught in the schools across the state but rather broad concepts within which local education decisions should be made. The academic achievement standards, however, describe content at grade ranges that correspond to the state assessment design, which tests students at the end of grades 3, 6, 8, and 12.	Frameworks for health and safety, physical education, and social studies are currently in progress. The science framework was re-edited and finalized in July 1996. Frameworks for all subject areas are expected to be in place by early 1997. Work on academic achievement standards continues.	The State Board of Education adopted frameworks in foreign languages, mathematics, and the visual and performing arts in November 1993. The English language arts framework was finalized and approved in 1996. Academic achievement standards for mathematics and English language arts were approved in 1996.

Appendix B

Standards Setting: State By State

State	Content Organization	Grade Range	AFT	Degree of Local Control	Timeline	Current or recently completed work
South Dakota	Standards and benchmarks	K-2, 3-4, 5-8, and 9-12	N	The standards will not be mandated, but their use by local districts and schools will be encouraged.	Science, mathematics, fine arts, civics, communication/language arts, world languages, health, geography, and history came out in draft form in March 1996 for public review.	Standards for all content areas were approved by the Board of Education in June 1996.
Tennessee	Curriculum frameworks	A curriculum framework is provided for each grade and subject.	Y	The frameworks are mandatory but are designed to allow districts freedom in curriculum and implementation decisions.	Frameworks for all subject areas are on a review cycle.	Frameworks have been developed for agriculture, the arts, computer technology, driver's education, health education and physical education, home economics, language arts, mathematics, science, and social studies.
Texas	Basic understandings organize essential knowledge and skills, which are matched with performance descriptions.	Content for K-8 is written for each grade level; content exclusively for Middle/High School is written at 7-HS or HS.	Y	The essential knowledge and skills in the foundation curriculum, which, according to state law, will be required for instruction, will also continue to serve as the basis for textbook evaluation and state assessments.	As required by board rule, the curriculum is reviewed and altered as necessary every five years. The first five-year review was completed in 1990.	Content material is circulating in draft form; a second, public draft will be issued in August and September 1996; adoption by the state board is scheduled for spring, 1997.
Utah	Standards organize objectives.	Organization varies among subjects. Content for K-6 is written for each grade level; content for 7-12 is written for each grade level or by course.	Y	Districts must teach the content described in the standards, and the state has assessments that are aligned with core content in math, science, and reading. However, the districts may choose to use their own assessments.	All subjects were revised in 1994; curriculum revision is on-going and done as deemed necessary, such as when updates are published by national groups.	Standards are available in visual arts, responsible healthy lifestyles, information technology, language arts, math, library media, music, science, social studies, vocational education.

Appendix B

Standards Setting: State By State

State	Content Organization	Grade Range	AFT	Degree of Local Control	Timeline	Current or recently completed work
Vermont	Vital Results Standards "cut across all fields of knowledge." Fields of Knowledge Standards are specific to content areas. Both types of standards are further described by the evidence required for demonstrating attainment of a standard. They are organized in a single framework.	PreK-4, 5-8, 9-12.	N	Local schools have flexibility in determining how their school and community can best achieve the standards. While the standards are not mandated by the state, state assessments are built on the standards.	A science assessment has been piloted. It was based on the state framework, which will be refined in June 1997 and reviewed again in 1999. Curriculum revision is ongoing and done as deemed necessary, such as when updates are published by national groups.	Standards effort was completed in spring, 1996, with vital results standards written for communication, reasoning and problem solving, personal development, civic and social responsibility; and field of knowledge standards written for the arts, language, and literature; history and social sciences; science, mathematics, and technology.
Virginia	Standards of learning	Each subject is organized differently. English and history/social science have content for each level, K-12; mathematics has content for each level K-8, then by course; science has content for each level K-6, then by course.	Y	The standards of learning are not intended to cover the entire curriculum nor to prescribe instruction. Teachers are encouraged to go beyond the standards and to select appropriate instructional strategies and assessment methods.	Currently work continues on aligning state assessments with content standards, with plans to assess at grades 3, 5, 7, 9, and 11.	In June 1995, the Virginia Board of Education approved standards in the fields of English, history and social science, math, and science.
Washington	Essential learnings organize benchmarks, which are grouped by components.	K-4, 5-7, 8-10	N	By legislation, all schools must have the essential learnings in place by the school year 2000-2001; state assessments will align with the essential learnings.	The Commission on Student Learning is now designing assessments for the standards; pilot tests were conducted in spring, 1996.	The Commission on Student Learning approved essential learnings in communications, mathematics, reading and writing in February 1995, in science, social studies, arts, and health and fitness in April 1996.
West Virginia	Instructional goals organize instructional objectives.	Content for K-8 is written for each grade level; at 9-12, content descriptions are by course.	N	Instructional goals and standards are mandatory, but the frameworks, which are developed by each school district in alignment with the state's instructional goals and standards, are voluntary.	All instructional goals and standards are currently being aligned with state assessments. Content areas are revised every six years.	All of the main subject areas (math, science, language arts, and social studies) are being revised and drafts will be sent to the state board in September 1996. Those goals and objectives will then be distributed for public comment.

Standards Setting: State By State

State	Content Organization	Grade Range	AFT	Degree of Local Control	Timeline	Current or recently completed work
Wisconsin	Content and performance standards	Elementary, middle, and high school	N	Standards will serve only as a model for local schools and districts. At some point assessments at grades 4, 8, and 10 may be aligned with content standards.	Tentative date for content standards is fall, 1997.	Currently, social studies, science, mathematics, foreign languages, and English language arts are in working draft form. Work on content standards and performance standards is ongoing.
Wyoming	The state's model content standards are organized under the common core of knowledge and the common core of skills.	Varies by school and/or district		The state has model performance standards which the districts can use if they wish. The state requires school districts to develop standards that cover 11 subjects, known as the Common Core of Knowledge, and six skills, known as the Common Core of Skills.	All of Wyoming's districts must have standards and assessments developed for the 1997-98 school year. A new set of model standards is in progress. Language arts and math will be finished by the end of 1997.	The common core of knowledge consists of applied technology, career options, fine and performing arts, foreign cultures including languages, health and safety, humanities, language arts, mathematics, physical education, science and social studies. The common core of skills consists of problem-solving, interpersonal communications, computer use, critical thinking, creativity, and life skills including CPR.
Washington D.C.	Content standards organize indicators; foundation skills describe general communication skills.		N	Incentives or consequences for students are not currently linked to the assessments, but plans call for a system in which assessment results will guide student promotion decisions.	Content standards in Health Promotion and Wellness and World Languages are in draft form and are scheduled for public draft in spring, 1997. Initial drafts of content standards in geography and career pathways are scheduled for spring, 1997. Draft content standards in the arts, economics, and government should soon follow. Tentative date for content standards is fall, 1997.	Content standards for mathematics and science and technology were recently revised; content standards for social studies and English/language arts have just been released to the public for review and revision.

Note: Information in this report, except as otherwise indicated, was gathered via telephone interviews with state education department personnel and through analysis of documents made available by the states. This review was conducted from April through August, 1996. Every effort was made to verify the accuracy of the data.

AFT: Y/N indicates whether or not, for the state indicated, "standards in all core subjects are clear and specific enough to lead to a common core curriculum" as determined in an annual report from the American Federation of Teachers (Gandal, 1996). A blank in the column indicates those states (Iowa and Wyoming) that have elected not to develop standards.

*Source: "Setting the Standards From State to State." (1995, April 12). *Struggling for Standards: An Education Week Special Report*, 23-35.

McREL Compendium Standards

Standards for Mathematics

1. Effectively uses a variety of strategies in the problem-solving process
2. Understands and applies basic and advanced properties of the concept of numbers
3. Uses basic and advanced procedures while performing the process of computation
4. Understands and applies basic and advanced properties of the concept of measurement
5. Understands and applies basic and advanced properties of the concepts of geometry
6. Understands and applies basic and advanced concepts of data analysis and distributions
7. Understands and applies basic and advanced concepts of probability and statistics
8. Understands and applies basic and advanced properties of functions and algebra
9. Understands the general nature and uses of mathematics

Standards for Science

Earth and Space
1. Understands basic features of the Earth
2. Understands basic Earth processes
3. Understands essential ideas about the composition and structure of the universe and the Earth's place in it

Life Sciences
4. Knows about the diversity and unity that characterize life
5. Understands the genetic basis for the transfer of biological characteristics from one generation to the next
6. Knows the general structure and functions of cells in organisms
7. Understands how species depend on one another and on the environment for survival
8. Understands the cycling of matter and flow of energy through the living environment
9. Understands the basic concepts of the evolution of species

Physical Sciences
10. Understands basic concepts about the structure and properties of matter
11. Understands energy types, sources, and conversions, and their relationship to heat and temperature
12. Understands motion and the principles that explain it
13. Knows the kinds of forces that exist between objects and within atoms

Science and Technology
14. Understands the nature of scientific knowledge
15. Understands the nature of scientific inquiry
16. Understands the scientific enterprise
17. Understands the nature of technological design
18. Understands the interactions of science, technology, and society

Standards for Historical Understanding

1. Understands and knows how to analyze chronological relationships and patterns
2. Understands the historical perspective

Standards for Grades K–4 History

Topic 1 Living and Working Together in Families and Communities, Now and Long Ago
1. Understands family life now and in the past, and family life in various places long ago
2. Understands the history of the local community and how communities in North America varied long ago

Topic 2 The History of Students' Own State or Region
3. Understands the people, events, problems, and ideas that were significant in creating the history of their state

Topic 3 The History of the United States: Democratic Principles and Values and the People From Many Cultures Who Contributed to its Cultural, Economic, and Political Heritage

4. Understands how democratic values came to be, and how they have been exemplified by people, events, and symbols
5. Understands the causes and nature of movements of large groups of people into and within the United States, now and long ago
6. Understands the folklore and other cultural contributions from various regions of the United States and how they helped to form a national heritage

Topic 4 The History of Peoples of Many Cultures Around the World

7. Understands selected attributes and historical developments of societies in Africa, the Americas, Asia, and Europe
8. Understands major discoveries in science and technology, some of their social and economic effects, and the major scientists and inventors responsible for them

Standards for United States History

Era 1 Three Worlds Meet (Beginnings to 1620)

1. Understands the characteristics of societies in the Americas, Western Europe, and West Africa that increasingly interacted after 1450
2. Understands cultural and ecological interactions resulting from early European exploration and colonization

Era 2 Colonization and Settlement (1585-1763)

3. Understands how the early Europeans and Africans interacted with Native Americans in the Americas
4. Understands how political institutions and religious freedom emerged in the North American colonies
5. Understands how the values and institutions of European economic life took root in the colonies and how slavery reshaped European and African life in the Americas

Era 3 Revolution and the New Nation (1754-1820s)

6. Understands the causes of the American Revolution, the ideas and interests involved in shaping the revolutionary movement, and reasons for the American victory
7. Understands how the American Revolution involved multiple movements among the new nation's many groups to reform American society
8. Understands the institutions and practices of government created during the revolution and how these elements were revised between 1787 and 1815 to create the foundation of the American political system

Era 4 Expansion and Reform (1801-1861)

9. Understands the United States territorial expansion between 1801 and 1861, and how it affected relations with external powers and Native Americans
10. Understands how the industrial revolution, the rapid expansion of slavery, and the westward movement changed American lives and led to regional tensions
11. Understands the extension, restriction, and reorganization of political democracy after 1800
12. Understands the sources and character of reform movements in the antebellum period and what the reforms accomplished or failed to accomplish

Era 5 Civil War and Reconstruction (1850-1877)

13. Understands the causes of the Civil War
14. Understands the course and character of the Civil War and its effects on the American people
15. Understands how various reconstruction plans succeeded or failed

Era 6 The Development of the Industrial United States (1870-1900)

16. Understands how the rise of big business, heavy industry, and mechanized farming transformed American society
17. Understands massive immigration after 1870 and how new social patterns, conflicts, and ideas of national unity developed amid growing cultural diversity
18. Understands the rise of the American labor movement and how political issues reflected social and economic changes
19. Understands federal Indian policy and United States foreign policy after the Civil War

Era 7 The Emergence of Modern America (1890-1930)

20. Understands how progressives and others addressed problems of industrial capitalism, urbanization, and political corruption
21. Understands the changing role of the United States in world affairs through World War I
22. Understands how the United States changed between the post-World War I years and the eve of the Great Depression

268

Era 8 The Great Depression and World War II (1929-1945)
23. Understands the causes of the Great Depression and how it affected American society
24. Understands how the New Deal addressed the Great Depression, transformed American federalism, and initiated the welfare state
25. Understands the origins and course of World War II, the character of the war at home and abroad, and its reshaping of the U.S. role in world affairs

Era 9 Postwar United States (1945 to early 1970s)
26. Understands the economic boom and social transformation of post-World War II America
27. Understands how the legacy of the New Deal in the post World War II period
28. Understands the Cold War and the Korean and Vietnam conflicts in domestic and international politics
29. Understands the struggle for racial and gender equality and for the extension of civil liberties

Era 10 Contemporary United States (1968 to the present)
30. Understands developments in foreign and domestic policies between the Nixon and Clinton presidencies
31. Understands the major social and economic developments in contemporary America

Standards for World History

Era 1 The Beginnings of Human Society
1. Understands the biological and cultural processes that shaped the earliest human communities
2. Understands the processes that contributed to the emergence of agricultural societies around the world

Era 2 Early Civilizations and the Rise of Pastoral Peoples, 4000-1000 BCE
3. Understands the major characteristics of civilization and the development of civilizations in Mesopotamia, Egypt, and the Indus Valley
4. Understands how agrarian societies spread and new states emerged in the third and second millennium BCE
5. Understands the political, social, and cultural consequences of population movements and militarization in Eurasia in the second millennium BCE

Era 3 Classical Traditions, Major Religions, and Giant Empires, 1000 BCE-300 CE
6. Understands technological and cultural innovation and change from 1000 to 600 BCE
7. Understands how Aegean civilization emerged and how interrelations developed among peoples of the eastern Mediterranean and Southwest Asia from 600 to 200 BCE
8. Understands how major religious and large-scale empires arose in the Mediterranean basin, China, and India from 500 BCE to 300 CE
9. Understands how early agrarian civilizations arose in Mesoamerica

Era 4 Expanding Zones of Exchange and Encounter, 300-1000 CE
10. Understands the Imperial crises and their aftermath in various regions from 300 to 700 CE
11. Understands the causes and consequences of the development of Islamic civilization between the 7th and 10th centuries
12. Understands major developments in East Asia in the era of the Tang Dynasty from 600 to 900 CE
13. Understands the political, social, and cultural redefinitions in Europe from 500 to 1000 CE
14. Understands state-building in the Northeast and West Africa, and the southward migrations of Bantu-speaking peoples
15. Understands the rise of centers of civilization in Mesoamerica and Andean South America in the first millennium CE

Era 5 Intensified Hemispheric Interactions, 1000-1500 CE
16. Understands the maturation of an interregional system of communication, trade, and cultural exchange during a period of Chinese economic power and Islamic expansion
17. Understands the redefinition of European society and culture from 1000 to 1300 CE
18. Understands the rise of the Mongol empire and its consequences for Eurasian peoples from 1200 to 1350
19. Understands the growth of states, towns, and trade in Sub-Saharan Africa between the 11th and 15th centuries
20. Understands patterns of crisis and recovery in Afro-Eurasia between 1300 and 1450
21. Understands the expansion of states and civilizations in the Americas between 1000 and 1500

Era 6 Global Expansion and Encounter, 1450-1770
22. Understands how the transoceanic interlinking of all major regions of the world between 1450 and 1600 led to global transformations
23. Understands how European society experienced political, economic, and cultural transformations in an age of global intercommunication between 1450 and 1750
24. Understands how large territorial empires dominated much of Eurasia between the 16th and 18th centuries

25. Understands the economic, political, and cultural interrelations among peoples of Africa, Europe, and the Americas between 1500 and 1750
26. Understands transformations in Asian societies in the era of European expansion
27. Understands major global trends from 1450 to 1770

Era 7 An Age of Revolutions, 1750-1914
28. Understands the causes and consequences of political revolutions in the late 18th and early 19th centuries
29. Understands the causes and consequences of the agricultural and industrial revolutions from 1700 to 1850
30. Understands how Eurasian societies were transformed in an era of global trade and the emergence of European power from 1750 to 1850
31. Understands patterns of nationalism, state-building, and social reform in Europe and the Americas from 1830 to 1914
32. Understands patterns of global change in the era of Western military and economic domination from 1850 to 1914
33. Understands major global trends from 1750 to 1914

Era 8 The 20th Century
34. Understands global and economic trends in the high period of Western dominance
35. Understands the causes and global consequences of World War I
36. Understands the search for peace and stability throughout the world in the 1920s and 1930s
37. Understands the causes and global consequences of World War II
38. Understands how new international power relations took shape in the context of the Cold War and how colonial empires broke up
39. Understands the promises and paradoxes of the second half of the 20th century

Standards for Language Arts

Writing
1. Demonstrates competence in the general skills and strategies of the writing process
2. Demonstrates competence in the stylistic and rhetorical aspects of writing
3. Writes with a command of the grammatical and mechanical conventions of composition
4. Effectively gathers and uses information for research purposes

Reading
5. Demonstrates competence in the general skills and strategies of the reading process
6. Demonstrates competence in general skills and strategies for reading literature
7. Demonstrates competence in the general skills and strategies for reading information
8. Demonstrates competence in applying the reading process to specific types of literary texts
9. Demonstrates competence in applying the reading process to specific types of informational texts
10. Demonstrates competence in using different information sources, including those of a technical nature, to accomplish specific tasks

Listening and Speaking
11. Demonstrates competence in speaking and listening as tools for learning

Language
12. Demonstrates an understanding of the nature and function of the English language

Literature
13. Demonstrates a familiarity with selected literary works of enduring quality

Standards for Geography

The World in Spatial Terms
1. Understands the characteristics and uses of maps, globes, and other geographic tools and technologies
2. Knows the location of places, geographic features, and patterns of the environment
3. Understands the characteristics and uses of spatial organization of Earth's surface

Places and Regions
4. Understands the physical and human characteristics of place
5. Understands the concept of regions
6. Understands that culture and experience influence people's perceptions of places and regions

Physical Systems
7. Knows the physical processes that shape patterns on Earth's surface
8. Understands the characteristics of ecosystems on Earth's surface

Human Systems
9. Understands the nature, distribution, and migration of human populations on Earth's surface
10. Understands the nature and complexity of Earth's cultural mosaics
11. Understands the patterns and networks of economic interdependence on Earth's surface
12. Understands the patterns of human settlement and their causes
13. Understands the forces of cooperation and conflict that shape the divisions of Earth's surface

Environment and Society
14. Understands how human actions modify the physical environment
15. Understands how physical systems affect human systems
16. Understands the changes that occur in the meaning, use, distribution, and importance of resources

Uses of Geography
17. Understands how geography is used to interpret the past
18. Understands global development and environmental issues

Standards for the Arts

Art Connections
1. Understands connections among the various art forms and other disciplines

Dance
1. Identifies and demonstrates movement elements and skills in performing dance
2. Understands choreographic principles, processes, and structures
3. Understands dance as a way to create and communicate meaning
4. Applies critical and creative thinking skills in dance
5. Understands dance in various cultures and historical periods
6. Understands connections between dance and healthful living

Music
1. Sings, alone and with others, a varied repertoire of music
2. Performs on instruments, alone and with others, a varied repertoire of music
3. Improvises melodies, variations, and accompaniments
4. Composes and arranges music within specified guidelines
5. Reads and notates music
6. Knows and applies appropriate criteria to music and music performances
7. Understands the relationship between music and history and culture

Theatre
1. Demonstrates competence in writing scripts
2. Uses acting skills
3. Designs and produces informal and formal productions
4. Directs scenes and productions
5. Understands how informal and formal theatre, film, television, and electronic media productions create and communicate meaning
6. Understands the context in which theatre, film, television, and electronic media are performed today as well as in the past

Visual Arts
1. Understands and applies media, techniques, and processes related to the visual arts
2. Knows how to use the structures (e.g., sensory qualities, organizational principles, expressive features) and functions of art
3. Knows a range of subject matter, symbols, and potential ideas in the visual arts
4. Understands the visual arts in relation to history and cultures
5. Understands the characteristics and merits of one's own artwork and the artwork of others

S tandards for Civics

What Is Government and What Should It Do?
1. Understands ideas about civic life, politics, and government
2. Understands the essential characteristics of limited and unlimited governments
3. Understands the sources, purposes, and functions of law and the importance of the rule of law for the protection of individual rights and the common good
4. Understands the concept of a constitution, the various purposes that constitutions serve, and the conditions that contribute to the establishment and maintenance of constitutional government
5. Understands the major characteristics of systems of shared powers and of parliamentary systems
6. Understands the advantages and disadvantages of federal, confederal, and unitary systems of government
7. Understands alternative forms of representation and how they serve the purposes of constitutional government

What Are the Basic Values and Principals of American Democracy?
8. Understands the central ideas of American constitutional government and how this form of government has shaped the character of American society
9. Understands the importance of Americans sharing and supporting certain values, beliefs, and principles of American constitutional democracy
10. Understands the roles of voluntarism and organized groups in American social and political life
11. Understands the role of diversity in American life and the importance of shared values, political beliefs, and civic beliefs in an increasingly diverse American society
12. Understands the relationships among liberalism, republicanism, and American constitutional democracy
13. Understands the character of American political and social conflict and factors that tend to prevent or lower its intensity
14. Understands issues concerning the disparities between ideals and reality in American political and social life

How Does the Government Established by the Constitution Embody the Purposes, Values, and Principles of American Democracy?
15. Understands how the United States Constitution grants and distributes power and responsibilities to national and state government and how it seeks to prevent the abuse of power
16. Understands the major responsibilities of the national government for domestic and foreign policy, and understands how government is financed through taxation
17. Understands issues concerning the relationship between state and local governments and the national government and issues pertaining to representation at all three levels of government
18. Understands the role and importance of law in the American constitutional system and issues regarding the judicial protection of individual rights
19. Understands what is meant by "the public agenda," how it is set, and how it is influenced by public opinion and the media
20. Understands the roles of political parties, campaigns, elections, and associations and groups in American politics
21. Understands the formation and implementation of public policy

What is the Relationship of the United States to Other Nations and to World Affairs?
22. Understands how the world is organized politically into nation-states, how nation-states interact with one another, and issues surrounding U.S. foreign policy
23. Understands the impact of significant political and nonpolitical developments on the United States and other nations

What Are the Roles of the Citizen in American Democracy?
24. Understands the meaning of citizenship in the United States, and knows the requirements for citizenship and naturalization
25. Understands issues regarding personal, political, and economic rights
26. Understands issues regarding the proper scope and limits of rights and the relationships among personal, political, and economic rights
27. Understands how certain character traits enhance citizens' ability to fulfill personal and civic responsibilities
28. Understands how participation in civic and political life can help citizens attain individual and public goals
29. Understands the importance of political leadership, public service, and a knowledgeable citizenry in American constitutional democracy

S tandards for Economics

1. Understands that scarcity of productive resources requires choices which generate opportunity costs
2. Understands characteristics of different economic systems, economic institutions, and economic incentives
3. Understands the concept of prices and the interaction of supply and demand in a market economy
4. Understands basic features of market structures and exchanges

5. Understands unemployment and income distribution in a market economy
6. Understands the roles government plays in the United States economy
7. Understands aggregate supply and aggregate demand
8. Understands basic concepts of United States fiscal policy and monetary policy
9. Understands how Gross Domestic Product and inflation and deflation provide indications of the state of the economy
10. Understands basic concepts about international economics

Standards for Foreign Language

1. Uses the target language to engage in conversations, express feelings and emotions, and exchange opinions and information
2. Comprehends and interprets written and spoken language on diverse topics from diverse media
3. Presents information, concepts, and ideas to an audience of listeners or readers on a variety of topics
4. Demonstrates knowledge and understanding of traditional ideas and perspectives, institutions, professions, literary and artistic expressions, and other components of target culture
5. Recognizes that different languages use different patterns to communicate and applies this knowledge to the native language

Standards for Health

1. Knows the availability and effective use of health services, products, and information
2. Knows environmental and external factors that affect individual and community health
3. Understands the relationship of family health to individual health
4. Knows how to maintain mental and emotional health
5. Knows essential concepts and practices concerning injury prevention and safety
6. Understands essential concepts about nutrition and diet
7. Knows how to maintain and promote personal health
8. Knows essential concepts about the prevention and control of disease
9. Understands aspects of substance use and abuse
10. Understands the fundamental concepts of growth and development

Standards for Physical Education

1. Uses a variety of basic and advanced movement forms
2. Uses movement concepts and principles in the development of motor skills
3. Understands the benefits and costs associated with participation in physical activity
4. Understands how to monitor and maintain a health-enhancing level of physical fitness
5. Understands the social and personal responsibility associated with participation in physical activity

Standards for Behavioral Studies

1. Understands that group and cultural influences contribute to human development, identity, and behavior
2. Understands various meanings of social group, general implications of group membership, and different ways that groups function
3. Understands that interactions among learning, inheritance, and physical development affect human behavior
4. Understands conflict, cooperation, and interdependence among individuals, groups, and institutions

Standards for Life Skills

Thinking and Reasoning
1. Understands and applies basic principles of presenting an argument
2. Understands and applies basic principles of logic and reasoning
3. Effectively uses mental processes that are based on identifying similarities and dissimilarities (compares, contrasts, classifies)
4. Understands and applies basic principles of hypothesis testing and scientific inquiry
5. Applies basic trouble-shooting and problem-solving techniques
6. Applies decision-making techniques

Working With Others
1. Contributes to the overall effort of a group
2. Uses conflict-resolution techniques
3. Works well with diverse individuals and in diverse situations
4. Displays effective interpersonal communication skills
5. Demonstrates leadership skills

Self-Regulation
1. Sets and manages goals
2. Performs self-appraisal
3. Considers risks
4. Demonstrates perseverance
5. Maintains a healthy self-concept
6. Restrains impulsivity

Life Work
1. Makes effective use of basic tools
2. Understands the characteristics and uses of basic computer hardware, software, and operating systems
3. Uses basic word processing, spreadsheet, database, and communication programs
4. Manages money effectively
5. Pursues specific jobs
6. Makes general preparation for entering the work force
7. Makes effective use of basic life skills
8. Displays reliability and a basic work ethic
9. Operates effectively within organizations

Documents Used to Construct the McREL Database

American Council on the Teaching of Foreign Languages. (1995, April). *Standards for Foreign Language Learning: Preparing for the 21st Century*. (Draft). Yonkers, NY: Author.

Australian Education Council. (1994). *English: A Curriculum Profile for Australian Schools*. Commonwealth of Australia: Curriculum Corporation.

Bradley Commission on History in the Schools. (1988). *Building a History Curriculum: Guidelines for Teaching History in the Schools*. Washington, DC: Educational Excellence Network.

California Department of Education. (1989). *Recommended Literature, Grades Nine Through Twelve*. Sacramento, CA: Author.

California Department of Education. (1989). *Visual and Performing Arts Framework for California Public Schools: Kindergarten Through Grade Twelve*. Sacramento, CA: Author.

California Department of Education. (1990). *Recommended Readings in Literature, Kindergarten Through Grade Eight*. Sacramento, CA: Author.

California Department of Education. (1990). *Science Framework for California Public Schools: Kindergarten Through Grade 12*. Sacramento, CA: Author.

California Department of Education. (1991). *Model Curriculum Standards: Grades Nine Through Twelve*. Sacramento, CA: Author.

California Department of Education (1993). *The Writing Assessment Handbook: High School*. Sacramento, CA: Author.

California Department of Education. (1994). *Health Framework for California Public Schools: Kindergarten Through Grade Twelve*. Sacramento, CA: Author.

California Department of Education. (1994). *1994 Elementary Performance Assessments: Integrated English-Language Arts Illustrative Material, Grade 4*. Sacramento, CA: Author.

California Department of Education. (1994). *1994 Middle Grades Performance Assessments: Integrated English-Language Arts Illustrative Material, Grade 8*. Sacramento, CA: Author.

Carnevale, A. P., Gainer, L. J., & Meltzer, A. S. (1990). *Workplace Basics: The Essential Skills Employers Want*. San Francisco: Jossey-Bass.

Center for Civic Education. (1994). *National Standards for Civics and Government*. Calabasas, CA: Author.

Center for Occupational Research and Development. (1995). *National Voluntary Skills Standard: Hazardous Materials Management Technology*. Waco, TX: Author.

Colorado Council on Economic Education. (1994). *Economics: Conceptual Content Standards, Grades K-12*. (Draft). Denver: Author.

Colorado Department of Education. (1995, August). *Content Standards for Foreign Language*. (Draft). Denver: Author.

Committee on the Junior High and Middle School Booklist of the National Council of Teachers of English & Nilsen, A.P. (Ed.). (1991). *Your Reading: A Booklist for Junior High and Middle School Students* (8th ed.). Urbana, IL: National Council of Teachers of English.

Committee on the Senior High School Booklist of the National Council of Teachers of English & Wurth, S. (Ed.). (1992). *Books for You: A Booklist for Senior High Students* (11th ed.). Urbana, IL: National Council of Teachers of English.

Consortium of National Arts Education Associations. (1994). *National Standards for Arts Education: What Every Young American Should Know and Be Able to Do in the Arts*. Reston, VA: Music Educators National Conference.

Crabtree, C., Nash, G. B., Gagnon, P., & Waugh, S. (Eds.). (1992). *Lessons From History: Essential Understandings and Historical Perspectives Students Should Acquire.* Los Angeles: National Center for History in the Schools.

Edison Project. (1994). *Student Standards for the Elementary Academy.* New York: Author.

Edison Project. (1994). *Student Standards for the Junior Academy.* New York: Author.

Edison Project. (1994). *Student Standards for the Primary Academy.* New York: Author.

Gagnon, P., & Bradley Commission on History in the Schools (Eds.). (1989). *Historical Literacy: The Case for History in American Education.* Boston: Houghton Mifflin Company.

Geographic Education National Implementations Project. (1987). *K-6 Geography: Themes, Key Ideas, and Learning Opportunities.* Washington, DC: Author.

Geography Education Standards Project. (1994). *Geography for Life: National Geography Standards.* Washington, DC: National Geographic Research and Exploration.

Gillespie, J. T. (Ed.) (1991). *Best Books for Junior High Readers.* New Providence, NJ: Bowker.

Gillespie, J. T. (Ed.) (1991). *Best Books for Senior High Readers.* New Providence, NJ: Bowker.

Gilliard, J. V., Caldwell, J., Dalgaard, B. R., Highsmith, R. J., Reinke, R., & Watts, M. (with Leet, D. R., Malone, M. G., & Ellington, L.). (1989). *Economics, What and When: Scope and Sequence Guidelines, K-12.* New York: Joint Council on Economic Education.

Hirsch, E. D., Jr. (1987). *Cultural Literacy: What Every American Needs to Know.* Boston: Houghton Mifflin Company.

Hirsch, E.D., Jr. (Ed.). (1993). *What Your 1st Grader Needs to Know: Fundamentals of a Good First-Grade Education. The Core Knowledge Series: Resource Books for Grades One Through Six, Book I.* New York: Delta.

Hirsch, E.D., Jr. (Ed.). (1993). *What Your 2nd Grader Needs to Know: Fundamentals of a Good Second-Grade Education. The Core Knowledge Series: Resource Books for Grades One Through Six, Book II.* New York: Delta.

Hirsch, E.D., Jr. (Ed.). (1993). *What Your 3rd Grader Needs to Know: Fundamentals of a Good Third-Grade Education. The Core Knowledge Series: Resource Books for Grades One Through Six, Book III.* New York: Delta.

Hirsch, E.D., Jr. (Ed.). (1993). *What Your 4th Grader Needs to Know: Fundamentals of a Good Fourth-Grade Education. The Core Knowledge Series: Resource Books for Grades One Through Six, Book IV* New York: Delta.

Hirsch, E.D., Jr. (Ed.). (1993). *What Your 5th Grader Needs to Know: Fundamentals of a Good Fifth-Grade Education. The Core Knowledge Series: Resource Books for Grades One Through Six, Book V.* New York: Delta.

Hirsch, E.D., Jr. (Ed.). (1993). What Your 6th Grader Needs to Know: Fundamentals of a Good Sixth-Grade Education. *The Core Knowledge Series: Resource Books for Grades One Through Six, Book VI.* New York: Delta.

Joint Committee on Geographic Education. (1984). *Guidelines for Geographic Education: Elementary and Secondary Schools.* Washington, DC: Association of American Geographers.

Joint Committee on Health Education Terminology. (1991). Report of the 1990 Joint Committee on Health Education Terminology. *Journal of Health Education, 22*, (2), 97- 107.

Joint Committee on National Health Education Standards. (1995). *National Health Education Standards: Achieving Health Literacy.* Reston, VA: Association for the Advancement of Health Education.

Law in a Free Society. (1977). *Authority I (Elementary): A Civic Education Unit* (Teacher's Ed.). Calabasas, CA: Author.

Law in a Free Society. (1977). *Privacy I (Elementary): A Civic Education Unit* (Teacher's Ed.). Calabasas, CA: Author.

Law in a Free Society. (1977). *Privacy II (Elementary): A Civic Education Unit* (Teacher's Ed.). Calabasas, CA: Author.

Law in a Free Society. (1979). *Justice I (Elementary): A Civic Education Unit* (Teacher's Ed.). Calabasas, CA: Author.

Law in a Free Society. (1983). *Responsibility I (Elementary): A Civic Education Unit* (Teacher's Ed.). Calabasas, CA: Author.

Michigan Department of Education. (1995, September). *Physical Education: Working Draft Content Standards and Benchmarks.* (Draft). Lansing: Author.

Michigan State Board of Education. (1988). *Michigan Essential Goals and Objectives for Health Education.* Lansing, MI: Author.

Music Educators National Conference. (1986). *The School Music Program: Description and Standards.* Reston, VA: Author.

National Assessment of Educational Progress. (1989). *Science Objectives: 1990 Assessment.* Princeton, NJ: Educational Testing Service.

National Assessment of Educational Progress. (1992). *Description of Writing Achievement Levels-Setting Process and Proposed Achievement Level Definitions.* Iowa City, IA: American College Testing Program.

National Assessment of Educational Progress. (n.d.). *Framework for the 1994 National Assessment of Educational Progress U.S. History Assessment.* Washington, DC: Author.

National Assessment of Educational Progress. (1992). *Item Specifications: 1994 National Assessment of Educational Progress in Geography.* Washington, DC: National Assessment Governing Board.

National Assessment of Educational Progress. (1992, March 26). *Content Specifications for the 1994 National Assessment of Educational Progress Mathematics Assessment.* Washington, DC: Aurhor.

National Assessment of Educational Progress. (1992, March 31). *Framework for the 1994 National Assessment of Educational Progress Mathematics Assessment.* Washington, DC: Author.

National Assessment of Educational Progress. (1992). *Provisional Item Specifications: 1994 National Assessment of Educational Progress in U.S. History.* Washington, DC: National Assessment Governing Board.

National Assessment of Educational Progress Arts Education Consensus Project. (1994). *Arts Education Assessment Framework.* Washington, DC: National Assessment Governing Board.

National Assessment of Educational Progress in U.S. History. (1994). *Provisional Item Specifications.* Washington, DC: Council of Chief State School Officers.

National Assessment of Educational Progress Geography Consensus Project. (1992). *Geography Assessment Framework for the 1994 National Assessment of Educational Progress.* (Draft). Washington, DC: National Assessment Governing Board.

National Assessment of Educational Progress Reading Consensus Project. (1990). *Assessment and Exercise Specifications: 1992 NAEP Reading Assessment.* Washington, DC: National Assessment Governing Board.

National Assessment of Educational Progress Reading Consensus Project. (1990). *Reading Assessment Framework for the 1992 National Assessment of Educational Progress.* Washington, DC: National Assessment Governing Board.

National Assessment of Educational Progress Science Consensus Project. (1993). *Science Assessment and Exercise Specifications for the 1994 National Assessment of Educational Progress.* Washington, DC: National Assessment Governing Board.

National Association for Sport and Physical Education. (1995). *Moving Into the Future, National Standards for Physical Education: A Guide to Content and Assessment.* St. Louis: Mosby.

National Association for Sport and Physical Education. (1992). *Outcomes of Quality Physical Education Programs.* Reston, VA: Author.

National Center for History in the Schools. (1994). *National Standards for History for Grades K-4: Expanding Children's World in Time and Space.* Los Angeles: Author.

National Center for History in the Schools. (1994). *National Standards for United States History: Exploring the American Experience.* Los Angeles: Author.

National Center for History in the Schools. (1994). *National Standards for World History: Exploring Paths to the Present.* Los Angeles: Author.

National Committee on Science Education Standards and Assessment. (1994, November). *National Science Education Standards*. (Draft). Washington, DC: National Academy Press.

National Council for the Social Studies. (1994). *Expectations of Excellence: Curriculum Standards for Social Studies*. Washington, DC: Author.

National Council of Teachers of English. (1982). *Essentials of English: A Document for Reflection and Dialogue*. Urbana, IL: Author.

National Council of Teachers of English. (1989). *The English Coalition Conference: Democracy Through Language*. Urbana, IL: Author.

National Council of Teachers of English and the International Reading Association (1995, October). *Standards for the English Language Arts*. (Draft). Urbana, IL: National Council of Teachers of English.

National Council of Teachers of Mathematics. (1989). *Curriculum and Evaluation Standards for School Mathematics*. Reston, VA: Author.

National Science Board Commission on Precollege Education in Mathematics, Science and Technology. (1983). *Educating Americans for the 21st Century*. Washington, DC: National Science Board Commission.

New Standards. (1995, June). *Draft Performance Standards for English Language Arts*. Washington, DC: Author.

New Standards. (1995, June). *Draft Performance Standards for Mathematics*. Washington, DC: Author.

New York State Education Department. (1994). *Curriculum, Instruction, and Assessment: Preliminary Draft Framework for English Language Arts*. Albany: Author.

Pearsall, M. K. (Ed). (1993). *Scope, Sequence, and Coordination of Secondary School Science. Vol. 1. The Content Core: A Guide for Curriculum Designers*. Washington, DC: National Science Teachers Association.

Project 2061, American Association for the Advancement of Science. (1989). *Science for All Americans*. Washington, DC: Author.

Project 2061, American Association for the Advancement of Science. (1993). *Benchmarks for Science Literacy*. New York: Oxford University Press.

Quigley, C. N., & Bahmmeller, C. F. (Eds.). (1991). *Civitas: A Framework for Civic Education*. (National Council for Social Studies, Bulletin No. 86). Calabasas, CA: Center for Civic Education.

Ravitch, D. & Finn, C. E., Jr. (1987). *What Do Our 17-Year-Olds Know?* New York: Harper & Row.

Saunders, P., & Gilliard, J. (Eds.). (1995). *A Framework for Teaching Basic Economic Concepts With Scope and Sequence Guidelines, K-12*. New York: National Council on Economic Education.

Secretary's Commission on Achieving Necessary Skills. (1991). *What Work Requires of Schools: A SCANS Report for America 2000*. Washington, DC: U.S. Department of Labor.

Standards Project for English Language Arts. (1994, February). *Incomplete Work of the Task Forces of the Standards Project for English Language Arts*. (Draft). Urbana, IL: National Council of Teachers of English.

Stotsky, S., Anderson, P., & Beierl, D. (1989). *Variety and Individualism in the English Class: Teacher-Recommended Lists of Reading for Grades 7-12*. Boston, MA: New England Association of Teachers of English.

Vignette Depicting One District's Efforts to Design Standards and Benchmarks

In 1991, the Arkansas Legislature passed Act 236 to provide Arkansas schools with the flexibility and tools to achieve the national education goals. Better known as the Restructuring Act, Act 236 requires school districts to write curricula that reflect the state-developed frameworks, which place a strong emphasis on teaching students to think critically and to apply content knowledge.

In 1993, the Arkansas Legislature followed up on the requirements of the Restructuring Act with Act 846. This act provides for a comprehensive competency and outcome-based assessment program for evaluating the performance of Arkansas students relative to the new curricula.

In August 1994, Lonoke School District, under the direction of Superintendent Dr. Paul Dee Human, determined that McREL could provide direction in setting content standards that would serve as the basis for writing new curricula. Chairpersons of the math, language arts, science, and social studies committees were invited to accompany Sharon Havens, curriculum coordinator, and Dr. Human to Aurora, Colorado, in October 1994, where the group met with McREL consultant Diane Paynter to discuss how McREL could most effectively support Lonoke.

The scope of the work was dependent upon Lonoke procuring outside funding. In November 1994, the district received a Goals 2000 grant that provided the resources for training and work sessions during the summer of 1995. During these sessions, committees wrote content standards and benchmarks in language arts, mathematics, science, and social studies. College professors from Harding University and Hendrix College worked with the committees providing content expertise.

Concurrent with this work, Lonoke staff were trained by McREL in complex reasoning processes and the construction of performance tasks. Teachers were expected to develop complex reasoning tasks for their classrooms during the 1995-96 school year.

In November 1995, the Lonoke School District received a second grant that allowed the district to continue its work. The content standards and benchmarks that had been completed by the Lonoke staff during the summer of 1995 were sent to McREL for revisions. McREL's task was to examine each standard and benchmark and determine if Lonoke's document reflected the Arkansas frameworks and the national standards in each content area. During the spring of 1996, Lonoke curriculum committees reviewed the recommendations made by McREL and determined which recommendations to accept, reject, or revise. In addition, Lonoke teachers assigned grade-level or course-level designations to the benchmarks. The revised document was returned to McREL in June 1996.

Once content standards and benchmarks had been identified, teachers needed training in instructional strategies to implement the new standards and benchmarks. The instructional model that was selected to create a link between standards and classroom practice was Dimensions of Learning, developed collaboratively by McREL and ASCD. During June 1996, all Lonoke teachers and district staff participated in staff development workshops on the Dimensions of Learning model. Additional training and assistance in writing performance tasks was provided by Diane Paynter.

Curriculum committees began work on the development of content standards and benchmarks for foreign language and fine arts. Professors from Harding University and Hendrix College once again provided additional content-area expertise and helped facilitate the work done by the committees.

In July 1996, principals met with Diane Paynter to develop a supervision model for monitoring the implementation of the new standards and benchmarks and the strategies in Dimensions of Learning.

Additional training in Dimensions of Learning during the 1996-97 school year is scheduled. Grade-level assignments have been determined for the comprehensive teaching of complex reasoning throughout the district. Plans are being made for the development of units that will incorporate the strategies learned in Dimensions of Learning and the content in the district standards and benchmarks. Assessments will be developed during the 1996-97 year to assess the performance of students on selected standards in grades 2, 5, and 9. Assessments will be developed for the remaining grades in the 1997-98 academic year.

During the summer of 1997, content standards and benchmarks in physical education and health will be developed. Work done during the previous years will continually be examined and revised as necessary. The Lonoke School District will continue to work with McREL to provide teachers with the knowledge and skills needed to prepare its students for success in the 21st century.

References

Aldridge, B. G. (Ed). (1995). *Scope, Sequence, and Coordination of Secondary School Science: Vol. 3. A High School Framework for National Science Education Standards*. Arlington, VA: National Science Teachers Association.

Aldridge, B. G. & Strassenburg, A. A. (Eds.). (1995). *Scope, Sequence, and Coordination of National Science Education Content Standards: An Addendum to the Content Core Based on the 1994 Draft National Science Education Standards*. Arlington, VA: National Science Teachers Association.

Allina, A. (1991). *Beyond Standardized Tests: Admissions Alternatives That Work*. Cambridge, MA: Fair Test: National Center for Fair and Open Testing.

Alverno College Faculty. (1985). *Assessment at Alverno College*. Milwaukee: Alverno College Products.

American Federation of Teachers. (1985, September). "Critical Thinking: It's a Basic." *American Teacher*, p. 21.

Anastasi, A. (1982). *Psychological Testing* (5th ed.). New York: Macmillan.

Anderson, J. R. (1982). "Acquisition of Cognitive Skills." *Psychological Review, 89*, 369-406.

Anderson, J. R. (1983). *The Architecture of Cognition*. Cambridge, MA: Harvard University Press.

Anderson, J. R. (1990a). *Cognitive Psychology and Its Implications*. New York: W. H. Freeman and Company.

Anderson, J. R. (1990b). *The Adaptive Character of Thought*. Hillsdale, NJ: Lawrence Erlbaum.

Anderson, J. R. (1993). *Rules of the Mind*. Hillsdale, NJ: Lawrence Erlbaum.

Anderson, J. R. (1995). *Learning and Memory: An Integrated Approach*. New York: John Wiley & Sons.

Archbald, D. A., & Newmann, F. M. (1988). *Beyond Standardized Testing: Assessing Authentic Achievement in the Secondary School*. Reston, VA: National Association of Secondary School Principals.

Arter, J. A., & Salmon, J. R. (1987). *Assessing Higher Order Thinking Skills: A Consumer's Guide*. Portland, OR: Northwest Regional Educational Laboratory.

Atwell, N. C. (1987). *In the Middle*. Portsmouth, NH: Heinemann.

Bailey, J., & McTighe, J. (1996). "Reporting Achievement at the Secondary Level: What and How." In T. R. Guskey (Ed.), *ASCD Yearbook, 1996: Communicating Student Learning* (pp. 119-140). Alexandria, VA: Association for Supervision and Curriculum Development.

Baker, E. L., Aschbacher, P. R., Niemi, D., & Sato, E. (1992). *CRESST Performance Assessment Models: Assessing Content Area Explanations*. Los Angeles, CA: National Center for Research On Evaluation, Standards, and Student Testing (CRESST), UCLA.

Baron, J. (1990a, October). Panel Presentation at the Annual Meeting of the State Assessment Directors. New York.

Baron, J. B. (1990b). "Performance Assessment: Blurring the Edges Among Assessment, Curriculum, and Instruction." In A. B. Champagne, B. E. Lovitts, & B. J. Calinger (Eds.), *Assessment in the Service of Instruction* (pp. 127-147). Washington, DC: American Association for the Advancement of Science.

Baron, J. B. (1991). "Strategies for the Development of Effective Performance Exercises." *Applied Measurement in Education, 4*, 305-318.

Baron, J. B., & Kallick, B. (1985). "Assessing Thinking: What Are We Looking For? And How Can We Find It?" In A. Costa (Ed.), *Developing Minds: A Resource Book for Teaching Thinking*. Alexandria, VA: Association for Supervision and Curriculum Development.

Bereiter, C., & Scardamalia, M. (1982). "From Conversation to Composition: The Role of Instruction in a Developmental Process." In R. Glaser (Ed.), *Advances in Instructional Psychology* (Vol. 2, pp. 1-64). Hillsdale, NJ: Lawrence Erlbaum.

Bereiter, C., & Scardamalia, M. (1985). "Cognitive Coping Strategies and the Problem of 'Inert Knowledge.'" In S. F. Chipman, J. W. Segal, & R. Glaser (Eds.), *Thinking and Learning Skills: Vol. 2. Research and Open Questions* (pp. 65-80). Hillsdale, NJ: Lawrence Erlbaum.

Berk, R. A. (1986a). "Minimum Competency Testing: Status and Potential." In B. S. Plate, & J. C. Witt (Eds.), *The Future of Testing* (pp. 88-144). Hillsdale, NJ: Lawrence Erlbaum.

Berk, R. A. (Ed.). (1986b). *Performance Assessment: Methods and Applications*. Baltimore, MD: The Johns Hopkins University Press.

Berliner, D. C. (1979). "Tempus Educare." In P. L. Peterson & H. J. Walberg (Eds.), *Research On Teaching*. Berkeley, CA: McCutchan.

Berliner, D. C. (1984). "The Half Full Glass: A Review of Research in Teaching." In P. L. Hosford (Ed.), *Using What We Know About Teaching*. Alexandria, VA: Association for Supervision and Curriculum Development.

Berliner, D. C., & Biddle, B. J. (1995). *The Manufactured Crisis: Myths, Fraud, and the Attack on American Public Schools*. Reading, MA: Addison-Wesley.

Block, J. H. (Ed.). (1971). *Mastery Learning: Theory and Practice*. New York: Holt, Rinehart & Winston.

Block, J. H. (Ed.). (1974). *Schools, Society and Mastery Learning*. New York: Holt, Rinehart & Winston.

Block, J. H., & Burns, R. B. (1976). "Mastery Learning." In L. Shulman (Ed.), *Review of Research in Education, 4*, 3-49. Itasca, IL: Peacock.

Block, J. H., Efthim, H. E., & Burns, R. B. (1989). *Building Effective Mastery Learning Schools*. White Plains, NY: Longman.

Bloom, B. S. (1968). "Learning for Mastery." *Evaluation Comment, 1*(2), 1-12.

Bloom, B. S. (1984). "The Search for Methods of Group Instruction as Effective as One-to-One Tutoring." *Educational Leadership, 42*(3), 4-17.

Board of Education, Commonwealth of Virginia. (1995, June). *Standards of Learning for Virginia Public Schools*. Richmond, VA: Author.

Bond, L. A., Braskamp, D., & Roeber, E. (1996). *The Status of State Student Assessment Programs in the United States*. Chicago: North Central Regional Educational Laboratory.

Bond, L., Friedman, L., & van der Ploeg, A. (1994). *Surveying the Landscape of State Educational Assessment Programs*. Washington, DC: Council for Educational Development and Research, and the National Education Association.

Borko, H., Flory, M., & Cumbo, K. (1993, October). *Teachers' Ideas and Practices About Assessment and Instruction: A Case Study of the Effects of Alternative Assessment in Instruction, Student Learning, and Accountability Practice* (CSE Tech. Rep. No. 366). Los Angeles: National Center for Research On Evaluation, Standards, and Student Testing (CRESST), UCLA.

Brandt, R. (1995). "Overview: What to Do With Those New Standards." *Educational Leadership, 52*(6), 5.

Bransford, J. D., & Franks, J. J. (1976). "Toward a Framework for Understanding Learning." In G. H. Bower (Ed.), *Psychology of Learning and Motivation* (Vol. 10, pp. 93-127). New York: Academic Press.

Braven, M., O'Reilly, F., & Moore, M. (1994). *Issues and Options in Outcome-Based Accountability for Students With Disabilities*. College Park, MD: University of Maryland at College Park.

Brookhart, S. M. (1993). "Teacher's Grading Practices: Meaning and Values." *Journal of Educational Measurement, 30*(2), 123-142.

Bruner, J. S. (1960). *The Process of Education*. Cambridge, MA: Harvard University Press.

Burns, R. B. (1987). *Models of Instructional Organization: A Casebook On Mastery Learning and Outcome-Based Education*. San Francisco: Far West Laboratory for Educational Research and Development.

Burns, R. W., & Klingstedt, J. L. (Eds.). (1973). *Competency-Based Education: An Introduction*. Englewood Cliffs, NJ: Educational Technology Publications.

Calfee, R. C. (1994). *Implications for Cognitive Psychology for Authentic Assessment and Instruction* (Tech. Rep. No. 69). Berkeley, CA: National Center for the Study of Writing, University of California.

Calfee, R. C., & Hiebert, E. H. (1991). "Classroom Assessment of Reading." In R. Barr, M. Kamil, P. Mosenthal, & P. D. Pearson (Eds.), *Handbook of Research On Reading* (2nd ed., pp. 281-309). New York: Longman.

Calkins, L. M. (1986). *The Art of Teaching Writing*. Portsmouth, NH: Heinemann.

Carnevale, A. P., Gainer, L. J., & Meltzer, A. S. (1990). *Workplace Basics: The Essential Skills Employers Want*. San Francisco: Jossey-Bass.

Carroll, J. B. (1963). "A Model of School Learning." *Teachers College Record, 64*, 723-733.

Carroll, J. B. (1964). "Words, Meanings and Concepts." *Harvard Educational Review, 34*, 178-202.

Carroll, J. B. (1982). "The Measurement of Intelligence." In R. J. Sternberg (Ed.), *Handbook of Human Intelligence* (pp. 29-122). London: Cambridge University Press.

Case, R. (1985). *Intellectual Development: Birth to Adulthood.* New York: Academic Press.

Cazden, C. B. (1986). "Classroom Discourse." In M. C. Wittrock (Ed.), *Handbook of Research On Teaching* (3rd ed., pp. 432-463). New York: Macmillan.

Center for Civic Education. (1994). *National Standards for Civics and Government.* Calabasas, CA: Author.

Chion-Kennedy, L. (1994). "What's in a Name? The Semantics of Outcome-Based Education." *The School Administrator, 51*(8), 14.

Clark, H. H., & Clark, E. V. (1977). *Psychology and Language.* San Diego, CA: Harcourt Brace Jovanovich.

Clark, J. P., & Thomson, S. D. (1976). *Competency Tests and Graduation Requirements.* Reston, VA: National Association of Secondary School Principals.

Clay, M. M. (1979). *The Early Detection of Reading Difficulties* (3rd ed.). Birkenhead, Auckland, New Zealand: Heinemann Education.

Clay, M. M. (1991). *Becoming Literate: The Construction of Inner Control.* Portsmouth, NH: Heinemann.

Clinton, W. (1996, March 27). *Remarks by the President at the National Governors Association Education Summit.* Office of the Press Secretary: The White House.

Cohen, D. (1995). "What Standards for National Standards?" *Phi Delta Kappan, 76*(10), 751-757.

Coleman, J. S. (1972). "The Evaluation of Equality of Educational Opportunity." In F. Mosteller & D. P. Moynihan (Eds.), *On Equality of Educational Opportunity* (pp. 140-161). New York: Vintage Books.

Coleman, J. S., Campbell, E. Q., Hobson, C. J., McPartland, J., Mood, A. M., Weinfield, F. D., & York, R. L. (1966). *Equality of Educational Opportunity.* Washington, DC: U. S. Government Printing Office.

College Board, The. (1983). *Academic Preparation for College: What Students Need to Know and Be Able to Do.* New York: College Entrance Examination Board.

Conley, D. T. (1996). "Assessment." In R. E. Blum & J. A. Arter (Eds.), *A Handbook for Student Performance Assessment in an Era of Restructuring* (Sec. I-4, pp. 1-8). Alexandria, VA: Association for Supervision and Curriculum Development.

Consortium of National Arts Education Associations. (1994). *National Standards for Arts Education: What Every Young American Should Know and Be Able to Do in the Arts.* Reston, VA: Music Educators National Conference.

Core Knowledge Foundation. (1992, January). *Core Knowledge Sequence: Grades 1-6.* Charlottesville, VA: Author.

Costa, A., & Liebman, R. (1995). "Process Is as Important as Content." *Educational Leadership, 52*(6), 23-24.

Countryman, L. L., & Schroeder, M. (1996). "When Students Lead Parent-Teacher Conferences." *Educational Leadership, 53*(7), 64-68.

Covington, M. V. (1983). "Motivation Cognitions." In S. G. Paris, G. M. Olson, & H. W. Stevenson (Eds.), *Learning and Motivation in the Classroom* (pp. 139-164). Hillsdale, NJ: Lawrence Erlbaum.

Covington, M. V. (1985). "Strategic Thinking and the Fear of Failure." In J. W. Segal, S. F. Chipman, & R. Glaser (Eds.), *Thinking and Learning Skills: Vol. 1, Relating Instruction to Research* (pp. 389-416). Hillsdale, NJ: Lawrence Erlbaum.

Cronbach, L. J., Bradburn, N. M., & Horvitz, D. G. (1994). *Sampling and Statistical Procedures Used in the California Learning Assessment System.* Palo Alto, CA: Report of the Select Committee.

Darling-Hammond, L., & Ancess, J. (1994). *Graduation by Portfolio at Central Park East Secondary School.* New York: National Center for Restructuring Education, Columbia University.

Darling-Hammond, L., Ancess, J., & Falk, B. (1995). *Authentic Assessment in Action: Studies of Schools and Student Work.* New York: Teacher's College Press.

de Beaugrande, R. (1980). *Text, Discourse and Process. Toward a Multi-Disciplinary Science of Text.* Norwood, NJ: Ablex.

Dewey, J. (1916). *Democracy and Education.* New York: Macmillan.

Diegmueller, K. (1995, April 12). "Running Out of Steam." *Struggling for Standards: An Education Week Special Report.* Washington DC: Education Week.

Dorr-Bremme, D. W., & Herman, J. L. (1986). *Assessing Student Achievement: A Profile of Classroom Practices.* Los Angeles: National Center for Research On Evaluation, Standards, and Student Testing (CRESST), UCLA.

Dossey, J. A., Mullis, I. V. S., & Jones, C. O. (1993). *Can Students Do Mathematical Problem Solving?* Washington, DC: U.S. Department of Education, Office of Educational Research and Improvement.

Doyle, W. (1992). "Curriculum and Pedagogy." In P. W. Jackson (Ed.), *Handbook of Research in Curriculum* (pp. 486-516). New York: Macmillan.

"Draft Standards Tackle Slippery Subject: English." (1995, October 25). *Education Daily, 28*(206), pp. 1, 3.

Drake, S. M. (1993). *Planning Integrated Curriculum: The Call to Adventure.* Alexandria, VA: Association for Supervision and Curriculum Development.

Durm, M. W. (1993). "An A Is Not an A Is Not an A: A History of Grading." *The Educational Forum, 57*(Spring), 294-297.

Education Commission of the States. (1996). *Standards and Education: A Roadmap for State Policymakers.* Denver, CO: Author.

Educational Policies Commission. (1961). *The Central Purpose of American Education.* Washington, DC: National Education Association.

"Educators Weigh High Price of Performance Assessments." (1996, January 4). *Education Daily, 29*(3), 1-3.

Eisner, E. W. (1995). "Standards for American Schools: Help or Hindrance?" *Phi Delta Kappan, 76*(10), 758-764.

"ETS Loses Cheating Arbitration." (1995-1996, Fall/Winter). *Fair Test Examiner, 9*(4), and *10*(1), 11, 13.

Evans, K. M., & King, J. A. (1994). "Research On OBE: What We Know and Don't Know." *Educational Leadership, 51*(6), 12-17.

Falk, B., & Darling-Hammond, L. (1993, March). *The Primary Language Record at P.S. 261: How Assessment Transforms Teaching and Learning.* New York: National Center for Restructuring Education, Schools, and Teaching.

Farkas, F., Friedman, W., Boese, J., & Shaw, G. (1994). *First Things First: What Americans Expect From Public Schools.* New York: Public Agenda.

Feuerstein, R. (1980). *Instrumental Enrichment: An Intervention Program for Cognitive Modifiability.* Baltimore, MD: University Park Press.

Finn, C. E., Jr. (1990). "The Biggest Reform of All." *Phi Delta Kappan, 71*(8), 584-592.

Fischer, K. W. (1980). "A Theory of Cognitive Development: The Control and Construction of Hierarchies of Skills." *Psychological Review, 87*(6), 477-531.

Fitts, P. M. (1964). "Perceptual-Motor Skill Learning." In A. W. Melton (Ed.), *Categories of Human Learning.* New York: Wiley.

Fitts, P. M., & Posner, M. I. (1967). *Human Performance.* Belmont, CA: Brooks Cole.

Fitzpatrick, K. A., Kulieke, M., Hillary, J., & Begitschke, V. (1996). "The Instructional Resource Network: Supporting the Alignment of Curriculum Instruction and Assessment." In R. E. Blum & J. A. Arter (Eds.), *A Handbook for Student Performance Assessment in an Era of Restructuring* (Sec. iv-3, pp. 1-6). Alexandria, VA: Association for Supervision and Curriculum Development.

Flavell, J. H. (1977). *Cognitive Development.* Englewood Cliffs, NJ: Prentice-Hall.

Florida Department of Education. (1996). *Curriculum Framework for Social Studies.* Tallahassee, FL: Author.

Flower, L. A., & Hayes, J. R. (1980a). "The Cognition of Discovery: Defining a Rhetorical Problem." *College Composition and Communication, 13,* 21-32.

Flower, L. A., & Hayes, J. R. (1980b). "The Dynamics of Composing: Making Plans and Juggling Constraints." In L. W. Gregg & E. R. Steinburg (Eds.), *Cognitive Processing in Writing* (pp. 31-50). Hillsdale, NJ: Lawrence Erlbaum.

Flower, L. A., & Hayes, J. R. (1981a). "A Cognitive Process Theory of Writing." *College Composition and Communication, 32,* 365-387.

Flower, L. A., & Hayes, J. R. (1981b). "Plans That Guide the Composing Process." In C. H. Frederiksen & J. F. Dominic (Eds.), *Writing: The Nature, Development, and Teaching of Written Communication* (Vol. 2, pp. 39-58). Hillsdale, NJ: Lawrence Erlbaum.

Fogarty, R. (1991). *The Mindful School: How to Integrate Curriculum.* Palatino, IL: IRI/Skylight Publishing.

Frederick, W., & Walberg, H. J. (1980). "Learning as a Function of Time." *Journal of Educational Research, 73,* 183-194.

Frederiksen, C. H. (1977). "Semantic Processing Units in Understanding Text." In R. O. Freedle (Ed.), *Discourse Production and Comprehension* (Vol. 1, pp. 57-88). Norwood, NJ: Ablex.

Frederiksen, J. R., & Collins, A. (1989). "A Systems Approach to Educational Testing." *Educational Researcher, 18*(9), 27-32.

Frederiksen, N., Mislevy, R. J., & Bejar, F. I. (1993). *Test Theory for a New Generation of Tests.* Hillsdale, NJ: Lawrence Erlbaum.

Frost, D. B. (1996). Personal communication.

Futtrell, M. H. (1987, December 9). "A Message Long Overdue." *Education Week, 7*(14), 9.

Gaddy, B. B., Hall, T. W., & Marzano, R. J. (1996). *School Wars: Resolving Our Conflicts Over Religion and Values.* San Francisco: Jossey-Bass.

Gagne, R. M. (1977). *The Conditions of Learning* (3rd ed.). New York: Holt, Rinehart & Winston.

Gandal, M. (1995a). *Making Standards Matter: A Fifty-State Progress Report On Efforts to Raise Academic Standards.* Washington, DC: American Federation of Teachers.

Gandal, M. (1995b). "Not All Standards Are Created Equal." *Educational Leadership, 52*(6), 16-21.

Gandal, M. (1996). *Making Standards Matter, 1996: An Annual Fifty-State Report on Efforts to Raise Academic Standards.* Washington, DC: American Federation of Teachers.

Gardner, H. (1983). *Frames of Mind.* New York: Basic Books.

Gardner, H. (1991). *The Unschooled Mind.* New York: Basic Books.

Gardner, H. (1992). "Assessment in Context: The Alternative to Standardized Testing." In B. R. Gifford & M. C. O'Connor (Eds.), *Changing Assessments: Alternative Views of Aptitude, Achievement and Instruction* (pp. 77-120). Boston: Kluwer Academic Press.

Gearhart, M., Herman, J. L., Baker, E. L., & Whittaker, A. (1993). *Whose Work Is It? A Question for the Validity of Large-Scale Portfolio Assessment.* Los Angeles: CRESST: Center for the Study of Evaluation.

Geography Education Standards Project. (1994). *Geography for Life: National Geography Standards.* Washington, DC: National Geographic Research and Exploration.

Gifford, B. R. (1992). "Introduction." In B. R. Gifford & M. C. O'Connor (Eds.), *Changing Assessments: Alternative Views of Aptitude, Achievement and Instruction* (pp. 1- 7). Boston: Kluwer Academic Press.

Glaser, R. (1984). "Education and Thinking: The Role of Knowledge." *American Psychologist, 39,* 93-104.

Glaser, R., & Linn, R. (1993). "Forward." In L. Shepard, *Setting Performance Standards for Student Achievement* (pp. xiii-xiv). Stanford, CA: National Academy of Education, Stanford University.

Glasser, W. (1981). *Stations of the Mind.* New York: Harper & Row.

Glickman, C. (1993). *Reviewing America's Schools.* San Francisco: Jossey-Bass.

Goodman, Y. M. (1978). "Kid Watching: An Alternative to Testing." *National Elementary School Principal, 57,* 41-45.

Goodman, Y. M., & Burke, C. (1972). *Reading Miscue Inventory: Procedure for Diagnosis and Evaluation.* New York: Macmillan.

Grissom, J. B., & Shepard, L. A. (1989). "Repeating and Dropping Out of School." In L. A. Shepard & M. L. Smith (Eds.), *Flunking Grades: Research and Policies On Retention* (pp. 92-113). London: The Falmer Press.

Guilford, J. P. (1967). *The Nature of Human Intelligence.* New York: McGraw-Hill.

Gulliksen, H. (1950). *Theory of Mental Tests.* New York: John Wiley & Sons.

Guskey, T. R. (1980). "What Is Mastery Learning?" *Instructor, 90*(3), 80-86.

Guskey, T. R. (1985). *Implementing Mastery Learning.* Belmont, CA: Wadsworth Publishing Co.

Guskey, T. R. (1987). "Rethinking Mastery Learning Reconsidered." *Review of Educational Research, 57,* 225-229.

Guskey, T. R. (1990a). "Cooperative Mastery Learning Strategies." *Elementary School Journal, 91,* 33-42.

Guskey, T. R. (1990b). "Integrating Innovations." *Educational Leadership, 47*(5), 11-15.

Guskey, T. R. (1994). "Introduction." In T. R. Guskey (Ed.), *High Stakes Performance Assessment: Perspectives On Kentucky's Educational Reform* (pp. 1-5). Thousand Oaks, CA: Corwin Press.

Guskey, T. R. (1995). "Mastery Learning." In J. H. Block, S. T. Everson, & T. R. Guskey (Eds.), *School Improvement Programs: A Handbook For Educational Leaders* (pp. 91-108). New York: Scholastic.

Guskey, T. R. (Ed.). (1996a). *ASCD Yearbook, 1996: Communicating Student Learning.* Alexandria, VA: Association for Supervision and Curriculum Development.

Guskey, T. R. (1996b). "Reporting On Student Learning: Lessons From the Past—Prescriptions for the Future." In T. R. Guskey (Ed.), *ASCD Yearbook, 1996: Communicating Student Learning* (pp. 13-24). Alexandria, VA: Association for Supervision and Curriculum Development.

Guskey, T. R. (1996c). Personal Communication. May, 1996.

Guskey, T. R., & Gates, S. L. (1986). "Synthesis of Research On the Effects of Mastery Learning in Elementary and Secondary Classrooms." *Educational Leadership, 33*(8), 73-80.

Gutek, G. L. (1986). *Education in the United States: An Historical Perspective.* Englewood Cliffs, NJ: Prentice Hall.

Guyton, J. M., & Fielstein, L. L. (1989). "Student-Led Parent Conferences: A Model for Teaching Responsibility." *Elementary School and Guidance Counseling, 23*(2), 169-172.

Halliday, M., & Hasan, R. (1976). *Cohesion in English.* London: Longman.

Hampel, R. L. (1986). *The Last Little Citadel.* Boston: Houghton-Mifflin.

Hansen, J. (1987). *When Writers Read.* Portsmouth, NH: Heinemann.

Hansen, J. (1991, Winter). "My Portfolio Shows Who I Am." *Quarterly of the National Writing Project and the Center for the Study of Writing and Literacy, 14*(1), 5-9.

Hansen, J. (1992). "Literacy Portfolios: Helping Students Know Themselves." *Educational Leadership, 49*(8), 66-68.

Hansen, J. (1994). "Literacy Portfolios: Windows On Potential." In S. W. Valencia, E. H. Hiebert, & P. P. Afflerrbach (Eds.), *Authentic Reading Assessment: Practices and Possibilities* (pp. 26-44). Newark, DE: International Reading Association.

Hawkins, D. (1973). "I, Thou, It: The Triangular Relationship." In C. Silberman (Ed.), *The Open Classroom Reader* (pp. 25-40). New York: Random House.

Herman, J. (1996). "Technical Quality Matters." In R. E. Blum & J. A. Arter (Eds.), *A Handbook for Student Performance Assessment in an Era of Restructuring* (Sec. I-7, pp. 1- 6). Alexandria, VA: Association for Supervision and Curriculum Development.

Herman, J. L., Aschbacher, P. R., & Winters, L. (1992). *A Practical Guide to Alternative Assessment.* Alexandria, VA: Association for Supervision and Curriculum Development.

Herman, J. L., & Winters, L. (1994). "Portfolio Research: A Slim Collection." *Educational Leadership, 52*(2), 48-55.

Hieronymus, A. N., & Hoover, H. D. (1986). *Manual for School Administrators: Levels 5- 14: ITBS, Forms G/H.* Chicago: Riverside Publishing Company.

Hillocks, G. (1987). "Synthesis of Research in Teaching Writing." *Educational Leadership, 44*(8), 71-82.

Hirsch, E. D., Jr. (1987). *Cultural Literacy: What Every American Needs to Know.* Boston: Houghton Mifflin.

Hirsch, E. D., Jr. (Ed.). (1993a). *What Your 1st Grader Needs to Know: Fundamentals of a Good First-Grade Education. The Core Knowledge Series: Resource Books for Grades One Through Six, Book I.* New York: Delta.

Hirsch, E. D., Jr. (Ed.). (1993b). *What Your 2nd Grader Needs to Know: Fundamentals of a Good Second-Grade Education. The Core Knowledge Series: Resource Books for Grades One Through Six, Book II.* New York: Delta.

Hirsch, E. D., Jr. (Ed.). (1993c). *What Your 3rd Grader Needs to Know: Fundamentals of a Good Third-Grade Education. The Core Knowledge Series: Resource Books for Grades One Through Six, Book III.* New York: Delta.

Hirsch, E. D., Jr. (Ed.). (1993d). *What Your 4th Grader Needs to Know: Fundamentals of a Good Fourth-Grade Education. The Core Knowledge Series: Resource Books for Grades One Through Six, Book IV.* New York: Delta.

Hirsch, E. D., Jr. (Ed.). (1993e). *What Your 5th Grader Needs to Know: Fundamentals of a Good Fifth-Grade Education. The Core Knowledge Series: Resource Books for Grades One Through Six, Book V.* New York: Delta.

Hirsch, E. D., Jr. (Ed.). (1993f). *What Your 6th Grader Needs to Know: Fundamentals of a Good Sixth-Grade Education. The Core Knowledge Series: Resource Books for Grades One Through Six, Book VI.* New York: Delta.

Holmes, C. T. (1989). "Grade-Level Retention Effects: A Meta-Analysis of Research Studies." In L. A. Shepard & M. L. Smith (Eds.), *Flunking Grades: Research and Policies On Retention* (pp. 45-75). London: The Falmer Press.

Hubert, B. D. (1989). "Students Belong in the "Parent-Teacher" Conference, Too." *Educational Leadership, 47*(2), 30.

Hunter, M. (1969). *Teach More Faster!* El Segundo, CA: TIP Publications.

Hunter, M. (1976). *Rx: Improved Instruction.* El Sequndo, CA: TIP Publications.

Hunter, M. (1982). *Mastery Teaching.* El Segundo, CA: TIP Publications.

Hunter, M. (1984). "Knowing, Teaching, and Supervising." In P. Hosford (Ed.), *Using What We Know About Teaching.* Alexandria, VA: Association for Supervision and Curriculum Development.

Innerst, C. (1995, July 27). "States Found Lacking On School Standards." *Washington Times,* p. A4.

Jacobs, H. H. (Ed.). (1989). *Interdisciplinary Curriculum: Design and Implementation.* Alexandria, VA: Association for Supervision and Curriculum Development.

Jaeger, R. M., Hambelton, R. K., & Plake, B. S. (1995, April). *Eliciting Configural Performance Standards Through a Sequenced Application of Complementary Method.* Paper presented at the annual meeting of the American Educational Research Association, San Francisco.

Johnson, P. E. (1967). "Some Psychological Aspects of Subject-Matter Structure." *Journal of Educational Psychology, 58,* 75-83.

Johnson, P. E. (1969). "On the Communication of Concepts in Science." *Journal of Educational Psychology, 60,* 32-40.

Joint Committee on National Health Education Standards. (1995). *National Health Education Standards: Achieving Health Literacy.* Reston, VA: Association for the Advancement of Health Education.

Jones, B. F., Friedman, L. B., Tinzmann, M., & Cox, B. E. (1985). "Guidelines for Instruction-Enriched Mastery Learning To Improve Comprehension." In D. U. Levine & Associates (Eds.), *Improving Student Achievement Through Mastery Learning Programs* (pp. 91-145). San Francisco: Jossey-Bass.

Jones, L. R., Mullis, I. V. S., Raizen, S. A., Weiss, I. R., & Weston, E. A. (1992). *The 1990 Science Report Card.* Washington, DC: Department of Education, Office of Educational Research and Improvement.

Kattri, N., Kane, M. B., & Reeve, A. L. (1995). "How Performance Assessments Affect Teaching and Learning." *Educational Leadership, 53*(3), 80-83.

Kendall, J. S., & Marzano, R. J. (1996). *Content Knowledge: A Compendium of Standards and Benchmarks for K-12 Education.* Aurora, CO: Mid-continent Regional Educational Laboratory.

Kenney, E., & Perry, S. (1994). "Talking With Parents About Performance-Based Report Cards." *Educational Leadership, 52*(2), 24-27.

Kentucky Institute for Education Research, The. (1995, January). *An Independent Evaluation of the Kentucky Instructional Results Information System (KIRIS): Executive Summary.* Frankfort, KY: The Kentucky Institute for Education Research.

Kifer, E. (1994). "Development of the Kentucky Instructional Results Information System (KIRIS)." In T. R. Guskey (Ed.), *High Stakes Performance Assessment: Perspective On Kentucky's Educational Reform* (pp. 7-18). Thousand Oaks, CA: Corwin Press Inc.

Kintsch, W. (1974). *The Representation of Meaning in Memory.* Hillsdale, NJ: Lawrence Erlbaum.

Klausmeier, H. J. (1980). *Learning and Teaching Concepts.* New York: Academic Press.

Klausmeier, H. J. (1985). *Educational Psychology* (5th Ed.). New York: Harper & Row.

Knight, P. (1992). "How I Use Portfolios in Mathematics." *Educational Leadership, 49*(8), 71-72.

Koretz, D., Stecher, B., & Deibert, E. (1993). *The Reliability of Scores From the 1992 Vermont Portfolio Assessment Program* (Tech. Rep. No. 355). Los Angeles: National Center for Research On Evaluation, Standards, and Student Testing (CRESST), UCLA.

Kozol, J. (1991). *Savage Inequalities.* New York: Crown Publishers.

LaHaye, B. (1994). "A Radical Redefinition of Schooling." *The School Administrator, 51*(8), 28-29.

Lake, K., & Kafka, K. (1996). "Reporting Methods in Grades K-8." In T. R. Guskey (Ed.), *ASCD Yearbook, 1996: Communicating Student Learning* (pp. 90-118). Alexandria, VA: Association for Supervision and Curriculum Development.

Lane, S., Liu, M., Ankenmann, R. D., & Stone, C. A. (1996). "Generalizability and Validity of a Mathematics Performance Assessment." *Journal of Educational Measurement, 33*(1), 71-92.

Lehman, P. R. (1995). "What Students Should Learn in the Arts." In A. A. Glatthorn (Ed.), *Content of the Curriculum* (2nd ed., pp. 1-22). Alexandria, VA: Association for Supervision and Curriculum Development.

Levine, D. V., & Associates. (1985). *Improving Student Achievement Through Mastery Learning Programs.* San Francisco: Jossey-Bass.

Lewis, A. C. (1995). "An Overview of the Standards Movement." *Phi Delta Kappan, 76*(10), 744-750.

Lindsay, P. H., & Norman, D. A. (1977). *Human Information Processing.* New York: Academic Press.

Linn, R. (1994). "Performance Assessment: Policy Promises and Technical Measurement Standards." *Educational Researcher, 23*(9), 4-14.

Little, A. W., & Allan, J. (1989). "Student-Led Parent Teacher Conferences." *Elementary School Guidance and Counseling, 23*(3), 210-218.

Lord, F. M., & Novick, M. R. (1968). *Statistical Theories of Mental Test Scores.* Reading, MA: Addison & Wesley.

Madaus, G. (1993). "A National Testing System: Manna From Above? An Historical/Technological Perspective." *Educational Assessment, 1*(1), 9-26.

Madden, N. A., & Slavin, R. E. (1989). "Effective Pullout Programs for Students at Risk." In R. E. Slavin, N. L. Karweit, & N. A. Madden (Eds.), *Effective Programs for Students at Risk* (pp. 52-72). Needham Heights, MA: Allyn & Bacon.

Mager, R. (1962). *Preparing Instructional Objectives.* Palo Alto, CA: Fearon Publishers.

Magnusson, D. (1966). *Test Theory.* Reading, MA: Addison & Wesley.

Manno, B. J. (1994). *Outcome-Based Education: Has It Become More Affliction Than Cure?* Minneapolis, MN: Center for the American Experiment.

Maryland Department of Education. (1992). *Maryland School Performance Report, 1992.* Baltimore, MD: Author.

"Maryland Performance Assessment Update." (1995, Spring). *Fair Test Examiner, 9*(2), 8-10, 12.

Marzano, R. J. (1983). *A Quantitative Grammar of Meaning and Structure: A Methodology for Language Analysis and Measurement* (Technical Report). Denver, CO: Mid-continent Regional Educational Laboratory. (ERIC Document Reproduction Service No. ED 239 491)

Marzano, R. J. (1990). "Standardized Tests: Do They Measure General Cognitive Abilities?" *NASSP Bulletin, 74*(526), 93-101.

Marzano, R. J. (1991). *Cultivating Thinking in English and the Language Arts.* Urbana, IL: National Council of Teachers of English.

Marzano, R. J. (1992). *A Different Kind of Classroom: Teaching With Dimensions of Learning.* Alexandria, VA: Association for Supervision and Curriculum Development.

Marzano, R. J. (1994). "Lessons From the Field About Outcome-Based Performance Assessments." *Educational Leadership, 51*(6), 44-50.

Marzano, R. J. (1995). Teacher Report of Use of Variables When Constructing Grades. Unpublished Data. Aurora, CO: Mid-continent Regional Educational Laboratory.

Marzano, R. J., & Costa, A. L. (1988). "Question: Do Standardized Tests Measure Cognitive Skills? Answer: No." *Educational Leadership, 45*(8), 66-73.

Marzano, R. J., Hagerty, P. J., Valencia, S. W., & DiStefano, P. P. (1987). *Reading Diagnosis and Instruction: Theory Into Practice.* Englewood Cliffs, NJ: Prentice-Hall.

Marzano, R. J., & Kendall, J. S. (1991). *Analysis of Effects on Standard Error of Measurement of Using Interim Scores.* Aurora, CO: Mid-continent Regional Educational Laboratory.

Marzano, R. J., & Kendall, J. S. (1992). Unpublished Data. Aurora, CO: Mid-continent Regional Educational Laboratory.

Marzano, R. J., & Paynter, D. E. (1994). *New Approaches to Literacy: Helping Students Develop Reading and Writing Skills.* Washington, DC: American Psychological Association.

Marzano, R. J., Paynter, D. E., Kendall, J., Pickering, D., & Marzano, L. (1991). *Literacy Plus: An Integrated Approach to Teaching Reading, Writing, Vocabulary, and Reasoning.* Columbus, OH: Zaner-Bloser.

Marzano, R. J., Pickering, D. J., Arredondo, D. E., Blackburn, G. J., Brandt, R. S., & Moffett, C. A. (1992). *Dimensions of Learning: Teacher's Manual.* Alexandria, VA: Association for Supervision and Curriculum Development.

Marzano, R. J., Pickering, D. J., & McTighe, J. (1993). *Assessing Student Outcomes.* Alexandria, VA: Association for Supervision and Curriculum Development.

McCombs, B. L. (1984). "Processes and Skills Underlying Intrinsic Motivation to Learn: Toward a Definition of Motivational Skills Training Intervention." *Educational Psychologist 19,* 197-218.

McCombs, B. L. (1989). "Self-Regulated Learning and Academic Achievement: A Phenomenological View." In B. J. Zimmerman & D. H. Schunk (Eds.), *Self-Regulated Learning and Academic Achievement: Theory Research and Practice* (pp. 51-82). New York: Springer-Verlag.

McCombs, B. L., & Marzano, R. J. (1990). "Putting the Self in Self-Regulated Learning: The Self as Agent in Integrating Will and Skill." *Educational Psychologist, 25*(1), 51-69.

McDonald, J. P., Smith, S., Turner, D., Finney, M., & Barton, E. (1993). *Graduation by Exhibition: Assessing Genuine Achievement.* Alexandria, VA: Association for Supervision and Curriculum Development.

McLaughlin, M. J., & Warren, S. H. (1992). *Issues and Options in Restructuring Schools and Special Education Programs.* College Park, MD: University of Maryland at College Park.

McNeir, G. (1993, April). "Outcome-Based Education: Tool for Restructuring." *Oregon School Study Council, 36*(8), 1-29.

McREL Institute. (1994). *A Summay Report of Studies of the Effectiveness of Standards-Based Education in the Aurora Public Schools.* Aurora, CO: Author.

McTighe, J., & Ferrera, S. (1994). *Assessing Learning in the Classroom.* Washington, DC: National Education Association.

McTighe, J., & Ferrera, S. (1996). "Performance-Based Assessment in the Classroom: A Planning Framework." In R. E. Blum & J. A. Arter (Eds.), *A Handbook for Student Performance Assessment in an Era of Restructuring* (Sec. I-5, pp. 1-9). Alexandria, VA: Association for Supervision and Curriculum Development.

Meeker, M. N. (1969). *The Structure of Intelligence: Its Interpretation and Uses.* Columbus, OH: Charles E. Merrill.

Menahem, M., & Weisman, L. (1985). "Improving Reading Ability Through a Mastery Learning Program: A Case Study." In Levine & Associates (Eds.), *Improving Student Achievement Through Mastery Learning Programs* (pp. 223-240). San Francisco: Jossey-Bass.

Meyer, B. J. F. (1975). *The Organization of Prose and Its Effects On Memory.* New York: American Elsevier.

Meyer, C. A. (1992). "What's the Difference Between Authentic and Performance Assessment?" *Educational Leadership, 49*(8), 39-40.

Minnesota Department of Education. (1993). *Graduation Standards.* Minneapolis, MN: Author.

Mitchell, R. (1992). *Testing for Learning: How New Approaches to Evaluation Can Improve American Schools.* New York: The Free Press.

Mitchell, R., & Neill, M. (1992). *Criteria for Evaluation of Student Assessment.* Washington, DC: National Forum On Assessment.

Murphy, P. D. (1974). *Consumer Education Modules: A Spiral Process Approach.* Curriculum Development in Vocational and Technical Education, North Dakota State University, Fargo. Washington, DC: Office of Education.

National Assessment of Educational Progress. (1992, March 31). *Framework for the 1994 National Assessment of Educational Progress Mathematics Assessment.* Washington, DC: Author.

National Assessment of Educational Progress. (1992). *Item Specifications: 1994 National Assessment of Educational Progress in Geography.* Washington, DC: National Assessment Governing Board.

National Association for Sport and Physical Education. (1995). *Moving Into the Future: National Standards for Physical Education: A Guide to Content and Assessment.* St. Louis: Mosby.

National Center for History in the Schools. (1994a). *National Standards for History for Grades K-4: Expanding Children's World in Time and Space.* Los Angeles: Author.

National Center for History in the Schools. (1994b). *National Standards for United States History: Exploring the American Experience.* Los Angeles: Author.

National Center for History in the Schools. (1994c). *National Standards for World History: Exploring Paths to the Present.* Los Angeles: Author.

National Center for History in the Schools. (1996). *National Standards for History: Basic Edition.* Los Angeles: Author.

National Commission on Excellence in Education. (1983). *A Nation at Risk: The Imperative for Educational Reform.* Washington, DC: Government Printing Office

National Council for the Social Studies. (1994). *Expectations of Excellence: Curriculum Standards for Social Studies.* Washington, DC: Author.

National Council of Teachers of English and the International Reading Association. (1996). *Standards for the English Language Arts.* Urbana, IL: National Council of Teachers of English.

National Council of Teachers of Mathematics. (1989). *Curriculum and Evaluation Standards for School Mathematics.* Reston, VA: Author.

National Council on Economic Education. (1996, August). *Content Statements for State Standards in Economics, K-12* (Draft). New York: Author.

National Council on Education Standards and Testing. (1992). *Raising Standards for American Education: A Report to Congress, the Secretary of Education, the National Education Goals Panel, and the American People.* Washington, DC: Government Printing Office.

National Education Commission on Time and Learning. (1994). *Prisoners of Time.* Washington, DC: Author.

National Education Goals Panel. (1991). *The National Education Goals Report: Building a Nation of Learners.* Washington, DC: Author.

National Education Goals Panel. (1993a). *Handbook for Local Goals Reports: Building a Community of Learners.* Washington, DC: Author.

National Education Goals Panel. (1993b, November). *Promises to Keep: Creating High Standards for American Students.* A Report on the Review of Education Standards From the Goals 3 and 4 Technical Planning Group to the National Educational Goals Panel. Washington, DC: Author.

National Education Standards and Improvement Council. (1993). *Promises to Keep: Creating High Standards for American Students.* A Report On the Review of Education Standards From the Goals 3 and 4 Technical Planning Group to the National Educational Goals Panel. Washington, DC: National Goals Panel.

National Governors Association. (1996, March). *1996 National Education Summit Policy Statement.* Washington, DC: Author.

National Research Council. (1996). *National Science Education Standards.* Washington, DC: National Academy Press.

National Science Board Commission on Precollege Education in Mathematics, Science and Technology. (1983). *Educating Americans for the 21st Century.* Washington, DC: National Science Board Commission.

National Standards in Foreign Language Education Project. (1996). *Standards for Foreign Language Learning: Preparing for the 21st Century.* Lawrence, KS: Allen Press, Inc.

"National Update on America's Education Reform Efforts." (1995, November 20). *The National Report Card, 5*(62), 1-4.

"NCTE, IRA Say Standards Effort Will Continue." (1994, June). *The Council Chronicle, 3*(5), pp. 1, 4. The National Council of Teachers of English.

New Standards. (1995, June 12). *Performance Standards: Draft 5.1.* Washington, DC: Author.

New Standards Project. (1995a). *Performance Standards: English Language Arts, Mathematics, Science, Applied Learning: Volume 1: Elementary School.* (Consultation Draft). Pittsburgh, PA: LRDC, University of Pittsburgh.

New Standards Project. (1995b). *Performance Standards: English Language Arts, Mathematics, Science, Applied Learning: Volume 2: Middle School.* (Consultation Draft). Pittsburgh, PA: LRDC, University of Pittsburgh.

New Standards Project. (1995c). *Performance Standards: English Language Arts, Mathematics, Science, Applied Learning: Volume 3: High School.* (Consultation Draft). Pittsburgh, PA: LRDC, University of Pittsburgh.

Newell, A., & Simon, H. A. (1972). *Human Problem Solving.* Englewood Cliffs, NJ: Prentice Hall.

Newmann, F. M., Secado, W. G., & Wehlage, G. G. (1995). *A Guide to Authentic Instruction and Assessment: Vision, Standards and Scoring.* Madison, WI: Wisconsin Center for Educational Research, University of Wisconsin.

News Press. (1995, March 29). "School District Launches Efforts to Establish Academic Standards," pp. 1B-8B.

Nixon, R. M. (1970). *Special Message to the Congress On Educational Reform* (March 3). Washington, DC.

Norman, D. (1969). *Memory and Attention.* New York: John Wiley and Sons.

North Dakota Department of Public Instruction. (1996). *North Dakota English Language Arts Curriculum Framework.* Bismarck, ND: Author.

Nunnally, J. C. (1967). *Psychometric Theory.* New York: McGraw-Hill.

O'Donnell, A., & Woolfolk, A. E. (1991). *Elementary and Secondary Teachers' Beliefs About Testing and Grading.* Paper presented at the annual meeting of the American Psychological Association, San Francisco.

O'Neil, J. (1992). "Putting Performance Assessments to the Test." *Educational Leadership, 49*(8), 14-19.

O'Neil, J. (1994). "Aiming for New Outcomes: The Promise and the Reality." *Educational Leadership, 51*(6), 6-10.

O'Neil, J. (1995). "On Using Standards: A Conversation With Ramsay Seldon." *Educational Leadership, 52*(6), 12-14.

Office of Technology Assessment. (1992). *Testing in American Schools: Asking the Right Questions.* Washington, DC: U.S. Government Printing Office.

Olson, L. (1995a, April 12). "Standards Times 50." *Struggling for Standards: An Education Week Special Report,* 14-22.

Olson, L. (1995b, June 14). "Cards On the Table." *Education Week,* 23-28.

Oregon Department of Education. (1994). *Certificate of Initial Mastery Orientation Materials.* Salem, OR: Author.

Ornstein, A. C. (1994). "Grading Practices and Policies: An Overview and Some Suggestions." *NASSP Bulletin, 78*(561), 55-64.

Osterlind, S. J. (1989). *Constructing Test Items.* Boston: Kluwer Academic Press.

Payne, D. A. (1974). *The Assessment of Learning.* Lexington, MA: Heath.

Pearsall, M. K. (Ed.). (1993). *Scope, Sequence, and Coordination of Secondary School Science. Vol. 1. The Content Core: A Guide for Curriculum Designers.* Washington, DC: National Science Teachers Association.

Perkins, D. N. (1981). *The Mind's Best Work.* Cambridge, MA: Harvard University Press.

Perkins, D. N. (1986). *Knowledge as Design.* Hillsdale, NJ: Lawrence Erlbaum.

Perkins, D. N. (1992). *Smart Schools: From Training Memories to Educating Minds.* New York: The Free Press.

Pinar, W., Reynolds, W., Slattery, P., & Taubman, P. (1994, April). *Understanding Curriculum: A Postscript for the Next Generation.* Paper presented at the annual meeting of the American Educational Research Association, New Orleans.

Plake, B. S., Hambelton, R. K., & Jaeger, R. M. (1995). *A New Standard-Setting Method for Performance Assessments: The Dominant Profile Judgment Method and Some Field-Test Results.* Paper presented at the annual meeting of the American Educational Research Association, San Francisco.

Pliska, A. M., & McQuade, J. (1994). "Pennsylvania's Battle for Student Learning Outcomes." *Educational Leadership, 51*(6), 66-69.

Popham, W. J. (1972, April). "Must All Objectives Be Behavioral Objectives?" *Educational Leadership,* 605-608.

Popham, W. J. (1994). "The Instructional Consequences of Criterion-Referenced Clarity." *Educational Measurement: Issues and Practices, 13*(4), 15-18, 30.

Powell, A. G., Farrar, E., & Cohen, D. K. (1985). *The Shopping Mall High School.* Boston: Houghton-Mifflin.

Powers, W. T. (1973). *Behavior: The Control of Perception.* Chicago: Aldine.

Presseisen, B. Z. (1987). *Thinking Skills Throughout the Curriculum.* Bloomington, IN: Phi Lambda Theta.

Project 2061, American Association for the Advancement of Science. (1989). *Science for All Americans.* Washington, DC: Author.

Project 2061, American Association for the Advancement of Science. (1993). *Benchmarks for Science Literacy.* New York, NY: Oxford University Press.

Ravitch, D. (1983). *The Troubled Crusade: American Education 1945-1980.* New York: Basic Books.

Ravitch, D. (1995). *National Standards in American Education: A Citizen's Guide.* Washington, DC: Brookings Institution.

Reckase, M. D. (1995). "Portfolio Assessment: A Theoretical Estimate of Score Reliability." *Educational Measurement: Issues and Practices, 14*(1), 12-14, 31.

Redding, N. (1991). "Assessing the Big Outcomes." *Educational Leadership, 49*(8), 49-53.

Resnick, L. B. (1987a). "Learning in School and Out." *Educational Researcher, 16*(9), 13-20.

Resnick, L. B. (1987b). *Education and Learning to Think.* Washington, DC: National Academy Press.

Resnick, L. B., & Nolan, K. (1995). "Where in the World Are World-Class Standards?" *Educational Leadership, 52*(6), 6-10.

Resnick, L. B., & Resnick, D. P. (1992). "Assessing the Thinking Curriculum: New Tools for Educational Reform." In B. R. Gifford & M. C. O'Connor (Eds.), *Changing Assessments: Alternative Views of Aptitude, Achievement and Instruction* (pp. 37-76). Boston: Kluwer Academic Press.

Roach, V. (1991). "Special Education: New Questions in an Era of Reform." *The State Board Connection: Issues in Brief, 11*(6), 1-7.

Robinson, G. E., & Craver, J. M. (1989). *Assessing and Grading Student Achievement.* Arlington, VA: Educational Research Service.

Rosenshine, B. (1983). "Teaching Functions in Instructional Programs." *Elementary School Journal, 83*(4), 335-351.

Rosenshine, B. (1986). "Synthesis of Research On Explicit Teaching." *Educational Leadership, 43,* 60-69.

Rothman, R. (1995a). *Measuring Up: Standards, Assessment, and School Reform.* San Francisco: Jossey-Bass.

Rothman, R. (1995b). "The Certificate of Initial Mastery." *Educational Leadership, 52*(8), 41-45.

Rowe, H. (1985). *Problem Solving and Intelligence.* Hillsdale, NJ: Lawrence Erlbaum.

Schulz, E. (1993, September). "Putting Portfolios to the Test." *Teacher Magazine,* 36-41.

Secretary's Commission On Achieving Necessary Skills, The. (1991). *What Work Requires of Schools: A SCANS Report for America 2000.* Washington, DC: U.S. Department of Labor.

"Setting the Standards From State to State." (1995, April 12). *Struggling for Standards: An Education Week Special Report,* 23-35.

Shavelson, R. J., & Baxter, G. P. (1992). "What We've Learned About Assessing Hands-On Science." *Educational Leadership, 49*(8), 21-25.

Shavelson, R. J., Gao, X., & Baxter, G. R. (1993). *Sampling Variability of Performance Assessments* (CSE Tech. Rep. No 361). Santa Barbara, CA: UCLA, National Center for Research in Evaluation, Standards and Student Testing.

Shavelson, R. J., & Webb, N. M. (1991). *Generalizability Theory: A Primer.* Newbury Park, CA: Sage Publishing.

Shavelson, R. J., Webb, N. M., & Rowley, G. (1989). "Generalizability Theory." *American Psychologist, 44,* 922-932.

Shepard, L. (1989). "Why We Need Better Assessments." *Educational Leadership, 46*(7), 41-47.

Shepard, L. (1993). *Setting Performance Standards for Student Achievement.* Stanford, CA: National Academy of Education, Stanford University.

Shepard, L. A., & Smith, M. L. (1989). *Flunking Grades: Research and Policies On Retention.* London: The Falmer Press.

Shepard, L. A., & Smith, M. L. (1990). "Synthesis of Research On Grade Retention." *Educational Leadership, 47*(8), 84-88.

Sizer, T. (1985). *Horace's Compromise.* Boston: Houghton-Mifflin.

Slavin, R. E. (1987). "Mastery Learning Reconsidered." *Review of Educational Research, 57,* 175-213.

Slavin, R. E. (1989). "Students at Risk of School Failure: The Problem and Its Dimensions." In R. E. Slavin, N. L. Karweit, & N. A. Madden (Eds.), *Effective Programs for Students at Risk* (pp. 3-22). Needham Heights, MA: Allyn & Bacon

Slavin, R. E., & Madden, N. A. (1989). "Effective Classroom Programs for Students at Risk." In R. E. Slavin, N. L. Karweit, & N. A. Madden (Eds.), *Effective Programs for Students at Risk* (pp. 23-51). Boston: Allyn & Bacon.

Slavin, R. E., Karweit, N. L., & Madden, N. A. (Eds.). (1989). *Effective Programs for Students at Risk.* Needham Heights, MA: Allyn & Bacon.

Smith, M. L., Noble, A. J., Cabay, M., Heinecke, W., Junker, M. S., & Saffron, Y. (1994, July). *What Happens When the Test Mandate Changes? Results of a Multiple Case Study* (CSE Tech. Rep. No. 380). Los Angeles: National Center for Research on Evanluation, Standards, and Student Testing (CRESST), UCLA.

Spady, W. G. (1988). "Organizing for Results: The Basis of Authentic Restructuring and Reform." *Educational Leadership, 46*(2), 4-8.

Spady, W. G. (1992). "It's Time to Take a Clear Look at Outcome-Based Education." *Outcome, 11*(2), 6-13.

Spady, W. G. (1994). "Choosing Outcomes of Significance." *Educational Leadership, 51*(6), 18-22.

Spady, W. G. (1995). "Outcome-Based Education: From Instructional Reform to Paradigm Restructuring." In J. H. Block, S. T. Everson, & T. R. Guskey (Eds.), *School Improvement Programs* (pp. 367-398). New York: Scholastic.

Spady, W. G., & Marshall, K. J. (1991). "Beyond Traditional Outcome-Based Education." *Educational Leadership, 49*(2), 67-72.

Sperling, D. (1996). "Collaborative Assessment: Making High Standards a Reality for all Students." In R. E. Blum & J. A. Arter (Eds.), *A Handbook for Student Performance Assessment in an Era of Restructuring* (Sec. iv-11, pp. 1-6). Alexandria, VA: Association for Supervision and Curriculum Development.

Standards Project for English Language Arts. (n.d.). Incomplete Work of the Task Forces of the Standards Project for English Language Arts. Urbana, IL: Author.

Staton, J. (1980). "Writing and Counseling: Using a Dialogue Journal." *Language Arts, 57,* 514-518.

Sternberg, R. J. (1979). "The Nature of Mental Abilities." *American Psychologist, 34,* 214-230.

Sternberg, R. J. (1984). *Beyond IQ: A Triarchic Theory of Human Intelligence.* New York: Cambridge University Press.

Sternberg, R. J. (1991). "Theory-Based Testing of Intellectual Abilities: Rationale for the Triarchic Abilities Test." In H. A. H. Rowe (Ed.), *Intelligence: Reconceptualization and Measurement* (pp. 183-202). Hillsdale, NJ: Lawrence Erlbaum.

Stevenson, H. W., & Stigler, J. W. (1992). *The Learning Gap: Why Our Schools Are Failing and What We Can Learn From Japanese and Chinese Education.* New York: Touchstone.

Stiggins, R. J. (1994). *Student-Centered Classroom Assessment.* New York: Merrill.

Stodolsky, S. S. (1989). "Is Teaching Really by the Book?" In P. W. Jackson & S. Haroutunian-Gordon (Eds.), *Eighty-Ninth Yearbook of the National Society for the Study of Education, Part I* (pp. 159-184). Chicago: University of Chicago Press.

Sulzby, E. (1986). "Writing and Reading: Signs of Oral and Written Language Organization in the Young Child." In W. H. Teale & E. Sulzby (Eds.), *Emergent Literacy: Writing and Reading* (pp. 50-89). Norwood, NJ: Ablex.

Taba, H. (1967). *Teacher's Handbook for Elementary Social Studies.* Reading, MA: Addison-Wesley.

Tchudi, S. (1991). *Travels Across the Curriculum: Models for Interdisciplinary Learning.* New York: Scholastic.

Tennyson, R. D., & Cocchiarella, M. J. (1986). "An Empirically Based Instructional Design Theory for Teaching Concepts." *Review of Educational Research, 56*(1), 40-71.

Tennyson, R. D., & Park, O. (1980). "The Learning of Concepts: A Review of Instructional Design Research Literature." *Review of Educational Research, 50*(1), 55-70.

Thaiss, C. (1986). *Language Across the Curriculum in the Elementary Grades.* Urbana, IL: ERIC Clearinghouse On Reading and Communication Skills, and National Council of Teachers of English.

Thompson, S. (1977). *Competency-Based Education: Theory and Practice.* Burlingame, CA: Association of California School Administrators.

Trimble, C. S. (1994). "Ensuring Educational Accountability." In T. R. Guskey (Ed.), *High Stakes Performance Assessment: Perspectives On Kentucky's Educational Reform* (pp. 37-54). Thousand Oaks, CA: Corwin Press.

Tucker, M. (1992, June 17). "A New Social Compact for Mastery in Education." *Education Week: Special Report,* S3-4.

Turner, A., & Greene, E. (1977). *The Construction of a Propositional Text Base.* Boulder, CO: Institute for the Study of Intellectual Behavior, The University of Colorado at Boulder.

Tyack, T., & Tobin, W. (1994). "The 'Grammar' of Schooling: Why Has It Been So Hard to Change." *American Educational Research Journal, 31*(3), 453-479.

Tyler, R. W. (1932, 1989). "Constructing Achievement Tests." In G. F. Madaus & D. Stefflebeam (Eds.), *Educational Evaluation: Classic Works of Ralph W. Tyler* (pp. 17-86). Boston: Kluwer Academic Publishers.

Tyler, R. W. (1949). *Basic Principles of Curriculum and Instruction.* Chicago: University of Chicago Press.

Uchida, D., Cetron, M., & McKenzie, F. (1996). *Preparing Students For the 21st Century.* Reston, VA: American Association of School Administrators.

Valencia, S. (1987, April). *Novel Formats for Assessing Prior Knowledge and Measures of Reading Comprehension.* Paper presented at the annual meeting of the American Educational Research Association, Washington, DC.

Valencia, S. W., & Place, N. A. (1994). "Literacy Portfolios for Teaching, Learning and Accountability: The Bellevue Literacy Assessment Project." In S. W. Valencia, E. H. Hiebert, & P. P. Afflerrbach (Eds.), *Authentic Reading Assessment: Practices and Possibilities* (pp. 134-156). Newark, DE: International Reading Association.

van Dijk, T. A. (1980). *Macrostructures.* Hillsdale, NJ: Lawrence Erlbaum.

Waters, T., Burger, D., & Burger, S. (1995). "Moving Up Before Moving On." *Educational Leadership, 52*(6), 35-40.

"What's Wrong With Outcome-Based Education?" (1993, May). The Phyllis Schlafly Report. *Eagle Trust Fund, 26*(10), 1-3.

Wiggins, G. (1989). "Teaching to the (Authentic) Task." *Educational Leadership, 46*(7), 41-47.

Wiggins, G. (1991, February). "Standards, Not Standardization: Evoking Quality Student Work." *Educational Leadership, 48*(5), 18-25.

Wiggins, G. (1993a, November). "Assessment, Authenticity, Context and Validity." *Phi Delta Kappan* (pp. 200-214).

Wiggins, G. P. (1993b). *Assessing Student Performances: Exploring the Purpose and Limits of Testing.* San Francisco: Jossey-Bass.

Wiggins, G. (1994). Toward Better Report Cards. *Educational Leadership, 52*(2), 28-37.

Wiggins, G. (1996). "Honesty and Fairness: Toward Better Grading and Reporting." In T. R. Guskey (Ed.), *ASCD Yearbook, 1996: Communicating Student Learning* (pp. 141-177). Alexandria, VA: Association for Supervision and Curriculum Development.

Wilde, S. (Ed.). (1996). *Notes From a Kid Watcher: Selected Writings of Yetta M. Goodman.* Portsmouth, NH: Heinemann.

Williams, P., Phillips, G. W., & Yen, W. M. (1991). *Some Measurement Issues in Performance Assessment.* Paper presented at the annual meeting of the American Educational Research Association, Chicago.

Willis, S. (1996, March). "Student Exhibitions Put Higher-Order Skills to the Test." *Education Update, 38*(2), 1-3.

Winograd, P., & Perkins, F. D. (1996). "Authentic Assessment in the Classroom: Principles and Practices." In R. E. Blum & J. A. Arter (Eds.), *A Handbook for Student Performance Assessment in an Era of Restructuring* (Sec. I-8, pp. 1-11). Alexandria, VA: Association for Supervision and Curriculum Development.

Winograd, P., & Webb, K. S. (1994). "Impact On Curriculum and Instruction." In T. R. Guskey (Ed.), *High Stakes Performance Assessment: Perspective On Kentucky's Educational Reform* (pp. 19-36). Thousand Oaks, CA: Corwin Press.

Wisconsin Department of Public Instruction. (1994, February). *Wisconsin Learner Goals, Outcomes, and Assessment: A Special Issue of Education Forward.* Madison, WI: Author.

Wolf, D. P. (1988). "Opening Up Assessment." *Educational Leadership, 45*(4), 24-29.

Wolf, D. P. (1989). "Portfolio Assessment: Sampling Student Work." *Educational Leadership, 46*(7), 35-39.

Yoon, B., Burstein, L., and Gold, K. (n. d.). *Assessing the Content Validity of Teacher's Reports of Content Coverage and Its Relationship to Student Achievement.* (CSE Report No. 328). Los Angeles, CA: Center for Research in Evaluating Standards and Student Testing, University of California, Los Angeles.

Young, A., & Fulwiler, T. (Eds.). (1986). *Writing Across the Disciplines.* Portsmouth, NH: Heinemann.

Zimmerman, B. J. (1990). "Self-Regulated Learning and Academic Achievement: The Emergence of a Social Cognitive Perspective." *Educational Psychology Review, 2,* 173-201.